W9-BDA-420

LOPEZ SPEAKING

LOPEZ SPEAKING

an autobiography by Vincent Lopez

THE CITADEL PRESS
NEW YORK

FIRST EDITION

 Library of Congress Catalog Card Number 60-9381. Manufactured in the United States of America. Published by The Citadel Press, 222 Park Avenue South, New York 3, N. Y.

CONTENTS

PREFACE

It's quite the custom now for veterans of show business to write their autobiographies. Some do it out of a desire to relive the past; others see in it a chance to improve their future; still others are interested only in the money-making possibilities of a best-selling book and a hit movie.

My major motivation in writing *Lopez Speaking: My Life and How I Changed It,* is to tell people how I straightened out a life that was being misspent—not in the sense that I had become an addict of some sort (the theme of so many such autobiographies) but simply that my life held little personal satisfaction for me, despite success in a number of directions, until I acquired, quite gradually, a new sense of values, a real orientation point, a fundamental purpose in being on this earth, and peace of mind.

My childhood had been closely associated with the strong Old World religious concepts of my parents, and under the guidance of a determined father, I studied for the priesthood. It was Father Sebastian who persuaded me to end these studies, to my father's consternation and my great relief. But I remained deeply spiritual throughout my life, although many times I put personal pleasure and even sensual enjoyment of life far above its spiritual values. However, a great spiritual force always brought me back to a better realization of the true values, the only values on which a complete and satisfying life can be built.

In that process, I slowly and painfully learned the importance of the right "timing" in the things we do, the major decisions we make. My friends know that I became a believer, then an exponent, and finally an advocate of numerology. It isn't a religion, but it acknowledges a creating force in nature which has balanced not only the universe upon certain mathematical relationships but has also placed those relationships in our individual lives.

Numerology helped me find a definite and sensible pattern to follow in life, but there were many other forces and events that had an important role. I didn't write this book for the followers of numerology. In it, I relate how and why I became interested in the subject and the part it played in my life. After all, this is the story of my life, and numerology has been involved in it.

However, I believe this book will be of interest to anyone who has followed show business in our time and of direct concern and practical value to people who somehow feel, as I once did, a vague discontent with the loose ends of life . . . a strong desire to seek a new and better path toward the future . . . perhaps a somewhat frantic impulse to find that improved way promptly before the sands of time flow all the faster in the hourglass.

For them, my book should be much more than just the autobiography of a band leader who has been up and down the chutes of success (quite a few times). It should help them find a new orientation point as I did, get their compass of life back on its bearings . . . change their dissatisfactions and fears into the serenity and peace of mind which all religions promise, but which all people must find for themselves.

I hope you enjoy reading my book, but far more I trust and believe that if you want to find a straighter course to life and a greater significance in it, this story of how I changed my own life toward those ends will be of inspiration and benefit to you.

Sincerely,

Vincent Lopez

LOPEZ SPEAKING

Chapter 1. CHILD WITHOUT A CHILDHOOD

Considering my life-long love affair with the piano, it may seem odd that I once hated the sight of one. This was because the piano cheated me out of a childhood. From the time I was six until I left for the monastery at the age of twelve, I practiced four to eight hours a day after school, leaving me no playtime such as other children enjoyed.

"Vincent," my father would explain, "to learn to play the piano properly you must practice, practice, practice until your fingers get a mind of their own! Can you accomplish that out in the street playing stickball?"

My father was a piano teacher and was home most of the time, so I almost never could evade practice. My own escape was in my imagination. Like most young kids, I wanted to be a fireman, and I devised a fire-alarm game I could put to music, and play, in my mind, while practicing.

I'd start the piano scales slow and easy, so as not to disturb the sleeping firemen. Then the alarm would sound and I'd clang out the signal on the treble notes. Back to the scales at a quickened tempo. Hit the bass as the heavy firetruck rolled into the street. Then the scales again as we'd pick up speed . . . slow up for corners, swoop around pushcarts, shout people out of the way, then put the tempo at top pace as we rushed along the open road to the beckoning blaze! This child's game, invented out of a child's need, built up such technique that I developed the fastest hands in the business.

Sometimes, when my father left the house for some reason, I'd sneak to the little cement court alongside the high stoop of our house, put on a pair of roller skates and play the fireman game by scooting around on wheels, now and then glancing out the front gate to see if Dad was returning. He never caught me at the game directly, but circumstantial evidence might convict me. Being a bum skater I took many a fall—and if he noticed a bruised knee when he got back to the house, I could hardly tell him I fell off the piano stool!

The trial was always short and the sentence unsweet. "Get the strap!"—about as cruel to a child as making a doomed man adjust the rope around his own neck. It wasn't that my father was a sadistic man, but his concept of the duties of fatherhood made him tyrannical. Every child takes in more of their conversations than the parents realize. I recall protests my mother made about our way of life. "What has happened to us, Antonio?" she would plead. "You were so gay and happy when I first met you, but now you find no joy in life—only duty and obligation."

"If your father had stressed those things more," he would answer, "you would still be the Baroness Gonsalves, living in luxury in Lisbon instead of the wife of a middle-class music teacher in Brooklyn."

"My father made his mistakes," mother would admit, "but they were mainly political mistakes. I'm not sorry we had to come to America and I was glad about it when I met you. My father's mistakes shouldn't concern us now."

"I made mistakes, as well," my father would reply, "and they were due to lack of discipline. I should have remained in Portugal instead of yielding to this wish to be a sailor and go off to America. My better-disciplined brothers, who stayed in Portugal, followed my father's footsteps and now are wealthy and respected jewelers. Children need such discipline."

And that would end the conversation. Either one or both would draw into a shell of silence that might last a week or more before another word was exchanged! I never dared ask my father about his background; and my mother was also very reticent. This much I pieced together from her reluctant answers. They had met at a champagne dinner given by the Portuguese Ambassador in New York; the forty-seven-year-old Antonio Lopez was the gayest and most charming man she'd ever met; a champagne romance had followed; then two perfect years of married life that thereafter was suddenly transformed into a tortured existence.

"Your father is a good man, Vincent," my mother often told me. "He loves us all deeply, but he fears what life can do to people and he tries to protect those he loves by raising a wall of iron discipline.

He wants you to become a priest because that life of discipline and devotion will keep you safe from the world."

"I want to become a priest, too," I'd assure her. "Not because I'm afraid of anything but because the church is so beautiful. But I don't think I can be as religious as father is. Why must he go to church three times a day and then burn candles and pray at home for hours? Was he always that way?"

"No, Vincent, for years he hardly ever went to church, but when the children were born—your father felt a deep need to bring you up righteously and he returned to the church. I wanted him to, but I never thought he'd carry his religious interest to such an extreme. I should have known, though. He's that way in everything.

"On your sixth birthday he decided you should learn the mandolin and the guitar, since those are the instruments he plays so well. Remember how difficult the lessons were he gave you? You don't know how I argued and pleaded with him to let you learn more gradually. But no, he said he was teaching you the far more important lesson in life—discipline."

"So you got him to let me study piano instead?" I asked.

"No, your father made that decision because you showed more ability at the piano. Fortunately that was what you wanted. But if you had preferred the mandolin he'd have *made* you change to the piano. Your father really believes that discipline is the most important thing. But sometimes I wonder if most of the unhappiness in life doesn't come because people do what they believe they *should* do instead of what they want to."

I didn't quite understand her words then, but later years have disclosed their full meaning. My father's discipline became a cancerous obsession that killed each thing it touched, including my mother's love.

There were times when he relaxed a bit. One summer afternoon he had no lessons to give and I had finished my day's practicing, so off we went on a trolley ride to the Upper Bay looking toward Staten Island. As he watched the passing ships Antonio Lopez, the music master, suddenly became the seafaring young Anthony of thirty years ago.

"Look there, Vincent," he exclaimed, "that's a Cunard line steamer on the way to England. It will be there in six or seven days, beautiful days on the ocean. That other ship, painted white, is bound for South America, probably Buenos Aires, a wonderful city." He got really excited when he made out a tramp steamer flying the Portuguese flag. He told me he had come to America on a ship very much like it.

"Father," I said, timidly, "do you think I could become a sailor some day, or at least travel to places?"

It was the wrong question! Down he came from his glowing memories, and back I went to our bleak world of discipline.

"Don't talk such nonsense!" he forbade. "You have a far greater destiny in the priesthood. Come, let's walk back to the trolley. It's getting late."

Our comfortable four-story house was next to the Swedish Lutheran Church on the corner. In the middle of the block was my school, P.S. 47. Like the other houses ours had its front court and a large backyard that could have been a world of enjoyment for a child. My sister Marie had more chance to play there than I did, for she was younger, she was a girl, and my father expected (or at least required) less of her.

Whenever my father left on a visit or a business matter that would keep him away at least an hour, my piano scales suddenly ceased and I would climb the side fence to visit either Evelyn Jacobson, daughter of the Lutheran minister who lived on one side of us, or Ruth Robinson, our neighbor on the other side. Ruth's side of the fence took most of the climbing, for her older brother, Lawson, was an Olympic sprinting champ, and his stories of athletic meets were better than Arabian Nights fare to a lonely heroworshipping kid.

Ruthie was my favorite chum. She seemed to understand and felt sorry for me on account of my strange home life. Many times mother's voice ringing out "Vincent, your father is coming!" would bring our talks to an end but save me from a beating.

Ordinarily, though, my mother was reticent and reserved toward my sister Marie and me. I think now that she felt somewhat responsible for the restricted life we had to lead but could do nothing except retreat from it herself. I suppose a psychologist would say that she withdrew from reality and found refuge in silence. Our home was probably the most silent one in the neighborhood.

Years later, my sister Marie said this was perhaps her greatest regret of our childhood: that we grew up apart, a brother and a sister without real affection or understanding for each other. We might as well have been four strangers living together; we weren't a family at all. A family grows on love and affection, not on discipline and fear.

I don't think a psychologist could say it any better!

Chapter 2. LITTLE LEAGUE OF NATIONS

However, the neighbors liked us and no doubt regarded us as a model family. People in our part of Brooklyn took pride in their well-kept houses and their well-brought-up children. Juvenile delinquency was as unknown there as the equation for atomic energy. Many racial stocks were represented—Swedes, Irish, English, Scotch, and Germans. The Lopez family was Portugal's sole representative in this small United Nations.

My mother made friends among the neighboring women; she loved to escape the restrictions of our own home by visiting during the day. Equally, my father had admirers among the older neighborhood men. They respected him as a good musician and a successful business man, a pretty rare combination.

"It's a pleasure to hear your father play his mandolin of a summer night," Mr. McNulty would tell me. "Please ask him to keep the windows open. We love the music."

"Tell your father he's doing wonders with my Ingrid," Mr. Swenson might say. "And I didn't know he was a composer and that he wrote a music instruction book, too. My daughter showed it to me the other evening as she was playing the piano. Your father has a fine talent, Vincent."

What impressed the Lutheran Reverend Jacobson the most, however, was my father's sudden decision to quit smoking." It takes character to do what your father did, Vincent," he told me on one of my backyard visits to his daughter. "After having been a heavy smoker for years he was able to stop. I heard your father say to your mother, 'Virginia, smoking is a dirty, useless habit and it's bad for the health. I'll never smoke again.' And I saw him throw the cigar he was smoking into the street. I understand he has never smoked since then. That takes character!"

The famous Dr. Lorenz once said that the secret of a happy life is to experience everything, but in moderation. I wish my father had understood that principle. Instead, he did things in extremes. Just as he impetuously and almost violently quit smoking, he took up religion with equal intensity. He stayed up until milkman hours, reading strange religious tracts and even experimenting with "psychic" communication (especially guided writing from beyond). He received "messages" that he was going to come into a lot of money and would go back to Portugal, the land of milk and honey. I'm sure he didn't mention these activities to Father McCarthy in the confessional!

He was a firm believer in miracles, and I well remember a minor miracle that happened to me while I was with him. (Believe me I needed a miracle at the time.) I had a typical kid's love for frankfurters, but my father frowned on them as an inferior food. One day when he took me on a shopping trip to the grocery-and-butcher shop around the corner on Dean Street and Third Avenue, I spotted a lone cold frankfurter on a display plate. I couldn't resist the temptation; but a split second after I poked it into my overcoat pocket I heard the Voice of Doom cry out, "Mr. Lopez, your kid just stole a frankfurter!"

"Vincent would never do a thing like that," my father glared. "I have absolute trust in the boy!"—and to prove his trust he began fishing in my coat pocket!

"The other pocket," the indignant butcher directed, and when my father dug into it, I thought I was a goner. But the frankfurter wasn't there! I quickly reviewed the list of possible saints to whom I owed this salvation, while father and the irate Mr. Schultz argued. ("I seen him take it, I tell you!" "Well, what did he do with it—eat it while you were looking?" "But Mr. Lopez, if he done it, he should be punished, that's all." "Why don't you have your eyes examined? In fact, if you ever think it's me coming in this store again, you better have them examined!", etc.)

Once home, I solved the mystery. The frankfurter had slipped through a hole in the pocket lining, down to the hem of the coat! I fished it out and promptly devoured it (miracle or no miracle), then promptly got half-sick on it and learned that crime doesn't pay.

It was almost a miracle, too, when my father would unpredictably take us all to Coney Island. Whatever was the reason, the pendulum would suddenly swing all the way over to an arc of leniency (and even love) which my father expressed in the only way he knew: a trip to Coney Island.

Then Marie and I would scurry around the neighborhood postponing music lessons scheduled for that day, and by 11 o'clock we'd be off. The usual restrictions were off, too. We kids were allowed to do pretty much what we chose, whatever rides enticed us, whatever exotic foods the boardwalk offered from apple-on-the-stick to frankfurters smothered in mustard and relish (yes, they were exotic foods for us, as I'll explain in a moment).

My father enjoyed it too. Still an expert shot from earlier days when he had been an avid sportsman, he would proudly knock down every target at the rifle games and we'd go home loaded with the gewgaws the galleries gave away in the profaned name of prizes.

The next day Marie and I usually had upset stomachs from our boardwalk binge and that was the signal for resuming a strange diet that my father thought could put all the gastrointestinal specialists back into general practice! Possibly it was a food ritual of the Old Country (although I doubt it—the Portuguese are such healthy people). It was a strict regimen of dried codfish, barley, and boiled potatoes at every meal! The beverage was barley coffee. Anyway, that would become the Lopez family diet for a month or more, until dad decided the danger was over and we could go back to ordinary food.

Little did he know that in between the codfish-barley-potato breakfasts, lunches, and suppers, Mother Lopez was slipping us fresh fruit to take to our rooms—or, if father went out long enough, broiling us lamb chops to take away the taste of that dried codfish.

However, there was never any codfish around at Thanksgiving or Christmas. Then food fads were forgotten, and mother would heap the table with roast turkey, roast beef, sweet potatoes, nuts, candy, plum puddings—the works (and we gave it the works). On these holidays also my father relaxed his stern disciplines and let some emotional warmth brighten up our home.

Father's discipline included rejection of the new-fangled electricity. Electricity belonged to God for use in lightning, not to man for use in lighting! As a result, we had to do with old gas jets that from mid-afternoon on spluttered and flared in a futile attempt to remove the shadows from our windowless middle rooms.

But promptly on January 2, out went the Christmas tree and the holiday dispensation. Discipline again reared its many shapes and some of them cost my father money. For instance, one afternoon soon after the holidays a woman student of my father's asked what I enjoyed most of my Christmas gifts.

"I guess it was the candy, I just love candy."

When she returned for her next lesson she brought a small box of chocolates. I was delighted, but father was furious.

"Give it back, Vincent," he commanded.

"But a little candy won't hurt him," she protested in surprise.

"I will decide what my children will eat, Madam!" father shouted.

There was a hurricane of an argument, and she stormed out of the house and never came back.

We lost other students through father's stubbornness. For instance, he insisted the guitar could be played properly in only one position—while sitting down, with the left foot daintily poised on a low stool. (Can you imagine how that would have cramped Elvis Presley's style?) One day my father was giving a mandolin lesson to an advanced new student whose previous instructor had died.

Practicing the piano several rooms away, I could nevertheless sense an argument.

"But, Mr. Lopez," the woman's voice insisted, "Professor Edelman told me that ragtime is becoming popular."

"Forget what Professor Edelman or anyone else told you," my father boomed. "Other teachers are imposters. Here you will learn the correct way to play or you won't be a student of mine."

Then, realizing I had left off the piano scales to listen, he stomped through the intervening rooms and thrust his short but impressive figure into the doorway. He was red with rage and his handsome black mustache bristled.

"Vincent!" he commanded. "Pay attention only to the important things of life. Get back to your practicing!"

When he got back to his studio, another cash customer had removed herself from the books. But that was immaterial to Antonio Lopez. He wanted discipline from his family, and the world. He always put principle above principal-and-interest! As his students dwindled he pawned family jewels that he had brought from Portugal so that we could have simple gifts and lavish food at the holidays. It was a price worth paying, in his judgment.

Chapter 3. TO THE MONASTERY

There's a popular religious slogan today that the family that prays together, stays together. Prayer helped keep our family apart, not because of the nature of prayer itself but through the almost violent manner in which it was indulged.

"The Lopez family is full of devils," my father would often announce dramatically, and looking at me would go on: "Vincent, you have fifty-one devils in you! We must drive them out with prayer." This made me think, "What kind of religion is this?"

Driving out the fifty-one devils meant leaving the meal unfinished to pray before an improvised altar in an upper-floor room for what was probably an hour, but seemed close to eternity.

When I was about eleven I began to pick up the popular tunes of the day, especially ragtime. I smuggled a piano copy of "Cannonball Rag" into my room and practised it when my father was away. One afternoon I didn't hear him come home, and the strap wasn't sufficient punishment for this fall from grace. I had to spend extra time at church for the next week, though that was no punishment to me. I enjoyed church where I served as an altar boy.

In my earliest memories I knew myself to have been dedicated to the priesthood by my father. One afternoon, Carl Fischer, the New York music publisher, was at our house discussing a new instruction book my father had written. I had to play the piano for him for it was the custom of that generation to show off the family accomplishments.

"You're really good, Vincent," our visitor said. "I suppose you want to be a concert-artist when you grow up?"

"No sir," I replied earnestly, "a priest."

I can still see the warm smile on my father's face, a look unusual for him, a deep effusion of joy within. There I caught a glimpse of the man he might have been.

And so it was taken for granted that some day I would study for the priesthood. There was an Irish family on our block, the McNultys, who had the same plans for their son, John. He was four years my senior but our common objective often brought us together. The McNultys were a big and jolly family and it was a delight to visit them. My father encouraged me to make a friend of John, but the age barrier was too great and his best pal remained another Irish lad of the neighborhood, Jimmy O'Connor. I wished I could be as carefree and gay as Jimmy, but we came from different families and might as well have been from different worlds.

On my return from school one afternoon, soon after my twelfth birthday, I spotted my father waiting for me in the doorway. My first fears were allayed when I saw the glow on his face.

"Vincent, Vincent! Wonderful news," he said, "you've been accepted at St. Mary's! You're going to become a priest!"

It wasn't entirely an unpleasant shock, but I guess we all resist major changes in our lives and I objected, "I'm not old enough."

"I took care of that," came the prompt reassurance. "I've been corresponding almost a year now with Father Fidelis about you. Do you know who *he* is, Vincent?"

I didn't know—or care, at the moment.

"He's the Provincial of the Passionist Order for the whole United States. I've even been over to see him several times at St. Michael's Monastery in West Hoboken, New Jersey. And now he's agreed to let you start your studies, and you can thank me! I assured him you've never been contaminated by the Outside World!"

Contaminated? How contaminated can one get in an isolation booth!

"Will I have to live in Hoboken?" I asked.

"Oh, no. You'll begin your studies at St. Mary's Monastery, in Dunkirk, upstate New York. It's near Buffalo."

It might as well have been near the North Pole, considering the frigid touch of fear that gripped me.

"But you won't be alone up there, Vincent," my father went on, "you're to go with your friend, John McNulty. Yes, they've accepted John also, but the big thing is that they've accepted you. Vincent, my prayers have been answered!"

Even at that moment of supposed delight, I couldn't help wondering if my prayers might not have been consulted, too. But then the excitement of the new venture swept away my doubts. I ran over to the McNultys with the good news. Mrs. McNulty acted surprised but she must have known, for she had an apple pie waiting for John and me to celebrate with. If there was any reluctance left in me at the moment, the first bite removed it. It's marvelous what an apple pie can do for a twelve-year-old lad whose breakfast and lunch had been dried codfish!

Several weeks went by, which John McNulty and I spent in preparation for our new life. My father was living on a cloud, and

I could do no wrong. At church I was singled out among the altar boys for special notice; and I must admit I enjoyed all of it.

But one muggy, rainy August morning I woke up with the sharp realization this would be my last day at home. I climbed reluctantly out of bed and gazed out the window at familiar Pacific Street. In spite of the rain and the litter it looked like a Heaven from which I was being banished.

A soft knock on the door was followed by the equally soft voice of my mother saying, in the liquid Portuguese accent that she never lost. "Vincent, are you awake?"

"Yes, mother." And she entered.

"I've brought you your new black suit. Isn't it nice?"

My slender mother still showed signs of the great beauty which she once had possessed. But that morning she was tired with a fatigue she couldn't hide—and sad with a questioning doubt she tried her best to conceal. When I didn't answer her, she placed the new suit carefully on the bed, then took my hands and held them with a tenderness that gave me courage and my voice.

"You're frightened, my son." It was a statement, not a question.

"I've never been out of Brooklyn, mother," was my choked-up explanation. "Now to be going away, never to live here again . . ."

"It is as your father wills."

"I think I *want* to be a priest, mother," I added after a long silence, "but I'm so young to be going so far away. John McNulty and the other boys there will be at least sixteen. Shouldn't father have waited?"

"Once your father knew there was a chance for you to go, nothing would stop him. He told the priests that you're ready, that he has allowed no evil thoughts to enter your head."

"You mean he allowed no thoughts at all to enter my head, unless they were his!" I rebelled finally.

"Hush, Vincent," my mother urged (but it was no command). "Your father has always done what he believed was right for you. Besides, he is a very religious man, and he wants this great honor for our family. If it is not to be, a greater wisdom than his will change all this, I'm sure. Trust in that wisdom now. And get dressed quickly. Father's waiting."

With that she pulled me to her with a desperation that shocked me, it was so different from her usual reserve. She held me close for a magical moment, kissed me, then walked proudly from the room. It was that attitude of pride which I needed. I hurriedly dressed.

Downstairs, my father was pacing back and forth. Every few seconds he would tug a huge gold watch from his pocket and shout, "What's keeping that boy, Virginia? This is the greatest day of his life. He should be all dressed and ready, and down on his knees thanking God for the opportunity he's been given. Doesn't he know we have to pick up the McNulty boy on the way? A thousand things still to do! Why is he so slow?"

I heard this last sentence as I came into the room. "Good morning, father," I said. "I tried to hurry, but the suit was new."

"No excuses, son. You're entering a life of dedication and study where excuses for failure have no place. . . . Virginia, will you be good enough to leave us alone? I wish to talk to Vincent."

My mother gave me a reassuring smile as she left, and I needed it.

"Vincent," my father began, "this is the most important day in your life. To be a priest is the greatest calling for man."

"I know, sir."

"You know nothing!" my father roared. "If I hadn't watched you night and day, you'd be out in the street like all the other boys, wasting away the years. The day you become a priest will be the day I've always waited for!"

Here were the dictatorial voice and views of the Old World—accepted by youth, perhaps, in Portugal—but alien and hateful to youth in the new America.

Ten minutes and a hundred admonitions later, my father left to pick up young John McNulty. That gave me a brief time for a final good-bye with mother. I knew she'd been crying, and when she held me off at arm's length I sensed it was because she did not want to cry again.

"Before you go, Vincent," she asked, "do one thing for me. Play the piano and sing my favorite song."

This was exactly what I needed to help me hold back my own tears. My young soprano voice wasn't the best in the world but it was the only one in the world for her that moment as I sang "At Dawning."

"When the dawn flames in the sky,
I love you . . .
When the birdlings wake and cry,
I love you . . .
When the swaying blades of corn
Whisper soft at breaking dawn . . ."

I got no further. I suddenly realized she was weeping softly so I shouldn't hear, and a moment later I was in her arms—with so many years of enforced distance between us to make up . . .

My father herded me and John along like a couple of balky steers. My new straw hat, a half size too large, kept slipping down, blotting out my view and the umbrella I shared with John kept poking me in the back of my neck. And while the rain poured, my father poured advice and admonitions over the two of us.

When we reached the New York Central depot the excitement of the railroad trip took over. Our excitement was intensified by the surprise visit of a score of John McNulty's school pals, led by irrepressible Jimmy O'Connor. At the track gate they spread a long roll of old towels in our path, imitating a plush carpet rolled out for royalty. With O'Connor leading, the boys with the loudest voices simulated a brass band. A crowd collected, and everyone thought it was hilarious—including John McNulty and me.

Did I say everyone? Omit my father from the list. Recovering from his stunned surprise, he furiously ordered, "Stop your laughing, Vincent, have you no pride? Is the devil in you, as it is in these wild boys?"

Sobering up, I stood aside with my father and the happy group left us behind. "I didn't mean to spoil your departure, son," my father softened, "but this is no occasion for silly fooling. I'm glad we're alone a minute, for I have a gift for you."

With that he took a package from his pocket and thrust it into my hands. "Drink this with every meal," he instructed, "no matter what they serve you at the monastery. When it's gone, write me and I'll send some more."

It was a pound of barley coffee!

With Jimmy O'Connor and his happy revelers in tow, John McNulty rejoined us and shook hands seriously with my father. Then it was my turn for this final good-bye. Impulsively I stretched out both my hands to embrace my father, but he froze into a rigid straightness, thrust his right hand toward me in a very formal handshake, and boomed, "Remember, Vincent, do exactly as you are told at St. Mary's."

"Yes, father," I stammered in embarrassment. I turned and leaped up the coach steps after John. We picked a seat on the platform side—and there was Jimmy O'Connor right below us, signalling for us to open the window. His group turned serious and began to serenade us with a melancholy song, "So Long, Pal."

So long, Pal, we hate to see you go,
We've got to let you know,
The Gang will miss you so,
And though you may wander far away,
We'll be there to share each care
That's sure to come your way.
So long, Pal—no tears, no sad farewell—
No sounding of the bell,
For you will always dwell
In our fondest memory,
Good-bye, so long, old Pal!

John and I tried to grin our way through it, but it was an age of sentiment and we both found it hard to gulp our feelings down. Was my father affected too? He tugged his big bandana handkerchief out of his back pocket and gave his nose a tweak with it. Was he choking up a bit? More likely the rainstorm was giving him a cold!

Then two blasts on the signal cord and we started rolling out of the station, headed toward the small town of Dunkirk in the northwest corner of New York—and a monastery where I was to find that discipline can be taught a youngster without sacrificing understanding, warmth and love.

Chapter 4. FIRST DAYS AT THE MONASTERY

ST. MARY'S PASSIONIST MONASTERY, said the sign on the huge, red brick building. "This end of the building is obviously the church, Vincent," John decided, "so the school and the dormitory must be back there. Think we'll like it?"

"I wish it wasn't surrounded by these big walls. Must be six feet high. Makes it seem like a prison . . ."

"That's not the way to look at it," John corrected me. "St. Mary's is to be our home for perhaps a year. Then we go to Pittsburgh for our novitiate—or back to Brooklyn if we don't have the calling. I hope I make good."

"So do I!" I said. We rang the bell and the massive door swung open revealing two priests in the darkened hallway. "We're the students from Brook . . ." John began, but the older priest raised a finger to admonish silence, smiled in welcome, then beckoned us to follow. The way led through several long corridors and I nudged John McNulty in delighted surprise when I caught sight of farm fields back of the monastery with cows grazing. But John shook me off with an impatient glance that held all the annoyance a sixteen-year-old youth has toward a kid. He was concentrating on trying to walk as quietly on the hardwood floors in his heavy shoes as the two priests in their sandals.

Passing a number of closed doors that seemed hewn into the bare walls we reached one, larger than the others and of darker oak. There the priests stopped and motioned for us to go in.

"What's the matter with them?" I whispered to John, "are they deaf and dumb?"

I think John gave me his shocked answer only to shut me up. "It's the morning silence they're observing. We'll do it, too."

Any amazed reaction I might have had to this was quickly smothered by the sight of Father Sebastian at his big desk. He was an impressive-looking man with cheeks like large red apples and a generous nose that he was indulging at the moment with a pinch of snuff. It was the first time I had seen a person use it, and the prodigious sneeze that followed startled me.

"Geezunheid!" was my reflex reaction and poor John almost wilted in embarrassment. But Father Sebastian welcomed us to St. Mary's in a booming voice that showed his pleasure.

"I'm Father Sebastian," he began. "You're John McNulty, I take it, since you're the older one—and you'd be Vincent Lopez. Well, sit down, lads, and make yourselves comfortable. "We'll get to know each other well in the time ahead, boys," he went on, deepening the attraction I already felt toward him. "How long you remain here depends on you, and you alone. You are now confraters. A confrater stays with us anywhere from six months to a year and a half. When he shows us he's ready, we send him on to Pittsburgh for his novitiate —or" (and he looked squarely at me) "we send him back home the very moment it's clear to us or to him that he wasn't meant for this life. I'm looking at you, Vincent, because you're the youngest boy ever to enter St. Mary's and you might be with us a bit longer than the rest.

"By the way, Vincent, we haven't learned what Saint's name you'll take. You may keep your own, if you like, since there was a St. Vincent, or take another."

"I've talked with my father about that," I answered, "and I'd like to take the name of St. Anthony."

"A wonderful choice," Father Sebastian agreed. "What made you select it?"

"Because," I half choked, "it's my father's name."

"Fine, fine," came the booming response. "Now let me tell you something about your life here. It's a life of strict discipline. Just as

Jesus applied the utmost discipline and denial to himself—He who could have had the world and the universe—so must we who would follow Him. The religious life is one of great denial, and discipline is the only way to accept that denial willingly and humbly. You will also find that a priest must have unlimited love and compassion for others, and self-indulgence and self-pity would leave him little room for those qualities.

"We start learning discipline from the very first day here. A bell rings in the dormitory at 5:20 in the morning. You get up at once and dress in your cassock and surplice. You must be in the chapel no later than 5:30. Our Holy Father, the Pope, has given a special indulgence each day for the boy who gets there first.

"We have an hour of prayer and Mass at the chapel, and you'll learn to sing the Gregorian chants with the priests and brothers. You return to the dormitory to clean up and make your beds." (NOTE: The "beds" were straw-filled mattresses on wooden slats.) "You then change into your regular clothes, your black suits, for the rest of the day, and by that time we'll be ready for breakfast."

I gave a practically famished sigh of relief, and Father Sebastian went on.

"Breakfast is at 7 A.M. sharp, and must be finished by 7:30. It's simple but good. We wouldn't want too much food in us then for we go into our hour of personal meditation. Now, boys, let me emphasize this. From the time you get up in the morning straight to the end of this hour of meditation, you're not to talk, not a single word, do you understand? If there's something you must communicate do it by gestures or not at all. Holiness is built on meditation, and meditation is built on silence!"

There were many other instructions; but I had stopped taking them in. I learned by doing, not by listening. Some of the doing proved to be pleasant, some not. My first disappointment was the "breakfast" which meant dry bread and coffee! On that meagre meal we prayed and studied until noon. By eleven on many a morning, a plate of my father's codfish and boiled potatoes would have been a banquet!

Let me piece together the schedule for the rest of our day.

8:30 A.M.—Individually assigned chores, from cleaning up Father Sebastian's study to dittoing the "Boys' Room."

9:00 A.M. until 12—Classes in Latin, Greek, English, religious philosophy, mathematics, et cetera.

12:00 NOON—Dinner in the refectory with the priests. Plain but wholesome food—no desserts—and no talking except for religious texts we were called on to read.

1:00 P.M.—Talking and general recreation, but not much noise on the playground please—the priests are taking their siesta.

2:00 P.M.—Back to classes until four. "No talking" reinstated.

4:00 P.M.—Another recreation break, then another hour of prayer, followed by supper. Then we were free until "Lights Out" at 9:20.

Still, I really enjoyed life at the monastery. Discipline was strict, but it was purposeful and consistent, not the erratic sort my father had imposed. The chance to live with and play with a group of boys (even though somewhat older) brought out the repressed boyhood in me, and I was the most talkative kid inside and the most exuberant one outside.

The first chance I had up at bat in baseball must have been under the guiding eye of the guardian angel of .300 hitters, for I plunked a long drive between two outfielders. But I stood there at the plate, not knowing what to do until John McNulty and the others yelled for me to run! I ran in the right direction to first base, but then I kept running straight on out to right field. Meanwhile the ball was being pegged back to the first baseman, whereupon Father Sebastian (a very bewildered umpire that day) called me out.

The age difference between twelve and sixteen sets up barriers even at play, and I began to feel left out of things. Nothing I could do seemed to interest the older boys until the invention of Bartolemo Cristofori, which I had come to regard as an instrument of torture, came to my rescue. I mean, of course, the piano.

Chapter 5. RETURN TO THE PIANO

There was a big old upright in our recreation room, and John often urged me to play; but memories of practice drudgery made me shun it. One evening, though, when the boys had split up into common-interest groups and I was left alone again, that ancient upright beckoned like an old friend. I went over and began to play it softly.

In a few minutes the boys had gathered round. They asked me to play their favorites, most of which I knew or could improvise. Soon it became the happiest night of our entire term, for I guess we were all a bit lonely and the songs we sang took us back home in memory.

All except me. I was having a much grander time playing than I'd ever had at home. At last I'd found an audience to play for—an audience that enjoyed every minute and wanted to hold back the clock as its hands sped toward "Lights Out." Music had suddenly become not a chore but a joy, because others found pleasure in it. I think that's why the concert pianist will put a lifetime of effort and practice into his playing, so he can transmit to people a relatively few hours of the beauty and the meaning that music holds. That evening, my own life was given over to a pattern in which it would become fixed.

Father Aloysius, who was our recreation counselor that night, took a keen interest. He was past eighty, but young at heart. The next afternoon he waited for me to finish classes and then asked me to teach him the piano. I saw that his gnarled hands would never get past the simplest tunes, but his ambition was to learn the "Cannonball Rag" right up to my tempo! He was never discouraged and month after month the wonderful old man kept practicing. Finally, though, he found a way to accept defeat: "Confrater Anthony," he said, "I'm afraid I've been guilty of the sin of pride. I believe the Lord wishes me to be content to perform the five finger exercise without error."

I sometimes wonder if Father Aloysius realized that each moment I spent helping him learn the piano subtracted something from my drive toward priesthood. In the evening recreations, and even in the practice I put into learning the popular songs of the day, I found that music was much more than technique. It's soul can be found only through enjoyment of it. Once that understanding comes there is a need to re-experience it again and again. Had there been no piano at St. Mary's, I believe that today I would be Father Anthony Lopez, not maestro Vincent Lopez.

If Father Aloysius and I didn't perceive it, a confrater named Joe Quillan did. One night after I finished a number he requested, Joe whispered, "Boy, if I could play the piano like you, I wouldn't stay here."

"You shouldn't say things like that," I protested. But an inner voice whispered the same idea to me. To drown it out, I doubled my prayers and devotions. A deep fervor followed. There are no words to describe the heights to which religious emotion can lift the soul. While praying in the chapel I'd forget my very surroundings and hunger or fatigue. I welcomed the long silences of the night when prayer seemed deepest and most meaningful. I passed up baseball games at recreation for solitary walks in the chapel yard—all in a subconscious effort, I suppose, to keep in the path of the priesthood. Yet all the while, the voice of the dormitory piano rang louder!

This inner conflict drove me to seek punishment. On my turn to read during meals I would deliberately make an error in pronunciation. When Father Sebastian corrected me I made the same error again. The first punishment for such wilful disobedience was an assignment of three "Hail Mary's" which I had to recite kneeling on the hard, wooden floor with my hands under my knees. If the error occurred again (which it always did) the next order was "three lines." That meant kneeling down and licking the floor three times (with your tongue)—about the ultimate in humiliation. I felt grateful for it, believing it would straighten out my thinking. It didn't.

Soon Father Sebastian realized that I was seeking out such punishments, but I think he placed the wrong interpretation on my conduct as attention-seeking. He stopped calling on me to read at meals and one afternoon he summoned me to his study.

"How is your music progressing, Confrater Anthony?" he asked. "Do you enjoy playing for us here?"

"I love it, Father," I told him. "I hope you'll let me continue playing, because the other confraters want me to, you know."

"Oh, yes, you may continue playing," he answered. "But you must learn not to be prideful of it. Pride is a grievous sin, Confrater Anthony, and the antidote is humility."

The lesson in humility was an assignment to scrub the old porcelain fixtures in the washroom until they were white! Since the porcelain had long since chipped away, it was a job for the patience of a saint and the cleverness of the devil himself. I know it gave me a devil of a time.

But I went at it with a will if not a way. I even whistled at my work—because my piano privileges hadn't been revoked!

Chapter 6. EXIT JOHN McNULTY— ENTER JIMMY KEEGAN

The railroad tracks were near St. Mary's, and to this day when I hear a train whistle in the distance, memory rushes me back to my straw-filled bed at the monastery, and once again I listen to the approaching hum, then the thunder of the early morning freights.

There was one time, however, when the screaming whistle of a locomotive froze me in fright. A group of us confraters had gone out for a meditative walk on a cold January afternoon. We were several miles away from St. Mary's when a blizzard struck, so we decided to return along the dependable path of the railroad, which the sharp wind swept clear of drifts. Near a road crossing, a flyer running behind schedule in the storm bore down on us. Its sudden scream just a few hundred feet behind us acted like an electric shock, setting the rest of the boys on the run but *paralyzing me!*

I froze in my steps! All I can remember of that moment was the headlight beam of the locomotive, then a figure running toward me from the side, grabbing me around the hips, and hurling me to the safety of the cinder bed. It was John McNulty! I owed him my physical life, and not long after that he tried to help me retain the spiritual life into which we had entered jointly.

One afternoon he came to me to say good-bye. "Father Sebastian just told me I'm to leave for my novitiate in Pittsburgh this evening."

We didn't question the suddenness of it, for quick good-byes are considered best in the religious life.

"That's wonderful, John," I congratulated him. "I certainly wish I was going with you."

"Do you really?" he questioned. "What if there's no piano at Pittsburgh?"

"Oh, I wouldn't miss the piano," I lied. "It's just a hobby with me. Like photography is with Father Ronan. I still want to become a priest more than anything else in life. Look how hard I try in my subjects, even though I'm the youngest one in class."

"Trying isn't enough. It may even be a sign we really wish for something else. I mean we try extra hard at our studies and devotions in order to forget what we really want to do. Promise me, Anthony, you'll think it over when I'm gone. It would be worse if you came to Pittsburgh and then had to leave."

"Don't you want me to become a priest like you?" I asked him.

"I want you to be whatever will make you happiest, and whatever you can make people happiest by doing."

Those were John's last words of advice to me and I haven't yet found a better expression of what a person should seek to do in life.

Several years later, John was ordained Father Casimir of the Passionist Order, and became an outstanding missionary. He passed on to the rewards of Heaven a little while ago. I never had the chance to meet him again, in this life.

I did not become fully conscious of the change in my life until

Jimmy Keegan joined us. His arrival set off a dynamite charge that blasted tons of my religious zeal and purpose into the whirlpool.

Jimmy and I didn't hit it off at first. For one thing, he was a couple of years older. Secondly, I was in a self-imposed silence and meditation period when he joined us, and he naturally made his first friendships with the other boys.

It was the piano that brought us together. Jimmy loved to hear me play—and I loved to listen to his talk of the outside world. An orphan, he had spent most of his seventeen years with reluctant relatives or at indifferent orphanages. He had had periods of self-support when he worked at menial jobs and slept in hallways or broom closets of third-class hotels. These experiences had toughened him without spoiling his innate good nature. He had the gift of cheerfully accepting a bad situation till something better turned up.

One night I asked him why he wanted to become a priest, a question I asked everyone, because it was so much on my own mind.

"Back at the orphanage I heard a visiting missionary talk about the faraway places he's seen," Jimmy explained. "Well, I love to travel, so why not be a priest? Anyway, I couldn't stand that orphanage any longer. This place ain't much better, though. They're both like prison!"

"You shouldn't say that," I protested, though that thought was churning in a secret recess of my own mind. I walked away from Jimmy, as I knew I should, but a magnetic force had been set up, pulling me toward the outside world. From then on, Jimmy Keegan replaced John McNulty in my life, and I was on my way to "cross the Rubicon" back to Brooklyn.

The fascination Jimmy held for me was his worldly knowledge. Moreover he had the Irish gift of weaving a commonplace story into a tapestry warmly tinted with humor and imagination. My life at home and at St. Mary's had been empty of such things, and like a starving boy I ate up his stories; probably I overate. Then one afternoon, when we were picking apples in the orchard, Jimmy talked of the forbidden fruit.

"Anthony," he began hesitantly, "have you ever kissed a girl?"

"No, I haven't," I half whispered, "and you know we're not supposed to talk about that."

"Well, I've kissed plenty of them," he went on, "and I don't see what's wrong with it."

"It's wrong if you're going to be a priest. You'd better talk it over at confession."

"I did," Jimmy said. "Father Paul got mad and told me to pray very hard every time such thoughts return to me. Pray all night if necessary."

"That will do it," I assured him. "Pray as hard as you can and you'll forget about girls."

"I'm not so sure I want to," Jimmy retorted. "Why should I spend the rest of my life marrying other people, and never have a girl myself?"

A fierce sex drive burned in Jimmy Keegan. Some spark of it caught in me that day that couldn't be extinguished by prayer, meditation, confessions, and the other weapons religion has devised against Mother Nature and sex. Unless the sex drive can be sufficiently sublimated in a man, there is no sensible place for him in a life that requires the vow of celibacy. Jimmy Keegan never belonged there; and, possibly it was not for me either. The spark of sex interest he struck that day (or the spark he transferred from my subconscious to my conscious mind) lit a fire that gave off at least enough smoke for me to lose the way!

To offset that conversation with Jimmy Keegan, I plunged into new excessess of religiosity: intense prayers, long devotions, special penances, even the sacrifice of giving up the piano for a month. One night, Jimmy left St. Mary's in a dismissal so abrupt he wasn't even given the privilege of saying good-byes. He managed to sneak a note under my pillow with the name of the orphanage where I could write to him. However, my letters went unanswered and I never heard from or about Jimmy again. Our questions to the fathers about him didn't bring forth much information. They clearly wanted to write him off their books, though Father Aloysius once said that Jimmy was a fine lad and would make a good Catholic layman.

With Jimmy gone, I felt that an obstacle had been removed from my own path to priesthood; yet I soon found myself again stumbling over doubts and dissatisfactions. I could erase them through music, not prayer. The piano became the "rod and staff" on which I leaned more heavily as the months dragged by. As purpose and direction seemed to drain away from my regular studies and activities, an overpowering love of music swept over me.

Chapter 7. I LEAVE THE MONASTERY

It was while under Jimmy Keegan's influence that I experienced my first crush. I was undergoing elaborate dental surgery at the time. (More about that later.) The treatments were painful, but there was balm in the lovely blonde nurse in the dentist's office.

I was too shy to speak, or even look at her when she spoke to me. But the moment her head turned my eyes devoured her. Finally I decided to put into a letter what I couldn't manage to tell her.

I wrote her from the monastery, pouring out the story of my love. It was a respectful love—tempered by the holiness with which Catholic worship surrounds womanhood. Nevertheless, it was one piece of mail that the U.S. Post Office failed to deliver—for an excellent reason. They never got it! All our mail was "reviewed" by the priests—and I found out, a long time later, that my first love missive wound up in Father Sebastian's wastebasket.

Other memories of letters during my monastery days take me back to the mail distributions. This often held a pleasant surprise for the confraters—candy or homemade cake or cookies. But the mail for Confrater Anthony was limited to brief home news and lengthy exhortations to study hard, obey the priests, etc. Finally I found the courage to write back that the other boys often treated me to their gifts from home and that I hoped to return the favor sometime.

My father "got the message." Back came a half-pound bag of Woolworth's best jelly beans for my friends—and another pound of Anthony Lopez's best barley coffee for me!

I have most of the letters my father wrote to me. In that respect he never failed me, while my mother seldom dropped me a line and I never heard from my sister. Father wrote every week, and more if I wrote home asking for something such as new sheet music or a pair of ice skates. And his letters never mentioned how tough things had become for the family, financially. His odd character and unpredictable temper had lost him most of his music pupils. And he was selling the jewelry pieces he had brought from Portugal. I did not know until years later at what sacrifices the ice skates or the hockey stick or the three or four dollars' worth of sheet music that I asked for at a clip had been bought for me.

Still speaking of letters, there's one I prize as a memento of my monastery days, though it was written many years later. It came from China from Father Raphael Vance, C. P. who had been Confrater Aloysius at St. Mary's.

"As a missionary," he wrote, "I've been privileged to christen a great many babies, Vincent. Yesterday I seemed to have run out of names when I was about to baptize a boy with unusually long fingers. Somehow I thought he might make a good pianist in the unpredictable future, and I remembered the wonderful nights at St. Mary's when you were our Paderewski. So I want you to know that here in distant China there is a young Christian named Vincent Lopez Yee!"

On his first visit back from China, Father Vance brought me Chinese musical instruments, and many tales of strange Chinese customs. The next time Father Vance returned to the United States, he was a broken man physically. The Chinese Reds had imprisoned him for years and subjected him to torture. I wanted to pay him a visit, but I was told he wasn't quite up to seeing even old friends after his ordeal.

Saturday night at St. Mary's wasn't merely bath time; it was barbershop night as well. We confraters were given a few lessons in Perry Como's original art to enable us to give one another haircuts. One

Saturday, a confrater who probably got sick on my jelly beans *shaved* my head! Everyone got a big laugh out of it, and as the youngest member of the crowd, I went along with the laugh.

But it wasn't funny the following morning when we filed out into the church and took our places as altar boys at High Mass.

There must have been a sell-out crowd that morning, judging from the buzz my appearance drew. A few minutes later Father Sebastian signaled to me to walk into the sacristy. What a bawling out I got for my Yul Brynner appearance! Loyalty to St. Mary's traditions obliged me to "take the rap" and claim that I had *asked* for the special haircut.

For punishment I was taken off altar-boy duty for weeks. Aside from the humiliation this was a real deprivation to me, I so much enjoyed the beautiful ritual.

In particular I enjoyed the early morning services when the priests and the students sang the Gregorian chants. It was back in the Sixth Century that Pope Gregory I started a Schola Cantorum (singing school) at Rome to establish the singing of church music on a standardized basis throughout the Church. It has become universal since then; and in no other form does the beauty of the human voice find deeper expression.

Its majestic form never ceased to thrill me. Though I was sometimes dog-tired from a long night of study or discouraged with the monastic life, joining in the chants always restored me. To this day the solemn beauty of the Gregorian chants seems to me man's closest approach to the Infinite.

As senior confrater, I was in charge of the vestments used for Mass on special holy days. I had to have them in proper order to place on the priest's shoulders at the proper moments of the Mass. It was an assignment I was proud of, but pride is not permitted in monastery life. Maybe my face showed it . . . maybe there was some other reason for the discipline—but at the midnight Easter Mass, as I stepped forward with one of the vestments, Father Sebastian pulled me back, took the robe from my hands, then indicated that Confrater Stephen was to perform my duties. The next day Father Sebastian called me to his office and said I must relinquish that special assignment.

"But why, Father?" I protested. "I've handled it with reverence."

"Anthony," he explained. "I'm afraid there's a touch of exhibitionism in you. If it's to be corrected, we can't begin too soon."

I started to protest, but he turned to his work and beckoned for silence. Maybe it was a test to see if I would accept the rebuke willingly, or turn to some other calling in life where "exhibitionism" is another word for stage presence.

My acceptance of the incident was anything but willing. Brooding over it, I built it from molehill to mountain size; then it changed from mountain to volcano. I was scrubbing Father Linus's room when all my discontent, unhappiness, uncertainty welled up beyond control. *"What am I doing here?"* I shouted. *"All meaning went out of this for me long ago. God must have decided I'm not to be a priest!"*

Scrub brush in hand, I headed for Father Sebastian's study and poured everything out. He didn't interrupt; he even endured the dripping of the scrub brush on his waxed floor, realizing how agitated I was.

Then he smiled—sadly. "Anthony, I've seen this coming for some time, but I wanted you to see it for yourself. I thought originally you were too young to start these studies, but your father persisted. He persuaded me that your isolation from the world was in your favor. Now I believe it was a mistake. Perhaps living in the world awhile, seeing things for yourself, making your own decisions, will help you decide whether or not this calling is for you. Would you like to try that for a year or so?"

"Yes, father," I agreed. "I think that would help a great deal."

"And what would you like to do with yourself that year?" he questioned. "Continue at school, perhaps?"

"No, father, I'd like to make some money on my own now, so I can decide things for myself. Perhaps I could make a living playing or teaching the piano. It's what I've grown to love, here at St. Mary's."

"And I've been waiting for you to make that decision, too," Father Sebastian nodded. "I really believe music is your true vocation—"

He stood up. "Suppose you say goodbye to the others now. . . . There's a train for New York at four o'clock—*Vincent!*"

It was over. I had ceased to be Confrater Anthony. Father Sebastian came out from behind his desk, put his arm around my shoulder.

"Once a decision is made, Vincent, never look back and waste time wishing it had been different. Instead, look on . . . move forward."

"But one thing worries me," I said. "My father will be angry. I don't know what to tell him."

"I'll help out there," was the kind reply. "We know your Heavenly Father understands. Surely your earthly father will, also."

But Father Sebastian knew my Heavenly Father's reaction much better than he understood those of some human beings. My earthly father never forgave me!

Chapter 8. BE IT EVER SO HUMBLE!

A heavy thunderstorm hit Dunkirk as I was saying my good-byes to my friends at St. Mary's, but it only thickened the heat and the atmospheric tension. So also with my psychological thunderstorm; it not only failed to discharge old doubts, but added new ones. What would I do with my freedom? Would I be able to take the old pattern of life at home since I had been unable to tolerate the milder discipline at St. Mary's? How would my mother take this change? (I well knew how my father would!)

To have the fewest possible reminders of the abandoned priestly role, I gave away most of my possessions. On the other hand, I jammed into my cardboard suitcase every piece of music that was mine, except a copy of "Cannonball Rag" that I left with Father Aloysius.

The monastery door closed behind me as silently as it had opened more than three years before. Perhaps there is joy in heaven over the one lost sheep that is found, but at a monastery the lost sheep must be forgotten and the remaining ninety-nine made more snug in the fold. I felt no resentment over the quick and even casual leavetaking. I even preferred the lack of ceremony since it gave me time to buy some sandwiches at a nearby luncheonette for my supper on the train. At sixteen, spiritual and emotional distress can become secondary to hunger!

I was comfortable enough in my rigid coach seat—there were no luxurious swivel seats in those days—as long as daylight (and the sandwiches) lasted. Then in rode a quick curtain of outer dusk and inner uncertainty. Freedom can be a frightening thing.

Musically inclined, I received rhythmic messages from the clicking wheels: "You shouldn't have gone, you shouldn't have gone . . . You ought to go back, clickety-clack, you ought to go back. . . ."

The next thing I knew, the conductor was bending over me with a half-concerned, half-amused look on his face.

"You had a bad dream, sonny—you were yelling. You were shouting, 'No more barley coffee!' Do you feel all right?"

"Yes," I said, but sleep ended for the night. The events of the past twenty-four hours kept parading before me—interspersed with the forebodings about the probable happenings of the next twenty-four. To distract myself, I opened my suitcase, just to riffle through my sheet music. There were a couple of new songs I wanted to study.

While digging for them I came across a batch of holy pictures I had somehow mixed up with my music—and Jimmy Keegan's orphanage address in Manhattan. I looked at them with both astonishment and a little superstition. Was some supernatural force giving me another chance to decide my future? The religious pictures pointed back to Dunkirk and the monastery. . . . Jimmy's address beckoned me on to New York and my music.

In the rising light of dawn, Jimmy's address looked better and better to me. I was suddenly struck with the idea that maybe I needn't go back to the Lopez home in Brooklyn. Maybe Jim could get me into the orphanage! By the time the train chuffed into New York, I was determined to try my new-found wings of freedom in flight.

But Jimmy wasn't at the orphanage. The minute he had turned eighteen he had applied for his discharge, and on the strength of a promised job he'd been allowed to try life on his own. . . . No, he had never written them how he was doing, but if I was a good friend of his from the monastery I could have his address—and would I please remind him he had taken two orphanage towels with him that he should return. I walked away, feeling let-down and fearful.

Having got the address, I went to see Jimmy Keegan, but was unprepared (though I shouldn't have been) to find him already a married man.

"I'm Vincent Lopez, Mrs. Keegan," I stuttered to the irritable looking young woman who opened the door. "And congratulations on your marriage."

"You can skip the congratulations," said Mrs. Keegan. "We both wish we'd waited a couple of years. Living in this awful place sure takes the glow out of a honeymoon. I'm sorry we don't have a nicer place to receive you in, but maybe the next time you call it'll be different."

"Sure, Vincent," Jimmy chimed in. "Next Thursday's my night off," he continued. "Why don't you drop by, Friday afternoon, and we can chew the rag about old times at St. Mary's. Vincent and I have some stories you'll get a kick out of, Grace. Could you make it Friday, pal?"

"Well, to tell you the truth," I blurted out, "I need a place to stay, Jimmy. I'm afraid my father will kick me out if I go home now. Do you think I could stay a while at the orphanage? I mean just until I found a job."

"Not a chance if you're not a genuine orphan," Jimmy explained. "Besides, you wouldn't like it there. Why do you think I rushed to get married? Anything's better than having somebody tell you what to do every minute of the day. Right, honey?"

Honey wasn't in the mood to agree. After a long minute of embarrassed silence I popped the big question: Could I stay with them temporarily?

"It's out of the question," Jimmy explained. "I work nights, and what would the neighbors think? I don't believe you know much about life, Vincent. The only place for you is your own home."

It was not what I wanted to hear; but ten minutes later we left Jimmy's flat to telephone my parents from a corner drugstore. To get them we had to call our neighbors, the Jacobsons, since the Lopezes could not afford a phone. When Jimmy put thru the call he asked Mrs. Jacobson to get Antonio Lopez.

"No, no!" I protested. "Get my mother first"—but Mrs. Jacobson was already on the way. A Purgatory-sentence wait ensued; then I heard my father's voice.

"Just a minute, Mr. Lopez," Jimmy requested—and thrust the receiver into my shaking hand. "Say something! Say something!" he ordered.

"Hello, father?" I piped. "This is Vincent."

"Vincent? Where are you?"

"In Manhattan," I explained. "I just came in on the train from Dunkirk."

"But why?" my father demanded. "Is there something wrong?"

"Oh, no, no." I fumbled. "They're making some repairs on the school and they gave us a vacation." That white lie drew a big black explosion.

"Nonsense!" the voice shouted. "You're in trouble! Come home at once!"

"He wants me to come home," I whispered to Jimmy, not knowing enough to cover the mouthpiece.

"Then that's the thing to do," Jimmy recommended with relief. "It's three squares a day. That's better than we could give you—and you've got a piano home, too."

"All right, father," I choked into the receiver. "I'll do what you say"—and I handed the phone to Jimmy, not knowing what to do with it. He listened a moment to the shouted instructions and admonitions, shrugged in disbelief, and hung up.

"C'mon up and have lunch with us before you go, Vincent," he sympathetically suggested. "It won't be much, but make believe you're having breakfast at St. Mary's." With my departure assured, Jimmy's spirits and generosity were picking up.

It was a miserable meal, eaten in a miserable atmosphere. Whatever urges had brought them to marriage had waned long ago. They kept a bitter edge of animosity turned toward each other—an edge ground sharp on the wheel of poverty. I was glad when the sour, reheated coffee had been downed and the time arrived for our good-byes. Jimmy thumped me on the back and said they wanted to see me real soon, but I had a hunch it was our last meeting. I went back several months later to find the flat empty. The neighbors said they had moved at night in order to beat the landlord out of the back rent. They had left no forwarding address.

Five minutes after I left their flat my decision to return home wavered. Instead, I spent the rest of the afternoon and early evening wandering around New York. My last seventy cents was spent on ice cream and sodas, with a nickel left over for the ride to Brooklyn. It was like the final meal permitted the doomed prisoner. But by nine o'clock there was no further dallying, so I climbed the elevator steps and headed for Pacific Street.

Both my parents were waiting up, my mother worried by my absence, my father impatient for the overdue explanation. When it came, he refused to accept it. But climbing those old steps at Pacific Street had taken the last ounce of my strength and hope for a new way of life. I sagged into a husk of a tired boy, not yet sixteen.

For once my mother took charge. Brushing aside my father's protests, she helped me toward my bedroom where the yielding springs and soft mattress lulled me into the deepest night of sleep I've ever enjoyed. For fourteen hours I found blessed oblivion.

It was noon next day when I awakened. Several rooms away I heard my father enumerating the seventy-five devils that had taken possession of me! Then my mother knocked on my door and came in with a glass of orange juice. Two quick gulps and it was down. Two quick sentences and the story of my dismissal from St. Mary's was out.

"Dress now, Vincent," my mother said, "and don't be afraid for a moment. I'll tell your father about this."

A moment later there was a vocal explosion outside. "So he's to think things over a year!" came my father's voice. "So his true vocation is music! When does he start his concert tour? What have I done to deserve such a son? The chance of a lifetime and he rejects it!"

Then his voice came nearer, the bedroom door flew open, his angry face glared at me. "I'm putting you back on the train for Dunkirk tonight! You'll be a priest or nothing!"

But my mother was right behind him. "Vincent," she suggested, "why not run over to Mrs. McNulty's and tell her about John. I'll talk this over with your father." In no time I was at the McNultys.

Wise, old Mrs. McNulty seized up the situation when I tried to gloss it over. "Your father is no doubt shouting his head off. Well, the important thing is to let him have his say. He wasn't a young man when you were born, Vincent, and you must understand what that means. Young fathers still have their own lives to lead, but an older man often wants his son to do the things he secretly wished to do—become what he wanted to become. The more such a father is disappointed with his own life, the more he demands from his son. I don't say it's right but I know it happens.

"Sooner or later," she continued, "such a man admits he can't mold the life of another, especially when his son shows he has a mind and purpose of his own. Your only chance is to stand up to him and make him see that."

In those few words, Mrs. McNulty gave me my first hope and my first idea of improving my situation at home. My attitude brightened, and we spent the next hour in delightful recollections of the experiences John and I had shared at St. Mary's. When I left after lunch she kissed me gently and said, "Remember, Vincent, be kind to your father. You have your whole life ahead of you. He has only his past, which he feels was largely wasted, and your future, which he can no longer control."

He certainly tried to control it when I got home. He was all for boarding a train with me and forcing Father Sebastian to take me back!

"You'll get on the train alone if you go, father," I told him. "There isn't a chance of my getting back in, but if you want me to, I'll write them a letter applying for readmission. That's all I can do!"

Maybe there was a new tone in my voice. To my mother's obvious surprise he reluctantly agreed. I got pen and paper and wrote out a simple request for readmission, to which my father added a three-page postscript of pleadings, promises, and implied threats (of leaving his religion). The letter completed, he left at once to mail it at the main post office. The corner mailbox wouldn't do.

There was a three-day truce while we waited for an answer. When it came father called my mother and me into his study. "Vincent," he promised, "here is where the gates of heaven reopen for you. Father Sebastian couldn't possibly resist my appeal."

But as he read it silently, his jaw went slack, his gaze fastened itself to the page in disbelief. Then he read it to us.

"It's as you said, Vincent," he conceded. "I thought you had run away, but Father Sebastian says the priesthood is not the proper vocation for you at the present time." And he slowly added, "If it isn't your vocation now, it never will be. God's will be done."

Chapter 9. FATHER FINDS ME A NEW CAREER

Ever the one to give God's will a helping (and directing) hand, however, Antonio Lopez immediately began reshaping young Vincent's career. He spent all that afternoon at the Jacobson's telephone.

At supper he announced, "Vincent, we can't let the decision at St. Mary's permit you to drift. You've had a specialized education there that won't fit in well with high school training, so the sensible thing to do is to send you to business college and equip you for the outside world. So I enrolled you today in Kissick's Business College. You start this coming Monday morning."

His making decisions for me, without even a word or whisper of consultation, shocked me now and I thought of Mrs. McNulty's advice to start living my life somewhat on my own. However, his accepting Father Sebastian's letter that morning without a temper tantrum decided me not to push my luck at the moment. Instead of telling him that I still wanted to follow music, I thanked him and promised I'd study hard.

"I'm sure that attending this business school will help you find your right place in life," said my father, speaking, though he did not know it, with the tongue of prophecy. For in my very first day at Kissick's I met a beautiful girl classmate through whom I found my right place in life—show business!

Making another important decision in my life so pleased my father that he became close and even confidential toward me. He spoke to me of his absorbing new interest, spiritualism (or at least communication with the beyond), which he pursued despite the Church's disapproval. He now practiced automatic writing late into the night. He showed me a sample of the automatic writing.

"See, Vincent! This note is in someone else's handwriting—someone long dead. I didn't write it; it was merely my hand being guided. It promises that we shall all return to Portugal soon, that I'm to inherit a great sum of money and we'll be rich, and you can attend a monastery in Europe not dominated by the Irish clergy. They turned you away but accepted John McNulty. Almost all the priests over here are Irish. . . ."

His rambling took even stranger turns. Excess of religious zeal is a wandering thing unless it is disciplined and guided. He confided to me that he sometimes had the power to see apparitions, relatives long dead and forgotten. He suggested that I concentrate to see if I had the same faculty.

I didn't mean to be cruel, but curosity about his reactions led me to play a trick on him. Once while he was talking about spiritual communication, I put on a terrified look and whispered, "Father, I see three spirits—there in the corner!"

He leaped from his chair in excitement, not fright, and peered where I was pointing.

"I can't see them, Vincent," he admitted. "What are they like? Is there anything unusual about their appearance that might be a message?"

"They had heavy chains across their shoulders," I improvised, recalling a holy picture I had seen.

"Is that all?"

"They dropped the chains before they disappeared."

"Wonderful!" enthused my father. "That means freedom! We'll all be free!" He didn't say free from what. However we ran out of barley coffee next morning and my father didn't get a new supply for weeks.

His spiritualistic interests continued but suddenly he stopped discussing them with me, although often I heard him late at night invoking the "spirits" to guide his hand.

At supper the Sunday night before I started at Kissick's, my father gave me an intent look and remarked that my appearance had changed while I was at school. "Your jaw is different. It looks better than when you left for the monastery."

I explained that during my first year at St. Mary's I had been sent to a Doctor Ellis, an orthodontist in Buffalo. Dr. Ellis found that, because of some baby-teeth extractions which my father had executed upon me at home (the hard way, via a pair of pliers), my second teeth had grown in such a way as to push my jaw out of shape, giving me a bulldog look. He told the priest who accompanied us that the condition would get progressively worse, unless expensive prosthetic work was done. A week later I was called into the study and introduced to a kind old gentleman whom I had frequently seen visiting the monastery.

"This is Mr. Powers, Anthony," Father Sebastian explained. "He is a good friend of ours and we owe a great deal to him. I've told him about your unfortunate jaw condition and how important it is that you have dental work to correct it. Mr. Powers has offered to pay the cost. Will you undergo the treatments?"

I expressed my thanks in a rather tremulous voice, and added that I would say a prayer for Mr. Powers each day of my life—a promise I've kept.

"The treatments will be somewhat painful," warned Father Sebastian. "Worse still, you won't be able to eat solid foods for a day or so after each treatment."

For the next year I existed on chopped meat (or mushed fish on Fridays). My gums would just about be feeling good again when another Wednesday, and a trip to Buffalo, would arrive. Without those treatments a public career would have been impossible.

Years later I stopped off in Buffalo to thank the doctor for his expert care. He was delighted to know that the Confrater Anthony he had treated was the pianist-maestro Vincent Lopez he often listened to on radio! When I tried to find Mr. Powers, however, to repay the money, I learned to my regret that he had passed on.

A few months after the treatments began, Father Sebastian told me he had not consulted my father in the matter because he was aware of the poor financial condition of the Lopez family, and he was afraid my proud father might oppose the corrective work. It was a wise move judging from my father's reaction now.

"To pay out that money for nothing, this Mr. Powers must have had evil designs! Are the Lopezes so poor they must accept charity? If it was God's will that your face should be shaped one way, who was this evil man to change that will? What suggestions did he make to you? Did you ever see him without Father Sebastian present?"—and the raving continued.

I decided it was time to put Mrs. McNulty's advice into practical action. I stood up and raised my voice to my father for the first time.

"If there was any evil in all this," I shouted, "you have created it from an evil mind. In your search for a god, find one who would not prefer to see a boy's jaw twisted and deformed!"

There was a gasp of disbelief from the other side of the table (joined in by my mother). Then Antonio Lopez rose slowly from his chair and walked out of the room in silence.

Chapter 10. HONKY-TONK CIRCUIT

Kissick's wasn't a diploma mill, but it devoted little time to the humanities. Typing, stenography, bookkeeping, elementary accounting, etc., made up its curriculum. It was the distillation, in six months, of what the commercial high school courses now offer in four years. There was little time for teen-age interests or "school spirit." Indeed, many of the students were long past their teens, anxious to get at least ninety-eight cents worth out of each tuition dollar.

My first minute in the typing classroom, though, brought a pleasant surprise. One of my classmates was Phyllis O'Connor a sister of John McNulty's pal. Seeing her brought back a lightning-flash recollection of the day we had left for the monastery, with her brother, Jimmy O'Connor, leading the group that rolled out a tattered-towel carpet for us. My father had predicted a criminal windup for him. Jimmy did wind up connected with crime. He became a private eye.

I got this information (and other neighborhood news) from Phyllis in our noon-time break for lunch on opening day. She told me her brother had a good voice and suggested that I play for him some time.

I dismissed the idea as just making conversation, even when she invited me to her house to do the playing. It was one thing to have lunch with Phyllis in the school cafeteria, but the idea of visiting her home and perhaps being alone with her brought my emotions up sharply at the end of the reflex-action chain that my repressed childhood at home and my religious conditioning at St. Mary's, had fashioned for me. I wasn't merely shy about girls. I equated them with temptation and trouble—at the same time hoping I'd run into plenty of trouble later on!

At home that night, you can be sure I made no mention of Phyllis—or the other nineteen young (and reasonably young) females who were in my classes at Kissick's. Somehow, naive Antonio had assumed that, since business was man's province, the business school was as male as a monastery. On graduation day nine months later, I was afraid my father might suffer a stroke when he discovered that sixty percent of the students wore petticoats.

But he was much too preoccupied with the news that he'd landed me my first office job as a stenographer at the Alexander Campbell Milk Company, and the disposition he would make of my salary. Out of my eight dollars a week, I could have two,—and if I kept lunch down to a quarter a day that meant a whole half dollar to splurge! I didn't resent this. Further depletions in his music-student ranks had left the Lopez exchequer at subsistence level. My father respected my contribution to the family kitty as much as he required it. Later on I found that he had spent only four dollars out of the six and put the rest in a bank account for me.

The tall, gray-haired principal was winding up his speech: "In conclusion, on behalf of the entire faculty, I want to say that when you walk thru these doors today, as you have done these past pleasant months, don't make it the last time. Feel free to visit us whenever you wish. Your world from now on will be the world of business. Think of Kissick's as your first home in that world . . ."

It was the usual hail-and-farewell bunkum of graduation day the world over. However, with the formal ceremony out of the way, he became warm and human again and gave a personal greeting to each of us as he handed out the certificates.

"Vincent," he smiled at me, "you came to us a mere boy, but we've watched you grow suddenly into a fine young man—fine looking, too."

"Thank you, thank you," I stammered, "Er, *the same to you!*"

Had prizes been given that afternoon for idiot responses, I'd have taken first. Shyness, or downright fear of girls, had thrown me!

But it was a girl who rescued me from my embarrassment. Phyllis O'Connor came over, introduced herself to my father and added, "Mr. Lopez, my mother is giving me a little graduation party tonight. Could Vincent come over for a while?"

Phyllis had the face of a young saint. I could see my father was lost for an answer. Finally he nodded permission, then half spoiled it with the warning to be home early.

During my nine months at business school my relationship with my father had improved. It never reached a true father-son quality, and too much time had run out for any real warmth to develop; nevertheless, we got along much better.

I went to Phyllis's party with the 9:30 deadline hanging over me like the Sword of Damocles. I found myself a seat in the corner and didn't join in the fun.

Phyllis took steps to fix that. "Let's shut off the phonograph a while and sing instead of dancing," she suggested. "My arm's tired from winding it." Nobody else seemed to like the idea but she carried it through in the manner of an experienced chairman.

So the crowd gathered around the old upright, and Phyllis sat down to play. Anyone who laughed would have had a good excuse. Beyond a recognizable chopsticks she did no better than stiff-fingered old Father Aloysius! When her best friends told her it was quite awful she agreed. The minx had a plan in mind, and when the trap sprang I was caught in it.

"Vincent can play the piano like a professional," she announced. "Let's get him over here." When I shook my head a couple of strong Irish arms lifted me out of my chair and plunked me down on the piano bench. A sweep or two across the keys and I was back at St. Mary's again in imagination and memory. It was my first audience since those days, and their enjoyment brought back the old thrill of performance—and the hope of a future in music instead of at a milk company.

We were running into a lull in the proceedings about an hour later when the shot in the arm needed to galvanize things arrived. It was Jimmy O'Connor, through with his private investigation work for the evening and ready for fun. Phyllis reintroduced us.

"I heard you playing when I came in, Vincent," he said. "I liked what I heard. Will you play a tune for me? I'm in a singing mood tonight."

He certainly was. He gave us "Gee, But It's Great to Meet a Friend From Your Home Town," "Put Your Arms Around Me, Honey," "Strike Up The Band, Here Comes a Sailor," "I Want a Girl," "If You Talk in Your Sleep," and a slew of others. Then he swung over into some Irish tune, leading off with George M. Cohan's "Harrigan," and scoring a home run with "River Shannon." By that time the house was rocking hard enough to make the termites hold hands and pray the place wouldn't collapse!

When the refreshments came, I was giddy from the champagne of success. I'd played again and people enjoyed it. No less an authority than grown-up Jimmy O'Connor had given me a big wink of approval when I helped him over the high notes with quick arpeggios. Then the grandfather's clock in the living room, with its twelve midnight bongs, brought me back to earth.

As I started to leave Jimmy said, "Let me walk to the trolley with you. I'd like to talk about a couple of things." He seemed serious . . . even a bit excited. "A friend of mine and I do entertaining on the side," he explained when we were in the street. "Maybe you know him—Neil O'Hare; he plays violin and wants to have a dance band of his own some day. He could use you, and I'd love to have you play for me on my singing jobs. It'd be two dollars a night, Vince. Will you think it over?"

"I don't even have to think it over, Jimmy," I replied. "Tonight I found out for sure what I want to be in life. They said, at St. Mary's, that I was too much interested in music to devote myself to the priesthood, and they were right. "Meeting you was the luckiest thing ever happened to me. My father got a job for me in an office, but I can't settle for that. I want to play the piano."

"Well, I don't want to get you in trouble with your dad," Johnny deliberated, "but I think he's wrong."

"I think I'll sort of compromise on this," I said. "I'll take the job at Campbell's. But I'll join you fellows, too. How late would those dates keep me out?"

"Midnight, most of them. Sometimes a bit later if we play a date that's out of the way," Jimmy admitted.

"I don't know how, but I'll manage it," I decided. "I'll find an excuse for staying out late. I'll say I was working overtime at the office. If I get the two dollars I'll keep one and say I got a dollar overtime."

"It's a deal, Vince," Jimmy pumped my hand. "I'm singing at Sanger Hall in Williamsburg this Thursday night. How about coming over to the house tomorrow to rehearse a bit."

We heard the last trolley for the night clanging over the tracks and I didn't dare miss it. The whole ride home I tried out explanations to give my father for my lateness. I decided to say I had boarded the wrong streetcar and been taken far out of my way. But I needn't have bothered. I noticed a light on in my father's study on the top floor. He was busy with his spirit contacts!

As I slipped in the front door and soft-shoed toward my bedroom, my mother's door opened and she whispered, "Is that you, Vincent? Did you have a good time?"

Five minutes later, I was dreaming of Thursday night and a smash success in Williamsburg.

My piano-playing career began on the rickety old upright at Sanger Hall in Williamsburg. There were keys that didn't play and I couldn't understand why. The crowd was getting impatient but Jimmy asked for a moment to tell a joke while I took a look inside. I found several sandwiches there! The heavy action was breaking them up, but now and then a piece of bread or meat would jam a key. I lifted out as much of the junk as I could reach—and got a much bigger laugh than Jimmy's joke.

In my barroom piano-playing career such hilarious episodes were frequent. Once when I was playing with Neil O'Hare's orchestra at an amateur show, the diva had flung out her arms and asked when her luck in love would change when a black cat strolled out of the wings and all across the stage. It broke up the audience—and the play.

Another time, on Halloween, we played a barn dance, at a place then far out in the Brooklyn sticks, now a cement jungle. Not satisfied with cornstalks, pumpkins, etc., for decorations, real farm animals were tethered around the place for "atmosphere." Then a group of sailors from the Brooklyn Navy Yard arrived and liberated a pig. With that frantic animal on the waxed floor, there were more pratfalls than were ever seen in a Mack Sennett comedy.

Another night, our little band augmented to six musicians, found ourselves outnumbering the dancers. Finally a flock of customers showed up, toughs with girl friends dressed like Parisian Apache dancers. Several cops arrived at the same time. Everybody was frisked, yielding quite an arsenal of revolvers and knives. The sergeant explained to us that two rivals gangs were holding opposition dances on the same evening, and we had unwittingly been booked for one of the dates.

"That's the reason you had so few people here," the sergeant added. "The decent people of the neighborhood are afraid to come."

Just then a strong delegation from the rival gang showed up to see what orchestra had been naive enough to sign for their opponents' shindig! Cops or no cops, a roughhouse started, and we got out the back door without trying to collect our pay. In the hurry, poor Neil hadn't fastened his violin case well; and on the ten foot jump to the ground the case opened and his expensive Jacob Steiner instrument fell and shattered. To add to that loss Neil had to pay off the outside musicians he had signed for the night. We regulars told him to skip it. It was an early demonstration to me of the troubles of a band leader.

But there were many nights of sheer satisfaction rather then mere excitement in the dates we played. For one thing, my interest in the piano was enlarging to a love for the entertainment field. I enjoyed the feel of an appreciative audience. People were becoming an important part of my life. A few years before, silence and meditation had been my emotional meat and drink. Now it was the sounds of crowds. I was becoming a theatrical hambone.

A date I always looked forward to was a once-a-month engagement at the Atlantic House at Coney Island. It was a second-rate hotel for elderly people who, in those pre-television days, had little entertainment except card games and they loved us. Our chief admirer was an ex-operatic diva who had put more time on "bars" than scales. Every time we played there, she'd bring out whole opera scores for me to sight-read frantically while she sang the passages she remembered. In response to the applause she would wave a magnanimous hand in my direction and say, "Your applause, please, for my accompanist, Mr. Lopez, who will some day conduct at the Metropolitan."

That "some day" was to happen within a few years!

Of course, playing these dates kept me at the O'Connors' a good deal of the time. Without my realizing it, a warm relationship developed between Phyllis and me. At first, I took it as merely being included in her sisterly interest in Big Brother Jimmy.

I understood very little about girls at the time. I found them fascinating—until they gathered around the piano at our dates. Then they became a bit unnerving and I'd keep my eyes fixed on the keys. When a conversation started, my part of it would be monosyllables.

It was different with Phyllis. I enjoyed being with her, talking with her, or just sharing a wonderful silence when we were alone. We were falling in love—but I didn't know it.

"Vincent," my father questioned, "you were out playing with Jimmy O'Connor three nights this week—until two last night. I won't have any more of this."

We had been observing a truce about my nights out, so his question startled and worried me. I thought the extra money I was bringing in had won him over to the idea, so I played that up in my reply.

"They liked us," I explained, "so they asked us to stay an hour overtime. We each got an extra dollar for it."

"I knew that. The spirits told me so! Look at this message!"

He thrust a scrawled sheet into my hands. It read, "Vincent will succeed in what he is doing now. Do nothing to stop him." And father said, "I don't know whether it means your job at Campbell's or the music. They both have my blessing."

Maybe he was in touch with some departed financial wizards.

Their cryptic advice kept me working night and day!—but I was contented.

Strangely, my mother seemed unconcerned by my late hours. Satisfied that I enjoyed what I was doing, she let it go at that. I resented it then, feeling that she lacked interest in me, but looking back at it now I realize that she was vicariously enjoying, *through me,* the good times she had been denied.

As for my sister, while I had been away at St. Mary's she found friendships and interests of her own. There was nothing to bring us together again, and until a long while later we were quite literally strangers toward each other.

So moved the months, drifting on toward a new year. Between the two jobs, plus rehearsals and my visits to the O'Connors, my thread-like connection with my own home frayed thinner. I believe I could have improved relationships with my father, but I didn't dare press the good luck of his acquiesence.

The only one expressing any concern over my night-owl habits was my employer, Alexander Campbell. He had a half interest in my health, and was concerned over the goofs I was perpetrating because of so little sleep. Mixing up people's milk bills can make trouble. Maybe our cows were contented, but our customers weren't!

Jimmy O'Connor was concerned about me, too, but for a different reason. "Vincent," he repeatedly said, "you're good enough for the big time. You've got to get started there. All it takes is the right break, and if you're not gonna get it for yourself, I'll have to get it for you!"

The theme of the less talented member of a vaudeville act deliberately breaking up the act to enable his partner-pal to make Broadway may sound like a corn ball. But it is founded on reality. I know, because it happened to me.

Jimmy O'Connor delivered on his promise to get me that all-important break even though it meant laying down his professional life for me. It was Phyllis who brought me the news.

Chapter 11. **PIANNER KID**

Somehow, I had stopped seeing Phyllis O'Conner so often. Jimmy and I were getting along better and better as a team, pulling real applause even at the more discriminating dates. That knowledge satisfied me, gave me what I wanted out of life at the time—and Phyllis became secondary in my thoughts for a while. The same thing probably happens in some marriages when the husband gets ahead fast in business or professional life and starts taking his wife for granted.

Nevertheless, I was delighted to find Phyllis waiting for me outside Campbell's at quitting time one afternoon. "You're to have supper with us tonight, Vincent," she explained. "It's all fixed. I telephoned the Jacobsons to tell your mother."

"I don't know," I said, "I'm not working tonight, so I thought I'd catch up on some sleep. I made three more mistakes at the office today. I don't know why they keep me."

"Well, maybe you won't need to work at Campbell's," Phyllis said enigmatically, but wouldn't say a word further. I was in a talkative mood, though, and confided some recent broodings. I had been sharpening my musical senses all right but what of the other values of life, like religion. Seeing the wonderful family relationships of people like the O'Connors and the McNultys made me want something like it for myself.

"Maybe I'm mainly to blame there, Phyllis," I admitted. "I never was close to my father but since I've been back from St. Mary's I've even got out of touch with my mother. We're a silent family even at mealtime. I really think they dislike me now. Why? Why?"

"Maybe it's just a phase you're going through, Vincent," Phyllis suggested. "There's a poem I read once about adolescence. It said that the teen-age years are a time to doubt everything except that the sun is warm, food is good, and life is to be lived rather than pondered."

I took her hand and said, "Then help me live it, Phyllis. I wish I could live it with you."

But life had other plans.

There was an air of mystery as well as merriment during the meal at the O'Connors'. (In an Irish household of that era, "dinner" was something served on Sunday afternoons.) Jimmy dropped some questions about how satisfied I was with our dates.

"I wouldn't want to feel that I was responsible for getting you into a line you'd later regret," he solemnized. "After all, if I hadn't asked you to be my accompanist you might make good at Campbell's and become a business tycoon."

"Forget that, Jimmy. It's father, anyway, who's responsible for my piano playing. If he hadn't enrolled me at the Business School, I'd never have met Phyllis—and then you."

Jimmy laughed. "Then I feel better about what I'm going to tell you. Dick Harding's going to drop by about eight. He's just about the best singing waiter in Brooklyn. He runs the show at Clayton's Restaurant. Well, you're going to be the relief pianist there!"

So the cat was out of the bag, although in ten minutes I felt nervous enough to crawl inside the bag myself. All the old insecurity showed up, and I was building an excuse to get me home (an imaginary stomach-ache), when Jimmy winked knowingly to Phyllis and left the two of us alone.

She talked with such conviction that when Harding arrived and we got the audition going, I kept the butterflies locked up in my stomach instead of letting them escape to my fingertips. He liked what he heard, but suggested a tryout at Clayton's itself. If the other singing waiters liked me, to say nothing of the audience, I could fill in while the regular pianist took his rest breaks. It meant about two hours of actual performance a night, and I'd be through around two A.M. The pay would be four dollars a night, seven nights a week, but no sharing in the waiters' tips. Only the regular pianist cut in on that melon.

Visions of possible trouble at home because I'd be out *every* night of the week, of getting sacked at Campbell's as my error record soared; but worst of all, a likely nipping of my budding romance with Phyllis . . . it was the last point I gave voice to.

"Phyllis, I've missed you a lot because of the dates Jimmy and I played. This job at Clayton's would be every night. We'd never see each other."

"Oh, we'll find time, Vincent," she assured me. "Even if it's just Sunday afternoons—and I want you to get ahead so much."

Brooklyn is still called the City of Churches, but some forty years ago it was also Borough of Bistros. Frank Clayton's was one of a cluster of cafés (or saloons) at Pearl and Willoughby Streets. Its competitors included Billy Watson's Cozy Corner where that great burlesque comic surrounded himself with ex-burlesque dancers who had gone well above the 160 mark; hence, the Billy Watson Beef Trust Chorus. Billy figured they were good advertising for the good food he featured, in that era of the king-size calory count. Then there was the café run by Jimmy La Panna, who figured that a good pianist could outweigh Billy's Beef Trust in pulling the cash customers. He paid his pianist a few bucks more, and even at thirty a week Jimmy Durante was quite a bargain!

A third competitor, Casey's, dispensed with other attractions and appealed only to the inner man. The food there was plentiful and good. Casey provided unscheduled entertainment, though. An ex-wrestler with underworld know-how through match fixes, he and his wonderful meals were a magnet to punks and toughs. Brawling being their profession they often took a motorman's holiday by mixing it up right at the tables. Many a mobster finished the meal with red stuff on his vest that wasn't ketchup, and this pulled a lot of ordinary people to the place, hoping to see trouble.

Clayton's grabbed off most of the carriage trade, though his place was famed for providing the biggest free-lunch in town. There was free stimulation for the esthetic senses, too. Oil paintings covered every square foot of wall space, disclosing the varied postures beautiful women—"tomatoes" as the customers called them—could assume while getting into or out of their clothes!

Clayton made up for it with his own elaborate attire, usually a pearl-gray coat, striped trousers, and a fancy weskit crossed by a heavy gold chain on which dangled an enormous hunk of jade. His clothes made quite an impression once you got your dazzled eyes off his six-carat diamond ring or his diamond-ringed pearl stickpin.

I thought I was somewhere in the middle of the Arabian Nights when Jimmy O'Connor half-led, half-pushed me inside Clayton's that night. We arrived just as a bouncer was tossing out a drunk. Figuring that inadequate piano players might rate the same treatment, I wanted to turn back, but Jimmy would have none of such chickening-out.

We glided up a thick red carpet to the plushy room where the entertaining was done. We arrived just as Dick Harding and three other singing waiters got started on "Play That Barbershop Chord." They were really good, especially Harding with his beautiful Irish tenor voice. He nodded hello in the middle of a note and indicated a nearby table we were to take. Then he tossed me a cue to study what the pianist did, and I forgot everything else.

I sat there entranced as they went through a repertoire I later learned by heart myself. I can still dream back to it and hear every rich chord they had worked into such wonderful old numbers as "Shine On, Harvest Moon," "That's How I Need You," "Dear Old Girl," "By The Light of The Silvery Moon," etc. Will today's Rock'n' Roll leave such memories, I wonder?

Their numbers finished, Dick came over to ask what I thought. I struggled for words to communicate my enchantment. Then I asked, "Who are those three girls at the table in the corner. The ones who smiled at us when we came in. Are they actresses?"

"Well," Dick hedged, "you might say they put on a show—a show of their own. They're here to meet the big spenders, Vincent. We don't exactly like to have them around, but they do bring in the guys who'll spend the bills instead of silver."

Incidentally, the big spenders in those days were the beer drinkers! A bottle of beer cost a quarter; whisky was fifteen cents. An unattached male who wanted to attract an unattached female proceeded to down four or five bottles of suds which the waiter left on the table as an unmistakable sign of opulence in search of amour.

"Eddie's finishing up a set of piano numbers now," Dick Harding observed. "C'mon over, Vince, and meet him."

Somehow my legs made those fifteen feet. I found Eddie Moebus very affable. All fear he'd think I was after his job vanished in the first minute.

"It's not a bad racket, kid," he explained. "A grind, it's true, but you get used to it. Only thing is, I absolutely got to have a relief pianist sit in now and then, and I hope that's you. Let's find out if you are good enough—right now. C'mon. Sit in for me while I take a break."

This time the butterflies were getting loose from their stomach prison in droves. I stammered an excuse, my knees buckled a bit, and I had to lean against the piano. But Dick Harding knew the antidote.

"Just do a number for me, like you did at the O'Connors' tonight. A simple one. Make it 'Let Me Call You Sweetheart' and I'll get everybody to sing."

Jimmy O'Connor whirled the revolving piano stool with one hand and pushed me on to it with the other. Dick gave me the downbeat with a friendly finger. We were off. . . "Let me call you sweetheart . . . I'm in love with you. . . ."

It was clear immediately that the crowd was in love with the tune. Dick skillfully brought them into a chorus but kept one ear tuned to how I was handling the piece. Then he suddenly waved for the singing to stop and said, "Go to it, Vincent; show 'em what you can do."

With all that skillful handling—more care than goes into presenting a newcomer on television—I couldn't miss. My attack of nerves was submerged in a wave of intense enjoyment. On Dick's signal to keep going, I slipped into "Alexander's Ragtime Band" . . . then "Maple Leaf Rag." The ragtime beat was the perfect complement to the schmaltz and I knew I had the crowd with me when people left their tables and gathered round the piano. That has happened many times since, but it's never brought the same thrill as the night I knew I was "going over" at Clayton's.

When I figured they had enough ragtime I switched back to the sentimental winding up with Father Aloysius' favorite, "Gee, But It's Great to Meet a Friend From Your Home Town." Maybe he was saying a prayer for me that evening, because the crowd loved it. The applause when I finished was something I could actually feel. The proof that it was genuine, came when six waiters brought up beers listeners were buying for me and lined them along the piano top.

Eddie Moebus explained it. "They liked you, kid," he smiled, "and it's their way of saying so. You were a real surprise to me, I'll admit. I didn't think you were old enough to play a good game of marbles. C'mon, drink up."

"But I don't drink," I blurted out. "Except celery tonic."

"Then take a couple of these over to your friend," Eddie suggested, "and I'll finish the rest . . . Oh, CHARLIE!" (he suddenly boomed out to a distant waiter) "Bring the kid a celery tonic!"

The crowd laughed as I walked back to Jimmy's table, but it was a good-natured laugh. I'd gone over with them—gone over big!—and all my doubts dissolved in that wave of applause. I even felt grateful to my father for tyrannically imposing those long hours of childhood practice.

I knew for certain now where I wanted to go in life—show business! Other circumstances, other opportunities might have directed me to the concert stage. But I'm not a bit sorry my professional life began at Clayton's. In the concert field one meets people from a very small cross-section of life. But in show business I've met them all, from punks to princes . . . from dames to dowagers . . . from Park Place to Park Avenue.

And it's been a ball!

A few weeks after I took the pianist relief job, Eddie Moebus decided night life wasn't for him. (Maybe his wife decided it for him!) He joined the Shapiro-Bernstein music publishing house as a tune demonstrator. On Dick Harding's say-so, Clayton okayed me as Ed's successor at the customary twenty-eight per week and twenty five per cent of the waiters' tips. Nevertheless, I stayed on at Campbell's. Maybe it was lack of confidence, maybe just deference to my father's wishes, maybe the inability of a seventeen-year-old youth to back up his decisions with appropriate action.

Whatever it was, I doubled in brass but good! The desk job at Campbell's ran from nine to five. . . . Clayton's hours were nominally nine to two plus occasional overtime. One night Clayton had a private party after closing time, and it was well after 5 A.M. when I eased my way toward my room. Suddenly I realized my father was coming downstairs. The childhood terror came charging back. I threw my hat and coat on a chair and walked over to the sink in the kitchen, hoping he'd miss that room.

He didn't. Wearing a bathrobe and an excited look, he greeted me almost casually, "Vincent, what are you doing up so early?"

"I couldn't sleep, father," I white-lied. "So I came down to get a drink of water. Maybe I'll go to early Mass" (it was Sunday morning).

"Never mind Mass," he insisted, "let me tell you a dream I had."

He was still interpreting that dream a half hour later when I slumped over in the kitchen chair and fell fast asleep on the table. I woke at eight o'clock with my father's bathrobe across my shoulders.

When I took over, Clayton's didn't hire a relief pianist. They auditioned several but none seemed to do, or maybe Frank Clayton saw the chance to save four dollars a night.

One evening a young fellow came barging up the stairs with six beautiful girls around him. I was just finishing up a solo set and he walked right over to the piano and stuck his nose in my face.

"Kid," he told me, "you look like you need a rest. Take a powder and I'll keep the keyboard warm for you."

That he did. He kept the audience warm, too, with his clowning and tap dancing. Yes, tap dancing while he played the piano, for he sent the piano stool spinning away with a kick.

I asked Dick Harding who the guy was.

"Oh, he's Jimmy Durante, that show-off pianist from La Panna's. I'm keeping an eye on him, because he likes to take a piano apart for laughs. I'll throw the bum out if he tries it here."

To the impressionable kid I was then, this left me goggle-eyed. To me Jimmy Durante was no "show-off pianist," but about the greatest entertainer in the world—and this opinion hasn't changed.

"Well, folks," the stand-in Cyrano announced some forty minutes later, "I got to get over to La Panna's, where there's real entertainment, but before I leave the jernt let me turn over this wunnerful instrument, which I haven't damaged a bit tonight, to the regular ivory tickler here. I don't know his name and he ain't old enough to be called mister anyway, so I'll just call him the Pianner Kid."

From then on Pianner Kid was my name at Clayton's. Thank you, Jimmy, for dubbing me with it.

Chapter 12. FIRST KISS

Sunday afternoon was the loveliest time of the week for me. It meant a date with Phyllis, a real date, not just supper at the O'Connors', and an hour or so of family conversation before I left for Clayton's. When I look back, I realize those Sunday afternoons were my closest touch with a normal, balanced life. Everything else was either boring or hectic—boring on my clerical job, hectic at the cafe.

The scientists tell us that for every action there is an equal and opposite reaction. The reaction from my transports over landing the pianist spot at Clayton's was a long time coming, but it lingered a long time, too.

"I'm not saving any money on the job," I complained to Phyllis on one of our long walks. "When friends come in or that reporter from the Brooklyn paper who says he'll write me up some day, I order drinks for them or foot the bill for dinner. That's what keeps me broke."

"We've been over that before, Vincent," she chided me. "You've got to stop trying to make a big impression on people."

"But I want people to like me," I protested—"and remember me, too. After all, making friends is good business."

After a silence Phyllis replied, "I don't like to say this but you've got to learn that you can't buy friendship that way. You've got other things to give to people. . . . I mean that" she continued when I looked hurt. "You're so shy just now that the good things you can offer can't seem to get through—except with me. . . . That's better. I like your smile. Now tell me, what else is bothering you?"

As I began pouring them out, those troubles, real or imagined, that had felt like a flood to me, ebbed to a trickle.

"Seems to me you're still worried about your situation at home," Phyllis suggested. "Can't you have an understanding once and for all? You say your mother has grown distant and indifferent to you. Ask her why. And tell them you want to give up the job at Campbell's. Working around the clock, like that, is hurting you—and it's hurting us, I'm afraid. Being with you part of the time is wonderful, but *not* being with you so much of the time—well, it simply hurts. This way, life isn't happy for me, either; I, too, have loneliness to endure."

"I think that's why I work as hard as I do, Phyllis," I explained. "So I won't miss you so much. Gee, that doesn't make sense, does it? I guess the real trouble is that I'm afraid to have a showdown at home about the job at Campbell's, and I've worked all the harder to run away from that problem.

"At first it seemed enough just to be doing well at Clayton's," I stumbled on, "but now I can see why I'm so dissatisfied. Doing what a fellow wants to do and succeeding at it—well, it's wonderful only if —if he's got someone to share it with him. Will you do that with me, Phyllis?"

"I always have, haven't I?" she whispered. "Why do you think I met you at Campbell's the night Jimmy had Dick Harding over to the house?"

"You've been a wonderful friend, but we're a lot more than friends now. I don't think I realized how dear you are to me until this minute. If I can get the price together before payday, will you wear my ring?"

"Vincent," she brought her lovely mouth to my cheek, "don't borrow anything. A ring is round and people use it because it symbolizes something without an end. I'll try to make my lips look something like a ring—if you'll kiss me forever."

It was a Sunday kind of kiss—warm but tender . . . full of yearning and sweetness, too.

It was my first kiss—and ours was a Sunday kind of love!

Back at the O'Connors' the news of our engagement started quite a celebration. Dad O'Connor broke out a special brand of Irish whisky he'd been saving for an event. Mrs. O'Connor garnished the corned beef with extra care. Jimmy bought himself a second cigar for the evening. In no time at all, I was late for Clayton's and they were waving good-bye to me from the front porch.

Phyllis walked over to the trolley with me, and on the wings of another kiss I promised I'd quit the job at Campbell's soon so we could have more time with each other.

"I'm twenty-five dollars in debt now," I explained. "Suppose I keep the job for just three more weeks and use every cent of my pay on what I owe?"

"I've been waiting for you almost three years," she smiled. "Guess I can put up with three more weeks."

Chapter 13. INITIATION INTO SEX

There are periods in a person's life when things don't "go right." Phyllis and I weren't engaged a week before the serious illness of an aunt took Mrs. O'Connor and her lovely daughter on a mercy mission to Boston. The aunt was apparently a cancer victim, but cancer was an unmentioned word those days. It was a time when hospital care for such cases was only for the very rich or the very poor. Phyllis's aunt had reached the point where she needed round-the-clock attention, and Mrs. O'Connor and Phyllis left to provide it. We made up a little pretence between ourselves that the patient would improve and Phyllis be back in my arms; but her absence stretched over two months.

When I announced my engagement at Clayton's it brought a lot more than mere congratulations! Advice on the "facts of life" poured in, part of it well-intentioned, part sly innuendo, part right out of the sex-joke sewer.

I certainly was ignorant. Sex had been a fiercely tabood subject at home; St. Mary's had ignored it in the classroom and castigated it in the confessional. My condition was realized by my rough and ready friends at Clayton's (ready with their advice, rough at imparting it). My painful ignorance soon became agonizing confusion in which I even doubted my "manhood."

One night when some of the singing waiters and imbibing customers were ribbing me, a sympathetic voice cut in and quieted the others. "Leave the kid alone. If he believes some of that stuff you're telling him, you can't tell what might happen!"

The voice was Rose Flaherty's, and as far as sex matters were concerned it was the Voice of Experience. Rose was one of the lovelier ladies of the evening who attracted the big spenders to Clayton's and left with her pick of the Johns at midnight.

But she passed up several opportunities that evening to chat with me during the piano breaks. She was a kind, generous girl in her late twenties, very much out of place in that old profession. She belonged in woman's *truly* oldest profession—motherhood. Usually our conversation was pretty casual, much in the manner of mothers with teen-age sons: my piano work, my other job at Campbell's, my girl Phyllis, our plans for the future. That night, however, Rose tried to fathom just how deep my sex ignorance was.

Rose must have mentioned my naïveté (hardly the word she'd use for it) to some of her girl friends at the bar. The next night a willowly creature named Violet lisped, "Vincent, when you finish up here, let's you and me get a hotel room."

"I don't have any money," I gasped, now that opportunity was breaking down the door. It was the truth about my fiscal condition at the moment, although my answer was more a feint to ward off the proposition.

"Then why don't you give me your watch," Violet persisted, "and I'll go pawn it."

Out came the big silver watch my father had given me back in my St. Mary days and out went Violet to pawn it—at one o'clock in the morning! She wasn't back when we closed at two (it was a slow night)—or at three-thirty where I was still waiting outside, not so much wanting Violet as my watch. When I didn't see her the following evening I mentioned it to Dick Harding. He got sore.

"I guess you're even stupider about dames than I thought! Don't trust any one of them around here, except Rose Flaherty. Don't worry about the watch, though. We'll get it back."

Dick brought over a detective named Mike Melee who listened to my story without comment, then buttonholed a few "knowledgeable" customers who had Violet's address. After work I went with Mike to a slum, where we climbed three flights of rickety stairs in the dark. Mike picked out flat 3A with his pocket torch, then pounded on the door. Violet opened it an inch, and Mike's strong-arm push wrenched the chain lock out of its socket.

"What's the big idea?" Violet pleaded, clutching her cheap bathrobe to her ribs. "I ain't done nothing. Oh, the Pianner Kid," she added, seeing me in the hallway.

"Yeah, the Pianner Kid," Mike agreed. "Where's his watch?"

"I ain't got it," Violet whimpered. "I hocked it to get something to eat."

"What's the matter with Clayton's free lunch?" asked Mike. "And let's have the pawn ticket, plus whatever dough you got for it—*pronto* . . . and get your clothes on. You're goin' to the freezer."

In the background I was protesting to Mike that I wanted no trouble—to let Violet go. But Mike insisted and next morning a plainclothesman came to Campbell's to take me to court. John Campbell's eyebrows flipped into his hairline when he learned this, but the detective said I had witnessed an accident and was needed to testify.

"Of course, of course," Mr. Campbell agreed. "Go right ahead,

Vincent. I'm always glad to have an employee of mine do his duty."

But when we reached the courtroom and I saw Violet sitting there, her eyes frightened into a stare, I knew I couldn't press a complaint against her. Mike and the judge were very angry when I said so.

"How do you figure we can clean up this part of town," Mike demanded, "if you suckers won't press charges after we get your property back!" He looked sore enough to sock me, but the judge intervened, and I got out.

Strangely, I never did get the watch back. I didn't even bother to find out where the pawnship was located, to redeem it. I should have treasured the timepiece as a gift from my father, but sentiment was swallowed by necessity. The two dollars recovered from Violet went too fast.

The episode was a laugh to everybody at Clayton's except Dick Harding and Rose Flaherty. With Dick's connivance, no doubt, Rose became my bodyguard around the place. She filled me in on some of the sterner details of life in general and certain people in particular, with emphasis on "girls like that bum, Violet!" In appreciation, I often bought her one of the choicer suppers on the menu if she seemed to be broke (and it's amazing what a loose hold women who make a "loose living" have on money).

We used to go to other places after Clayton's closed for the night. One of our favorites, for choice food if not ditto company, was Hogan's, the hangout of that era's version of Murder, Inc.

One night a shifty-eyed character passed some pink envelopes around the tables. Some took the packets, poured the white powder contents on their wrists, and sniffed it eagerly. You could do things like that at Hogan's without attracting a curious stare, let alone a member of the narcotics squad.

"Want a buzz, kid?" the creep suggested, holding out an envelope to me. Rose leaped from her seat, stretched across the table, and slapped the envelope to the floor.

"You gahdamzonofabitch," she screamed at the character, who made a record-breaking dash out Hogan's front door while Rose tossed beer glasses and epithets after him. As the dope pusher fled into the night he carried with him a lurid (and probably accurate) description of his family tree.

Rose came back from the door, to warn me, "Kid, never touch that dream stuff, y' hear!"

The excitement and exercise had whetted her appetite and I ordered her another lobster!

"Lobster's my favorite food," Rose told the admiring table. "My mother used to feed me on it when I was six months old. I couldn't hold on to my food then, so Ma gave me food that would hold on to me!"

It was Rose's favorite joke and always got a laugh. It's still getting laughs on television.

A week or so later, Violet showed up at Clayton's again. First thing she did was assure me she had intended to follow through on our deal but had felt sick that evening and the next night. When she suggested we might still consummate the deal, I was ready to go, when Dick Harding walked over to break things up. Later that night, he told Rose Flaherty.

It was a Friday and when we closed around three in the morning Rose asked me to keep the following night free after Clayton's shuttered, to try a new hangout she'd discovered.

"Have they got a piano there?" I wanted to know. "Will I be expected to entertain?"

"You certainly will," Rose added, with a Mona Lisa smile.

The following night she showed up a bit late but looking very radiant. There were more mysterious smiles as it got toward closing time. As soon as I was through Rose was at my side, hurrying me out to a waiting hansom. The driver knew where we were going, which was certainly more than I did. Ten minutes later we pulled up before one of Brooklyn's classiest hotels.

When we were shown into the room Rose had reserved, bells of understanding began to ring!

"Vinnie," she whispered as she embraced me, "you got to find out about women sometime. I don't want you learning from a tramp like Violet. I don't want you to get your first impression of love that way."

"And something awful could happen in the way of a disease, couldn't it?" I voiced a suppressed fear. "From Violet, I mean."

"Yes," Rose agreed, "but a lot worse than that could happen to you. You could miss what's beautiful and wonderful about it, and think it's disgusting. . . . I was engaged once to a young fellow just a couple of years older than you are now. Some of the boys took him out a week before our wedding to learn about women. He left New York a few days later and wrote that he couldn't marry me. No, it wasn't a disease. I found out, years later, from one of the boys. Frank was young and innocent and unknowing. From what happened that night he thought he lacked manhood. He was *afraid* to marry me!"

"Maybe he was that way, really," I suggested. "I've heard that Olson, one of the singing waiters, never got married because he couldn't."

"Forget all that nonsense they've been telling you, Vinnie. Let me show you how marvelous love-making can be."

She certainly didn't have a reluctant pupil.

Emerging from the bathroom, where she had taken a shower, Rose gave me my first understanding of how beautiful a nude woman can be. The cheesecake photographs of that time, plus my own imagination, had left an uncertain picture in my mind. Rose created a vision where there had been a mirage.

Rose's kisses spoke for all womanhood—to all the longing and desiring and wondering the adolescent suffers . . . then finds the suffering forgotten in urgent ecstasy.

To me, the next few hours were ecstatic, but I realized that Rose didn't quite share that ecstasy. She was warm, tender, even passionate—but through it all I got the impression that some other purpose was stronger than sex desire.

I didn't really comprehend why she took the initiative, made all the arrangements I would have bungled, then offered herself so tenderly to a naïve youth. I didn't really comprehend her motivation until years later when I saw the Broadway production of *Tea and Sympathy.*

For me, Rose Flaherty was the headmaster's wife, helping a naïve boy across the bridge of a difficult experience, to the side of understanding and joy!

However, by the time I got home around ten that Sunday morning, the traditions of religious training and paternal raving on the subject of sex had set up a reaction. I didn't suffer a revulsion of feeling about the night; it had been too beautiful for that. But I wondered if I "should have waited," brought male virginity to my marriage, etc.

The pendulum of my emotional reaction swung all the way to guilt when I read the note my mother had left on the kitchen table, on her way to Mass: "Vincent, Phyllis O'Connor called twice this morning. She's back from Boston for a few days. Wants you to drop over there this afternoon. Give her our love . . . Mother."

It was wonderful to see Phyllis again. The ordeal of physical suffering that she was helping relieve had somehow added another dimension to her loveliness. I've seen the same luminous glory in the faces of men and women giving their lives to religion.

My own thoughts weren't exactly luminous that afternoon. I did a questionable thing, but I suppose the rules of my upbringing required it. In words that couldn't possibly convey the full story and meaning of the night before, I blundered into confessing my threshhold step into sex experience. Phyllis was shocked, hurt, bewildered —and I deeply penitent. I asked her if she wanted to stop seeing me.

Phyllis looked into my eyes for a very long minute. Then she turned out the light over the sofa where we were sitting. I could barely see her in the dimness of the late afternoon, but I could feel her arms bring my face to her lips and I could hear her voice murmur, "Could I do any less for you—than Rose?"

Strangely, I never saw Rose Flaherty again except at a distance, and a distance more emotional than physical. She stopped coming to Clayton's, and since Phyllis's return had put me back on Cloud Nine I couldn't have cared less. I think Phyllis managed to get in touch with Rose that Sunday evening of our reconciliation (or her brother Jimmy did it for her), and an understanding was reached that Rose wouldn't see me. I came across her from time to time, but her greeting was strictly on the platonic side, and Rose drifted out of my life without a ripple.

Chapter 14. I LOSE TWO JOBS IN HALF A DAY

At Campbell's, one warm spring Saturday afternoon, I went over to a file cabinet to look up some bills. My next recollection was of Mr. Campbell shaking me gently by the shoulder and saying, "Is there anything wrong, Vincent? Are you feeling well?"

"Yessir, I'm all right," I said.

"You had us worried a minute," he explained. "I couldn't rouse you. I thought you were ill."

"Well, that's right," I agreed. "I was feeling kind of dizzy and I just leaned up against the cabinet." I was playing along with the lead he had suggested, that I hadn't been asleep but was feeling ill. P. S.—it didn't work.

"I've noticed you haven't seemed well lately," Mr. Campbell observed. "You're too intelligent a young man to make all the mistakes you do unless you're sick. Maybe the job is too hard for you . . . or you're not really suited for it. Anyway, suppose you get well, Vincent, and come back here when you're feeling better. We'll give you a week's wages and shake hands on it."

So I got home earlier that Saturday afternoon than usual. I knew I'd need a couple of hours shut-eye for the big night ahead at Clayton's, so I asked my mother to call me at six. That deep sleep earlier in the day at the office was the tip-off on my utter exhaustion. I hardly heard what my mother answered. I was dead to the world by the time my head touched the pillow.

I woke up sluggishly, with a vague impression that things weren't quite right. I knew my mother had just knocked on the door and called me. But the light was peculiar for that time of the evening.

As I washed and dressed I planned some of the medleys I'd piece together at Clayton's. I called a quick good-bye to my mother in the kitchen and said I'd have something to eat at the restaurant. She answered vaguely about attending Mass. This was incomprehensible to me. Who goes to Mass on Saturday evening?

On my way to the trolley it seemed that Pacific Street was deserted except for Mr. Gilhooley who was just coming down his front steps.

"Doesn't it seem kind of quiet for this time of the evening?" I answered when he greeted me.

"Time of the avening!" he popped incredulously. "Vincent, this is Sunday morning! I'm on me way to Mass."

The next moment I was on my way to Clayton's, sans trolley car. I ran all the way and called on every saint I'd made friends with at St. Mary's to end this silly dream. But it was no dream. When I reached Clayton's and pounded on the locked door with my little remaining strength, it was opened by Eddie Bolger, bartender and cleanup chief. He was amazed to see me.

"Where the hell were you all night?" he demanded. "Out buying another watch for Violet?"

"Where's Clayton?" I gasped. "Something awful happened."

"I'll say it did," Eddie agreed. "And you're lucky Clayton isn't here to say it in person. A big Saturday night and you don't show up. So half the customers are gone by the time he lands a fill-in pianist. I never seen him boil like that."

"But I want to tell him what happened," I spluttered.

"Don't bother," Eddie comforted me with a sneer. "Clayton said if you had the nerve to show up, I should tell you you're through. Your pay's in an envelope behind the bar."

I guess I was tight-roping on tears when I came out. Eddie stopped sweeping a moment and called after me, "I'm sorry, kid. You never should have did that to Clayton. But good luck, anyway."

There I was, fired from two jobs in half a day with probably less than half a chance of getting another. As for clerical positions, any reference Campbell gave me would hardly be glowing. As for cafés, failure of an entertainer to appear as scheduled was a capital crime. That old axiom "The show must go on" was created by theatrical employers rather than by actors. Many a performer went on when he should have been carried off to a hospital. It was a choice between physical or professional oblivion—and it's obvious which one a hambone would pick.

I walked back home, trying to understand what had happened. I couldn't. My thoughts were too emotional. I even considered going back to St. Mary's in the belief this setback might be a sign that I had the calling after all. But then I thought of Phyllis, and I knew that life without her simply wasn't for me. That gave me some degree of resolution to fight back against the two bad breaks. When I came home an old-fashioned greeting from my father put backbone in my resolve.

"Vincent," he shouted from his study. "Mr. Campbell telephoned to ask how you're feeling today. He told me he let you go there until you're well again. What sort of lies are you telling him about your health? Go to Mass immediately and see me when you get back, do you understand!"

The clerical job he had saddled me with was over, but he still meant to ride herd on my life. With that came my decision. I would leave home, for good!

Ever the practical soul in the provender department, after I packed my belongings I made a pile of sandwiches to take along. To my mother, away at Mass, I wrote this brief letter:

"I lost my job at Campbell's. I'm going to stick to music instead of getting another job as a clerk. That would only cause trouble here, so I think it's best that I leave home. Please don't worry about me. I'll be all right and I'll let you know how I'm doing . . . Love, Vincent."

There was only one thing I regretted as I left the house: I couldn't take my old piano along.

I resolved not to burden the O'Connors with my troubles. They had difficulties enough coping with the illness in their family. So I headed through a heavy rain, for the Harding's—and woke them out of the sound Sunday-morning sleep that Dick so much depended on. Dick was speechless when he answered the door and saw me soaked to the skin, with my cardboard suitcase ready to fall apart.

"I've run away from home," I announced, miserably.

Dick knew at once that the moment called for a joke. "It looks like you swam away," he observed. "Shake yourself and c'mon in."

"Ann," he called as I oozed my way toward the living room (parlor in those days)—"we've got a visitor badly in need of a cup of coffee." Then he turned to me and asked where I'd been the previous night. I told him the crazy, mixed-up story and he began to laugh.

"What's there to laugh about?" I demanded. "What am I gonna do? No job. No place to live."

"Well, you're better off without that job at the milk company. As for a place to live, you bunk with us for awhile."

"And what about my job at Clayton's? I certainly can't get that back."

"You'd have lost it in another week, anyway," Dick answered. "Clayton is closing the upstairs place this summer after Decoration Day. I postponed telling you till I could line up something for both of us. Well, McLaughlin's wants me to head the entertainment at their place out at Sheepshead Bay. That means you'll be the pianist there, as soon as you satisfy Old Man McLaughlin you're as good as I told him."

"Gee, that's wonderful!" I beamed. "But what will your wife say about my staying here a while?"

"She'll say here's your hot coffee," Ann Harding announced from the kitchen doorway, "and be sure you see my husband comes straight home from work with you each morning."

We all had a laugh on that, and for the first time in my life I realized how enjoyable bacon and eggs can be for breakfast!

That enjoyable late morning breakfast opened a delightful two weeks vacation for me. The Hardings insisted that I take a much needed rest before starting at McLaughlin's, and they wouldn't accept any board money until the new job began.

That meant that Phyllis and I had fourteen days (and nights) and twenty-eight dollars to spend with and for each other. It was only two dollars per day but to a couple in love that's a million. And we were a million dollars in love!

Chapter 15. CONEY ISLAND DOWN THE BAY

I didn't have to display a nickel's worth of talent auditioning for the job at McLaughlin's. Dick introduced me to the stocky, ruddy-faced, cigar-chewing owner of the place with a buildup a modern press agent would envy.

"But I *got* a piano player," the impeturbable McLaughlin replied, taking another bite at his soggy cigar.

"Sure you have," Dick agreed, "and a good one. But Billy Little can't handle the grind all by himself. His work's bound to suffer. This way you get two top pianists. And the Piano Kid here will be sensational. Just give a listen."

"Naw," Bert McLaughlin decided, and looked me up and down. "Okay, Kid, you can have the job. Twenty bucks a week, and you can sleep upstairs."

The reduction in salary didn't please me, but I liked the idea of a room of my own, so I looked at Dick, got a quick nod that okayed the offer, and we shook on it. And, the hours were much better than at Clayton's (I was to split a twelve-hour shift with Billy Little) which left me a lot more time to be with Phyllis.

I soon found that although the hours were shorter the work was more strenuous. I wasn't there simply to play for the customers when they came in; I was also to help the singing waiters *get* them in! McLaughlin's was situated at a trolley-transfer point of the Ocean Avenue and Seagate lines, and we used every trick in the sales book (plus some) to entice the people who were waiting to make the transfer. Many a returning husband whose trolley was a few minutes late reached home several hours late, with a shirtfront inflated with McLaughlin's hot frankfurters and cold beer.

Every time a trolley came in, the singing waiters who weren't busy at a table would rush out to extol our hot dog stand, and add some free entertainment with a song or two. If a potential customer seemed half-sold, we elbowed him in the rest of the way!

We were up against plenty of competition! Lundy's and Jake the

Old Reliable were across the avenue. But we had a great aid in a dance hall right next to McLaughlin's, where Johnny Nolan's orchestra played. Johnny's music would get the dancers hot and thirsty, McLaughlin's beer and hot dogs would cool them off. It was a great one-two punch.

A dependable source of customers was the old Vitagraph movie studio nearby. Movie stars were a lot more democratic in those days, or a lot more easily satisfied. Francis X. Bushman, Maurice Costello, Earle Williams, John Bunny, Flora Finch, Pauline Fredericks, Anita Stewart—all big names of the day, were big spenders at McLaughlin's.

The way to the "powder room" took the ladies past my piano. Some paused to exchange smiles with me. One suspicious male escort resented this so much he came back the next night to throw rocks onto the porch in the general direction of my piano! I had to keep on playing, but Dick Harding ran outside and fixed matters with a little unfriendly persuasion.

I'd been at McLaughlin's just a couple of weeks when Billy Little was caught at some infraction of the few rules that weren't to be broken, and Bert gave him the sack. Then he bestowed a great honor on me.

"Kid," he announced, "you're the head piano player here now, and you can handle it full time, too."

The thrill over the promotion departed when I learned, on payday, that it carried no increase—except the doubled hours! Still twenty bucks a week and the room upstairs. McLaughlin did add one nice touch, though. He put a screen in my bedroom window and reduced the hordes of Sheepshead Bay mosquitoes almost fifty percent.

I was kept so busy I even ate most of my evening meals (hot dogs and celery tonic) right at the keyboard. I kept the melody going with my right hand while stuffing the food in with my left.

The singing waiters made up a betting pool on what day I'd collapse. But I fooled them and we used the money for a farewell party in the fall. They didn't realize that twelve hours a night at McLaughlin's was a vacation compared to the winter I'd put in at Clayton's and Campbell's.

Things were always hot enough at McLaughlin's, but my first Fourth of July there got much too hot for comfort. Just after dark a dozen young punks wearing identical caps and blue celluloid "H. K." buttons pinned to their shirt collars rushed in the front doors and began setting up a barricade of chairs and tables!

"Give the call, Vincent!" Dick Harding yelled. "These are the Hell's Kitchen Boys!"

Instantly I thumped out "The Wearing of the Green" on my piano. It was our equivalent of the "Hey, Rube" cry of the circus for all hands to come a-running and ready for trouble. The trouble began when a horde of Hudson Dusters stormed the barricades to get at their gang rivals. The feuding gangs had picked McLaughlin's for their July Fourth battleground.

I played on and on, in an unbelieving trance, while beer mugs and crockery and fists sailed through the air.

Our regular customers had exited, and some of them had the good sense to send the cops.

But it was not yet the era of rapid communications, with prowl cars alerted by radio signals; so it was the longest half-hour since time began until the advance squad of police showed up and promptly signalled for reinforcements! Meanwhile several of the Hudson Duster mob unloaded "cannons," as revolvers were then called, and took pot shots at their gang rivals. Their code of ethics kept them from aiming at our singing-waiter group, even though we were bombarding them with beer mugs. Finally the mounted police arrived and ran their horses right into the groups that were fighting in the street. But they didn't get things under control, until a smart police sergeant (who later became a captain) turned in a fire alarm. As we heard the fire sirens screaming toward us, Dick Harding paused a moment in his attempt to pry another gangster from the porch and asked, "Now, why didn't I think of that?"

High-pressure fire hoses turned the trick where police clubs and charging horses had failed. The fight went out of that sodden mob and they hightailed it for safety. About sixty of them didn't make it, for enough pie wagons to hold that many were filled with those that the police had cornered. They included seventeen ambulance cases, three of them gunshot victims.

Peace returned to McLaughlin's—although none of the terrified customers did that night. I suddenly realized it was very quiet, except for one sound I couldn't quite figure out. Then in came Dick Harding, his waiter's outfit torn and bloody, his right eye swollen shut. Despite his hurts, he burst out laughing. The incongruous sound still heard in the night was me. I was still playing the piano!

I was still playing though some of the middle scale notes would never sound again. A good-size rock had shattered the back of the piano and smashed the inner keyboard. If that rock had gone a couple of inches higher it would have got me in the head!

That was the second time my piano stool had been a post of danger. The first had been one morning at Hogan's where I had gone after Clayton's had closed. I was knocking out some request tunes on their piano. Suddenly a dope-crazed customer went beserk, pulled a revolver from a shoulder holster, and started pegging random shots at me!

Later it turned out he was just aiming at the piano, without even knowing I was on the other side of it. The crowd screamed and ducked for cover. I kept right on playing, although I guess I missed a few beats. Before he could improve his aim, 300-pound Mike Shaughnessy, the most feared bouncer in Brooklyn, roared onto the scene like a bull elephant. Mike was unarmed (as always) but the sight of him was enough to send the dope-happy gunman toward the nearest exit. He knew what was coming, although I didn't. Catching the poor hophead around the waist, Mike lifted him off the floor, pulled his face sharply upward, and in one quick motion *bit off the end of his nose*! The screaming victim of this mayhem—now sobered—staggered out the front door into oblivion.

Mike calmly displayed the severed nose tip to the startled crowd, then walked over to the bar where the bartender—an experienced hand at this routine—was already pouring a glass of gin.

I thought Shaughnessy needed the drink to steady his nerves, but no! Instead, he dropped his trophy in it and the glass was hoisted to a row of three other embalmed noses. The display (which I hadn't previously noticed) was renowned as Mike's Souvenirs. Nose ends of two of Brooklyn's toughest thugs were included in the collection.

Chapter 16. TEMPERANCE WAS MY UNDOING

But my memories of those early days recall lots of good times with good people, too. There was John Bunny from the nearby Vitagraph Film Studios. When we needed scenery and props for comedy skits, we simply told Bunny and next day whatever we needed would arrive from Vitagraph—without charge!

John Bunny's favorite of the comedy field was our singing waiter, Billy Dyke, and with good reason. His face was a comic valentine, and his Adolf Hitler haircomb was automatically good for a hearty laugh. Today, Dyke would be a television headliner. He had hundreds of hilarious skits and sketches, much in the Sid Caesar or Red Skelton manner. But his versatility stretched over into sheer slapstick as well, and he could improvise at the drop of a remark. Ragtime Jimmy Durante owes some of his mannerisms and style to Billy Dyke, whom he openly admired and even copied.

There was a class restaurant up the street called Osborn's, whose swank entertainer was "The Baron," a sort of early-20th-century Liberace of the violin. The Baron made beautiful women swoon with his violin and his shoulder-length blonde hair that would have made Elvis Presley look like Yul Brynner. The carriage trade from Park Avenue loved The Baron, but McLaughlin's plebeian customers demanded something a lot lustier. They got it in Billy Dyke.

Nevertheless, Osborn's began sending its Baron to our place as a paying customer, for the obvious purpose of luring some of our crowd away. This went on for several weeks until Billy Dyke proposed a skit in which our more muscular singing waiters would stumble over the Baron's feet by accident, muss him up a bit, and fling him out the door on his shiny coattails. When Dick Harding nixed that idea as too direct and drastic, Billy came up with another idea that was less strenuous but no more subtle. The next afternoon a big sign went up outside our place, reading:

THE BARON AND HIS FAMOUS VIOLIN!
WILL POSITIVELY APPEAR HERE
TONIGHT AT 9:30

John Bunny lent us a fright wig, a breakaway fiddle, and an oversize comic full-dress suit from the Vitagraph Studio props. He and the entire studio gang were on hand to watch the fun. A partly-puzzled, partly-angered Baron strode in at 9:25 and took a table down front.

At 9:30 sharp I gave forth with a fanfare on the piano—and out strolled Billy Dyke, in the movie props.

"I am der Baron—from Barren Island, yet," he announced. "This is the high tide of my career—und you can *still* schmell me a mile away!"

He weaved his way among the customers, kissing the ladies despite a big wad of chewing tobacco. His ad libs were worthy of a Joe E. Lewis, his low comedy grimaces as funny as a circus clown's. Exuding charm in every mincing step, he stopped to chew a Bermuda onion, so his charm would carry even further. John Bunny fell off his chair in a fit of laughter that almost choked him.

Finally, the fake Baron reached the stage and went into a concert on his stringless violin—with an offstage fiddler scraping out the tune. By this time, the whole audience were rolling out of their chairs—all except the legitimate Baron. His was not a fit of laughter; it was a plain fit. Seizing his gold headed cane, he wound his theatrical cape about his proud shoulders and stalked back to Osborn's, never to reappear.

I ended my first summer at McLaughlin's the same way I began it—flat broke. Aside from the fact that the pay wasn't much—there was always a singing waiter with a big family who needed a five-spot to tide him through the rent—and my romance with Phyllis took the rest. She wanted to stay home and save the money but I still loved to see the sights a couple of nights each week after closing time at Bert's. So, while we were more in love than ever, September found us further away than ever from a nuptial Mass.

McLaughlin's shuttered on Labor Day, and the best Dick Harding and I could do was sign for the winter at a place called The Cottage in the Williamsburg section of Brooklyn.

"It's not a classy dump at all," Dick conceded, "but it might make a good showcase for you, Vince. A lot of theatrical people hang out there, they tell me. Let's take it and see what happens." There wasn't much alternative. When the summertime job folded at McLaughlin's I lost more than my twenty-per-week. Gone also was a room to sleep in. That meant getting a boarding house and Brooklyn landladies wanted their payoff in money, not piano medleys.

The patrons at The Cottage were more theatrical hanger-ons than performers but I kept hoping someone really important would drop over from New York and like my style. Good pianists were class entertainment then—as they are once more today. I was aiming high and hoping I'd hit on-target soon, so I could rent a flat for the future Mr. and Mrs. Vincent Lopez.

Frank Hennessey, who managed The Cottage, could have doubled for a Keystone Comedy cop. He had the build—and the mentality. Illustrative of the latter was his dislike for one of his best customers, a juggler from vaudeville with a big red nose and (in those days) a friendly manner for people he favored. The juggler evidently enjoyed my piano style, for he left the bar long enough to come over to the piano and introduce himself.

"Greetings, lad!" he boomed, sticking out an affable right hand while juggling two billiard balls with his left! "You are so young, yet I am so inspired by your genius that I would quote from the first Pythian ode . . . But why bother? Suffice it to say that my name is W. C. Fields and I wouldst honor you with a beverage—a nectar from yonder bar."

"Thank you, Mr. Fields," I stammered. "I just drink celery tonic."

"Oh, the pain!" Bill Fields responded (though he obviously felt none at the moment). "Celery is a noble vegetable, no doubt, and if some poor misguided souls wouldst trample it under foot in the mistaken notion it is grapes, then perchance other misguided souls wouldst drink the awful brew! To make up for this misguidance, I'll step forth and offer myself in service. A celery tonic for the lad—and a *double* whiskey for me!"

That was my first meeting with the great W. C. Fields. He was very friendly in those days. I'm glad I knew him at the Cottage. He continued to want to buy me a drink whenever he dropped in, and I persistently held out for celery tonic.

"My lad," he sadly decided one evening when he took my glass and sniffed it with disdain, "keep drinking this stuff and you'll come to some unfortunate conclusion." Little did I realize that we would meet again in Earl Carroll's "Vanities."

I was staying at a boarding house run by a Mrs. White who gave me a black look each time I reached for seconds at the dinner table.

"Where do you put it?" she demanded as I whisked through my first meal there. "I know growing boys are hungry but you eat enough for the Siamese twins."

My dietary habits got me into worse trouble than at Mrs. White's. Right after Thanksgiving, Hennessey paid me for the week and told me to look for a job elsewhere.

"But why, Mr. Hennessey?" I pleaded. "The customers like the way I play. Have you had any complaints from them?"

"It's just a matter of business, Lopez," he explained. "You're good, all right; but when the customers want to buy you a drink, you order a ten-cent celery tonic. The last guy I had here drank enough to pay his own salary in the profits. Get it?"

So I was out of work again, in the middle of the season with just about all the regular jobs filled. It took all of Phyllis's love and understanding to bring me back from the Slough of Despond that night. I was a weary Pilgrim, making very little progress.

Chapter 17. **A TRAGIC DEATH**

The only job that turned up for me was one in Buffalo. "Can't you get a job closer?" Phyllis pleaded.

"Honey, I've tried everywhere," I repeated. "I've been out of work two months now and our nest egg is down to a few dollars. This pays thirty-five a week and the agent who got it for me says I can go to at least fifty. That means we could get married and live there. You'd like Buffalo, wouldn't you?"

"It has one advantage, Vincent," Phyllis smiled. "It's awfully close to Niagara Falls. But why wait till you make fifty. We can get along on thirty-five. Please, dear, I want to go with you. We shouldn't be separated again."

"If I had even a hundred dollars to start with, I'd marry you tonight," I whispered. "And look—out of that thirty-five I have to pay the agent three-fifty; I need fifteen to live on. I'll save every other nickel and we'll get married in Niagara Falls as soon as we get that hundred in the bank. We'll have to live in a furnished room a while, but that's okay, isn't it?"

The sweetest kiss this side of heaven showed me I needn't ask such silly questions. When Phyllis saw me off on the New York Central it was one of the coldest mornings of the New York winter, but I had my love to keep me warm.

I needed all the warmth that love and a cheap overcoat could provide when I reached Buffalo. There was a foot of snow on the ground and a wind that froze one's breath. But I resolved to save every nickel, and I walked all the way from the station to the garish sign that said "Paddy Lavan's." It was no better than Hogan's in Brooklyn and I'd travelled four hundred miles to get there.

"I'm Lopez, your new pianist," I told Harry Hart, the singing headwaiter as I stamped the powdery snow off my patent leather shoes. "A terrible night to break in. I don't think you'll have much of a crowd."

"Oh, we're used to this in Buffalo," he smiled. "They'll be out, wait and see. But you better look at this telegram that came for you a couple of hours ago. It beat your train in."

Telegrams have always bumped my blood pressure. They're so often bearers of bad news. This one, from Jimmy O'Connor, would have chilled me if it had been the hottest summer day.

The heavy upstate snow had hit New York when I got back. A stuttering, laboring taxi ploughed its way to St. Mary's Hospital.

"Phyllis O'Connor?" I asked the information clerk. As she consulted the register her face clouded and she said, "Er—that was Room 319—but you can't go up now." . . .

At the far end of the third floor corridor, a slumped figure was silhouetted against the window frame.

"Jimmy, Jimmy," I called out. I took Jimmy O'Connor by the shoulder and turned his face toward me. "Jimmy, it's me, Vincent. For God's sake, how's Phyllis?"

There was a convulsive sob. "She died an hour ago . . ."

Probably chilled by her trip to Grand Central, Phyllis had complained of a cold when she got home that afternoon. Nevertheless, she had written me a long letter after supper, then walked to a distant mail box where she knew there was a postal pickup late at night. The snow had started and she got back home with soaking wet feet. The sore throat of the early evening was the fulminating pneumonia of the next morning. People who remember the pre-penicillin days can write the rest of the hospital story. Earnest but ineffectual medication,—then the coverlet raised above the beautiful face.

I still have that faded letter from Phyllis, re-mailed to me from Paddy Lavan's in Buffalo.

Chapter 18. "THERE, BUT FOR THE GRACE OF GOD . . ."

Phyllis's death left me rudderless. I simply drifted in and out of the familiar places. It was more the instinct to live than to make a living that sent me hunting a piano job again. I didn't even try the better places. My low mood sent me downhill to the little joints I had recently disdained.

Dutchman Jimmy Hasenflug signed me on condition that I'd play a lot of Irish tunes. Hasenflug claimed he just loved Irish music. He'd kick up his heels on a reel, or wipe a tear from his eye at every line of "Mother Machree." But the only tune Jimmy really loved was played on the cash register. Half his regular customers were just a few years removed from County Cork.

But Irish songs now had a painful memory for me. Each time I played "When Irish Eyes Are Smiling," my own eyes could hardly see the keyboard, swimming as they did with memories of Phyllis, so I guess I didn't give Hasenflug his full share of the Auld Sod numbers, and he kept complaining. One night he came over to the piano and openly ragged me on the tune I'd just finished. Patience gone, I broke my rule against swearing and called him an ugly name.

Hasenflug whirled around and stamped into his private office off the bar. An hour later, I'd pretty much forgotten the incident, but Jimmy hadn't. One of the singing waiters said the boss wanted to see me in his office. I walked right in and sat down. But not in a chair. Hasenflug let me have it, smack in the nose! When the stars stopped revolving in my brain, Jimmy pointed me in the general direction of the piano and said, "Now go out and play 'Mother Machree'—LOUD!"

Later that night, when Dick Harding asked me about the swollen nose, he wanted to go after Hasenflug and return the compliment, but I staved him off.

I told him, "I had it coming to me. I broke my rule against swearing, and God showed me He didn't like it."

"I'd believe that if He'd sent an angel with a message," Dick replied, "not Hasenflug. They're not *that* short-handed in Heaven!"

Dick came up with a wonderful solution, though. He knew that Jimmy Bannon, the pianist at the nearby Broadway Inn, had a big Irish repertoire and loved to play it, whereas the Inn customers preferred more balanced musical fare. Dick arranged a deal that made everybody happy: I took over Bannon's job at the Inn, and Bannon moved to Hasenflug's. Bannon got the better part of the deal, for Hasenflug's hours were shorter. A gambling crowd hung out at the Inn and didn't go home until dawn.

The Broadway Inn was one of the best-protected hot spots of the town with all curfews ignored. The society swells, Manhattan sophisticates, and Brooklyn toughs who filled the place wanted more for their money than the bar and grill provided. That extra something was illicit games of chance. The Inn's "protection" didn't cover gambling; that was undercover.

Above the Inn was a Chinese restaurant. I enjoyed a late meal there many a night, just to tide my appetite over to breakfast time at the boarding house. After a while, I noticed that many a patron developed a late urge for Chinese food. But they weren't seated five minutes before they left the table and sauntered off into the kitchen! That would be the last I'd see of them until they showed up back at the Inn around closing time. My reading in Sherlock Holmes gave me the clue. There was a connection between the kitchen and the hidden gambling room.

"Hello, Lee," I casually remarked one night as I strolled into the kitchen. "Think I'll join the crowd for a little action tonight."

Deciding that, as the pianist at the Inn, I'd been let in on the secret, Lee walked me past the big stoves and sink, where a couple of very Occidental gorillas were leaning against the wall. There was a quick okaying signal between them, whereupon a press of a button opened a sliding door in the wall—and one of the gorillas started hauling on a rope. I knew the sound of a Brooklyn dumbwaiter, and sure enough an outsize one soon slid into view. Lee pointed for me to get in.

It was the day of banner headlines about tong wars and opium murders in Chinatown. My first thought was of a quick trip down the shaft into a subterranean sewer, but there wasn't much choice about it. I got in. A moment later I was plunging down and my next view was of a very swank gambling room where half the Inn's customers were enjoying a Las Vegas mood.

"Hey, don't let that kid out!" came a sudden yell down the dumb-waiter shaft. "Frank didn't okay him!"

The goons at the basement level got the message all right, and shoved me back in the coop. "Wait a second," they shouted back. "Mrs. Mitchell ain't feelin' so good. We're sending her up, too."

The spinning roulette wheels had been too much for Mrs. Mitchell's spinning head, so in beside me she crawled and ups-a-daisy we immediately started. In a couple of seconds I was back with the familiar chow mein smells. I think Mrs. Mitchell's presence saved me a punch on the nose from the top floor guardians.

"Nice try, kid," one of them commented, "but don't do it again unless you ask Frank."

Canton Lee was somewhat more concerned. "Why you try fool me?" he wanted to know.

"Just curious," I grinned.

"Confucius say," Lee hissed at me in first-rate Fu Manchu manner, *"Curiosity killed cat."*

That time I got the message!

Two months more at the place, though, and I was "one of the family." I was even invited to play at quite an intimate party they threw.

It was a benefit for a Broadway showman we'll call Montgomery James Bleeker, a real favorite with the Inn patrons. His ascent up the ladder of success had been slow but his descent had been fast—from the top rungs of operetta to burlesque, and then the stag-party bottom. A heavy fine for being caught at that had put Bleeker in the clutches of the loan sharks—and his friends threw the party to bail him out.

It cost fifty dollars a head, but plenty of entertainment was promised, both scheduled and impromptu. The former consisted of vaudeville and burlesque acts, and the Piano Kid. The latter—collaborating with the impromptu entertainment—supplied by some twenty girls from burlesque. They were the hit of the evening. Many of the patrons brought their own preference in girl friends, in case there weren't enough to go around. Montgomery James—although broke—had a string of three blondes to keep the evening from dulling up. His dramatic entrance with them just after the vaudeville performance finished, really began the affair!

"Play some Egyptian music, Vincent," Frank commanded. Out came a lovely dancer on the opening bars, to do the Dance of the Seven Veils. I hadn't finished one improvised chorus before she ran through her complete repertoire, and I might as well have stopped playing right then and there. The audience made their own music.

There were four bottles of champagne at each table but one of Bleeker's blondes wasted hers (she didn't need it!) by giving Monty a champagne shampoo. Since most of the champagne ran down through his clothes, the girls decided he couldn't risk pneumonia sitting around in wet clothes!

"Little Egypt" resented this interruption of her dance, and when Monty's blondes insisted on showing they could do the Seven Veils too she socked one of them. Fist fights broke out as the more gallant men of the group rushed to separate the veilless combatants, and a real shambles threatened.

Frank rescued the situation by dousing all the lights except for two tiny ones that must have been just out of Mr. Edison's incubator. "That's enough fighting," he roared. "Now everybody kiss and make up!"

The invitation was taken seriously. Half an hour later I decided that if Nero's wild parties had ruined Rome, America didn't have far to go, either. But, of course, the real America is entirely different from a bistro full of Brooklyn bums.

I played the piano right up to the time the last couple got in the dumbwaiter and left—but I don't think many of them listened.

Some of them must have *talked,* though. A few nights later a special vice squad shoved Lee Won and his gorillas against the wall at gun point, then raided the den by the dumbwaiter route and smashed all the gambling equipment. Frank was out of a restaurant "front"—and I was out of a job.

It was just as well I lost it. I've yet to know an entertainer who regularly performed in any capacity for such "stag" parties and kept his personal integrity or his professional ability. On my own road to the Broadway Inn, I'd become acquainted with many characters who ran the range from just rough and rowdy to dissolute and depraved. However, with the exception of the all-out party for Monty Bleeker, none of them ever tried to interest me in their offbeat pursuit of thrills. Possibly, it was their last shred of decency used to protect a young kid.

As I came up toward big-time success a few years later, many of the heavy spenders of my early days sought me out and put on a touch. I helped as much as I could, but so many of them were beyond any real help.

My experiences back in those Brooklyn dives gave me a lifelong lesson in humility, though. Knowing how close I came to the chutes that dump a man finally in Potter's Field, I never see a bum mooching a cigarette without saying, "There but for the grace of God . . . go I!"

Chapter 19. MY FIRST MARRIAGE

When the Broadway Inn closed (the hard way), I took the next few weeks off as a vacation until McLaughlin's opened at Sheepshead Bay on Decoration Day. Like the legendary motorman who spent his leisure Sundays riding rival trolley lines, I spent my vacation at the other restaurants. One of them, Lundy's, became *the* place for me when I saw their new cashier.

"Didn't you play the piano last summer at McLaughlin's?" she asked when I paid the tab for my sandwich and celery tonic.

"Yes," I said, "but how did you know? You never came in there."

"I did, but I looked different," she explained. "I suddenly grew up last winter. I added twelve pounds—and this is a new way I wear my hair. Do you like it?"

I loved it—and that twelve pounds, too, plus the name of Linda Groves that I thought so musical, plus a lot of other details about her, most of all her suggestion that I wait for her outside Lundy's and take a stroll along the waterfront. She had an hour break in about twenty minutes.

It turned out that Linda was from upstate New York (and that gave us a mutual interest!). Her mother recuperating from a serious illness, Linda was finishing up her high-school senior year in Brooklyn—and she'd be at Lundy's all summer. Yes, she loved music, especially the piano. The only rub in our getting along smoothly was young Bill Cooper, her boy friend.

"He thinks he owns me," Linda complained, when she joined me. "You hadn't left the place a minute, Vincent, before he was over warning me to stay away from you."

Despite a vivid mental image of the muscular Bill Cooper, I said, "We won't let him do that!" I was wrong. A minute later I heard a heavy pounding of feet, and up loomed the boy friend.

"I told you to stay away from this cheap piano player," he yelled at Linda as he grabbed her arm. "Now get back to the restaurant"—and he gave her a head start with a vicious push.

"Look, Cooper, you can't do that!" I protested.

"Sez who?" he wanted to know, but didn't wait for an answer. A Jim Jeffries right landed on my jaw. As Jackie Gleason would put it, I made my first trip to the moon!

Ten minutes later, maybe, I came to, thinking I was in heaven. An incredibly beautiful girl held my head in her hands, and tried to lift me to a sitting position.

"Are you ill?" she asked. "Should I try to get a doctor?"

"No," I explained. "I was in a . . . I was running along the beach for some exercise and I must have stumbled and hit a rock."

"In all this sand?" she said in disbelief. It was the first question Mae Kenny asked me, but by no means the last. Before our marriage broke up a few years later she would ask thousands of other questions for most of which I would have similarly poor answers.

Mae was a slender version of brunette Irish loveliness. Bards have sung praises to such beauty since St. Patrick's time. Any doubts I may have had about the claims of Irish songs about Irish colleens were dispelled when I saw Mae Kenny's face that evening.

She'd been visiting friends on a houseboat in the bay. They rowed her back to shore, and she had almost stumbled over me on her way to the trolley. It might have been best if she had walked past me.

I took her home, out to Gravesend Bay, where the Irish-Americans had set up a stronghold. Every time I hear Judy Garland sing "The Trolley Song," I recall how my heart went clang, clang, clang all the way.

Did I say the Irish had made Gravesend Bay a stronghold? Might as well call it a fort. On my third date with Mae we lingered a bit at the doorway when a heavy object came flying through the air and bounced off the porch post.

Mae was out of my arms in an instant, shouting after a dark figure running up the street: "John Clancy, you should be ashamed! Just because I have a date with a boy who isn't Irish, do you have to try to hurt him?"

Coming out of my bewilderment, I took a look at the missile that had landed almost at my feet. It was a neatly broken half of a brick! Irish confetti to let a Latin know he was an outlander!

An upstairs window banged open and Mrs. Kenny flung a few well-selected insults at the retreating Mr. Clancy. Then she spotted Mae on the porch steps.

"Is that you, Mae?" she demanded. "And what would that trouble be about?"

"It's only that jealous John Clancy," Mae explained. "He doesn't like it that I'm dating someone else."

"And who might this someone else be?" mother asked.

"Oh, mother, I forgot," Mae apologized. "This (and she took me out on the walk, where the corner street light gave some illumination)—this is Vincent Lopez."

"Lopez? Lopez?" came Mrs. Kenny's response. "What sort of a foreigner is that?"

"I'm not a foreigner, Mrs. Kenny," I said. "I was born right here in Brooklyn. My parents are Portuguese."

"Well, that's not too bad," the upstairs critic decided. "I was afraid you might be Eye-talian . . . in which case I'd wish Johnny had hit you with the brick! Say good night, Mae, and come right in."

"Don't be angry, Vincent," Mae pleaded. "It's just that mother thinks I should marry an Irish boy . . . People are like that, you know. Good night. Will I see you again?"

"See me again? If you think I'm angry about your mother, forget it, Mae. Let the old folks keep their old-world ideas—we live in a new world."

"I'm glad you're not narrow-minded, Vincent," Mae replied. "I've seen enough of it in my family, and I don't want it for the rest of my life . . ."

This made me realize Mae had marriage on her mind. I had her mother on mine, anticipating a dislike that took little time to develop. The very next night I took a chance with the bricks by dating Mae again, calling for her at her home instead of meeting her at Lundy's (that had been her suggestion, and now I knew why). And so I met the family—and was hit by something else.

Mae's dad liked me, it seemed. But unlike the Lopez home the Kenny home was dominated by the missus. I was to learn in time that Mae had inherited a good bit of her mother's disposition though not her intolerance toward people who'd been stupid enough not to pick Irish grandparents.

Mrs. Kenny's dislike for me was obvious from the start. Not even Mae's mention of my education at St. Mary's changed the picture.

"Sure and why didn't you stick to your vocation?" came Mrs. Kenny's prompt challenge. "Far better to be the comfort and inspiration a priest can give his people than go playing a pianner for them."

Two youngsters in love can overcome anything. There was the further problem of my job at McLaughlin's, which kept me working nights. But Mae met me there, usually, and that gave us an extra hour together, since it saved my transportation time. We were out quite late, of course, but somehow Mae managed the parental objections. By the time we got back to her house, the Kenny's were sound asleep.

During a breakup over something I've forgotten, I began seeing another brunette, with the Italian olive skin and dark eyes. One night, after I was through at McLaughlin's, she suggested visiting a café at Coney Island. I couldn't imagine why, but I went along. No sooner did we get comfortable at a table than Gina asked our waiter to tell Joe she'd like to see him.

"Who's Joe?" I got curious.

"Oh, just an old boy friend of mine," Gina confided. "I want him to see what a nice guy I landed after he shook me."

This didn't seem like a bad idea to my inflated ego at the moment—until Joe appeared. He was much bigger than my ego—and he obviously didn't feel he was the *ex*-boy friend.

"Who's this guy?" he asked. "Where'd you find him?"

"Oh, Joe, I want you to meet Vincent Lopez. He's a pianist. He's my new boy friend."

"Ye're kiddin'," Joe yelled. "You mean you'd leave me for *that*!" (This remark definitely finished off the ego for the evening.)

Two nights later, Gina dropped in at McLaughlin's to show me a big engagement ring. "That's wonderful," I exclaimed. "My very best wishes, Gina."

"Thanks, Vincent," she said. "I mean thanks for more than your best wishes, too. I owe this ring to you . . ."

The Kennys had a telephone, and on my first break from the piano that night I called Mae to ask if I could see her again. Our romance really went into high gear then. She came to McLaughlin's just about every night that summer, to sit alone at a wall table (where I'd join her in the breaks) and wait for closing time so we could have a brief hour together. A girl who can accept that deal as courtship, and settle for more of it in marriage, is out of her mind with love. . . . or just plain out of her mind.

One night I faked illness at McLaughlin's so I could take Mae to downtown Brooklyn and a big-time vaudeville show. It was an immense evening that we topped off with supper at a really nice restaurant, where the bill depleted my bankroll to sixty-five cents. But the El at Fulton Street was only a nickel, so I wasn't worried. Two hours later, though, Mae was a bit frantic. Like a couple of hicks, after seeing the sights we had fallen asleep on the elevated train, gone to the end of the line, and back again past Mae's station!

"Honey, it's almost four in the morning!" she wailed. "My mother will never believe we just went to a show and then fell asleep on the train." And she began to cry very softly, but oh so effectively.

"I know one solution," I blurted out. "Let's get married. We're on the way back to Fulton Street, anyway, and that's right near Borough Hall where we can get the license." (Magically, Mae's tears stopped!)

Clang, clang, clang went the trolley when I first met Mae. Now bong, bong, bong went the wedding bells!

We found a little coffee joint to linger in until the Marriage License Bureau opened, but even so we had to wait in the office almost an hour before the clerk showed up.

"You been here long?" he yawned.

"Since seven o'clock," Mae answered. I thought I heard him mutter, "How anxious can you get!"

But a horrible realization struck me. The ride on the El, six cups of coffee, and a tip left a very thin dime in my pocket and a marriage license cost two dollars.

"Wait here, darling," I yelled to Mae. "I have to see a man about our marriage license." And I pell-melled it for the office of politician Hughie Winters, whom I'd met at McLaughlin's. It took half an hour to find him at Borough Hall and borrow a five-spot. The license clerk was quite surprised when I turned up again.

"I've seen them get cold feet before," he explained, "but they don't usually run out as fast as you did. Now what are the names and ages, please?"

License in pocket, we still weren't ready for the ceremony. A trip to the five-and-dime got us a wedding ring, and Hughie Winters meanwhile rounded up a couple of witnesses (whom we'd never seen before and never met again). Hughie also had the good sense to check with "Missing Persons" and have them telephone Ma Kenny that we were safe and sound. By 9:30 that morning, we were Mr. and Mrs. Vincent Lopez. A couple of weeks later we made it "official" on the church records, too, by repeating the ceremony at St. Augustine's, where my father had donated one of my mother's diamonds to be placed in the center of the tabernacle door on the altar.

"Darling," Mae suggested as we emerged from Borough Hall and took a bright new look at our brand new world, "do you mind if we go home first and tell mother we're married?"

"I think that's a good idea," I agreed. "Er, the room where I'm boarding isn't much, Mae. Maybe your parents will let us stay with them awhile, till we save money for an apartment. Think so? Or wouldn't you like that?"

"Well, let's try it, but not for long, honey," she replied. "I want to be Mrs. Lopez, not the former Miss Kenny. Let's talk it over with mother. And I want to tell *your* parents, too."

As we walked from the trolley, I could see Mrs. Kenny waiting for us on the porch. Mae waved a happy greeting. Her mother waved—a fist!

"Niver mind any explanations," she yelled. "Just show me the license!"

"Here it is, didn't you believe us . . . mother?"

"Mother, is it?" she exploded. "From this day, I'm mother to neither of you—unless Mae wants to come back here alone!"

Mae began to cry but I held her tight and she went beautifully limp and yielding in my arms. Mrs. Kenny knew I'd won. She thrust the license back in my hands and shouted, "All right, then, Mae. You've made your bed. Now go sleep in it!"

The front door shook as it slammed shut with finality. Back we walked to the street car, hand in hand.

"What about *your* folks, Vincent?" Mae said, when the tears subsided. "They have a big house. Couldn't we rent a couple of rooms from them?"

"I've had enough of family reactions for a while, darling," I answered. "Let's see if we can make a go of it for a few weeks, anyway, at Mrs. Toner's."

Mae managed a smile. "All right, if that's your decision, dear."

It was the worst possible decision. Starting a honeymoon on the remains of a borrowed five-dollar bill, in a one-window room of a crowded Brooklyn boarding house, is like a baseball player coming to bat with two strikes against him. Looking back, I realize that Mae and I were lucky to stay in the game a couple of years, as we did.

Chapter 20. MAE AND MOM

About a week before our Labor Day closing at McLaughlin's that season I had an unexpected visit from a man who was writing a funeral march for the day of the singing waiters.

"M'name's Jimmy McLaughlin," he introduced himself. "Nope, no relation of your boss unless we're thirty-second cousins from back in Ireland. I'll come to the point. I'm handling the entertainment bill at Minden's and we want to try something new. Feature singles instead of group singers or acts. That stuff belongs in vaudeville, not clubs."

"What do you mean by clubs?" I said.

"It's a new sort of place where gentlemen can bring their wives or their girl friends for a bite to eat, a drink and some class entertainment. The main entertainment goes on late so we call the place a 'night club.' I'll let you in on a sensational idea of mine. One of our solo acts is gonna be a beautiful blonde singer named Blanche Evans, the first time a woman has done a single in Brooklyn."

"Outside of vaudeville, you mean."

"That's the idea," said Jimmy. "Vaudeville's the rage, but you can see it only at a big theatre. We'll give the customers vaudeville on an intimate basis, as they do at a private club. Get it?"

"Sounds good," I admitted. "But where do I come in?"

"We want to feature you at the piano. If the ritzy crowd will load

Carnegie Hall to listen to a long-hair pianist, why can't we aim at the middle and present a pianist at our place with a touch of class, too?"

"I got class?" I questioned.

"You got youth, looks, and you don't line the top of your piano with empty shot glasses. You're the one we want, and it could mean a great deal to you, Vincent."

"What about Dick Harding?" I wanted to know. "We work together."

Jimmy shook his head. "No singing waiters at Minden's. Class entertainment I told you."

"Well, if Dick isn't included, you can forget—"

"Wait a minute. I've already talked to Dick Harding about this, and he's all for it." With that, McLaughlin signalled Dick who'd been standing nearby. Dick smiled and walked over.

"Take the job, Vincent," he insisted. "I can always make a living like this and I'm satisfied with it. This is your chance to get out of the joints." And when I demurred, he added, "I'll kick some sense into you through the seat of your pants if you don't take this. There's just one team you've got to worry about . . . You and Mae. Besides," as he gave me a cuff on the neck, "I'm sick of playing dear old dad to you, boy. Let Mae worry about you now." And the laugh that followed gave me the assurance I needed.

"Okay, Mr. McLaughlin," I decided. "What's the pay?"

"Well, thirty-five to start with," he half apologized, "but if this night club idea catches on it'll be fifty. Come over for rehearsal tomorrow afternoon at three sharp."

In the next hectic week, Jimmy put quite a show together for Minden's, a series of "singles" (or solo) acts.

Nobody mentioned it during the rehearsals, but luckily Blanche Evans happened to remark, when Jimmy and I had a late lunch with her after the "dress" run-through that she thought I'd look "cute" in a tuxedo.

"I don't own one."

"*What?*" Jimmy yelled. "What about tonight? You'll have to wear a tux!"

"*Now* you tell me!" I said. "I can't buy one on—a dollar eighty" (I was counting the change.)

"You can't even rent one for that!" Jimmy moaned. "How much you got, Blanche? Three dollars? I've got about three. That ought to do it. C'mon. Let's get going!"

At Guttenburg's "Men's Tailoring Establishment" we got a model that had a little mileage left in it, for five dollars.

Luckily, the pants were a bit too long—they hid my high-button shoes! Unluckily, the sleeves were a bit too short.

A week's supply of waiter's dickeys, those old pasteboard shirt-fronts with imitation wing collar attached, set us back seventy cents. However, they weren't as economical as they sounded. They had no sleeves, of course, so that meant a further expenditure of funds for imitation cuffs at a nickel apiece. The cuffs were simply shoved up the sleeve where it was hoped the bulge would overcome the law of gravity. The idea worked for less strenuous performers, but, at the very first show that evening, when I went into high gear with the overture from *Zampa,* my cuffs worked down over my knuckles—to the delight of the crowd!

There are moments when you must make an instantaneous decision. I made mine, and it worked out very well. Realizing I couldn't get by flinging my arms every minute to shove the cuffs up to my wrists again, I simply stood up in the middle of "Moonlight Bay," ripped out the protruding cuffs, threw them on the floor with a comic gesture and went on playing.

It brought down the house. I think the customers had been getting too much of the class-act treatment and were in the mood for a real laugh. My cuff-shedding provided it, and I had to repeat it at every show until the novelty wore off. (Decades later, Victor Borge rediscovered it!)

Incidentally, Mae soon had saved enough out of my salary to buy me three regular dress shirts that I kept rotating and she kept washing and ironing.

There was a wonderful Italian chef at Minden's who deserted his big range each time I played "Oh, Marie," or "Oh Sole Mio." I could see him holding the kitchen door open an inch or two to hear the music. Since he enjoyed it so much, I included some of his favorites every night. Then he decided to return the favor—and it nearly killed me.

I had just finished my second "set" of numbers that closed the show when I heard a sharp "*psssst!*" from the kitchen door. "You like steak?" Pietro asked when I entered. "Sure you do. I know. I like the music you play for me. You like the steak I cook for you." And there it was—a juicy two pound Porterhouse. It was against the rules, of course. Minden didn't object to the talent finishing up left-overs but the Eleventh Commandment there was not to covet the boss's steaks.

One night I was halfway through my illicit steak dividend when Pietro yelled, "Here comes Minden, kid. Get in the refrigerator!" and he propelled me toward the huge walk-in ice box where the meats were kept. Inside the box I managed to finish the steak before the 10-below temperature froze it solid.

Minden decided to go over the menu for the week—and added a military inspection of the pots and pans. My five dollar tuxedo kept out very little of the cold, and I did an energetic soft shoe to keep warm. But my feet were getting numb and I was on the verge of banging on the big door and taking my chances with an angry Minden when I heard Pierto call out, in a voice loud enough to penetrate my igloo, "Good night, Mr. Minden. Glad you liked the kitchen."

A moment later he anxiously poked his face into the ice box and was relieved to find me still alive. The chill quickly passed, thanks to a bottle of Minden's best brandy that Pietro thoughtfully provided.

I ate more and played less at Minden's than had ever been my experience. We had just the four shows a night, and Mike Minden only wanted a little music in between. I had been conditioned to marathon playing until the place closed, and I started out at Minden's that way.

"Look, kid," Mike said. "I'll let you in on a show-business secret. The difference between a class place and a joint is that at the class place the customers get less of everything—and pay more."

It was a lesson I found hard to learn—if, indeed, I ever learned it. I often played straight through the evening at Minden's. The crowd seemed to like it, and Mike Minden finally gave up on it.

One night, though, he walked over to the piano where I'd been sitting for two hours. He leaned close as if to say something confidential. I stopped the music on the next bar and looked up at him inquisitively.

"Hey, Lopez," he whispered. "Tell me—don't you ever go to the bathroom?"

For the first few months, Mae came over to Minden's almost every night, but then she began to tire of the routine and we'd kiss goodbye for the evening when I left after supper. We were living at a nearby boarding house, where a bedroom and a little sitting room (the best suite in the house) cost me twenty a week with our meals.

We both needed clothes (that five-dollar tuxedo didn't last very long) and with other expenses we weren't saving much. I wanted to borrow $500 to furnish an apartment, but cautious Mae voted it down. She felt that going into debt was somehow sinful. But trying to live our first year of marriage in a noisy boarding house was sinfully foolish.

I knew, too, that Mae had "made peace" with her mother and was over there a great deal. But Ma Kenny's dislike for me had not lessened. When I mentioned paying the family a visit some afternoon, Mae changed the subject. Several times she introduced the idea that I give up the piano and get a "decent job" somewhere, and like a young fool, I got angry.

Meanwhile, although Jimmy McLaughlin and Blanche Evans had reached the point where they heard wedding bells in everything, a good "stag" evening still rang a bell in Jimmy's mind, too. Any time Blanche felt tired enough to call it a day when Minden's closed at one o'clock, Jimmy would suggest to me that we have a look around before retiring.

If it was a night Mae didn't come to Minden's, I'd be all for the idea and off we'd go. Strangely, Blanche got peeved at *me* for this;

on the other hand, when I'd drift in at four or later, Mae would speak her piece about that no-good McLaughlin!

Jimmy and I picked up some extra money that way. We'd still be in our formal clothes, and several places offered five apiece for our after-hours act. Often the hoods we played for specified sad songs, and Jim and I would prime the tear ducts with such songs as "All Alone," "The Curse of an Aching Heart," "Dear Old Gal," and "Melancholy Baby."

Once Jimmy was lending his tenderest tremolo to "Your Mother Is Your Best Friend After All" when he happened to glance over the heads of our enraptured audience to the locked door of the private banquet room that had been rented for the occasion. There was a peephole much like those that were later to become familiar at the speakeasies, and Jim suddenly realized that someone was poking the business end of a revolver barrel through it!

When he froze on a note (splitting poor "moth-er" in two) I looked up in astonishment—and followed his outstretched finger to the peephole in the door.

"Duck, Vince!" he shouted, and I lost no time following him under the nearest table. A moment later the shots began. Then a mobster inside recognized the voice of a colleague on the outside.

"Hulleegee, Joe," he shouted, "what you doin'?"

The shooting stopped, the gun barrel receded, and the mistake was cleared up. The raiding party had been given the wrong information on who was having the blowout. Nevertheless, there was still some tension in the air and the threat of more gunplay until Jimmy and I crawled out from under our sheltering table in our evening clothes. We had picked the table under which the cleaning lady parked her sweepings each night, and we were a mess. The sight of us got some of the girls laughing and in no time at all the party was on again. In fact, it ran overtime, so that Jim and I collected an extra five.

During one of our early morning arguments Mae came out with the plea that her mother had planted: Would I quit this uncertain life, get a decent job somewhere, and settle down as a married man should?

When I refused, she pouted, "You love your piano more than you love me. Why did you marry me, anyway, Vincent?"

"I think I know why I married you, Mae," I said, voicing thoughts that had been accumulating in me. "I married you because you're a beautiful girl. But there was something else, too. I was lonely. My family is as good as dead to me. And when we were going together, I began envying the married couples we knew. I thought I'd like that, too—all the wonderful things that marriage can add, but it hasn't worked out that way, has it?"

Mae nodded—then burst into tears.

"So you married me just because you were lonely," she sobbed. Then she ran from our room down the hall to the bedroom of a girl who boarded there. The next morning, I found a note that she was going to visit her mother. She returned that evening, but things were never right again.

The following week we made an important change that should have helped, had we been mature enough. We rented our first flat, a third-floor "railroad" apartment, so called because the rooms were strung out in a line like a train of cars. Time payments hadn't been brought to the scientific point whereby a young couple could go into perpetual hock for everything they needed in the way of furniture. So we had furniture only in the front room. In the absence of central heating, we fought off Jack Frost with a big kitchen range and a pot-bellied stove in the front room. The coal had to be hauled up in a dumbwaiter, and I put a labor-saving technique to use by doing the job all at once and storing a month's supply on the floor of an empty room.

We loved the place, but soon arguments began again. "Why do you spend so much time downstairs at the Raabs?" Mae would demand. "What's the big attraction?"

"Now you know, honey, that Phil and I plan to start a piano school," I'd explain. "Besides, we've got no piano and Phil has. I have to try out the new numbers somewhere."

Are you sure it isn't Florie you're trying out?" Mae accused. "Was Phil home while you were there?"

When she got off on that pitch I would retaliate with cutting remarks about her cooking, which was so bad that to get out of eating it, I sometimes made an excuse about a new tune I had to hear at Phil's.

"If you must know," I blurted out, "she was serving me some decent food—a piece of roast beef and it was delicious—instead of your special, eggs and fried baloney! What cook book did you get that out of?"

Then Mae would cry, and I'd say I was sorry, and we'd patch things up until the next time. Frankly, though, Mae *was* the world's worst cook.

Lovely as Mae was, my enthusiasm for her meals hit an all-time low the afternoon I bought some fresh-caught bluefish at Sheepshead Bay and took it home for supper. She cooked it without cutting off the head—and the taste, and those sad fish eyes staring up at me from the plate brought on a suddenly remembered date with a song plugger at Minden's!

It was a reasonable excuse, for we pianists were the disc jockeys of that day in popularizing a new tune, and the song pluggers were always at us for demonstration time. That's how I began to acquire an ear for a hit song—just listening to so many of them and learning to separate the wheat from the chaff. The great songs of that era included, "My Melancholy Baby," "Moonlight Bay," "Oh, You Million-Dollar Baby," and "Marcheta."

Our piano school in Phil Raab's downstairs apartment never got off the ground. Maybe times were too tough or we weren't good enough. I began to realize what my father had been up against trying to make a living that way. However, we impressed one of our students well enough for her uncle to offer me a partnership if I'd put my full time into a music-school chain he was starting. Had I accepted, I'd be half-owner, today, of a famous chain of music schools worth a million!

Too many of my students were on forced scholarships. When Mae's folks heard about the sideline piano school, thrifty Ma Kenny sent her four other children and a niece to get free lessons. I took them on gladly, hoping it might soften Ma Kenny's stony dislike for me, but I was soon disillusioned.

But first came a more shattering experience. I lost my job at Minden's! Their policy of providing too little (in food) for too much (in money) didn't pay off and the red ink ran all over their ledgers. Minden finally called it quits, and I took a job at a dive called Pabst's. They were looking for a piano player and I was looking for my next month's rent. It was an awful comedown from Minden's. The tuxedo went back into the mothballs, and I went back into the joints.

Chapter 21. STICK-UP AND PADLOCK

Frank Zagarino was a man you could never forget. Short, swarthy, and heavy-set, he looked like the classical extrovert, but inwardly he craved the approval of others. He sought it by flashing diamonds.

The night I started in his employ at Pabst's, he accented his instructions with diamond flashes from his gesturing hands.

"You play popular stuff and we get along fine. Keep playing songs like "What's the Use of Dreaming?," "Are You Sincere?," and "You Made Me Love You."

"I certainly will, Mr. Zagarino," I assured him.

"Another thing," he added. "Might as well tell you now. You'll get to know it later. I got a couple of silent partners who don't show on my liquor license because they want it that way. I could lose my license if somebody here developed a loose lip. Understand? . . . And confidentially, kid, the real money comes from special parties for the boys. You know some of them, from Clayton's and the other joints. They just want to have a sociable time, but the cops don't see it that way. Our license says we close at one o'clock, but what they gonna do the rest of the night? The license is silly, ain't it?"

I nodded absolute agreement.

"So we have a special room for those parties. It's downstairs and it's soundproof. You'll play the piano there, too, and there's extra money in it for you. *But*—keep your lips buttoned unless you'd like to feel your teeth comin' through some night. Understand?"

I understood.

Pabst's turned out pretty well for me. The pay was fair and some of the associations were wonderful. Quite a few up-and-coming vaudevillians used the place as a tryout for new material, among them Mae West, the Sunshine Boys, Tom Sharkey, Nemo Roth and Witt, Lewis and Dody, Fred Fisher, writer of "Peg o' My Heart," Al Piantadosi, composer of "That's How I Need You," Sophie Tucker, and Fannie Brice. Joe Schenk (later of Van and Schenk) introduced his famous "They Made a Miser of Me" at Pabst's; but what I looked forward to most were the occasional visits of Jimmy Durante.

Frank Zagarino was a Durante fan, too, and they'd sit around and talk about Jimmy's troubles. Ragtime Jimmy wasn't getting places fast enough. "The payroll for my band is killing me," Jimmy wailed.

"You got a band?" Zagarino asked in surprise. "How many pieces?"

"Well, let's see," Jimmy thought it out. "There's me at the pianner —and a drummer."

Zagarino roared, "Pianner and drums? You need some brass to make it a band!"

"Well," Jimmy replied, adjusting his tie and going into his famous pout, "don't you think I got a lot of brass *callin' it a band?* . . . Gee, if I could only get in some classy place instead of a jernt."

"Why not open a place of your own, Jimmy?" Zagarino suggested.

"Great idea," Jimmy agreed. "But what'll I use for money?"

"Are you really that broke?" Zag wanted to know.

"Listen, Frank," said Durante, "I joke about my nose bein' so big, but right now I wish it was full of nickels."

One night when we ran "overtime" down in the basement, I was playing a request for Tug Reilly and Spider Murtha, when I felt something cold, round, and very hard, pressed to the back of my neck!

"Just keep playin' good and loud," were the instructions. "This is a holdup."

"I got only about two dollars. . . ." I stammered.

"We're not after your dough," the voice ridiculed. "Just keep playin' like I said."

With that, three other hoods went into action. Two covered the crowd with "cannons" while the "master of ceremonies," Nemo Roth, announced the stickup and directed the ladies and gentlemen to lay their valuables right on the table *real quick!* To top the take, the crooks made poor Zagarino ring up "No Sale" on his cash register—which yielded over four hundred dollars more.

Meanwhile the muzzle of the gun in my neck hadn't relaxed a particle of an inch, but then the voice hissed, "We're leavin' now. We're gonna lock the door. If I don't hear this piano still goin' when we're a block away I'll be back some night and take care of you personally."

I was starting on the 'steenth chorus of the special request number when Frank Zagarino shook my shoulder and shouted, "Fer godzake, Lopez. Stop playin' that damned piano and help us get out of here!"

An hour later Zagarino and his silent partner were figuring out the cash-register loss.

"Four hundred and twelve bucks," Frank moaned.

"It could be worse," the silent partner commented.

"How could it be worse?"

"Next week is Christmas, right?" the partner explained. "The Christmas bonus we were going to give the employees would have come close to four hundred? So—we tell 'em there ain't no Santy Claus."

That meant we didn't get the extra money we'd been counting on; but there was even worse news for me. Zag broke it, not very gently, on Christmas night.

"Lopez," he confided, "I didn't tell you this earlier cause I hated to spoil your Christmas, but you're through here on New Year's. This gives you a week to look for another job."

"Is there anything wrong with my playing?"

"No, kid, that ain't it," Zag admitted. "It's just that I can get Ragtime Jimmy Durante. You're good, too, but with Durante I get a whole floor show!"

To my surprise, Mae took the news very well—to well, in fact.

"Maybe it's for the best, honey. Maybe now you'll give up show business."

"Gee, try to understand, dear," I said as I kissed her, "I can't imagine doing anything else in life. I guess I've got two great loves, —you—and the piano."

"I hope you never have to choose between us," she murmured, as we turned out our light and turned on the stars.

The police added a second man outside Pabst's on New Year's Eve to make sure the one o'clock curfew was obeyed. Evidently the the pair didn't count the house, for a lot fewer customers emerged around one o'clock than had gone in. The rest of them had made their way down the damp, brick-lined stairway to the special room in the basement. By 1:30 the renewed festivities had shifted into high gear.

Shortly after three, when heads were beginning to thump from too much champagne, there was a series of louder thumps on the big oak door that led upstairs.

"It's the cops!" somebody shouted, and one of the customers unlocked the door. All he got for his courtesy was first seat in the pie wagon. Though even the women had to take the trip to the station, the New Year's spirit wasn't dampened a bit. To the clang of the patrol wagon bells (this was the pre-siren era) they added the jangles of their own cowbells and the raucous toots of their horns. The unexpected ride simply added to the fun!

I fully expected to take the trip myself, but the cops were interested only in Zagarino. "Where is he?" the lieutenant demanded. "We know he was holed up here with the rest of you, and there's only one way out. How about you, kid—where's Zagarino?"

"Search me," I mumbled, not intending the wisecrack. The cops laughed anyway.

"Where did Zagarino go?" shouted the lieutenant. "Tell us, or *you* go to jail."

"He was over by the bar, talking to his partner," I said, letting the cat out of the bag. "Then he disappeared when the lights went out. Hey, they *both* disappeared!"

"So he's got a partner," the lieutenant trumpeted, jotting something down in a little black book. "It don't say so on his liquor license. That's another violation. Now let's see what you singin' waiters know. . . ."

Two hours later, the police squad gave up on capturing the boss and started to leave. The waiters and I stayed behind. "We just want to clean up the place," I explained.

"You ought to save your energy," said the lieutenant. "Pabst's is closed as of now and it ain't gonna reopen, not with Mr. Zagarino as the owner."

We were just getting some of the dishes cleared away when a section of the dance floor began rising. A quick flashback to my St. Mary's training made me think of Lazarus emerging from the tomb, but it was a very much alive Zagarino and his elusive partner who emerged. The partner was no longer "silent." He joined Zagarino in cussing out the New York police. Then he turned to us and explained, "I'm Jimmy La Panna and I own half this place. We'll get shut down, no doubt, but we can reopen somewhere else and I guarantee you your jobs back as soon as we do. I don't want to see any show-business people get hurt."

The singing waiters loved being referred to as show-business people (as they truly were), and a cheer went up for Jimmy La Panna. His interest in show business was genuine. Later on, in Prohibition days, he lost the fortune he made on liquor backing bad Broadway plays. A frustrated ham at heart, Jimmy became the most gullible angel on Broadway because he rushed in where even a fool would fear to tread.

Before leaving I asked Zagarino when I could collect my thirty dollars salary.

"Don't bother me now, kid," he replied. "Come around tomorrow at noon."

I did, and I was still sitting there at two o'clock, waiting for the boss, when Jimmy Durante walked in.

"What a break," he said. "I quit my band to come here, and they nail up the jernt!"

"I know how you feel," I commiserated. "Zagarino hasn't paid me my salary, and I sure could use that thirty dollars."

"Thirty bucks! Thirty?" Jimmy gasped, and his nosed swelled with indignation. "Why, the bum was only gonna give me twenty-eight!"

Mae prevailed on me to make a trip back to my old home on Pacific Street to wish my family a happy new year. I hadn't climbed the front stoop when a familiar scene was re-enacted. My father had seen me coming, and his grim face glared at me from the open door.

"Are you coming home now because you repent your sins?" he demanded.

"Repent my sins?" I exclaimed. "I just wanted to see you, father, and wish everyone the best of the new season. I wouldn't dream of coming back here to stay. I'm married now."

"So we learned from your friends. And we also learned where you were married—at a civil ceremony, ignoring our Mother the Church!"

"Wait a minute," I began, "We were—"

"And another thing," my father interrupted, "Do you still make your living playing the piano in those place of sin?"

"Yes, I still play at the cafés and the rathskellers," I retorted. "It's what I want to do in life."

"Then what I want to do in life is be rid of you! Go and let us hear no more from you while I'm alive."

The door slammed shut in my face. It was the last time I saw my father.

Avoiding Mae's questions about my family with a tale about illness that made a visit impossible, I then took Mae back to her old home in Gravesend Bay for an after-supper call. It simply wasn't my day. Mrs. Kenny was waiting on the front porch.

"Did you tell him, Mae?" she demanded.

"No, mother, not yet."

"Now's as good as any time. Vincent, you'll never be a son-in-law to me; but you're Mae's husband and I'll accept it if you'll do something for her."

"Do what for her?" I said, the Lopez Latin temper flaring up.

"Give up playing the pianner now that you've lost yer job in that

Pabst joint. Get a decent, honest job where she can be proud of you. Will you do that?"

"Mrs. Kenny," I said, "Mae and I have been over that many times and it's no use. Playing the piano is what I want to do, and she knew it when she married me."

"She didn't know what it meant, though," came her retort. "Living in boarding houses or cold-water flats, staying alone till all hours every night. Not knowing when there'll be work or no work. Now do you or don't you get a decent job?"

"Has this all been planned?" I turned to Mae accusingly.

I got the answer from her mother. "Yes, we planned it. We've talked it over a dozen times. And now I'll give you all the news. Mae is leaving you till you come to your senses! She's coming back to live with us until you get a regular job. Then you can take her back with you. Otherwise you go back alone to your pianner!"

"Is that the way you want it, Mae?" I asked her.

"I guess so, Vincent," she choked. "Let's try it this way, anyhow. If you love your piano more than you love me—then I think it's best we try a—well, a vacation from each other a while."

Suddenly the Latin temper won out. I whirled around and walked away.

Chapter 22. INTERLUDE WITH JENNIE

A telegram was waiting for me when I got back to our flat that evening. Up in Buffalo, Harry Weil (a singing waiter who had been at Clayton's) had read about Jimmy Durante replacing me at Pabst's Café. Harry wired me an offer of thirty-five a week at Paddy Lavan's.

Lavan's roused memories of Phyllis's death, but necessity overcame that. I got Mae on the telephone and told her the news.

"They want me there right away," I explained, "so come over first thing in the morning and we'll leave tomorrow night."

But Mae hesitated . . . said she really wasn't feeling well . . . thought perhaps I'd better try it alone for a few weeks to see if the job would last. I realized she didn't want to come along.

I arrived when the evening was well under way at Lavan's. Harry Weil took me over to Paddy Lavan for the introduction.

"This is the new pianist I hired—Vincent Lopez. He's played the best places in Brooklyn. Our customers will love him. His professional nickname is the Piano Kid."

"My professional name," said Paddy proudly, "was the same in the ring—Paddy Lavan. Fought the best of them, I have, and now I got a place that rates with the best of them."

"I'm sure I'll like it here, Mr. Lavan," I answered.

"Just be sure you play plenty of Irish tunes," Paddy advised. I didn't need any further cues. My imagination could still feel that belt in the nose Hasenflug gave me when I didn't follow such instructions.

"There are three reasons why my place is a hit," Paddy added. "Keep them in mind if you want to play here. We provide liquor, music, and women—and all of them have to be good except the women. Is there anything disagreeable in that to you, Mr. Lopez?"

"Er—no, nothing at all," I agreed.

"Harry tells me you used to attend St. Mary's at Dunkirk, and I just want to be sure we won't offend any monastery memories."

Paddy was in a talkative mood and it was at least an hour before he let me take over at the piano. In Harry Weil's introduction, I became the "Piano Kid from Manhattan," not Brooklyn.

I began with some of my specialties. The songs that went over best were "Where the River Shannon Flows," "Just One World of Consolation," and "Stack O'Lee."

I got a big hand, and some ladies of the evening draped themselves affectionately over my shoulders during the pauses. "If Father Aloysius could see me now!" I thought to myself. St. Mary's was just forty-two miles away.

"How about doing your specialty, the one you play every night?" boomed Lavan. "You know—where you play 'Yankee Doodle' with one hand and 'Dixie' with the other."

Obviously the boss man had me confused with his previous piano player. So I improvised the "specialty" on the spot—and I never forgot how to play it!

When I finally took a break, Harry Weil insisted that I meet a very special friend of Paddy's. From the way she was dressed I should have realized that she was Queen Bee of all those honeys at the tables. But she simply seemed a beautiful but overdressed woman in her thirties wearing enough jewelry to stock a counter at Tiffany's—a trademark, I learned later, of the Buffalo Madam.

Jennie—that was her name—loved music, especially the piano. New York was her idea of the ultimate in sophistication and gracious living. So the combination of her interests and my background got us off to a friendly start. I went back to her table every time I took a break.

"Vincent," she said, just before closing time—which was whenever the last customer left or was carried out, "striped silk shirts are the style for men in this town. If you need some, let me pick you up at your place tomorrow afternoon and I'll show you some good buys in the department stores."

It was a date.

In order to send Mae twenty dollars out of my week's wages of thirty-five—I held on to the tip money—I was staying at a cheap rooming house. Jennie's brand new car, which chugged up to the entrance the next afternoon, certainly looked out of place.

I jumped in beside her and got cosy with her while her chauffeur drove us to the department store.

When we walked in, the stares made me uncomfortable—but Jennie loved every bit of the attention we were getting.

"Why do they keep looking at us like that?" I whispered. "Is it because I'm younger than you? Do you suppose they think you're my mother?" This nearly doubled Jennie up with laughter.

"For goodness sake, Vincent," she finally gasped, "do I look that old?"

"Anything but," I tried to be gallant. "You look like a girl."

"Just wait till you see me tonight," she promised. "Now let's get those shirts."

We got them—one dozen of the best that Jennie picked—and paid for! I'd been under the impression that we were out to get three shirts at a buck apiece, but the tab on the twelve—plus two ties—was an even hundred! Jennie produced it over my not too vehement protests, then specified the one I was to wear that evening.

"You can buy me lunch now," said Jennie, "and pay the rest off playing the piano for me—at my house—I mean my home."

Jennie's place was unbelievably ornate, a swirl of plush upholstery and untamed color. A liveried butler at the door led me to the library while Jennie went upstairs to change. I was introduced to three middle-aged visitors—obviously business men but not the least bit tired! They were admiring an art collection of nudes. I joined the art lovers.

"Jennie's interest in art," said one of the gentlemen, "is based on the theory that no nudes are *not* good nudes! That's a twist on a pun, young man." (I hadn't laughed.)

"What Mr. Adams means," his friend explained, "is that each nude in these paintings has one thing on her mind."

Since the nudes were all either reclining on couches, or getting into bed, including a farmer's daughter on a bed of hay, I got the message!

Jennie completed it, a few minutes later, when she reappeared in a plunging-neckline gown that would have broken a television camera, and suggested that we "join the girls in the salon."

"The girls" were a dozen beauties in filmy gowns and black net silk stockings. Had I been an Arab, I'd have thought I had just died and was in heaven.

"Now do you know why we attracted so much attention in the department store?" Jennie asked. "I'm Jennie Relda, probably the most famous woman in Buffalo. The newspapers spell it notorious but it means the same thing. Doesn't it, Mr. Adams?"

"I'll instruct my reporters to refer hereafter to the famous Jennie Relda . . . and her infamous establishment."

There was a general laugh, but I didn't join in. My religious training and my marriage to Mae combined to give me a case of "cold feet."

"Jennie, you wanted me to play the piano. Mind if I do that now?"

While the other guests sauntered off with girls, I went through my repertoire. In between playing hostess to new arrivals, Jennie sat alongside and really enjoyed the numbers.

"Why don't you pick one of the girls and have some fun, Vincent?" she asked. "Sex is good for you; I don't mean just physically. It gives a man poise, and I think you could use a bit of that."

"I'm no angel," I replied. "But I'm married and I don't think it's right."

"I know *how* you're married," Jennie said. "Harry Weil told me."

"You mean about my wife staying in Brooklyn?" I asked.

"That's exactly what I mean. You call yourself married—with your wife in Brooklyn?"

I had no answer.

"If most women were real wives to their men, I'd be out of business!" Jennie went on.

"Mae will join me," I answered. "She just waited to be sure the job would last."

"If it doesn't last at Lavan's," Jennie offered, "you've got a job playing here."

Even I laughed at the remark. I could visualize telling Mae *that*.

Jennie went on, "Does Mae want to fix your tie, tell you not to eat so fast, advise you to get more sleep? Because that's the sort of a woman who'd really go for you, Vincent. I'm that type myself, inside. Motherly, they call it. When I meet a shy man—and you're really shy, except at the piano—I want to do something for him—like buying you those shirts today."

"Is that how you feel toward me?" I asked, a bit disappointed. "Motherly?"

"But not only that," was her admission. "There's more to it, Vincent. If that wife of yours doesn't come up to Buffalo soon, I'll show you the difference."

Mae came to Buffalo a month later, at my insistence. She was equally insistent about visiting Lavan's, although I succeeded in keeping her away for a whole week. We had a second honeymoon seeing Buffalo, but the honeymoon was over the minute she walked into Paddy's and spotted the unattached females prospecting for dates.

"Oh, Vincent," she half sobbed, "this is terrible. You've got to come home and give all this up."

"There you go assuming the worst," I accused. "Here I've been living like a saint and you believe I've been taking up with these girls. There were the same kind of girls in the Brooklyn places and you didn't object."

"But I was with you then," Mae protested.

Just then one of the men called loudly for his check, and the girl at his table went into the dressing room to get her fur coat. As they left, arm in arm a moment later, the guy cast a suggestive wink in my direction. On such incidents can a whole life turn. Mae grew furious.

"That does it!" she exclaimed. "Either you quit this job right now and we go home to Brooklyn, or I'm leaving by myself."

"What'll I do back in Brooklyn?" I wanted to know. "Do you know of a job open anywhere?"

"Yes, I do," she triumphed. "My brother Harry got you one—at the bank where he works. Twelve dollars a week and your lunches. We can get by on it."

"If you think I'm giving up the piano—" I began. But Mae pulled her coat tight around her and walked toward the door. I turned around and walked toward the piano.

When I got back to the hotel she was gone, leaving a brief note that amounted to an ultimatum: Either take the bank job in Brooklyn, or stay by myself in Buffalo.

I stayed in Buffalo, but not by myself. Not while there was Jennie for companionship—plus.

Chapter 23. I BECOME A FATHER

The job at Lavan's stretched into the spring and on through the summer. I heard regularly from Mae, but her letters grew more and more indifferent. The distance between us was lending no enchantment at all. However, I had some vague idea that we would pick up again as husband and wife, and said so in my letters. In fact, when I got a five-dollar raise I increased what I was sending her to twenty-five.

The psychologists claim that we learn (or improve) in sudden spurts, then stay on the new plateau for years. The Buffalo experience gave me a real push forward in technical proficiency, but not an inch in spiritual growth.

It was a telegram that took me away from Buffalo. It was from Mae's brother Harry and it read:

BABY GIRL BORN TO MAE THIS EVENING STOP EVERYTHING FINE STOP MAE DIDN'T WANT TO INFORM YOU EARLIER BECAUSE WE DON'T WISH THE CHILD TO INFLUENCE YOUR DECISION ON FUTURE LIFE STOP HOWEVER MAE FEELS YOU SHOULD BE HERE TO TALK THINGS OVER AGAIN CAN YOU MAKE IT THIS SUNDAY AT OUR HOUSE

HARRY

I groped for the nearest lobby chair, practically stunned. Fatherhood! A quick calculation showed me that our second honeymoon (when Mae visited me at Lavan's) had been more fruitful than the first. But to become a father so unexpectedly! I didn't know which way to turn . . . except to Jennie's . . . for some motherly advice this time.

"The child is just another reason why you should go back," Jennie told me "and maybe not the most important one, Vincent."

"What could be more important, Jennie? I'm a father now. I've got to go back to Mae."

"That could be a mistake," she explained. "When two people aren't right for each other, a child doesn't necessarily help the situation. And their being together may not be good for the child, either. The best reason for going back to New York is your career, Vincent. You've become a real professional at the piano the last few months. Maybe I was right about love bringing out the best in a man . . ." and she grinned slyly. "But let's stay serious about this. There's nothing more for you in Buffalo. You've got to go on from this point, or you'll slide back."

"Lavan's is as good a place as most of them in Brooklyn," I objected.

"Who said Brooklyn? You'd be foolish to settle for that. You're ready for Manhattan now—for the best on Broadway. And there's still another reason. It will be best for me to have you go back. We've grown very fond of each other the last few months, and in my business, there's one luxury I can't afford to indulge."

"What's that?" I pressed.

"One I thought I'd forgotten, but I haven't. It's jealousy."

That Saturday I finished up at Lavan's and took the express for Grand Central, then the elevated local to Brooklyn. Jennie wasn't at the depot to see me off. However, her car was there to take me from Lavan's to the station. It was her last touch of motherly interest in my welfare.

What I remember best about Jennie was her preference in songs. I once thought it odd that a member of the world's oldest profession was so deeply moved by the world's oldest type of song—the lullaby! She was just as fond of sad ballads.

Sometimes I'd protest, "How about some ragtime now?"

"Ragtime does nothing to me. Maybe it's too close to the tempo of my life, Vincent. That's why I like the sentimental numbers. Stop arguing, dammit, and play!"

Her girls had the same taste in music. They liked ragtime and such novelty tunes as "Ballin' The Jack" and "Mammy Jinny's Jubilee" well enough, but for their serious listening, they called for tearful tunes, "Curse of an Aching Heart," "Just One Word of Consolation," "I'm Tying the Leaves So They Won't Fall Down," and, above all, "Mother, a Word That Means the World to Me."

The same song preference was generally true of the gangsters, grifters, and gamblers of those days—and today! Maybe it's their sole touch with the thing they want above all—respectability!

I didn't exactly welcome the responsibilities of parenthood, but I accepted them. I convinced Mae we should give our marriage another try, and in this I had the unexpected support of her mother. The grandchild changed her attitude a lot, although the change didn't last. Two weeks after the birth of Kay (that's what we called her), we were back in a flat of our own in the Ridgewood section of Brooklyn.

Speaking of flats, I was almost flat on my back financially, for I had saved little at Lavan's and if Mae had put anything aside out of the money I'd sent her, she wasn't admitting it. I could find no piano job at the familiar joints. Brother Harry suggested a "position" at the bank again, and this time, with the rent and a big milk bill only two weeks away, I almost gave in. But remembering Jennie's admonitions, I decided to try Broadway.

My number came up by way of a chance meeting with a theatrical agent named Al Herman. By avocation Al was an amateur horse player, and a good friend of "Action" Klein, a reformed bookmaker who had gone into the restaurant business with popular Morty Lane. They owned Broadway's most fabulous place, the Pekin, on 47th Street and Broadway, facing Duffy Square.

Action Klein hadn't carried the reform movement too far. Just about every afternoon he was at one of the Broadway betting parlors, handling bets on the horses. Al Herman met Action one afternoon in a betting parlor and learned that the Pekin was in the market for a "class" pianist to accompany the vocal numbers of the floor show and keep the music going while Ed Fischelli's dance band was taking a break. I met Al that same evening in Brooklyn, and in two shakes of a gentlemen's agreement we were hurrying back to Broadway and a hoped-for audition at the Pekin.

Inside, the Pekin was built like a pagoda and Confucius might have felt at home there. Herman whisked me up to Klein's office.

"I got you the best piano player around," Al told Action. "Grab him while you can. They want him back up in Buffalo."

Klein interrupted the sales pitch with a nod of his head that signified "okay." "The band's off the floor now and we got a full house, so let's hear your boy play. I'll check first with Dan Dody. He's responsible for our shows. If Dan and Ed Fischelli like your boy, he's in. Nobody we heard today was good enough."

A quick call on an office phone brought Dan Dody to the scene. As we walked back in to the restaurant, the hum of voices from a capacity crowd sounded like a wall of indifference I'd never hurdle.

Dody walked to the stand and tapped on the piano for attention. "Ladies and gentlemen," he announced. "Hope everyone is enjoying himself, and we'd like to present a specialty act this evening. From Buffalo, where he starred at the famous Paddy Lavan's, we give you the Piano Kid, Vincent Lopez."

I suddenly realized that Al Herman would break my ribs with his nudging elbow unless I got up. I don't recall much about that walk across the dance floor except that I stumbled against the piano bench and somebody snickered. That did it! An electric charge, half anger, half determination, took over and I ran through "Ragging the Scales" with that certain extra something an entertainer knows he's put into his performance when it's there. The applause was solid, and I went right into "Maple Leaf Rag," followed by an imitation of bamboo bells and a music box. Now the applause really bounced off the walls and I had my encore ready: "The Entertainer's Rag," a novelty I'd learned at Lavan's, playing "Yankee Doodle" with the right hand and "Dixie" with the left.

With the then current patriotic stirrings of World War I, this last number brought down the house.

Back at Action Klein's table, I found my newly signed agent already talking a deal.

"Sure he's good," Klein agreed. "But twenty-five a week is our limit. Tell you what, if Ed Fischelli wants to use him in the band as well, he can work out his own deal."

I had made the grade on Broadway in my very first try. I was playing a pretty good piano, thanks to lots of practice, and the confidence I needed was coming along, too—thanks to Jennie.

Ed Fischelli wanted me for his band, it turned out, and offered me another twenty-five a week to join his outfit. Two weeks later I was also playing for his brother, Gerald, for tea dances at Bustanoby's at 39th and Broadway.

Incidentally, two of the "dance instructors" at Bustanoby's did pretty well for themselves later in Hollywood: George Raft and Rudolph Valentino. I could tell when the "dance instructor" business was slow (or shall we say inactive?). George and Rudy would drop by to see me at the Pekin in the late afternoon and casually drift over to the counters where we kept our rolls and condiments, which the waiters could conveniently pick up without making a trip to the kitchen. Valentino would load his roll with chili sauce to the point where it couldn't be told where the chili stopped and the roll began. I forget what George's preference in rolls and condiments was—but there was one thing both the boys loved about them. They were free!

Chapter 24. THE HOODS AND THE STAGE DOOR JOHNS

The fly in the ointment was that the work kept me away from home. The trip to Ridgewood took almost an hour, and pretty soon I was having just a late breakfast as my only meal with Mae. Our youngster was colicky and her attacks usually came on just when I was falling asleep. Let's face it. I did a lot of complaining to Mae about not keeping the baby quiet. On her part, despite the good money I was making, Mae wasn't pleased that I'd landed the Pekin job. She was sure I'd be better off at the bank. When that got nowhere, she suggested that we'd *all* be better off if I rented a room near the Pekin and come home only on Sundays. Then I knew that Mae and I would never again make beautiful music.

At the Pekin I got to know a brand-new type of customer and renewed my acquaintance with an old familiar type. The innovation was the Stage-Door John; the echo of the past from Casey's and Lavan's was the Mobster, who loves to mix with society in expensive restaurants. The Pekin had its share of them, impeccably tailored by the Fifth Avenue shops, but with the same bulge of the armpit holster.

The Pekin was famous for its stage show. That fame was built on the theatrical flair of our producer, Dan Dody, who had come up through burlesque and Broadway musicals, and the beautiful, talented showgirl-dancers whom Dody hired and then inspired. He turned the ordinary stage show into a capsule revue that sparkled for forty minutes as brightly as the best of the "Follies" or "Vanities." I think Dody was the top producer of his day. Every one of his successive shows was different; and even in a current show he'd introduce new bits of business, to replace what wasn't tops. Many later-day headliners owed their start to his coaching, one being Fannie Brice.

The Pekin was a happy hunting ground for the Stage-Door Johnnies. But they were gentlemen (I mean the true species). We had a beautiful French girl in the show, named Marie Legrand. *Two* of the Johns used to escort her around town—simultaneously.

"And you get fifty dollars from each of them whenever you go out?" I asked her incredulously.

"Yep," said Marie. "Six fifty dollar bills so far this week."

"Let's get very personal a minute. What do you have to do for that?"

"I'd slap your face if we weren't good friends," Marie laughed. "But so help me, nothing but go out with them after the Pekin closes. Then they take me back to my hotel in a taxi, and leave me in the lobby. Get that questioning gleam out of your eye!"

"Well, I'll be—" I admitted. "So they just want to be seen with a beautiful girl!"

"A lot of Johns are like that," said Marie. "Lonely men who want to imagine for a couple of hours that they're young again, courting a young girl. And they expect to pay well for it."

"But two of them romancing you at the same time; how come?"

"They're business partners and they both happened to take a liking to me. Oh, they're a bit sorry for me, too, or rather for my mother—there in Paris, you know, with the terrible war."

"Oh," I understood. "You told them about your mother in Paris."

"Yes," said Marie. "Mother does live in Paris; Paris, *Kentucky!*"

Death Valley Scotty, who struck it so fabulously rich, often played Santa Claus to our orchestra instead of to our chorus girls. When the mood and the song suited him, he would have the orchestra members line up near his table and he would pitch ten-dollar gold pieces into the bells of their instruments, for the lucky musicians to keep! Any coins he missed were supposed to be returned for another try, but some of our waiters, with chewing gum plastered on the soles of their shoes clumsily walked on the coin when he missed.

Two of the mobster habitués who loved piano music, usually took a table near me. I never knew their real names; they were known as Gyp the Blood and Lefty Louie! And nobody tried to keep them out.

Prohibition hadn't yet turned the billion-dollar liquor and restaurant business over to gangsterdom, but its rackets ranged from plate-glass window "protection" for the little business man to Big (but illicit) Business on the docks and wharves;—from selling a lone shot of cocaine to providing call girls for a business convention.

Inevitably, a few cops were caught taking protection money; and, of course, all of New York's finest suffered the stigma when the newspapers headlined the few. One of them was Police Lieutenant Charles Becker who banked $70,000 in two short years of gangland pay-offs. But he couldn't take it with him . . . in the electric chair at Sing Sing.

Becker engineered a plot to "remove" a gambler named Herman Rosenthal who was "singing" to the D.A. The legitimate "front" that Rosenthal employed was a vegetable business catering to the big restaurants and hotels, including the Pekin. He often dined here, and it was here that the two hoods, hired by Becker, planned the murder. At their table near me Gyp the Blood and Lefty Louie were arguing about how to handle the job, and Eddie Fischelli and I overheard them.

"The best place to let him have it is in the hall coming up here to the restaurant," Gyp insisted.

"Nuts!" Louie exclaimed. "Rosenthal knows he's in trouble and if he spotted us waitin' for him he could scram. Let's give it to him in the lobby the minute he walks in. That way, we can be in the street in a couple of seconds, with a car waitin' outside."

Then their voices trailed off into a more cautious tone, but I had heard enough. Finishing my set of numbers in a shaky mood, I headed for Klein's office. My story left him equally shaken and he sent for Dan Dody on the double.

"Tell him what you heard, Vincent," Action instructed me. I repeated the intelligence.

"Supposing I talk to Gyp the Blood about this," Dody suggested. "He owes us a favor. After all, we've let him hide packages in the restaurant safe from time to time—and always after some big jewel robbery!"

"We don't ask him no questions about the packages," Klein decided, "and so he don't owe us any favor as far as he figures it. No; we got to handle this more direct. Now, if we can't go to the mountain, why not go right to Mohammed?"

"You mean tell Rosenthal about this?" Dody wondered.

"Why not?" Action replied. "We're helpin' him and he ain't gonna squeal to anybody! Tell you what, Dody. Get him on the phone right now and say we got good reason to believe it'd be healthy if he stayed out of here a couple of weeks."

Dody picked up the phone.

"Is there any objection if I stop in at the neighborhood precinct and tell them what I heard?" I asked.

"Yes, there is an objection!" Klein thundered. "From two people: me—and your life-insurance agent!"

"Just forget the whole thing, kid," Dody added. "If Rosenthal has any brains, he'll get out of town after what I tell him. . . ."

Rosenthal planned to leave town but he took one night too long to clean up some business details. That night, he was shot at the Hotel Metropole on 43rd Street. A long trial and several appeals later, Gyp the Blood, Lefty Louie, Dago Frank, Whitey Lewis and Lieutenant Becker were executed for his murder.

Ed Fischelli and I got along fine. It was my first job with an orchestra, and I had the luck to pick a progressive leader who knew that the funeral march sets in for any band as soon as it grows complacent. Ed was forever experimenting. It was his band that introduced the laughing trombone; and he was also the first New York leader to use a saxophone in a dance band.

It was through Fischelli that I was able to introduce W. C. Handy's "St. Louis Blues."

"Mr. Lopez," the earnest composer said to me, "this is a good song I've written. It has something special. Would you look it over and show it to Mr. Fischelli if you like it? I need a good band to give this song a break."

"Sure," I said. "But don't be too hopeful. The blues are flooding the market today and I'm afraid the public's getting a little tired of them."

"Not this one," he insisted with a quiet confidence I couldn't help but notice. "This one they'll never get tired of."

I gave it a first run-through the following afternoon, and I could hardly wait for Ed to reach the Pekin that evening.

"This one is really great, Ed," I enthused. "It has everything."

Ed looked over the original copy and the words. "It's got an interesting lyric, anyway," he agreed. "And any customers we have from Missouri will like the title. Okay, we'll work up an orchestration and give it a try."

When we introduced the tune a week later, a classic was born Handy's immortal "St. Louis Blues."

It was summertime of 1916 and infantile paralysis warped not only the limbs of its poor victims but the mind of the entire city. When the disease struck in an apartment, the entire block went into a panic. Public places were shunned. Ed Fischelli became obsessed with the fear that he might pick up the germ at the Pekin and take it home to his youngsters. To play it safe, he sent his family to Connecticut. When the epidemic waned, Ed asked if he could have the weekends off to visit them.

"Okay, but who'll lead the band?" Action demanded.

"We've got two pianos," Ed suggested. "Why not use Lopez to start the beat . . . then sit in on each number? He's young but the crowd likes him and he can handle it."

Strangely, I wanted no part of the deal! I was quite content to remain a pianist. Klein cut my objections short. "Ain't nobody told you the facts of life yet? We need an orchestra leader and you need a job. Get it?"

The Pekin's colorful co-owner, Morty Lane, added a gift to his congratulations. "Now that you're a regular band leader, you'll be spending more than you make on clothes. And you'll need a lot more shirts, I suppose."

I wondered what was coming. Morty was a nut about expensive silk shirts. If it had been the thing in those days to go to psychiatrists, he'd have been on the couch trying to figure his strange compulsion never to wear a shirt a second time! Instead, Lane bought a brand new shirt every day, to the delight of Nat Lewis, Broadway's leading haberdasher. If Morty was caught short with only one new shirt over a weekend, he would wear it to bed on Saturday night, so it would still be on his back for Sunday!

"Your piano playing has given me a lot of personal enjoyment, Kid," Morty went on. "I'd like to say best wishes in your new job with half a dozen shirts."

"Thanks, Mr. Lane. Will you pick them out for me? I've always admired your taste in shirts."

"You have?" He grinned in delight. "In that case, I'll make it a dozen."

A couple of weekends later, Dan Dody noticed that I was starting each number while seated, kicking the tune off with the old "Ah-one, ah-two" method that Lawrence Welk uses so effectively today. But Dan didn't like it.

"I don't like it either, but I have to do it this way. My ankles are all puffed and they kill me when I stand up so much. Here, look for yourself"—and I rolled my socks down to show him the swelling.

"Gee, kid," Dody commiserated, "you got rheumatism! Why don't you see a doctor?"

"Aw, it isn't that bad," I replied. "Besides, I don't believe in doctors."

"You don't see many people who don't believe in doctors—because

Antonio Lopez (my Father)

Virginia Lopez (my Mother)

Me (McLaughlin days)

Bert McLaughlin and our sing
waiters on vacation.

With Father Sebastian and
brother confraters. (I am se
from the left in the second
from the top.)

overnor Alfred E. Smith at the opening of the Empire State Building. From left: Lopez, nidentified, Smith, Lou Holtz, Harry Hershfield.

I wield my baton for the Penetro Radio Show, with Bob Ripley and Ed Sullivan.

METROPOLITAN OPERA HOUSE

NEW YORK

SYMPHONIC "JAZZ" CONCERT

By

VINCENT LOPEZ

And His Augmented Orchestra of Forty Selected Soloists

SUNDAY AFTERNOON, NOV. 23, 1924

UNDER DIRECTION

WILLIAM MORRIS and S. HUROK

The program for our Jazz Concert at the Metropolitan Opera House.

Lopez and his Orchestra at the famous St. Regis Roof.

When in New York City, Don't Forget to Visit the Casa Lopez

ADDISON FOWLER and Florenz Tamara (below), featured dancers now at the Casa Lopez, will come here with George White's "Scandals" next June.

"LOPEZ SPEAKING"—you can almost hear his voice as the famous musician, Vincent Lopez (above), announces his next musical number before the orchestra begins playing, not only for the entertainment of those who visit the exquisite club (above at center), but also for those who "listen in" on Station WEAF and its associated chain of twelve radio broadcasting stations. To his beautifully decorated club the smartest folk from Broadway come to dance—and listen to Lopez's original musical conceptions.

The beautiful Casa Lopez

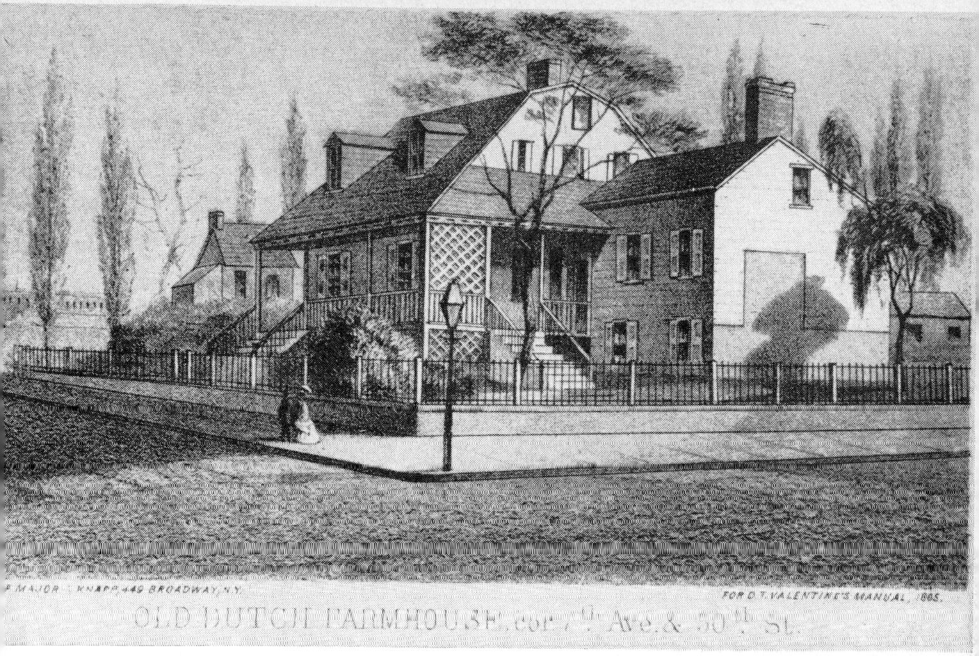
F. MAJOR & KNAPP, 449 BROADWAY, N.Y.
FOR D.T. VALENTINE'S MANUAL, 1865.
OLD DUTCH FARMHOUSE, cor 7th Ave. & 50th St.

Old Dutch Cottage, the first building on the site of the Hotel Taft.

Lopez and his Orchestra today at the Hotel Taft Grill Room.

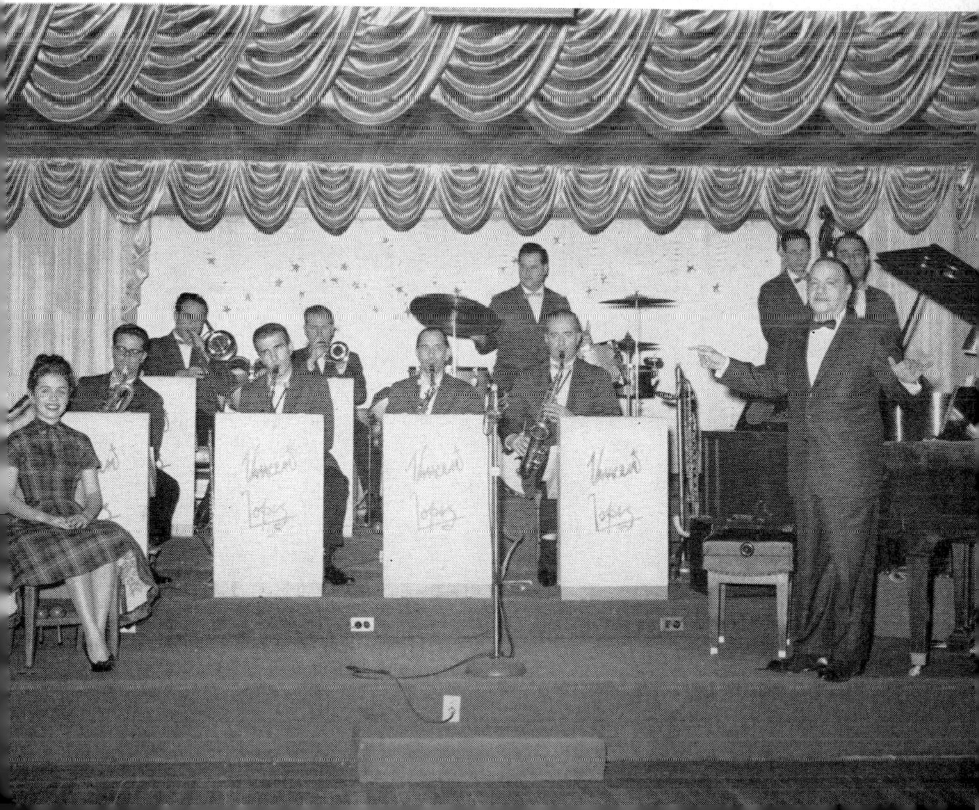
Vincent Lopez
Vincent Lopez
Vincent Lopez

DOWN MEMORY LANE: 1) With Pat Rooney, who taught me the art of sho business. 2) I forsake the piano to accompany my sister Marie, age 4, on t mandolin. 3) Wooing Sophie Tucker. 4) With W. C. Handy, composer "St. Louis Blues," who wrote "Evolution of the Blues" for our Jazz Conce at the Met. 5) Rudy Vallee in a familiar pose. Vallee's first job in New Yor Playing a club date for Lopez! 6) With Alfred Lewis, managing director of Ho Taft. 7) "Lopez and His Kings of Harmony," my original Dixieland jazz ba of 1919. Left to right, Tommy Gott, trumpet; Tony White, drums; Bill Hamilt clarinet; Lopez, piano; and Harold Geiser, trombone. 8) Irene Castle. 9) Jolson. 10) Yoshi Fugiwari, the "Caruso of Japan," and Grace Moore. 11) M protégé, Betty Hutton. 12) Texas Guinan and Jane Bertolli, winner of a beau contest. 13) Xavier Cugat and Abbe Lane, who was once a vocalist for m (Picture layout courtesy of The Morning Telegraph, New York.)

"America's Number One Jitterbug"—my protégé, Betty Hutton.

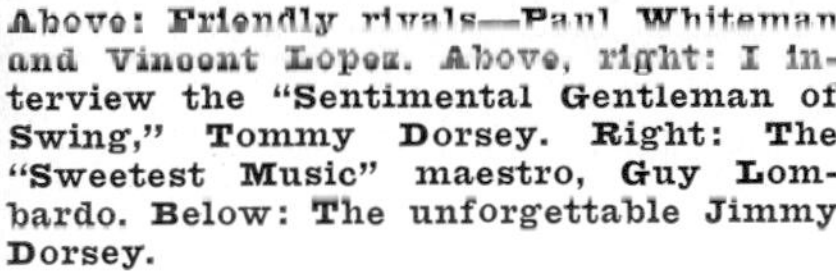

Above: Friendly rivals—Paul Whiteman and Vincent Lopez. Above, right: I interview the "Sentimental Gentleman of Swing," Tommy Dorsey. Right: The "Sweetest Music" maestro, Guy Lombardo. Below: The unforgettable Jimmy Dorsey.

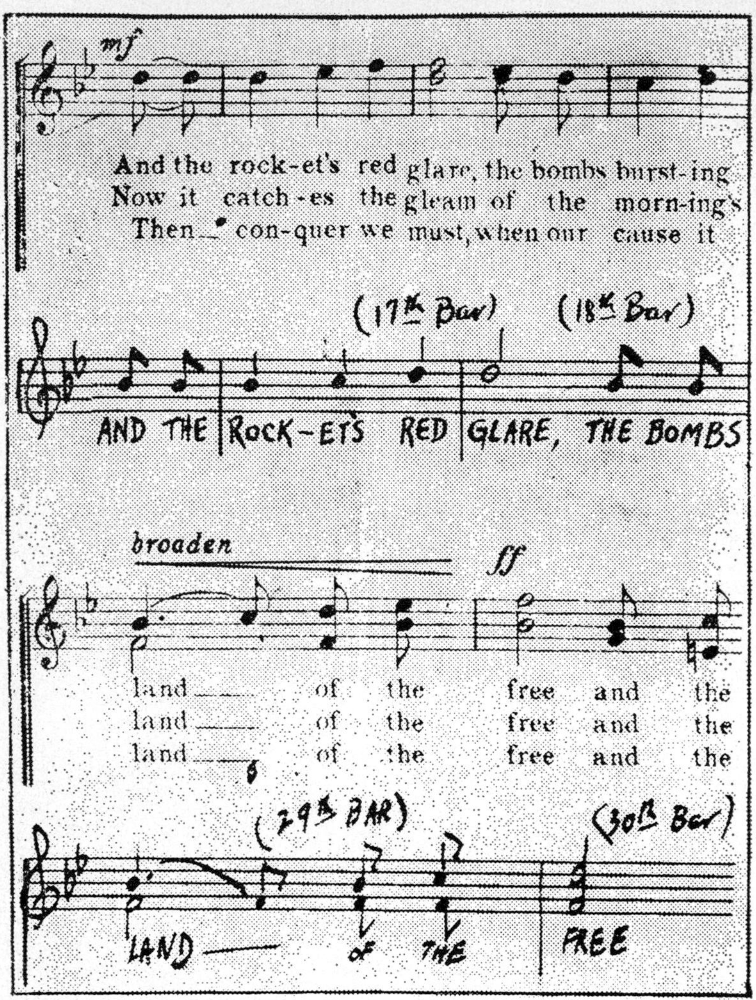

The changes I proposed to make our National Anthem more singable. (Try it on your piano.)

I appear on TV as Nostradamus in "Masquerade Party." (Produced by Ed Wolfe, my former press agent.)

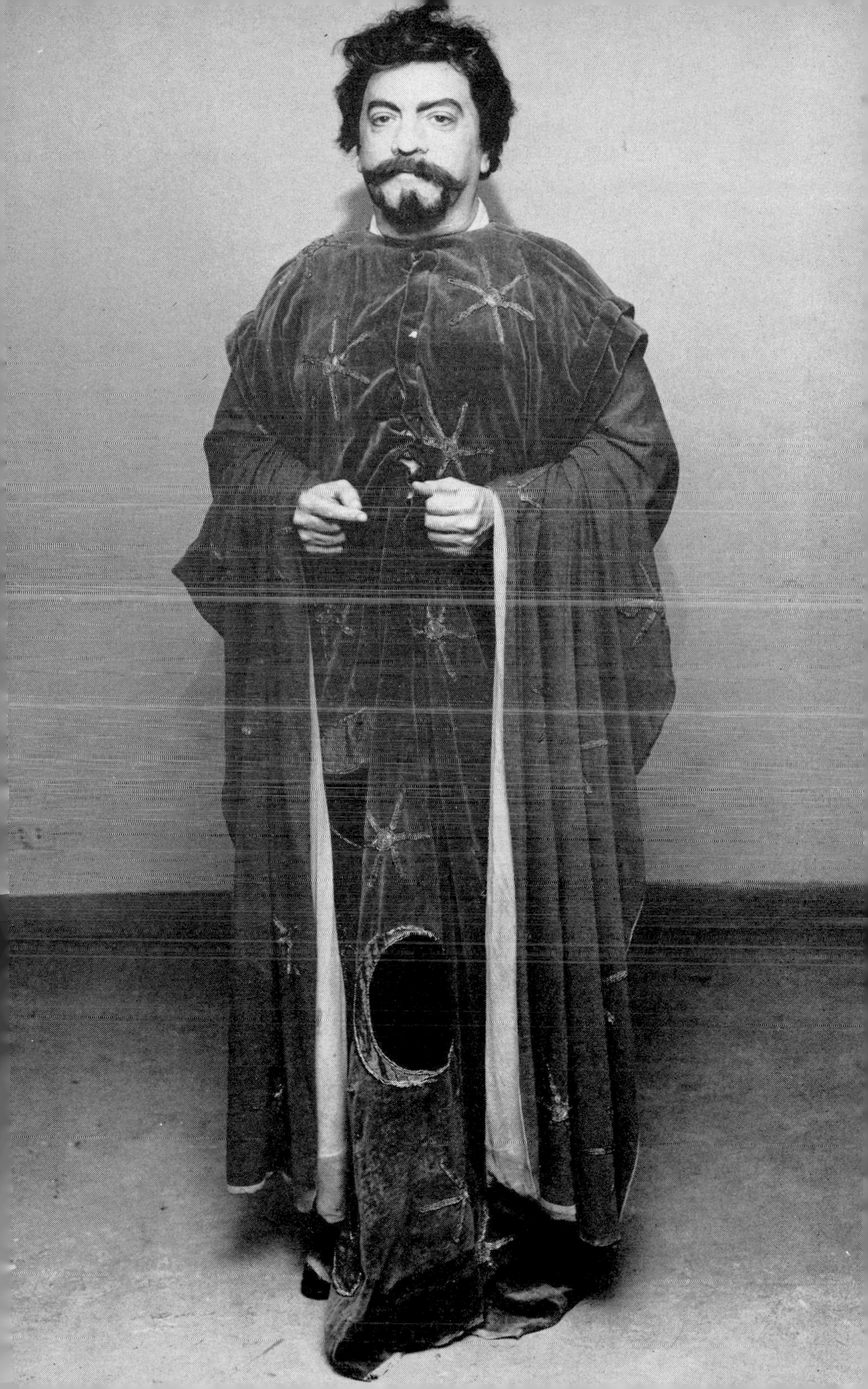

E. M. Statler, who gave me my start at the Hotel Pennsylvania (now the Statler Hilton).

MY THREE MENTORS

J. J. Atkinson, who signed my million-dollar contract at the St. Regis Hotel.

Alfred Lewis, executive vice-president of the Hotel Taft and a very important factor in my life.

Above, left: Toots Shor of Toots Shor. Above, right: John Perona of El Morocco. Left: Leo Lindy of Lindy's.

FAMOUS NEW YORK HOSTS, WHOM I FREQUENTLY VISIT. THEIR FRIENDSHIP COUNTED WHEN I NEEDED IT.

Right: Al Schacht of Al Schacht's Restaurant. Below, left: Ed Wynne of Harwin Club. Below, right: Max Asnas of the Stage Delicatessen.

The lady who changed my life—Mrs. Vincent Lopez.

most of them are in cemeteries," said Dody. "Anyway, I hope the rheumatism doesn't climb up to your fingers."

It was a pretty horrible thought, and I drowned it later in a delicious meal topped off with two pieces of strawberry shortcake.

Chapter 25. I BECOME A BANDLEADER—AND LOSE MY WIFE

Ed Fischelli decided to settle down in Connecticut, and asked Klein for his release. "I can get an easier job in the Vogue restaurant," he explained, "and local dates where I live. I'd like to take Vincent along, but he's got a better chance leading the band right here."

Action called me in and broke the news. Thinking poor Ed was getting the business I refused the job; but they soon straightened me out on that. A ten-dollar raise clinched matters. I walked out of Action's office the youngest orchestra leader in the Big Time.

Just two weeks later, Ed Fischelli came back to the Pekin to see me. "Vince, I'm sorry to do this, but I need a good clarinetist at the Vogue and Bill Darby wants to join me because he prefers the shorter hours even if there's less dough."

"If that's the way you both want it, swell," I said. "I'll send out the word we need a clarinetist here and twenty will apply tomorrow."

The word brought me a fellow with long black hair who had his wife on one arm and a saxophone case under the other. A musician in my aggregation who knew him said he was terrific with a licorice stick and I said okay, but at thirty-five like everyone else. This chap wanted seventy-five which was more than I was making. Picking up his hat, wife, and clarinet case, Ted Lewis strolled out of the Pekin and out of my professional life.

A little while later he was featured at Rector's and the Ziegfeld

Roof, wearing a battered silk hat, playing an elegant clarinet, and asking his jampacked audiences, "Is *every*body happy?"

There had been so much emphasis on President Wilson's election promise to keep us out of war that when America did go in, it caught me by surprise. Even though I was pretty far back in the draft ranks, as a husband-father, I felt it would be a good thing to enlist and pick my own branch of service instead of waiting for the Draft Board to decide that for me. Strangely enough, Mae agreed with that idea. Most wives were imploring their eager-beaver husbands to wait for the draft, but Mae was all for my enlisting at once.

It was several days after I signed the enlistment papers that I got my medical exam. My friends helped me through the waiting period with a round of farewell parties. I still didn't drink, but I could surely eat.

"You're about twenty pounds overweight now, Vince," Dan laughed, "but a month in the Army will take care of that."

"How long have you had that edema of the ankles?" the doctor wanted to know.

"That what?" I began. "Oh, you mean the swelling. A year, I guess. It comes and goes, but it's pretty bad now."

"You've got a real case of lithemia—*gout* to you. Too much uric acid in the blood. It's often hereditary. Did your father or grandfather have it? It's usually passed on through the males."

"I don't know about my grandfather," I answered, "but my father never had it."

"Then he probably took good care of himself," the doctor surmised. "Ate sparingly—simple foods?" I told him he had hit the nail right on the head, and I recounted the codfish, boiled potatoes, and barley-coffee routine.

"On that diet he'd never get gout," said the doctor. "Beri-beri maybe, but not gout."

"How long will it take for army life to put me in good shape?" I questioned.

"It depends on what war you mean. This one won't last another year. Maybe you'll get in the next one."

"You mean I can't get into service?" I said in disbelief.

"We're fighting a war, not running a clinic," he snapped.

The disappointment had largely worn off by the time I got home to Ridgewood that evening (I made a special trip to tell Mae about it). I resolved to see a doctor about my condition, do whatever he recommended, and try to enlist later. But a new disappointment faced me. It was the disappointment Mae plainly showed over the news.

"I thought the Army would straighten you out in your thinking," she told me. "Get you over the idea of playing a piano the rest of your life. Now what have I got to look forward to? Living alone here in Brooklyn, with you over in New York?"

"Why don't you live over there with me?" I countered.

"And leave my moth—. No, that's not it," she corrected. "Kay is growing up, and Manhattan's no place for her. Once and for all, Vincent, will you get a regular job so we can have a decent life together?"

I was silent, knowing how futile an argument would be. This infuriated Mae. "I don't know that I *want* to lead the rest of my life with you," she screamed. "If the Army won't have you, why should I? The gout! An old man's disease. You're an old man already."

"If I am," I yelled back, "you're not to blame."

"What do you mean by that?"

"The doctor says I got this from eating rich foods," I snapped. "It certainly wasn't anything you cooked!"

The words were said half in jest, but they ignited Mae's Irish temper. She ran into the kitchen, to emerge with a frying pan in her hand. I headed for the door and the downstairs stairway. She hurled the heavy pan after me.

The shock of her deadly intentions stopped me right on the stairs. I picked up the frying pan and looked back at her.

"Did you mean that, Mae?" I asked her. "Be honest now. Did you want to hurt me?"

"Hurt you!" she shouted. "I didn't care if I killed you!"—and she meant it.

"All right," I said. "This is it. We could never have any love or respect for each other after this. I know you won't give me a divorce, but we can have a separation as far as the Church is concerned. I'll send a lawyer over in the morning."

"Never mind the lawyer," Mae answered. "Just give me your word you'll support the baby."

"You've got it," I answered. "The baby—and you."

And I walked off not knowing that I was still carrying the frying pan.

Chapter 26. WARTIME ON BROADWAY

Broadway's normal tempo was lively enough, but the war spirit of 1917 raised it to a hectic peak. People simply didn't want to go home at night. They made the rounds from one place to another, moving on as one place closed to a spot with a later curfew.

The entertainers joined in. There was a gambling house on 42nd Street that should have used "Sunrise Serenade" as its closing theme. One night a performer named Bill Duffy won $90,000 in a dice game. But unlike TV's giant jackpot quiz programs it wasn't possible to quit while well ahead. The next two nights at the dice table cleaned him out.

There was a drop in our afternoon business, but we more than made it up at night. Our salaries didn't increase but the tips did. A new crop of free spenders making big money in wartime industries by day rivalled Death Valley Scotty and Dave Lamarr in getting rid of it at night.

I got right in the money-spending parade. I shared the feeling of national pride and confidence that surged through America. There was nothing like it in World War II when we were a much stronger nation. With our strength had come a sobering maturity.

Anyway, my willingness to "live it up," plus the money I sent Mae each week under our informal agreement, kept me on the borderline of insolvency. People marveled over the fact that I never missed a night on the bandstand. My health secret was a simple one: I couldn't afford to be sick!

"Be sure you play plenty of patriotic songs," Dan Dody advised me. "It's what the customers want."

"All right, Dan," I agreed. "We're putting plenty of war songs in as it is, but we'll use even more. Though how they'll ever dance to 'Bring Back My Daddy to Me,' I can't imagine. And look at some of the other numbers we play regularly: 'Good Bye, Broadway—Hello, France;' 'Liberty Bell, It's Time to Ring Again;' 'Till the Clouds Roll By;' 'The Rose of No Man's Land;' 'My Buddy;' 'Give My Regards to Broadway;' 'I Didn't Raise My Boy to Be a Soldier'—"

"That's the stuff to give 'em," Dan enthused. "And the 'mother' tunes, too—like 'I'm Proud to Be the Mother of a Soldier,' and 'That's a Mother's Liberty Loan.' Here's one I'd like you to learn in a hurry: 'Save Your Kisses Till the Boys Come Home.' I'm building a special production for that in the show next week. The girls will wear costumes native to all the countries on the Allied side."

"Why not back it up with their native music," I suggested.

"Great! Great!" Dan enthused. "You're graduating from just a musician, Vince. You're getting to be a showman."

"And I got a good song for the finale," I went on. "I think it will be the most popular song of the whole war."

"Something sentimental?" he asked, "like 'Roses of Picardy'?"

"Not this time. This is a rhythm number that will make people want to get up and march right off. George M. Cohan wrote it. It has a very simple title—'Over There!' "

When the afternoon slump in business reached the "let's face it" stage, Action Klein took action. He closed the Pekin to the matinee trade and put in more tables for the evenings. That left me with some afternoon time on my hands.

At first I spent (or misspent) a lot of it on the movies. Their major theme was psychopathic rather than patriotic. Norma Talmadge was ravished by enough Prussian officers (complete with

Kaiser mustaches and monocles) to assure Germany's defeat from exhaustion of its manhood. The Kaiser himself came in for treatment as a sex fiend in *The Beast of Berlin.*

This dementia infected vaudeville, too. Eva Tanguay got $3000 a week for an act in which she wore a gown trimmed with lumps of coal and sugar, very scarce items at the time. In his review Heywood Broun thought Miss Tanguay wasn't "long" on talent, either: "Miss Tanguay is billed as a bombshell. Would to heaven she were, for a bomb is something which is carried to a great height—and then dropped!"

Even the legitimate theatre deteriorated. The theatre-going crowd has always been more demanding than movie addicts, and not even such headline names as William Faversham, Grace George, and Billie Burke could save the turkeys that roosted in the Broadway theatres around Thanksgiving, 1917.

In the musicals I once again came across W. C. Fields. But Ziegfeld wasted his comic genius on a silly impersonation of Teddy Roosevelt.

The one aspect of show business that maintained reasonably good taste and made progress was popular music—and it prospered mightily in the Broadway restaurant, typified by the Pekin.

"The purpose of this meeting," Action Klein announced, "is to find out why receipts were down almost thirty percent last month. Any ideas?"

"It's the influenza epidemic," Dan Dody insisted. "People are afraid to go anywhere."

"Then why the hell are they breaking down the doors at Reisenweber's? Can you tell me that?" Klein countered. "Is that new band there so terrific?"

"No better than my band," I chimed in. "But they've got a new music style called Dixieland. That's what we're up against."

"Music styles come and go," Dan disagreed. "The thing that pulls in the customers is the floor show, not the music." I kept quiet, but Klein read disagreement in my face.

"Maybe Lopez has got something," he said. "Anyway, let's go up to Reisenweber's tonight and see what this Dixieland is like."

"By the way, Mr. Klein," I added. "We might not have a band soon. Three of our boys go in the Army next month, and two more got their draft notices today."

"So what's the problem?" Klein questioned. "Women can play in a band, too, can't they? They want to do everything else these days!"

Before the war ended, six of my eight "sidemen" were women!

Dixieland had spread from New Orleans to Chicago. Its leading exponent was the ODJB (Original Dixieland Jazz Band) which Reisenweber's hired away from its Chicago run. A Victor recording of "Tiger Rag" gave them national popularity, and for months it was almost impossible to get copies of their quickly released recordings of "Barnyard Blues," "Sensation Rag," "Skeleton Jangle," and "Fidgety Feet."

It was the music that most closely mirrored America's carefree World War I mood. I made up my mind to adopt it even before our trip to Reisenweber's, but I had to sell Klein and Dody on the idea. However, a sales spiel wasn't needed. The new music sold itself! One hour at Reisenweber's convinced Klein and Dody that I was right about the new style. They gave me the go-ahead. In a week, we made the switch from schmaltzy music with heart appeal, to the drive of Dixieland that does something to the adrenal glands!

Though we left Reisenweber's rather early we stayed long enough to catch the powerful and compelling voice of the new star, Sophie Tucker. No greater praise is possible than to say the crowd loved Sophie as much as it did the new-style music.

The advent of Dixieland on Broadway changed the entire fabric of the entertainment world. There were still a few more years left for the sweet stuff. But audience sophistication soon set in, and with it the demand for higher standards. Like the Renaissance, the new music brought a quickening of thought for all show business. It paved the way for today's Rodgers and Hammerstein musicals and the "hep" artistry of *Guys and Dolls*. In the legitimate theatre, it helped the transition to playwrights like Tennessee Williams, whose

Glass Menagerie wouldn't have been comprehended by the audiences of 1917.

However, there was one undesirable change the war brought to Broadway. World War I's version of the juvenile delinquent infested the side streets late at night.

When the draft made personnel inroads on New York's finest, New York's lowest climbed out of the sewers and had its terrifying fling. There were open assaults on late strollers right in well-lighted Times Square! I remember it not from newspaper headlines but from personal experience.

"Want me to call a taxi, Vince?" Dan Dody inquired as we finished up some late work on a new show. "It's after four o'clock and there have been some holdups around here."

"My room is only a couple of blocks away. I'll make it all right. You go ahead, Dan. I've still got a little work on a few numbers."

Half an hour later and a long block away from the Pekin, five young toughs began trailing me. Deciding that a bold front was the best defense, I turned on them and asked what they wanted. Two of them flashed knives. My only weapon was a rolled-up newspaper that we all carried late at night to cuff off a lone bum who might get rough making his touch.

One of the knife wielders came in fast and low, but a lucky shot with the newspaper sent his blade ringing along the sidewalk. The others began circling me for an all-sided attack when I saw my opening—a path down the middle and back to the Pekin, if I could make it.

I could always sprint with the best of the neighborhood kids, and my sudden fear was a marvelous anesthetic for my gouty ankles. I reached the Pekin door ten feet ahead of my pursuers. The Lopez who had abandoned church felt need for a prayer.

"Oh, God!" I implored. "Let that front door be open!"

It was. I jerked it open and threw myself inside. Before I could bolt the door, my pursuers were forcing it inward against my jammed foot, and I realized I couldn't hold them out. But the restaurant was pitch dark and that was what saved me.

I started sliding past the tables toward the stairs I knew led to a storage room where we kept the band instruments. It had a snap lock, and I had the key. The gang poured in, and I heard curses as they collided against a table. As I groped up the carpeted stairs, I heard one of them yell that he had a flashlight. Another silent prayer from Lopez to his Maker, and again it worked. The torch wouldn't switch on.

"Fiddle with the top that screws on," a voice advised. "Sometimes they work that way."

He was right. The narrow beam came on. But by that time, I had reached the door and was fumbling for the lock with my key. An eternity-like moment later, I found it, squeezed the door open carefully, and slid inside.

Those young hoodlums had determination. Maybe I had offended some strange pride in them by getting away. They searched under every table and then came up the stairs to look further! When the doorknob shook on my hideaway, I stopped breathing for a full minute.

"Locked," the voice on the outside said with disgust. "He can't be in there."

"Aw, let's quit and scram," another voice suggested. "It's gettin' light outside. Time for us to go over to Mike's place and split what we made tonight."

Ten long minutes later I was sure they had left, so I crept out of my bandroom sanctuary. Then I waited for the sun to come up and light the safe way back to my room.

In the meantime, I took care of another matter long overdue. Using the first step of the stairs as an altar, I gave my humble thanks to God for answering when I had twice called on Him so desperately!

Shuttering the Pekin during the afternoons meant a proportionate slicing of my pay. To make up the loss I took another job. Paul Cunningham, a song plugger and writer who later became President of ASCAP, suggested it, one of the nights he dropped in at the Pekin with Irving Berlin, to promote the songs they were plugging.

"Why don't you work for Earl Carroll demonstrating songs? You got the qualifications for it. You learn a tune fast and you can play it in any key."

"Who would I demonstrate the songs to?"

"That depends. Sometimes it's a headliner from vaudeville that Earl wants to interest in a number, sometimes it's a financier that Earl is trying to get to back a new show. That means selling the guy on the music, mainly—and that takes a good pianist! Earl's looking for one now; so take my card and go over to see him. I'll write on it that you're okay."

Carroll evidently agreed with Paul for I went to work for him that very afternoon. But two weeks later, he closed his office. His commission in the Air Force had come through.

However, I stayed in the song-demonstration game several months, mainly with the firm of Charles K. Harris who had written many hit songs himself around the turn of the century, topped by the all-time favorite "After the Ball Was Over." But the ball was largely over for his music company. The flood of jazz was sweeping him into oblivion.

I think it was because it was so quiet that Mae West and her pianist, Harry Richman, chose the place for their rehearsals. The only piece of music they ever used having the slightest connection with the Charles K. Harris office was a novelty titled "Everybody Shimmies Now." Joe Gold (the other pianist in the Harris office and who later worked for me) wrote it. When he mentioned it to Miss West as she was leaving the place one afternoon, she thought it over and said, "Okay, Joe. Keep it handy. I'll come up to see you sometime."

Now, *there's* a switch!

Joe Gold and I were putting the cobwebbed music files in order the afternoon of November 11, 1918, when all the whistles in the world seemed to go off around Broadway. The heavy sirens of the Hudson River boats joined in. Then the tootings were lost in the joyful shouts of what seemed a million voices. Joe and I ran to a side window and looked out.

As far down Broadway as we could see, people were milling around in wild elation, shaking hands, thumping backs, and kissing every pretty girl in sight. Some were simply running. All traffic stopped. People poured out of streetcars and popped out of the buildings. Hundreds of hats were tossed in the air, to drop and be tossed again and again.

A snake dance began that bobbed and weaved its way down every block and people shouted, yelled, thumped backs, cried without restraint or shame. The primitive emotion of naked joy had captured New York.

Not all were overcome by it. Many knelt at the curb in prayer. Some wandered along almost in a state of shock, as if afraid to hope, reluctant to believe.

Joe Gold and I were speculating what it was all about.

"They've gone nuts," Joe Gold decided. "Maybe it's some sort of Heinie nerve gas."

"That isn't it, Joe," I yelled. "Look down the street to the Times Building, Joe. That's where the crowd's really collecting. Must be important news."

When a truck pell-melled its way to the corner newsstand and tossed a bundle of fresh papers on the curb, they landed upright and three floors up we could read the banner headlines: ARMISTICE DECLARED! WAR ENDS!

With that, a trickle of papers began spilling out of office windows everywhere and promptly grew into a Niagara of swirling snow.

Joe and I looked at each other—then headed for the files. The next moment we were adding much of the Harris music library to the downpour. Old songs, original copies, late tunes, even some brand new manuscripts went out the window. But most of the stuff was war songs and we were well rid of them. The world had enough of war songs—and war.

Chapter 27. THE WAR THAT NEVER ENDS

My own personal "war" with women was very much on at the time. The battle of the sexes is one war for which I passed the physical—but should have had my head examined. Two weeks after Mae and I separated, I had a new sweetheart, Karole Sheridan from the

Pekin floor show. Her specialty act was high kicking, and to me a beautiful girl in full-length hose, balanced on one exquisite leg while flicking the other high over her pretty head—well, I couldn't resist!

It began after an exchange of compliments about my piano playing and her high kicking. Then she asked about my gout, why wasn't it getting better, and what was I doing about it. I explained that I was keeping off rich foods, as the doctor instructed, but I got up too late in the morning and home too late at night for the twice-a-day dunking in epsom salts that I was supposed to give my feet.

"Someone ought to take care of you," said Karole—and I hadn't the faintest idea that she was nominating herself!

At ten the next morning, there was an insistent knock on my door. Rolling out of bed and into a bathrobe, I answered it. There stood Karole with a five-pound box of epsom salts.

"Here." She handed me the box. "Get dressed and put some hot water on. I'll be back in ten minutes with sandwiches and coffee—if you'd like to have breakfast with me."

It was a wonderful breakfast. I don't know what was warmest: the coffee I drank, the epsom salts footbath, or my temperature as Karole talked, laughed, and looked so lovely just across the trunk that served as our breakfast table.

For a week, we made quite a ritual of it. Breakfast at my place with Karole at ten. She'd leave by eleven and I wouldn't see her until the Pekin that evening. Then after the place closed we'd go off somewhere else for a few wonderful hours together until I took her back to her apartment and left her there.

One night, though, I didn't leave her. We had breakfast as usual the next morning, but not at my place—at hers.

And I was madly in love again!

Karole knew about my marriage, of course, and of the religious roadblock Mae set up to divorce. But there were no questions, no arguments, no recriminations in the love Karole gave me.

I wish I had been capable of returning such love. I was crazy about Karole, found sheer rapture in the hours we spent together, but when we were separated by the illness of her mother in Portland, Oregon, she wasn't away from me two months before I was floundering in a shallow affair with another dancer, Dorothy Holt.

It was a letter from Karole that started me off.

"Dear Vincent," it read. "Mother's condition seems unchanged, but the doctors tell us it's just a question of time. She picked up a bit when I got home, for I'm her only daughter and she never did want me to leave for New York.

"I've suggested the idea to my father that I return to the Pekin soon, but he's terribly afraid it would set mother back. If only she could improve. It isn't that she needs me just emotionally, Vincent. There's a round-the-clock nursing job to be done, and I'm elected, I guess. Luckily I saved some money while it was coming in, and I hope it lasts. Dad's pay just isn't enough with all our expenses.

"But no matter what the expenses, I'm going to use enough of it for a trip back, to be with you at Christmas. In the meantime, know that my every second thought is of the love I have for you.

"My very first thought is of your love for me, darling. Keep it burning . . . Your Karole."

That Christmas visit was a wonderful promise—but the postmark on the letter was May 10 with December seven months away.

My love for Karole stayed bright, and clean and good . . . but even though I kept it burning, Dorothy, too, became my flame.

Like lint on a blue serge suit, Dorothy was easy to acquire but hard to brush off. She had an apartment facing the Hudson River, and when equatorial weather poured into New York in mid-July she suggested that I move in to enjoy the occasional cool breezes. A month later I tried to move out but Dorothy wasn't buying the idea. She put on a heat wave of her own. If loving persuasion didn't work, she used threats of bad publicity (BLONDE DANCER LEAVES SUICIDE NOTE BLAMING MARRIED ORCHESTRA LEADER).

Physical violence wasn't beyond her, either. One night on our way home from the Pekin I got up enough determination—and courage—to stop outside the apartment entrance and say I was going home to my own place.

"If you take ten steps away from here," Dorothy warned me, "I'll scream for the cops and say you tried to assault me."

"You're bluffing," I decided—and took the first step.

Her opening scream froze me in my tracks. Somewhere along the ancestral line, Dorothy must have had some Mohawk Indian blood. A rookie policeman came pounding over from Eighth Avenue, gripping his nightstick.

"Okay, Dorothy, you win," I whispered in defeat.

"It's all right, officer," she explained to the policeman. "I was frightened when my husband opened the door to our apartment here. Something ran out, but it was only a cat."

"Only a cat!" he exclaimed. "Lady, I sure hope you never meet up with a tiger. You'll scare a valuable circus animal to death."

Came the end of November and my prisoner-of-love situation grew worse. Dorothy wasn't just a clinging vine. She was a man-eating plant. But so lovely! Most of our Broadway friends who knew about the romance thought me lucky. I might have been, but I was in love with Karole.

When her next letter said she would reach New York on December 23 to stay with me until after New Year's, I wrote a letter of explanation full of love, shame, remorse and panic.

Karole's reply bawled me out for my infidelity but promised to bail me out of my dilemma. "Don't you do anything about it. I don't want Dorothy resorting to a desperate step we'd all regret. Let me handle her, please, and we can settle this decently. I have a plan. Just be there in her apartment the night of the 23rd."

Dorothy and I were just sitting down to a very late supper at 3 a.m. that morning when the apartment bell rang.

It was Karole—but not the Karole I expected. She could have been in the running for any Mother-of-the-Month contest.

For perhaps half a minute (that seemed half a year) she didn't say a word when I opened the door. She simply stood there, looking at each of us accusingly—and letting us get an eloquent look at her.

"They told me you'd be here, Vincent," Karole finally said. "And, Dotty, how could you play up to my husband when I went away.

It's not just that he's my husband. Think of his baby I'm going to have!"

"Husband? Baby?" Dotty echoed. "Honest, Karole, he never told me you were married—or about a child. He told me he couldn't get a divorce from his first wife."

"Is that what he told you?" Karole sympathized, flashing a big wedding band. "She divorced him last spring—so our child would have a name. Now that I see what he's been up to, I'm going to spread this story in all the papers."

Dorothy's face went a pasty white. "Don't do that, Karole," she implored. "I'd lose my job at the Pekin and I'd never get another one with such rotten publicity. Listen, you can have this guy back—if you want him. After this I couldn't stand the sight of him."

"Well, for the sake of the baby—" said Karole.

A few minutes later, Karole and I got a lucky taxicab and headed for my place. I sat well away from her in the back seat.

"Aren't you going to kiss me?" she demanded with a sweet pout.

"If I may—" but I was cautious as I embraced her, thinking of her condition.

"Oh, come on, darling, I'm not your sister," she complained.

"What about the baby?" I asked. "And how come you never wrote me about it?"

"I just didn't think of it, I guess," Karole confided as she snuggled toward me. "As soon as we reach home I'll get rid of these pillows under my coat."

Dorothy left the Pekin the following day for a part in the musical, *Good Morning, Judge.*

Chapter 28. PROHIBITION'S FIRST YEARS

Karole rescued me from a nightmare, and the next evening I did the same for John Cali, my guitar man, in an affair not of the heart, but the pocketbook.

In the post-war period unionizing of the entertainment world began, and believe me, it was needed. Exploitation of performers ranged from callous indifference toward their welfare, to outright cruelty. When a Broadway show failed to open after fourteen weeks of unpaid rehearsals, wonderful Marie Dressler joined the Chorus Girls Union to fix national sympathy on the performers' plight. Feeling against "management" reached such a fever pitch that poor George M. Cohan was forced to resign from The Lambs Club and The Friars. As producer of *Seven Keys to Baldpate,* he was an "owner" to the embittered actors.

The militant up and coming Musicians Union warned union men not to play in non-union outfits. But poor John Cali decided to ignore the fact that he held a union card while his boss (Lopez) was non-union. He kept on playing for me until an angry sergeant-at-arms walked across our dance floor one night, pointed an accusing finger at Cali, and said, "This outfit ain't organized, Cali, so take your banjo and get out of here. And be at headquarters to answer charges against yourself tomorrow afternoon."

"Vince," Cali implored, "can you do something about this? My family'll starve on my spare-time jobs."

"Why don't you resign from the union?" I suggested, not knowing what else to say.

"I can't," Cali replied, with the sergeant-at-arms listening in. "It's a matter of principle with me. I believe in the union."

"Don't worry, John," I reassured him. "I'll think of something."

My thinking included the memory of the thirty bucks Zagarino still owed me . . . the doubled hours McLaughlin had imposed without an added dollar of pay . . . owners chiseling on the entertainers' tips. All this called for reform!

So the next afternoon, I showed up at union headquarters just as John Cali's case was called.

"Gentlemen," I interrupted. "May I say something? This is mainly my fault. John Cali has tried to get me to unionize all along and I promised to think it over. I asked him to stay with my band, meanwhile, and he did that as a favor. Now let me return the favor. If you'll let John off with just a reprimand, gentlemen, the whole Lopez band will join up today."

It was a bargain—and one I've never regretted!

All America was on the brink of a great regret, however. On December 18, 1917, Congress submitted the 18th Amendment to the states. It didn't have a chance until propaganda pushed it in.

The Drys screamed that anarchy would ensue if our returning doughboys could indulge the drinking habits they had learned in France! There would be rape in the streets and a total collapse of law and order. Young Americans who could win the war couldn't be entrusted with the peace!

Rural America stampeded. Cotton-growing Mississippi was the first state to ratify the amendment; cornhusking Nebraska was the second. On January 16, 1920, Prohibition became the law of the land.

The Drys were right about the threatened breakdown of law and order. It materialized, the day after. Crime and gangsterism, once a small-time operation, was handed a billion-dollar, tax-free business to organize . . . through blood and bullets!

We got early hints at the Pekin of the careful look the criminal element was giving the restaurant business. Groups of deadly looking men dropped in. Action Klein tried to ignore them but they found means of getting his attention. Their proposition was short and to the point: half the profits, after Prohibition came in, for a continued supply of good liquor and "protection" in serving it.

"I don't know where I'm going with the Pekin, come next year," Klein admitted to Dody, "but jail is one place I'm going to stay clear of. I'll sell the place before I get into anything shady."

"Why doesn't Klein just continue the Pekin as it is?" I asked Dody. "Without serving liquor. Just good food and good entertainment."

"Vinnie," Dan replied. "What good entertainment costs can never be covered by the profits on food. It needs the liquor sales. It's a simple equation you and I are up against: No liquor, no jobs."

"You mean he'd let the band go?" I doubted.

"That's how he's thinking," said Dan. "Save the restaurant by putting up even better food, but skip the floor show and the dancing. You might be in luck, though, kid. He wants you to stay on as pianist."

On the night prohibition began Klein talked to the Pekin performers. "I'm sorry it has to end this way, but after tonight my hands are tied. I'd like to keep all of you, but, keeping the Pekin open at all isn't going to be easy. Without the money coming in from liquor we can't afford entertainment."

"We understand," someone shouted. "How about making this last night one to remember?"

No binge in history equalled the one on prohibition eve. The Pekin was a madhouse. People came with baskets and bought liquor by the quart to hoard. That night they used it for shampoo, in their soup, in finger bowls. . . . Someone came up with a stuffed dummy with a sign pinned on saying "John Barleycorn." As he was paraded around the Pekin, the band played,

"For he's a jolly good fellow . . ."

"Hey, let's have a funeral for John," someone suggested. So a mock funeral was staged while the band played the Funeral March. Everyone was having a good time until, as the clock struck midnight, Federal agents moved in to see that no more liquor was sold. As they moved about the Pekin, a hush fell over the crowd. All the fun seemed to drain away and they listened quietly to one of the agents who stepped in front of the band and announced that the Volstead Act was now the law of the land, and no more drinks would be sold. They could stay and finish what they had, he said. He walked off and not a sound could be heard. I had been seated at the piano through all this. As I sat there, my fingers automatically sought the keys and I started playing

"Should auld acquaintance be forgot and never brought to mind?"

The band joined in.

When I finished, one of the customers stood up on a table and shouted, "What are we all sitting here like the world came to an end? Come on, everyone, let's *really* celebrate."

The party started all over again, only wilder than before. The Pekin was a shambles as the first gray light of dawn peeped over Times Square. But I drank nothing that night. A very good reason kept me cold sober. No job. I walked slowly up to the storage room where the band members were putting away their instruments. One by one, my musicians left for home, shaking hands with me and agreeing to show up as soon as we had a job. But the promise had a hollow ring, and we all knew it.

The bedlam had died down. Those who had passed out were sprawled across tables, chairs, and on the floor. I stepped over some of them, as well as the overturned chairs, empty bottles, and tables as I made my way to the big bay window and looked out on the familiar sight of Times Square. Down below, three very drunk men in tails and top hats staggered by, each clutching a bottle.

I suddenly remembered the incident of the year before, when I found refuge from a pursuing group of young punks in that same small room. I recalled how I had prayed there.

I prayed again, not just for myself this time, but for the wonderful guys who were working for me.

"Dear God," I stumbled through toward what I wanted to say. "Often I've asked You not to fail me. This time, please help me not to fail them. And, most of all, don't let them see how scared I am about the future."

I'll buy the old adage that God helps those who help themselves. I'll go it one better, for I believe that while we're able to help ourselves, God requires us to do so.

The very next morning, with a good luck letter from Karole in my pocket (she was still in Portland) I made the rounds of the booking agents. Another girl helped me that day—the agent Lillian Bradley, who mentioned Perry's at Coney Island as a possible lead. "They're giving up on the sweet stuff, Vincent, a good jazz combination is what they want. Let me get Joe Perry on the phone right now and make a date for you to see him."

Perry had often heard our band at the Pekin and signed us to start immediately! He had a good bunch of acts lined up, including a new team billed as Gus Van and Joe Schenk.

"What kind of competition are the other places giving you?" I asked.

"Tough," he conceded. "Sophie Tucker and the Memphis Five down the street and Belle Baker at the College Inn. Kerry Walsh's restaurant has only a pianist, named Durante. Has a tremendous nose he gets laughs with, but I hear Ziegfeld is going to let Eddie Cantor play Kerry Walsh's again this summer. That'll be something. A comedian from the Follies at Coney Island!"

As it turned out, Eddie didn't do that return date for Kerry Walsh. Maybe Banjoeyes was still sore over something Kerry had done to him a few seasons previously.

Eddie was just a singing waiter then, and when he showed up late one afternoon (the hours were from 2 P.M. until exhaustion), tough old Kerry was sitting at the side entrance, cane in hand. Eddie wanted no part of it, so around to a back window he sneaked. But he got stuck midway and Kerry recognized Cantor from the seat of his shiny pants, and proceeded to put some more shine on with his cane! Poor Eddie worked like a beaver for the next two weeks; he couldn't sit down.

The famous juggling team of Bedini and Arthur dropped around to Walsh's for a look at the kid who'd caught it from Kerry. They liked his style and signed him up as a blackface stooge for laughs their act needed—and Eddie was on his way! That's why Eddie quipped that his career began at the bottom!

Our own career picked up at Perry's that summer. To our surprise plenty of the friends we'd made at the Pekin took the long trip to Coney to dance to our Dixieland beat again. And the chance to play Perry's meant a lot for our future. From Perry's many stars had been shot into orbit. It was the Copacabana of its day.

I made friends with the cop on the beat who pointed out the historical sights of Coney to me. One of them was Norton's Point, the site of a lighthouse that was to make bigger history.

"There's a wireless station out there now," he told me. "A feller named David Sarnoff started it, and that's where he picked up the news that the Titanic was sinking. They say he's playing around with a new gadget called radio that carries the human voice. Probably just a fad, but you can never tell."

"Say, Mr. West," I wondered. "You mentioned that your daughter is in show business. What name does she use?"

"What name would she use but her right one, Mae West. Remember it. She'll be famous some day."

Officer West was delighted to know I'd already met his daughter and that I agreed with his forecast on her future.

Chapter 29. I LOSE KAROLE

On a rainy, end-season night, with only four customers to hear us, we were finishing up when a dripping-wet party of five came in.

After we'd played some more numbers, one of the newcomers motioned to me and I walked over to their table.

"My name is Edgar Allan Wolf," he introduced himself. "Nice little band you've got here. Quite versatile, I notice, but basically you play jazz, don't you?"

"Dixieland, mainly. We're sold on it. It's going to be around quite a few years."

"Well, you'll be around with it," Wolf said. "We came out here tonight to hear the band at Henderson's. They feature strings, don't they?"

"Yes," I agreed, "but that's not our style. We're looking for something different."

"So are we," Wolf said with a smile. "Mind if we listen to some more of your music."

"Glad to play for you," I replied.

Back on the bandstand, I whispered my hunch that the late arrivals had some connection with show business and were looking for a band.

"Play up a real storm, fellows," I said. "We might get a couple of nights' work out of this."

Sure enough, after we'd given him some more, Wolf beckoned again.

"I guess you're the outfit we want, if you're available. Are you free after this week?"

"We can start any time you say. What restaurant do you represent?"

"This isn't a restaurant deal," Wolf explained. "I've just written a four-act stage presentation called *Rings of Smoke,* a sort of glorified vaudeville revue. You'll be travelling all over the country with it. We'll pay you $500 a week for the band and allow half salary for rehearsal time, which will be about two weeks. Are you interested?"

"Very much so."

"In that case meet the producer of our show, Mr. Carlton P. Hoagland. Joe Santley here wrote the musical score. I wrote the book and the lyrics. Two stars of our show are right here at the table with us. Meet Pat Rooney and his Mrs., Miss Marion Bent."

When I told the boys about our new job, only one showed no enthusiasm.

"I'm sorry, Vince," spoke up Dan Alvin, "but I thought we were through and I took another job a couple of nights ago."

"You been working here all week, Dan," I argued. "How could you find another job?"

Dan smiled. "Remember seeing Joe Gold and Sophie Tucker in here on Tuesday?"

"Sure," I said. "They dropped by to pay me a visit. Joe and I worked together at the Charles K. Harris Music Publishing Co."

"Well, he's working against you now. He's gonna lead the band for Sophie Tucker at Reisenweber's this winter; and they signed me to play clarinet for them. No hard feelings, Vince."

There were hard feelings at first toward my old pal, Joe. We didn't speak to each other for years. But his talent raid was really a break for us. My replacement was Bill Hamilton who was more than a good musician; he was a great showman. My band needed him if we were to make a hit in vaudeville.

Bill drove a hard bargain. He demanded a silent partnership in the band, and I okayed it when there was no other way out. We started a show-business association that was to move our band from dimly lighted dance floors to world-wide recognition.

It proved easy enough to replace my clarinetist, but the Rooney job cost me someone else I never replaced—Karole.

She had just come east again from Portland, for two wonderful weeks of reunion with me before she had to return to her mother's bedside. The doctors said their patient wouldn't live to Christmas. Karole had accepted their judgment with the passive resignation that comes from seeing a loved one in too much pain.

But my decision to join *Rings of Smoke* was something she couldn't, or wouldn't, accept. "Darling," she protested, "what sort of a life is that? Travelling from place to place, not even being with me for the holidays. This isn't what I've waited for."

"But it's a job, dear," I argued. "And a good one. Pat Rooney is a headliner. Joining him, we've got a real chance to make a name in this business. I can't pass this up."

"But in a few more months, you and I can be husband and wife to each other with everything but the license," she said. "A job is bound to show up where you can stay in New York."

Looking back, I can only guess that I didn't believe Karole meant her calmly-put ultimatum that if I didn't turn the band over to Bill Hamilton within two months and find myself a settled spot in New York or some other big city, she would never return to me.

Rings of Smoke was a hit, and I got caught up in it. My letters to Karole glowed with my enthusiasm, bidding her to share it. But she wasn't buying. Following a letter that offered me another two weeks to think things over, a registered package arrived containing all the presents I'd given her.

Despite my letters of protest, I never heard from Karole again—except for a wedding notice that arrived the following year.

So Karole wound up with a ring—and I with *Rings of Smoke*. . . .

Chapter 30. **FROM RESTAURANTS TO THE STAGE**

We rehearsed *Rings of Smoke* at Bryant's Hall at the corner of Sixth Avenue and 42nd Street. All the way it was Pat Rooney's show.

His big and loyal following enjoyed his every gesture no matter how often they saw it. Who else ever got a rave notice in *Variety* for sticking his finger in a pot of boiling coffee to see if it was hot!

Rings of Smoke was a dance review with a plot. It was spectacular and exciting. Pat dreamed of beautiful girls he had known in the different parts of the world. Successively he "smoked-ringed" his way to Ireland, France and then Spain, with appropriate songs and dancing.

He was generous and patient with me. In the fourth scene I was to be onstage with my band (now called the Kings of Harmony) and a typical Dixieland outfit—the piano, drums, clarinet, trombone and trumpet. In that scene, he arrived at the land of jazz. He worked hard to get me over my initial shyness, and make my bit a success.

I was shy about the on-stage appearance of my band and Pat was patient in his coaching and encouragement. Then he was generous about our success. For when our Kings of Harmony made a running exit from the pit, and on to the stage with our instruments, we brought down the house. Even at rehearsals it stopped the show as stagehands and hangers-on caught the rhythm and went into impromptu dancing on their own.

A lesser person than Pat Rooney, might have hired another band because of such show-stealing. But not Pat. He was delighted.

"Vincent," he enthused, "you've got a job with *Rings of Smoke* as long as we keep it going. And that could be for years."

He was right. We were an immediate hit when we opened in Mount Vernon, New York and we satisfied the critical tastes of the Palace audiences, too, when we moved into vaudeville's stronghold one week later. The Monday matinee at the Palace was rough because the audience was mostly composed of booking agents, newspaper and trade critics, and other actors. Going out there for the first time gave a performer a feeling something like walking into an undertaker's parlor.

But hit them with a socko act and they'd come alive. There was great applause for Pat Rooney on his opening appearance. Then Marion Bent kept them warmed up with "The Daughter of Rosie O'Grady." Pat's next dance started the sound waves thundering, and at last the Kings of Harmony were on for their jazz performance.

I have *Variety's* review of the opening framed under glass. The passing mention of us was brief, but couldn't have been better. "In their rendition of three jazz numbers, the Kings of Harmony held the audience spellbound."

Sitting at the piano, I didn't have to be a personality kid to get by. Bill Hamilton got most of the audience attention with his clarinet. He had the magic spark of showmanship that can light up the dullest audience with his pantomime and facial expressions. But I was improving my own stage presence. I had overcome the stage fright that floored me the afternoon we opened the show at Proctor's in Mount Vernon where the local band leader had to fill in for me while Joe Santley talked enough spirit into me to get me to take my place on the stage. Once there, I was all right. I had a dependable friend with me—the piano.

With Pat Rooney's coaching and Marion Bent's reassurances, I got to the point where I could even stand up, take a bow, and *smile*—though that often required an offstage cue from Marion. "Smile, Vincent, for the love of St. Patrick, *smile*!"

Whereupon I'd break out in a grin.

Rings of Smoke played all the big cities along the eastern seaboard and appeared with the top names of the entertainment world: Ethel Barrymore, Sarah Bernhardt, the Mosconi Brothers, Willie and Eugene Howard, Frank Fay, Eddie Dowling, Williams and Walker, Will Rogers, Moran and Mack, Frances White, Billy Roche and Nat M. Wills among others.

Most of us stayed at the same hotels and that meant getting together for dinner, for a card game afterward and frequently for a party following the show. And what parties Pat and Marion threw, especially in New York where they could use their lovely home in the Seminole Apartments, 68th Street and Broadway. I think Pat Rooney probably gave Arnold Ruben his biggest boost when Pat had him cater those affairs. Pat, a non-drinker, stuck to the same menu night after night—a chicken sandwich, a cup of tea and some cold pears. There was a wonderful warmth and friendliness among show people then that has somehow gone out of the entertainment world today. Maybe the Bigger Money has produced Smaller People.

Except for the greatest stars, though, the "bad press" that literature and pulpit had long given the theatre lingered on. Most performers simply weren't "socially accepted."

At a dance given in honor of President Wilson's sister Margaret, we were setting ourselves up next to the dance floor when the hostess politely explained that the orchestra would have to play from the antechamber, not out among the guests.

It was thirty-five bucks a man, and we'd have played from the powder room, so we did as instructed. I guess we gave them quite a ball for the dancing got real crazy as we blew up a Dixieland storm.

Midnight was our curfew, and just before we jumped into the last set at 11:45, our charming hostess arrived with a message from Miss Wilson. "Gentlemen, the President's sister wants to say that she enjoyed your music very much."

This gracious message cheered our antechamber exile!

At quite another party in Washington I had my first highball. After eating everything in sight, as usual, I was on my way to the bar for some soda when I bumped into Marion. When she heard I wanted something to drink she handed me a glass she was carrying. It didn't occur to me that it was a highball and I swallowed it in one gulp, the way I drank everything.

"Wow," Marion exclaimed, "where did you learn to drink like that!"

Three minutes later I was out colder than a Penguin's feathers. It was my first experience with a highball.

We were playing Boston another time when a party we were at ended at 1:30 A.M. with the night still young and everybody feeling beautiful. Someone mentioned that Meyer Davis and his thirty-piece orchestra were playing a big society date at the Copley Plaza Ballroom.

"What are we waiting for?" said Bill Hamilton. "Let's get our instruments and crash the place. Its worth the risk of being tossed out on our tubas for the publicity break it would be if we got on and the crowd liked us."

He was right. Meyer Davis was glad to accept our offer of a friendly breather for his band, whereupon we took over and gave the crowd the loudest, liveliest Dixieland Boston ever heard! And they loved it, demanding encore after encore. We got off the floor in half an hour with Hamilton announcing that we'd like to play for future dances at the Copley!

On the way out, a portly man stopped us and asked if we were serious about playing other dates. He offered us a fill-in date at a theatre in Lawrence, Mass. that Sunday night. We took it not worrying a bit about the winter weather in New England.

We started worrying, though, at 11:30 Sunday night, when we emerged from the stage door into a record blizzard! The taxis had quit so we hoofed it to the railroad station carrying our instruments over our heads. The next train, due at 5:20 A.M., was an hour late. We were using the last scuttle of coal for the undersize station stove when the belated train rescued us.

The following summer we enjoyed a vacation at Pat Rooney's beautiful home at Southhold, Long Island. But Pat had restless feet. The local fire company asked us to play a benefit to buy them some new equipment, so Pat put *Rings of Smoke* on in the firehouse—and what could be more appropriate?

The idea caught on with other fire laddies and other charity organizations. Soon we had the show going several nights a week all over Long Island—with a minimum of scenery, for the real stuff was packed in a Manhattan warehouse. In fact, some of the firehouses and big barns we played didn't even have gas light. The show lost nothing thereby. If anything, our audiences seemed warmer and the show more wonderful.

After Labor Day Pat got tired of *Rings of Smoke* and wanted to do a show of his own. He got interested in Max Wilner and Sigmund

Romberg's *Lovebirds*. The producer of *Rings of Smoke* took me aside and asked if I'd stay with the show even if Pat didn't.

"If Pat wants me in any new show I think I'd go along," I told him.

Carlton Hoagland tried to talk me out of it, but when Pat went into rehearsal of *Lovebirds* I was right along with him. Some of the others were Elizabeth Hines, Dick Boles, Eva Davenport, and Elizabeth Murray. Pat almost worked us to death rehearsing. He wanted everything perfect, and it was. As an extra, non-monetary reward, Romberg wrote a small part into *Lovebirds* for me. In addition to leading the Kings of Harmony, I appeared in a harem scene dressed in a long, silk robe and a shako-size turban.

The show was good but it lacked the zest of *Rings of Smoke*. Its overhead was too high for those days and the red-ink level kept rising. We held it together until the summer despite terrific competition that year, and then closed.

My finances couldn't stand another hot-weather stretch of playing for free at Long Island fire houses. When John Steinberg, one of New York's smartest Maître D's and manager of Ross Fenton Farms at Asbury Park, offered us a job in mid-July, we took it.

Ross Fenton Farms was incredibly beautiful, something out of a Hollywood musical. We played on a bandstand just six feet from the cool waters of Deal Lake. Young couples in canoes would paddle nearby and wax romantic to such numbers as "Avalon," "Margie," "Whispering," and "Japanese Sandman."

One night a good-looking lad paddled right up close to the bandstand and asked could we play a Vincent Youmans tune.

"Glad to oblige," I answered. "He's going to be one of the top song writers. Do you know him?"

"Pretty well," came the embarrassed answer.

"We'll play, 'Oh, Me, Oh My, Oh, You' from *Two Little Girls In Blue*. What's your name?"

"My name?" came the echo as the canoe paddled away, "is Vincent Youmans!"

A hat on the side of the upright piano on the floor was good for \$300 or \$400 in tips on a Saturday night, the idea being if more music was wanted the kitty had to be fed. But one night the kitty almost had indigestion. As an oilman from Tulsa, Oklahoma danced past, he dropped a bill into the kitty and asked me to play "Sheik of Araby." When we were finished, several people came over to me and said, "Do you know that man dropped in a thousand-dollar bill?" I looked into the kitty and there it was, with Grover Cleveland's face staring up at me. I went over to the oilman and said, "Do you know you dropped a thousand-dollar bill in the kitty?"

"Sure, I know," he answered, "it's for you and the band."

When that night was over our tips amounted to $1,800—a record according to an Asbury Park newspaper.

Another night, a man came up to me and said, "My name is Raymond Schindler, and I'm here to ask a favor of you." I told him it depended on what the favor was.

"It's this," he answered. "I'm a member of the Asbury Park Rotary Club, and we're having a luncheon tomorrow. Would you come over and play the piano for us?"

"How'd you like to have the whole band instead of just me?" I asked.

He said that would be fine except they couldn't afford it. I assured him he wouldn't have to worry about that. We'd do it on our own.

Schindler was so happy, he said, "Some day I'll return the favor."

The next day we went over to the Rotary luncheon and really put on a show. We were all hams at heart and we didn't pass up the chance to show off. Bill Hamilton did all his Ted Lewis tricks; I did everything I knew on the piano. It was a real ball.

I pretty much forgot about Raymond Schindler—we had other worries on our mind. The summer was coming to an end, and we were wondering where we'd go from Ross Fenton Farms.

When the Kings of Harmony were back in New York, on the verge once again of disbanding and even cheery Bill Hamilton admitting the booking chances looked glum, when "our" telephone (out in the hall of the rooming house we were reduced to) started ringing. Bill ran to answer it. "Vincent," he yelled, "it's for you."

"Maybe it's a weekend date," I said as I ran to get the call.

"Hello. Hello, this is Raymond Schindler. I've been trying to reach you. Remember you fellows played at our Rotary Club luncheon in Asbury Park two months ago."

"Oh, yes; hello, Mr. Schindler," I replied. "Good to hear from you. Want us to play again?"

"Well, not for us," he explained, "but I've got a lead you might want to follow up if you're not committed for the winter. My good friend, Mr. Statler, is looking for a band. I told him about you last night and he's interested. You've heard of him, haven't you—E. M. Statler?"

"Oh, yes, of course," I bluffed, for I had but a hazy knowledge of the name. "Where would he want us to play—a restaurant around town?"

"Better than that," Schindler explained. "A grill room of his. Get in touch with him right away at the Hotel Pennsylvania, Vincent."

"Hotel Pennsylvania," I repeated, writing it down on the wall. "What room number?"

"Oh, you don't need a room number when you ask for him," Schindler pointed out. *"Statler owns the hotel!"*

Chapter 31. HOTEL BANDLEADER

Our audition didn't start out well. One of our men arrived late—he thought I had said we'd meet at Pennsylvania *station*. We weren't even ready with the downbeat when E. M. Statler walked in with his secretary, Alice Seidler, who later became Mrs. Statler. I had no idea who they were. He certainly didn't look like a man who was putting together one of the world's greatest hotel chains. Had he appeared on "What's My Line" that day, with a clue that he was in the hotel business, they'd have probably guessed his occupation as a night clerk.

As he dictated to his secretary he looked us over. I thought he was criticizing our band suits which had been through a long summer at the Ross Fenton Farms. Later I found out he was dictating notes on ideas for better hotel service . . . provide free needles and thread in every room, and other such improvements.

We weren't getting very far with our opening numbers when poor Ernie Holtz finally figured out I must have said the Pennsylvania Hotel and showed up with his violin.

"If this Statler likes us," I alerted the fellows, "he'll get up and dance. That's what Ray Schindler told me this morning. So if he just sits there, it's a bad sign."

"Then let's hit him with our best jazz number," Bill said. We tried "The Sheik of Araby." It obviously did nothing to E. M. Statler. He kept on dictating.

"Ain't We Got Fun" didn't get him up out of his chair, either, and I had visions of the Kings of Harmony missing their union dues for several months. Then I called for a tune that featured the piano —"Canadian Capers."

Halfway through, Statler got up and waved his hand for silence. I figured it meant curtains for the audition. But no, "Play that from the beginning again, will you," he said. "Come on, Alice, let's dance."

We were in!

Play more numbers like that last one," said Statler, "with plenty of piano and featuring yourself. And one more suggestion—get your men some better-looking suits. Now here's Mr. Baylitz who'll take care of the business details. Come, Alice, we have work to do."

Baylitz came right to the point: Playing the Pennsylvania Grill was a prestige deal for a band. All they paid was $850 for seven men.

"Eighty-fifty?" Bill Hamilton moaned. "Why, we took in more than that in tips some weeks at the Farm."

"Oh, that's another thing," Baylitz added, "absolutely no tipping here. No hat on the floor—and if any gratuities are offered when you play a request number, send it back. *This* is the Pennsylvania Grill."

Although it meant jeopardizing our future, I nevertheless stood off a bit and thought things over. Bill Hamilton and I would be making less than some of the men on our payroll. Baylitz noticed my indecision.

"Of course," he added, "there are extra benefits playing here. Your price for outside dates will go up. Also the hotel publicity staff will do a lot of promotion on you, Mr. Lopez. We'll have your name in the paper almost every day. This will be a stepping-stone to a great future for you."

I signed.

Baylitz delivered on his promise to get up publicity, and we played most nights to a crowd that packed the Grill. I hired J. Bodewalt Lampe, one of the best arrangers in the business, at my own expense.

J. B. Lampe's arrangements certainly helped the band. Even the professional magazines took note. Baylitz got them mentioned in the Broadway columns.

This sound of success deluded the local Packard agency into sending a man around to show me their newest model. In actual fact, I was barely scraping along. The cost of improving the band, plus increased needs Mae kept informing me of by letter (our little girl was growing up, it's true) kept the red ink mounting in my personal accounts. I finally flipped one night when Baylitz suggested I add a few more men to the band.

"Well, you want to compete with Paul Whiteman, don't you?" he argued, aiming at my vulnerable spot. "You're the only challenger for his position as King of Jazz. It's worth a little sacrifice to top him, isn't it?"

"Not this time. The spirit is willing—but the pocketbook is weak. One more 'improvement' in the band and I'll have to give up eating."

"All right. Add a couple of men to give the band a bigger look and fuller sound. The hotel will pick up the tab on it."

One night when I arrived at the Grill, something looked different about the bandstand. The grand piano was missing!

"Where's my piano?" I asked the Maître D'.

"Didn't you know about it?" he asked blankly. "The men took it away this afternoon. I wonder why they haven't delivered the new one yet."

Frantic questioning confirmed my worst fears. Four men with strong backs and weak morals had appeared at the Grill about noon, presented a phony invoice that called for a piano exchange—and fast-talked the hotel into letting them dolly out their beautiful Steinway. It was never recovered. There were plenty of eyewitnesses, but none could describe the men well enough and of course the truck license plate had gone unnoticed.

Dancing was delayed at the Grill that evening, while a hurriedly assembled bunch of hotel porters moved a spare piano down from the main ballroom.

Our band was a hit at the Pennsylvania Grill. The men I had added, Bob Effros and Frank Reino, were the best in the business. Every night the big shots in the garment trade would bring the out-of-town buyers over to hear our band, and the buyers would bring the beautiful models they had met when the new lines were displayed during the day!

Saturday afternoon we played our one-and-only matinee of the week, for the flapper set, girls in short tight dresses and suits that had no shape, a bright feather stuck in their shoes and a matching feather in their hats. Then there were our "regulars"—the society set we had played for at Ross Fenton Farms, in from the Oranges, Montclair, Verona, or up from Spring Lake. Keeping them company were similar groups from Long Island and Westchester. But the Park Avenue socialites stayed strictly on their east side of Fifth Avenue. We were to meet them later when we became the hit of the St. Regis Hotel . . . and romance returned to my life through the "400."

Chapter 32. I PIONEER IN RADIO

Included in my press clippings is an item from a Boston newspaper, dated June 4, 1872: "A man about 46 years of age, giving the name of Joshua Coppersmith, has been arrested for attempting to extort funds from ignorant and superstitious people by exhibiting a device which he says will convey the human voice any distance over metallic wires so that it can be heard by listeners at the other end. He claims, further, that in time the *wires* will not be necessary in this performance!

"Well-informed people know that it is impossible to transmit the human voice over wires, although it may be done with dots and dashes of the Morse code. As for the preposterous idea of transmitting the voice *without wires,* the authorities who apprehended this swindler are to be congratulated and it is hoped his punishment will be prompt and fitting!"

Fifty years later, "ignorant and superstitious people" were still standing in the path of radio. I owe my start in radio to the bigotry that existed in 1921.

Tommy Cowan was the Director and Announcer of the first Westinghouse radio station WJZ in Newark, New Jersey. Tommy was a regular patron of the Pennsylvania Grill, and one Saturday night I noticed that he was irritable and depressed.

"What's the trouble, Tommy?" I asked. "Why the long face?"

"I had a real scoop all lined up," he said. "You know Carl Helm, the press agent for *Tangerine?* Well, I talked him into putting the entire show on our station out in Newark tomorrow night. Their only night off and they were willing to do it."

"I know, I know," I added. "Read about it in the papers this week. What happened? Did they back out?"

"They were forced out," Tommy explained. "The same Bluenoses who shoved Prohibition down our throats ran a crusade against desecrating the Sabbath by broadcasting a musical comedy on God's air!"

"You're kidding!" I exclaimed. "Who could object to a show with Julia Sanderson and Frank Crummit in it?"

"Not many, of course," he replied. "But it's the old story of the mouse panicking the elephant. The voice of that tiny minority frightened the Westinghouse people. They wanted to 'edit' the show. That made the producers sore, so now I've got no program tomorrow night—a million dollars worth of publicity down the drain!"

The publicity remark rang a very loud bell with me, and I said, "How about substituting my band?"

"You'd do it? You mean you'd travel out to Newark with the whole outfit?"

"The Hudson Tube's just a block away from the hotel," I answered. "We can get taxis to WJZ out there, I hope."

"Taxis my foot," said Tommy. "We'll shoot the expense budget and hire a couple of Pierce Arrows to meet you. But that'll be it, Vincent. We can't pay you for the show."

The WJZ Studio was located in an old cloakroom in an unused area of Westinghouse's Newark factory. There were no elevators, just a rickety stairway barely wide enough for us to haul our instruments upstairs.

The small room was lined with some absorbent material dyed an ugly shade of red to give it some semblance of uniformity. Old rugs had been laid down to deaden studio sounds. Somehow an old upright piano had been squeezed in. Clayton's in Brooklyn had owned a better one. But we were there, and we made the best of it.

"What does this Westinghouse outfit do?" I heard Bill Hamilton ask.

"I saw a big box outside in the hall marked BOLTS," Bob Effros said to him.

"Must be the place," Bill answered. "We're certainly a lot of NUTS to come over here."

We had been so worried about everything else, we hadn't given a thought about the program. I'll never forget Tommy Cowan turning to me and saying, "Vincent, why don't you announce the program?"

"Me announce the program?" I was so frightened as it was, I didn't know what to do. Tommy and I argued the point for a few minutes. I told him it was my first time near a mike, but he finally talked me into saying hello to the radio audience. When the program began I stepped up on a little platform and said, "Hello everybody. Lopez speaking."

Cowan jumped up alongside me and said right into the microphone, "Is that all you're going to say, Mr. Lopez?"

"That's enough for me," I answered.

Tommy took over and said, "The first selection will be 'Anitra's Dance.' " I called out to the orchestra, "Number 42, boys," and we were on our way.

During the program Cowan suggested that I play a piano solo. I motioned to the broken-down upright and said, "On that?" But Tommy paid no attention to me and brought the mike near the piano. There was no backing out then, so I played "Canadian Capers," which had been responsible for getting me the job at the Pennsylvania Hotel.

In those days there wasn't any time limit on programs. If something was good, it went on and on. Our show lasted an hour and a half—the first "live" broadcast of popular dance music. The date, November 27, 1921.

When the show was over the telephone started to ring. Many of the calls were from pleased Westinghouse officials. One came all the way from Washington, D. C. It was from Joseph Tumulty, secretary to President Wilson. Radio had no more ardent fan than Mr. Tumulty. He even came to New Jersey a few weeks later to watch us broadcast.

There was some additional talent on the show that night—a young baritone doubling in radio to help advertise his appearance at a Newark theatre. His name? John Charles Thomas.

Later Secretary Tumulty paid a visit to the station and Tommy Cowan had the inspiration to introduce him on the air and interview him about the world political situation. Cowan had chalked up another first for WJZ: the radio commentator.

Most of my band regarded our trip to Newark that night as a lark —or an annoyance. Paul Whiteman had already turned down such appearances for his band with the comment that radio was for kids who liked to build crystal sets and fool around with them. I believed radio would increase our popularity, but I didn't foresee the millions of fans it would soon create for us.

"Vincent," Tommy said as we rode back to New York after closing up the WJZ studio that night, "in the days to come when there are a hundred million sets in America and people depend on radio for their news, their ideas, and their entertainment, don't ever forget that tonight you became one of its real pioneers. A lot of stars in show business have turned me down cold, but I'm positive that radio will make your band the hottest thing in the entertainment field."

Tommy was playing Nostradamus, as so many of us like to do with a new medium, but it was such a nice prediction, who was I to disagree with him?

I had just an inkling that radio was the greatest genie ever held in a bottle—and I'm humbly thankful I had the chance to help pull the cork!

The mail response to our music had the Newark Post Office working overtime for days and Cowan asked us to broadcast regularly. However, E. M. Statler had no enthusiasm for that idea. He wanted us at the Pennsylvania Grill, quite naturally, not out in Newark.

"Can't you put a microphone right on our bandstand and send it out over the wires to Newark?" I asked Tommy.

"The telephone company says it isn't feasible," Cowan explained. "Let me see if Western Union can rig something up."

The rigging-up took a month and we went on the air one Thursday night, late in December—another radio first. We announced that we'd be broadcasting regularly right from the Grill.

We wondered if people would like to come in and watch the band do a program. Within an hour, we had our answer. Telephone calls had soaked up every table reservation for the following evening—and the calls kept coming in that night and all the next day.

Early Friday evening, Seventh Avenue and the two side streets looked like Ebbett's Field back in the old days when the New York Giants were fighting the Brooklyn Dodgers for the pennant. What's more, the entire hotel was sold out by midafternoon.

"Vincent," said an amazed E. M. Statler, "I couldn't build business up like this in a thousand years of hard work. You did it in an hour. I think radio has real possibilities." It was the understatement of the century.

The mail response to our next broadcasts was simply unbelievable. At the microphone one night, with my usual shy lack of words that took years to overcome, I blurted out an offer of a photograph to anyone who'd write us a letter. The next day's mail filled ten big clothes hampers, most of it on post cards. I couldn't possibly take care of it so I apologized on the air but offered an autographed photo to people who *telephoned* their requests to the Hotel Pennsylvania. The incoming calls so jammed the hotel switchboard the next two days that people calling for room reservations grew tired of getting a busy signal.

"Next time, Vincent," said Mr. Statler, "hire a switchboard of your own."

Radio music so conveniently at their finger tips made Miss America (and maybe Mrs. America, too) romance-minded. Many letters read like this:

"Dear Mr. Lopez . . . I start this letter quite formally, but I want to call you Dear Vincent—or My Darling Vincent. After listening to your sweet romantic music at night, I dream wonderful dreams of you. One who plays as you do about love must be a marvelous lover. I am said to be beautiful, and I have many admirers but they are all so matter of fact. . . .

"You have replaced them all. I want to meet you when I come to New York, but in the meanwhile I must have your photograph. Please autograph it tenderly. Think of what the state of my heart is toward you, and see if you can reciprocate.

"But even if we never meet, play on forever and I will be happy for I adore your music—and through it, I adore you. Remember that the woman who assumed the name of George Sand as a writer first fell in love with Chopin through his music, and theirs was an exquisite romance.

"I am a writer, too, but music is the true portrait of my soul. Through it, we shall always be together. . . ."

I didn't have to rely on her, however. Romance was waiting for me right at the Pennsylvania Grill. I had noticed her on our first night there, the cigarette girl, Alma Greer: five feet of provocative womanhood, who could wear clothes like a movie queen . . . and afford them too, on the tips her smile drew.

Correctly interpreting the rather formal "distance" I kept between us as shyness rather than indifference, she took the lead. She let me know she liked me very much—and hoped I liked her. I had the right answer there, believe me, but before we began dating I told her of my marriage that couldn't end in divorce. It made no difference to Alma. She became my girl without once questioning where it would wind up. . . .

Chapter 33. VAUDEVILLE HEADLINER

Now we had a marvelous band, and radio had given us a chance to rise to the top. One man stood in our way—Paul Whiteman. He knew we were out to top him, and that his lead in vaudeville and the record field was being narrowed by the jump we had secured through radio.

I went into vaudeville . . . and signed to make records for the Edison Company!

We had record hits with "Rose of the Rio Grande," "Bambalina," "Beal Street Mama," "Sweet Lovin' Mama," and others; but it was depressing to see Paul Whiteman keep hitting the million mark time after time.

After listening to our broadcasts, Thomas A. Edison wrote me this note: "Dear Mr. Lopez, I listen to your radio broadcasts from the Hotel Pennsylvania Grill. Why can't you get the same sound into the records you make for my company? Thomas Alva Edison."

Records had been around for twenty-five years by then but they still sounded tinny. It wasn't until phonographs were built for electrical instead of mechanical amplification that the big change came.

Another critic, an upstate New York farmer, felt that we had shortchanged him. He had this complaint: "Dear Mr. Lopez, I like your music on the radio a lot. I bought some of your records as well so I can hear your band when I get up early in the morning and make breakfast. Your records run four minutes, the way they read on the label. I got in the habit of dropping my eggs in the boiling water the second I turn the record on. When the music stops, my four minute eggs are ready, and I can't eat no other kind without indigestion.

"Well, you have let me down, for your recording of "Bambalina" runs only three minutes and 20 seconds. The eggs just weren't right. I thought maybe it was something I had been feeding my hens in the new mash, but then I got the idea of timing the record with my Ingersoll watch which is very dependable and has a second hand you can easily follow.

"Stop cheating your public on your records. If you say they run four minutes, be sure it's four minutes. I was blaming my hens but it was your new record that was at fault all along.

"P.S.—I'll still listen to you on radio."

I hope our farmer friend was satisfied when we switched to the Okeh label a short time later.

We were doing very well at the Hotel Pennsylvania when one day, at a band rehearsal, Bill Hamilton spoke to me and said, "Vince, Harry Fink and I have something to show you." He reached down under his chair and came up with a fez hat, complete with pony tail and all. Harry Fink, seated next to Hamilton, also reached down and brought out a pith helmet. The two of them stepped out in front of the band. Hamilton, carrying a curved soprano saxophone, Harry Fink with a brass sax, put on their hats and gave their impression of "Gallagher and Shean." Hamilton made his soprano sax talk like Mr. Shean. You could actually hear it say, "Oh, Mister Gallagher, Oh! Mister Gallagher."

And Harry Fink's bass sax answered, "Why Mister Shean, Why Mister Shean!"

I said, "That's terrific."

"We have lots more," Hamilton answered. "All the boys have been working on specialties and novelties in their spare time. How about our going into vaudeville?"

"Vaudeville? Gee, I don't know."

"Why not?" Hamilton asked. "We can catch up with Whiteman. Look at the hit he's been at the Palace. Now we want a crack at it."

"That's just it, Billy," I said. "I know we can do a great vaudeville show, but Whiteman was there first. We shouldn't follow him there unless we can do something entirely different—something that will make us stand out all by ourselves."

"Do you have anything in mind?" Harry Fink asked.

"No, I don't, but we'll find it."

Walking down Broadway, I got caught in a sudden downpour and ducked into the nearest store which happened to sell toys. From an adjacent record shop, a loudspeaker was blaring Al Jolson singing, "The Natchez and the Robert E. Lee." My gaze fell on a sort of miniature Mississippi River with river boats, complete with side-wheels and smoke. Al Jolson's record and the display blended into one in my mind and then. . . .

Thunder pealed along Broadway, but I knew where the lightning had struck. It had given me the idea I needed for our vaudeville show—scenic effects to back up our songs. Two steamboats moving slowly across the stage, with paddlewheels churning as we played "The Natchez and the Robert E. Lee"; the Statue of Liberty in New York Harbor, with a Navy blimp floating overhead as the background for John Philip Sousa's "Stars and Stripes Forever"; a steam-spouting train for "California, Here I Come"; etc.

Arranging the financing for my idea was tougher than anything I had yet done. With all I could borrow from my friends in the music field, I was still $5,000 short. Alma noticed me brooding at the Grill one night. Trying to cheer me up, she drew out the story of my financial plight.

The next day I had the money. Alma had withdrawn it from her own bank account and insisted on lending it to me as a business investment!

To start the ball rolling I called Harry Weber, Pat Rooney's booking agent, who handled Pat Rooney, and I sold him my idea. He sent his assistant, Walter Meyers, to the Penn Grill to see me and make arrangements to book us for a Sunday at Proctors-Fifth Avenue —no billing and no money. When the curtain opened on our first show we received an ovation. Scenic effects used by a band proved a sensation.

But Eddie Darling, the head booker of the Keith Circuit, remained skeptical. I told him the big date I wanted was the Palace and right away. "I heard you've got a cancellation on the bill next week. Put us on in any spot you want to pick, and if we don't pack the place you don't have to pay us."

With a gambler's instinct Eddie Darling took my bait. "You're in for one week, Lopez," he said. "Third spot on the bill. If you've got something we'll play along with you." For the rest of the week, I plugged our coming Palace date between every number we put on the air.

We opened at the Palace on Monday, August 7, 1922. It was Vincent Lopez and his Hotel Pennsylvania Band. The line outside the theatre extended around 7th Avenue and all the way down 47th Street toward 6th Avenue.

The Palace was full. The dance act in front of us was finishing and received a nice round of applause. The curtain went down and the signs on the side of the Palace stage changed to "Vincent Lopez Band."

An air of excitement swept through the crowd and as the curtain rose, a tremendous burst of applause could be heard. Darling was standing in back of the threatre with Walter Meyers. "What did your boy do, buy out the house?" he asked.

Meyers shook his head. "Not as far as I know."

"We'll soon find out," Darling answered.

With our very first number, "Stumbling," the crowd went delirious. And so it went number after number. The Gallagher and Shean routine rocked the house. My piano rendition of "Kitten on the Keys" was also greeted enthusiastically.

Finally, a scrim in back of the band opened revealing a little stage, and a set portraying the Mississippi River of fifty years earlier. Two scaled-down boats, the *Natchez* and the *Robert E. Lee,* all lighted up with smoke coming from the stacks and the side-wheels in motion began moving across the miniature stage.

I gave the downbeat and the band went into "The Natchez and the Robert E. Lee." Then the crowd really went wild.

Darling expressed it best. "In all my years in vaudeville I've never seen anything like it. Scenic effects with a band, it's ingenious!"

In the middle of the presentation, the band softened down, and I introduced L. Wolfe Gilbert, composer of "The Natchez and the Robert E. Lee." A narrator stood off to the side of the band. So effective was the lighting, he was completely in the shadow as he recited the story of the famous race between these two great river steamers.

It was very dramatic. The old Palace really rocked at the end of the number.

While the band was taking bows, an usher rushed up to Mr. Darling. "Mr. Darling, I think we've found out what you wanted to know. Lopez didn't paper the house. He announced on radio he was going to be here. All these people are radio fans of his. They hear him on radio and want to see him in person."

On the stage I was visibly shaken, tears welled in my eyes as I stepped forward. "Thank you," I said, "thank you," and ran off into the wings. That set the crowd off again.

Reporter Jack Lait, with *Variety* at the time, met Darling in the Palace lobby after our first show and said he would give us a sensational review.

"How come you've got them third on the bill?" he asked. "They're the show stopper."

"Just a mistake, Jack," Eddie assured him. "We're moving them down next to closing." Then he spotted a page boy and yelled, "Sid, get those photos of the Lopez band and put them in the display signs outside. Yes, I know. Never mind whose picture's in there now. Make the change right away."

The headlines in the daily press and the trade papers tell the story:

LOPEZ BAND A SMASH HIT
SCENIC EFFECTS REVOLUTIONARY
LOPEZ HAILED AS BELASCO OF BANDMEN
JOHN PHILIP SOUSA TO SEE LOPEZ' PRESENTATION OF "STARS AND STRIPES FOREVER" AT THE PALACE

"John Philip Sousa sat in a box, overlooking the Palace stage. The Lopez band was presenting his "Stars and Stripes Forever" complete with scenic effects. The band played in front of a drop which had New York Harbor painted on it, showing the Statue of Liberty and other landmarks of the turn of the century. The Harbor was lit up and a Navy blimp was shown floating over the Statue of Liberty. The crowd cheered and cheered. Lopez stepped forward and made a little speech about Sousa. When he was finished, Sousa stood up and took a bow. The audience gave him an ovation never before equalled."

Our tentative one week at the Palace stretched out to eleven.

Chapter 34. ON THE ROAD

That summer, when we took a "vacation" from the Hotel Pennsylvania Grill, we visited other cities. A vaudeville tour took us south to Washington and north to familiar Boston. We travelled first class on the railroads, our scenery in a hired special baggage car. The married members of the band talked me into letting their wives accompany them—at my expense. As a result, my net return on that tour was close to nothing.

But a financial break did show up that summer. I collected royalties from orchestras in vaudeville using my name, The Vincent Lopez Red Caps, the Vincent Lopez Cadets, the Vincent Lopez Debutantes, etc.

Later on I tried to extend this satellite band idea through additional financing and built my organization to fifty-one "Lopez Presents" orchestras.

While we were playing a quick date at the Keith Theater in Cleveland, I heard that a new band from Canada, playing at the Claremont Restaurant, had a special touch to their music. I went to hear them and was really impressed. I called the leader over to my table, told him I liked the band, and offered to get him better bookings if he would play under the "Vincent Lopez" billing. He asked for time to talk it over with his brothers, who were also in the band.

Two dance sets later he came back to my table and said, "Mr. Lopez, it's been tough getting started, and there have been times when we nearly quit. In fact, only this morning we were talking about going back to Canada and playing just local dates there; but your offer to sign us means a lot to us. It convinces us we have what it takes to make good. But if you don't mind we'll try to make good on our own."

They've come a long way since then with their "Sweetest music this side of heaven—Guy Lombardo and the Royal Canadians."

Within a few months I had rebounded to the black-ink side of the ledger. On one of our dates I proudly handed Alma Greer a $6,000 check for the $5,000 loan she had made when I needed it so desperately.

"What's the matter, honey?" I asked. "I thought you'd get a kick out of this. Getting your money back, plus a thousand dollars."

"It's very nice of you, Vincent," she answered. "But when you told me on the phone that you had something special for me tonight . . . well, I thought it might be . . . an engagement ring."

"Not just yet, Alma," I stammered the words. "Even if I could get married, I'd be too darned busy for it."

"Then you mean it about never getting a divorce because your religion forbids it?" she asked. "You don't seem such a religious person to me. Why do you have to be religious about that one point?"

"Alma, it's a funny thing," I tried to explain. "You can stop going to church and never even think about the sacraments and yet some parts of the religion . . . some beliefs in it you never get over. If God instituted marriage for mankind who am I to tell Him He was wrong?"

"I guess He's never wrong," Alma conceded, "but I've been wrong—in believing you loved me."

I never did settle the matter of divorce and remarriage in my own conscience. Maybe God is never wrong—but Alma Greer would have been oh-so-right for me!

I owed my financial comeback mainly to a good Samaritan deed of several months before. One day a couple of my musicians, Hank Waak and Bob Effros, ran into the late B. A. Rolfe, for whom they had worked when he was a headliner. It seemed to them that things were not going well financially for B. A., so they took him to a restaurant to talk things over.

"And when you get a chance," said Effros, "come backstage at the Colonial where we're playing and we'll talk Lopez into hiring you."

"I don't have an embouchure," B.A. said. But they told him I'd hire him long enough for him to get his lip back so he could get a good job somewhere. They then hunted me down and convinced me I couldn't do without B.A. He soon got his lip back and was hitting those high ones that had made him famous. What's more, he came through with great show ideas and soon he was making a thousand a week managing and putting together acts for me.

"Cast your bread on the water," I can hear Father Aloysius say. . . .

Months before I was out of the red financially, however, I received a telegram saying that a wealthy radio admirer whom our music had delighted in her last days, had left this earth to join the heavenly choir, naming me recipient of half a million dollars in her will! Of course, I should have known better but I wanted to believe it.

I wired back to the alleged firm of attorneys in Cleveland, asking for confirmation—and within an hour it came! For two days I walked around on air, thinking I was a rich man. E. M. Statler warned me that relatives might try to break such a will; then offered me the help of the hotel's attorney in representing my claim. I made hurried arrangements for a quick trip to Cleveland on the attorney's advice, whereupon the boys in my band chickened out and admitted it was a practical joke. The attorneys in Cleveland were a barber shop owned by cousins of one of my sidemen!

It took me several weeks but I got back at them. Pretending dissatisfaction with their playing, I harped on the need for more rehearsals. Then I sprang my novel idea: "Fellows, I really think success has gone to your heads. You're getting about $300 a week apiece now, and you've lost your spark. What we need is to work off these swelled heads. So starting next Monday we're going around town and play in the backyards of apartment houses. I'll pay you for it, of course, just regular scale; and gentlemen, this is for your own good. You'll thank me for it later on."

Nobody thanked me then—and when I distributed a backyard concert schedule on Saturday, with Brooklyn first on the list for Monday, I nearly had a strike on my hands.

"All right, then," I huffed. "If that's your attitude, we won't play the backyards. Of course we'll slide into mediocrity in time, but what do I care? I can always live on the money I inherited from that old lady in Cleveland"—and I waved the telegram as their faces broke into relieved (and sheepish) grins.

Unintentionally we nearly got into trouble with the SPCA one night. We had traveled to Buffalo to open the new Statler Hotel there and doubled in a vaudeville date at Shay's Hippodrome. "Tiger Rag" was Joe Tarto's encore number on the bass, and as a finale he would kick the instrument to spin it into the spotlight. This had worn a hole in the bottom of the big fiddle into which one of the backstage cats had crawled. As Joe thumped out his heavy rhythms, in "Tiger Rag," she began meowing wildly. Superstitious Joe first thought it was a ghost, but he was game and kept on with the tune. But when he gave the instrument the customary kick and spin, it hurled the startled cat out of the hole and off into the wings!

The audience howled with delight, thinking it was part of our act. The following morning we had quite a time convincing a representative of the Society for the Prevention of Cruelty to Animals that it wasn't!

Chapter 35. KEEPING UP WITH WHITEMAN

For years I worked and planned to beat Paul Whiteman—and he, to keep ahead of me. Paul would bid away my best musicians and I would do the same to his. If either of us added a musician the other would match him so that *Variety* could announce both.

When I took the lead in something, Paul would have to follow suit—but there was one venture he didn't follow me in. This was the stock boom of the 'Twenties. I sold stock when even bootblacks were speculating on Wall Street, thereby making the *Wall Street Journal* as well as the Broadway columns. I incorporated, and financing was needed for my ambition to have a Vincent Lopez Orchestra and a Vincent Lopez School of Music in every sizeable town; to have even more elaborate scenery for our vaudeville acts, etc. The idea of incorporating was sound, as many show-business stars have proved (Jack Benny, Bing Crosby, Arthur Godfrey, et al.)

The newspapers gave it a big play with headlines like LOPEZ TO PUT JAZZ ON STOCKMARKET; CORPORATION TO ORGANIZE BANDS UNDER LOPEZ BANNER; LOPEZ INCORPORATED: CAPITALIZED AT $400,000.

My brokers ran an ad in the newspapers offering our preferred stock. It read: "VINCENT LOPEZ, INC., A NEW YORK CORPORATION OFFERS, 20,000 SHARES 8% CUMULATIVE PREFERRED STOCK PAR VALUE $10.00 LOPEZ SPEAKING: *To all my friends: It is my hope to have a large number of you financially interested in my company. In this way only, can I hope to broaden and extend its scope and influence. I would rather have a thousand shareholders with a nominal investment than a single partner with the wealth of Croesus. . . . And for your protection, I have insured my life for $200,000 payable to the company, so you will be protected come what may!*"

The Hotel Pennsylvania public relations people had been doing well for me, but Jim Gillespie of the *Dramatic Mirror* nevertheless sold himself to me as a press agent for the band.

"You'll need a good publicity man who'll concentrate on you,

Vincent," he argued. "After all, Whiteman has one. Why not Lopez?"

"Er—Whiteman has one?" I questioned. "Doesn't the Palais Royale handle his publicity for him?"

"Yes, they help," Jim conceded. "But Paul has his own full-time man as well. You know what publicity means—and you don't want to let him get ahead of you. . . ."

The arrow hit smack in my Achilles heel again! I signed Jim on and he did a great job for me.

It wasn't long before I was getting reams of publicity.

"I set up a date that'll be good for mention in every paper," Jim informed me right after the Dempsey-Firpo fight. "You're to give Jack a cup naming him the heavyweight fighter with the greatest sense of rhythm in the world. You make the presentation at Roseland tomorrow night."

"Sunday night!" I half protested, "my only night off. I want to meet Dempsey of course, but does it have to be a stunt like this? Can't we get together socially. Maybe have him come to the Grill?"

"It'll be a social affair as well," Jim assurred me. "I had to work this out with a million people who are cutting in on the publicity. The Roseland owners started the ball rolling, so it's got to be held there. Afterward you all go to the Hotel Alamac for a big shindig with the press."

"What do you mean, we 'all' go there?" I asked.

"Oh," Jim added. "The Follies is in on this, too, and you've got a date with a beautiful Ziegfeld girl. So has Dempsey—with the girl who does the center nudes. You know, they advertise her as the girl with the most beautiful body in the world. . . ."

"Oh, Beryl Halley?" Why didn't you get her for *my* date? And who did you get for me, anyway?"

"Another real doll," Jim answered. "A brunette named Estelle Taylor."

The presentation at Roseland was no example of smash ad libs. Neither Jack Dempsey nor I were public speakers and we stumbled through the ceremony with a minimum of words. But on the way over to the Hotel Alamac later we certainly came alive. Beryl and

Estelle were just what the psychiatrist would order for an introverted patient. They had a lot besides beauty—wit and charm and gaiety.

Somehow, though, as the conversation warmed up, Jack fixed his attention on my date, Estelle Taylor. Believe me, I didn't get the least bit sore. If Luis Firpo had lost an argument with Jack, I didn't figure on starting one. Furthermore, I was satisfied to pick up where Jack left off in the conversation department with lovely Beryl Halley.

She mentioned that she was going to pose for one of the nation's leading sculptors the next afternoon. "Mr. Ziegfeld wants him to do a statue of me," she explained.

"The way you are now," I half choked, "or the way you look in that finale tableau scene?"

"Oh, the tableau scene, of course," Beryl answered—and I found myself wishing I'd been a sculptor instead of a pianist.

At the press party, some crazy arrangements separated us. Jack and Beryl were at a table perhaps twenty feet away from Estelle and me. Jack kept looking in our direction. Then I noticed him whisper intently to Beryl. She smiled—and he walked over.

"Hey, Vince," he suggested shyly, "Beryl and I think maybe they made the wrong dates for us tonight . . . I mean if it's the same to you . . . and if Miss Taylor here wouldn't mind . . . suppose we switch girls for the rest of the night. Okay?"

Estelle answered for me. "Yes, Jack," she said, "that would really be okay."

As things turned out, Estelle became Mrs. Jack Dempsey; and bandleader Lopez found that Beryl Halley could make the most wonderful music!

Beryl and I began having so many dates I talked myself into renting a limousine. Taxicabs would have been just as good, but my reason for wanting the car was to impress Beryl. For a hundred a week I got not only the use of the car, but the owner as well, a Broadway character nicknamed "Mother MacFadyen." He was right out of a Damon Runyon story, an Irishman with a foghorn voice who always wore a white bow tie, and a blue suit. Having a chaffeur was a big mistake because I haven't learned to drive to this day.

"Mr. Lopez," MacFadyen told me after a week, "I don't have enought to do just chauffeuring you and Beryl around. If you're going to have me on the payroll I want to earn my dough, so starting tomorrow I'm going to be your valet too." And there was no talking him out of it.

To impress people with an affluence that simply was not there, I talked MacFadyen into having my initials printed on both sides of his Packard. Not to be outdone, my partner, Bill Hamilton rented a Rolls Royce with BH emblazoned on each door. Success had come to both of us rather quickly—maturity was slower and more painful.

While my romance was a big success, I had quite a publicity setback when Paul Whiteman stole Jimmy Gillespie away from me with an offer of $500 a week—$100 more than I was paying. Henry Busse and Paul had quite an argument over the move. Busse thought that I was planting Jim Gillespie in the Whiteman organization to spy out their doings. On my end of things, Jim's sudden announcement that he was going with Whiteman made *me* wonder whether he'd been spying on my setup for Paul!

Chapter 36. JAZZ AT THE MET

While playing at Keith's Palace in Washington, D. C., who did I find taking tickets at a competing theatre but William Morris, Sr., then managing vaudeville headliner Harry Lauder. (I guess some of the Scotch thrift had rubbed off his famous client onto Mr. Morris, to make him work as a ticket taker!) This gave me an idea for a publicity break. President Coolidge had just expounded the importance of thrift, so I proposed that Morris have penny-pinching Lauder meet the President—with photographers present.

I was to be present, also, and somehow get into the photograph.

Morris liked the idea, and helped to arrange it. And that was how I got to meet President Coolidge at the White House.

"I like the way you introduce the numbers," he commented. "You just give the name of the song, then play it. Most announcers talk too much."

Mr. Morris talked the President into posing for a picture with Sir Harry, but I was eased out. Knowing it would make practically every paper I was glum in the taxi that took us back to my hotel. Mr. Morris tried to placate me.

"You gave me a good idea—so let me return the favor and give you an idea. You've done about everything in show business: radio, vaudeville, hotels, benefits. You can top all that with a jazz concert. You claim jazz is an art form of American music. Prove it with a concert!"

"Sounds good," I agreed, intrigued with the thought. "But where would I give it?"

"Right where it would get you the greatest attention," he explained. "The Metropolitan Opera House!"

"That sounds terrific. If I ever get the time, will you handle it for me?"

"It's a date, Vincent," he promised.

On the way north from Washington that day, I found the time to keep a promise I'd made to play the piano for the kids at St. Mary's Industrial School in Baltimore. It was a wonderful audience and the brothers thanked me for stopping by.

"Don't thank me," I explained, "somebody else really thought of this. A graduate of yours who's doing pretty well for himself in New York now. Maybe you remember the name: George Herman Ruth."

Sometime later Ed Wolfe was sounding me out for publicity leads he might plant in the New York columns. Thinking it would needle Paul Whiteman, I told Wolfe to start a rumor that I would give a concert at Carnegie Hall. Paul sure reacted! He immediately hired Aeolian Hall and commissioned a young song writer to create a brand new composition in the American idiom and gave him ten days to deliver. Each day, the composer turned in a few pages which Ferde Grofe orchestrated and Whiteman rehearsed at night.

Out of that spurious concert plan, spawned by our rivalry, came one of the great pieces of American music. The young man Whiteman hired was George Gershwin—and the composition he so feverishly put together was "Rhapsody in Blue."

1924 was a great year for me. For instance, walking along Broadway one summer afternoon, I ran into Harry Bestry, a booking agent. "Funny you should come along just now," he remarked. "Jones and Green are going to produce *The Greenwich Village Follies* starring the Dolly Sisters. How would you like to co-star in it with your band?"

That led to a contract a few days later, by which time Bestry had another deal—for me to play a New York night club, the Ostend.

"What are you trying to do, kill me?" I questioned. "I'm playing at the Pennsylvania Grill all week, plus theatre dates around town. You know we have to put in our share of the benefits, too. And here's the *Greenwich Village Follies* we're going into. Now you want me to add a night club! Look, Harry, *I* can take it, but it would give my life insurance agent a nervous breakdown."

"Don't be such a pessimist," he insisted. "I've got your routine all worked out. You're free after one o'clock just about every evening. You stay up the rest of the night anyway, so why not get paid for the time and play the piano at the Ostend Club?"

"What about my dates with Beryl Halley?" I asked.

"Bring her along," Harry solved it. "You take her out most every night anyway. So get paid for it."

An agent can talk so glibly. Anyway, I took the Ostend job. As things turned out, the Ostend was no great trouble—but I should have opened Pandora's box rather than the *Greenwich Village Follies*. After their first look at the lovely chorus girls heavy romancing began for my musicians. My rule about no fraternizing with the showgirls got about as much enforcement as—Prohibition!

To set a good example, I even turned down a date that I very much wanted to keep. With the première and some shakedown changes out of the way, the Dolly Sisters suggested one evening that I drop in at their dressing room for a glass of champagne, now that the show was settling down.

I regretfully declined, with an explanation about the rule I had set for the band. The Dolly Sisters understood—but my band didn't!

A month later, the Piccadilly movie theatre signed me at $750 a week, just to come in for a few minutes and conduct the opening overture in those pre-talkie days! Jones and Green immediately secured a restraining order against my appearance at the Piccadilly Theatre on the basis that the movies were a competitive medium. My publicity man said the legal battle would be great for publicity. It was; but getting up early the morning of the hearing almost killed me. I'd been out until six a.m., and I almost fell asleep in the courtroom. However, the decision handed down by Supreme Court Justice James O'Malley woke me up—we won it.

Although Whiteman's concert was a financial flop despite its artistic success, I decided to go ahead with my own jazz-concert plans. We had the band for it, but it takes promotion genius to move such a concert from the idea stage to actuality. So I reminded William Morris, Sr. of his promise. He asked, "Do you want to do this concert to get even with Whiteman?"

"Partly," I admitted. "But that's not the only reason."

"What's the other reason?" he asked. "It can't be money because you stand to lose money on this. That leaves Beryl Halley. You want to do a concert to impress her with how big you are in this business?"

"That might enter the picture, too, Mr. Morris, but there's another reason, and it's the big one. Outside of the spirituals and folk music, jazz is the only good music America has produced. Everything else we play had its roots in Europe. Now we've come up with a music form that's our own and we should be proud of it because it expresses the restless, vigorous tempo of our life."

Two weeks later, Morris had done the impossible—booked us into the Metropolitan for a jazz concert on Sunday afternoon, November 23, 1924. That left us a month for rehearsals. To match Paul Whiteman's coup in signing Gershwin, I bought original jazz compositions from the leading jazz composers; W. C. Handy whose "St. Louis Blues" I had helped introduce, refused to take a cent for his contribution. "Let's say it's my way of saying thanks for what you did for my St. Louis number." It was a brilliant musical history of the Blues. Next time you hear it in jazz recital—"The Evolution of the Blues"—remember it as the key point of our 1924 concert.

Besides the instrumental jazz presentation by our band, some inner sense of show balance told me we needed a novelty that would somehow belong in jazz. I found what I wanted in a harmonica player who was demonstrating the instrument behind a sales counter at Wurlitzer's. His name was Borah Minnevich.

Out of sheer curiosity, several Metropolitan Opera stars dropped in to watch our rehearsals. One of them, a great tenor whom I won't identify, saw Borah's name (and instrument) on our program and he exploded to me! "Mr. Lopez, the idea of a jazz concert in this opera house is preposterous enough, and I don't know what connections you have that got you permission. I'll even admit that your music has its own primitive qualities. But this plan of yours to present a harmonica player! It's—it's sacrilege!"

I calmed him down, "Why don't you postpone judging this performance until you hear it? I'll admit I was prejudiced against grand opera until I heard you in it. And I have tickets for your performance in *Manon*. I'd like you to be our guest at the concert. Where shall I mail a pair of tickets?"

"My apologies, sir. I shall, as you suggest, reserve judgment."

Luckily he didn't ask to see my opera tickets—I knew about his date in *Manon* from the billboards outside the Met! From that afternoon, the opera stars were more friendly. Word must have gotten around that Lopez was an opera fan!

Preparations for the concert included some lessons in conducting. At the Pennsylvania and even in vaudeville, I kept conducting to a minimum, preferring to set the beat from my piano. But for this occasion, with the band augmented to the symphonic size of fifty-six pieces, I'd have to take over the baton and give it the customary flourishes. To prepare for it, I contacted the Metropolitan's famous conductor, Bodansky.

Bodansky shared the animosity of most serious musicians to jazz and deplored my coming concert within the sacred walls of the Met; but he consented to audition me.

"How can you afford my fee of $50 a lesson?" he wanted to know. "How much you make leading a dance band?"

"Ten thousand," I answered offhand.

"Not bad, not bad," he agreed. "Most people in opera don't make ten thousand a year."

"Oh, I mean ten thousand a week," I explained.

The maestro was thunderstruck. I could see him doing some mental arithmetic as he stared at me in disbelief. Then he muttered, "Ten thousand a week! Lopez, maybe you better give *Bodansky* lessons!"

Despite Bodansky's coaching, at ten minutes before concert time that Sunday I took a look at the tremendous house awaiting us (there were scores of standees and even seats in the pit)—and got a terrible case of stage fright!

"You take it, Joe," I said to my concertmeister, Joe Nussbaum.

"But it's your concert, Vince," he argued. "It's your band."

"Sure, sure," I countered. "But everybody knows it's my band, so what's the difference who leads it?"

"Are you crazy?" Joe shouted. "You go six weeks with about three hours sleep a day, spend thousands on publicity, and now you want me to steal the spotlight."

"You'd be a fool not to," I persisted.

"You'd be the fool not to," he settled it. "And I'd be a fool if I took over 'cause this crowd came here to see *you* lead the band. Now get going, will you."

I got going, but I don't think I realized what was happening until the finish of our first number when the applause hit us. It came up over the footlights in a wave of sound heavy enough almost to grasp and feel. Turning toward the audience in a bow, I recognized a number of familiar faces, among them Statler and my favorite opera tenor, shouting the traditional "bravo" of the opera claques. Then I knew that, like the saints in the great jazz number, we were marching in!

To show you what a wide and difficult range we covered, the program of the concert is included here on the next three pages.

Later that evening we were sitting it out in Lindy's waiting for the first editions to see how the longhair critics liked us.

"We're a hit! A smash!" Bill Hamilton shouted as he brought in the papers. "Even Olin Downes in the *New York Times,* says 'It demonstrates the real promise in American music!' "

PROGRAMME

With Descriptive Notes by
FREDERICK H. MARTENS

Programme

PART ONE

1. RUSSIAN FANTASY . . . . LOPEZ-POLLA*

This fantasy suite, with the Rachmaninoff C sharp minor "Prelude" as an introduction presents well-known themes, among them Cui's "Orientale" and "The Volga Boat Song" in quasi-symphonic development. Especially interesting are: the dialogue development of the theme from Rimsky-Korsakow's "Song of India" between soprano saxophone, oboe and bass; and the rhythmic treatment of the brilliant climaxing "March of the Sirdar," by Ippolito-Ivanow.

* The orchestral development of the numbers of this programme has been carried out according to Mr. Lopez's creative indications with regard to instrumentation, dynamics, color and effect.

2. BY THE WATERS OF MINNETONKA . . . THURLAW LIEURANCE

(Orchestral Development by Lopez-Polla)

An orchestral version of this "Indian Love Song" by the well-known exploiter of the aboriginal melody of the Yellowstone region, in which the themes of the original have been subjected to special inflections of rhythm and tone color to stress their interesting primitive appeal.

3. BIBLICAL SUITE . . . . VLADIMIR HEIFETZ

(Orchestral Development by Lopez-Nussbaum)

A suite in three movements—1. Near the Ruined Wall of the Temple; 2. The Mysterious Moment; 3. Hebrew Dance—based on ancient traditional biblical melodies, whose fine themes admit of an especially sonorous orchestral development.

4. INDIAN LOVE SONG . . . . RUDOLF FRIML

(From "Rose-Marie")

(Orchestral Development by Lopez-Polla)

A specific orchestral development by Lopez-Polla, of an outstanding lyric number of one of the most popular of musical comedies now running in New York. There are interesting effects secured in the strings and double-reeds.

5. "THE MELODY THAT MADE YOU MINE" . . . . . . W. C. POLLA

(Orchestral Development by Lopez-Pol'

An orchestral version of a popular ballad waltz, in which the trumpet appears in the solo rôle, playing between B flat and G above the staff.

6. PELL STREET . . . . EMERSON WHITHORNE

From "'New York Days and Nights."
Op. 40

(Orchestral Development by Lopez-Nussbaum)

"Pell Street" is the third number of the virile suite for orchestra by this gifted American modernist. The composer has outlined its programme: It is night in Pell Street. An ancient Chinese melody, "The Fifteen Bunches of Blossoms," floats from a fan-tan house, where an old Chinaman, swaying as he rocks his bow, plays the exotic tune on his single-stringed fiddle. All the clever, colorful exotic possibilities of the composition have been kept in mind in this specific orchestral version.

7. ECCENTRIC . . . . R. ROBINSON

(Orchestral Development by Lopez-Nussbaum)

"Eccentric" (A Pure "Jazz" Fantasy) is an eloquent exposition of the rhythm and color effects possible in a genuinely imaginative handling of "jazz" values. Its "jazz breaks"—those two measure rests in the melody progression which the accompanying instruments "fill in" with a piquant mosaic of varied rhythm—are especially characteristic.

8. "WILD FLOWER" - - - - - - - - - - - VINCENT YOUMANS

(*Concert Paraphrase for Piano Solo with Accompaniment by Vincent Lopez*)

THE TRANSCRIBER AT THE PIANO

A brilliant and effective concert paraphrase of Vincent Youmans' attractive original, in which the special technique of piano syncopation and tone color is exploited in a series of contrasting variations, with an orchestral background.

9. FANTASY ON THEMES - - - - - - - - ARTHUR SULLIVAN

From Gilbert and Sullivan's "H. M. S. 'Pinafore'"

(*Orchestral Development by Lopez-Lampe*)

A "comedy" fantasy on themes which lend themselves to humorous instrumental effect. In them the principals in the comic opera, supported by an instrumental chorus, appear in solo rôles: the Captain (piano); Sweet Little Buttercup (cornet burlesque); Admiral (trombone); and Dick Dead Eye (baritone).

10. THE EVOLUTION OF THE "BLUES" - W. C. HANDY AND JOSEPH NUSSBAUM

(*Orchestral Development by Lopez-Nussbaum*)

This "symphonietta in 'jazz' style," as it has been called, presents in a free-form fantasy the evolution of that specifically American negro emotional quality known as "the blues." The composers have been notably successful—after a beginning in which the tribal drums of jungle villages beat—in presenting in a brilliant, stepwise progression the birth of "the blues" out of the profane song (negro tribal dance and occupational melody) and sacred song (the slave-day spirituals). These "blues" —the negro character combinations of a surface melody of carefree happiness on a ground bass of sorrow and melancholy—have been symphonically traced through their evolution in this tone-poem. It is a work rich in effect, and old negro spirituals and the famous "Blues"—Memphis, St. Louis, Beale Street, Harlem—are harmoniously interwoven in its pages to justify the title.

PART TWO

11. SCHEHEREZADE - - - - - - - - - - N. RIMSKY-KORSAKOW

(*Orchestral Development by Lopez-Polla*)

Themes from the different movements of the Russian composer's symphonic poem have been elaborated in free-form style and in a thoroughly symphonic manner, with effects of sonority peculiar to the special orchestral composite presenting the fantasy.

12. CIELITO LINDO (BEAUTIFUL SKY) - - - - - MEXICAN FOLK SONG

(*Orchestral Development by Lopez-Polla*)

A Spanish ballad in tango-rhythm presented in a novel orchestral color-scheme.

13. "FOLLOW THE SWALLOW" - - - - - - - - R. HENDERSON

(*Orchestral Development by Lopez-Polla*)

A popular song of the day in an original orchestral working-out of its rhythm and color possibilities.

14. TWO SOLOS FOR HARMONICA - - - - - - - - - - - - -

a. "My Heart at Thy Sweet Voice" from C. Saint-Saëns' "Samson et Dalila"

b. Rubeville Original Jazz Fantasy

Soloist*

MR. BORRAH MINEVITCH

* These numbers are introduced to prove that the mouth-harmonica, in the hands of an artist, has a valid claim to be taken seriously as a musical instrument.

15. "THE MEANEST BLUES" - - - - - - - - - FLETCHER HENDERSON

(*Orchestral Development by Lopez-Katzmann*)

This, a typical "jazz" number, is a composition of the genuine negro "jazz" variety, with all the instrumental "comedy" effects (clarinet *glissandi*, melodious wails, crooning, reproaches, insinuations, chuckles, etc., on the part of the other reeds and brasses) which, if spontaneous, as in this instance, are so unquestionably piquant.

16. A STUDY IN SYNCOPATION - - - - - - - - HENRY SOUVAINE
(*Orchestral Development by Lopez-Vodery*)

A brilliant orchestral two-minute-and-a-half "review" of practically all the forms of syncopation in colorful sequence,

17. a. "ALL ALONE" - - - - - - - - - - - IRVING BERLIN
b. IF LOVE WERE ALL - - - - - - - - - - - HUGO FREY
Ballad
YVETTE RUGEL, *Soprano*

A new song by this leading exponent of the "jazz" genre, with an orchestral accompaniment by Lopez.

18. "INDIAN LOVE LYRICS - - - - - - - AMY WOODFORD-FINDEN
(*Orchestral Development by Lopez-Polla*)

The popular song-cycle by Amy Woodford-Finden in a free orchestral transcription whose instrumentation brings out its exotic color with major effect.

19. "IN A LITTLE RENDEZVOUS" - - - - - - - - - TED SNYDER
(*Orchestral Development by Lopez-Polla*)

A light, popular number which allows the introduction of characteristic effects in color and rhythm somewhat outside the beaten track.

20. A JAZZ WEDDING - - - - - - - - - J. BODEWALT LAMPE
(*Orchestral Development by Lopez-Lampe*)

A programmatic tone poem on a miniature scale: the Richard Strauss "Domestica" in a jazz variant. With a characteristic wealth of humorous detail we have note-pictures of bride and groom, their wedding, the departure on the honeymoon (amid the realistic tonal patter of showered rice and old shoes) and—a year later, the introduction of the baby whose cries are convincingly voiced by the trap drummer.

ENCORES

JUNE NIGHT - - - - - - - - - - - - - - - - ABEL BAER
WHY LIVE A LIE - - - - - - - - - - - - - - WOLFE GILBERT
SALLY LOU - - - - - - - - - - - - - - - - HUGO FREY

CHICKERING PIANOS AMPICO RECORDING
OKEH RECORDS MARTIN INSTRUMENTS

But when Ed Wolfe said "I guess that'll show Whiteman who's King," the thrill was suddenly gone.

"Whiteman! Whiteman!" I shrugged Ed off. "Why am I always chasing after him, anyway? From now on, I don't care what Whiteman does. I'm going to be concerned with what only one orchestra leader does—and his name is Vincent Lopez."

So it is, in moments of letdown after triumph, that we mature a bit and are able to grow toward what life intended for us.

Chapter 37. I BRING AMERICAN JAZZ TO ENGLAND

Our symphonic jazz concert at the Met brought me international recognition, but nearly ruined me financially. I went in for more lavish publicity, hired a full-time accountant, referred legal problems to a top-drawer firm of attorneys, and signed up high-priced musicians. One man I wanted was on the coast. He wired acceptance of my offer ($200 a week) if I would also pay "the expenses of coming to New York." I telegraphed an okay, figuring it would cost $150. But he bought first-class accommodations for his family (wife and four kids!) and shipped his furniture east at my expense!

Xavier Cugat, the present Rumba King, was a man I didn't particularly want, but he kept pestering me for an audition. "So you can play the violin," I told him on the phone one day. "What else can you do? My men have to be versatile—real artists."

For the next three days a messenger delivered wonderful caricatures of me and the band in action at the Pennsylvania Grill. The enclosed notes simply said: "I hope this shows I'm an artist, too."

Such ingenuity caught my imagination, so I added Cugat and his violin to the band. His accent, those days, was closer to old Barcelona (where Cugat was born) than it is now. Romance was his middle name, for he had the Latin's appreciation of feminine beauty. Somehow this combination of Spanish accent, toreador zest for the best in girls, and the other things that make up Xavier Cugat as we see him on television, brought out the band's instinct for playing practical jokes—on poor Cugie. Most of the jokes were such corny things as planting a $10 violin in place of his expensive Stradavarius, but one joke would have killed a man with a weak heart.

Cugie had developed quite a crush on a showgirl who often came into the Grill with her escort. Bob Effros, our first trumpter, who knew her, persuaded her to give Cugie the ever-lovin' eye one evening. Then he fashioned a note which a waiter delivered to Cugat as the girl was leaving, giving a fictitious name and apartment number and saying she'd love to have him play the violin for her the next afternoon!

Cugie just couldn't keep the good news to himself.

"I know that girl quite well," Bob Effros confided. "The way to make a hit with her is bring her a strawberry shortcake. She's crazy about them."

So Cugat took both his violin and a big Lindy cake with him the following afternoon. The apartment the boys had picked for their joke was two flights up a dark stairway, on Tenth Avenue, in Hell's Kitchen! As Cugie stumbled up the last few steps, trying to see in the gloom, he suddenly heard a very angry masculine voice shout, "So you're the crumb who's been visitin' my wife while I'm woikin!"

With that, prankster Effros smashed a couple of electric light bulbs, and the echoes in the narrow hall sounded like revolver shots. Cugat took the stairs three at a time as he reversed direction. He sprinted a full block before he realized that the footfalls and shouts following him belonged to Bob Effros and his practical joke pals.

Incidentally, Cugat still had his violin under his arm and the strawberry shortcake box held tightly by its string in the other hand!

I capitalized on our Metropolitan Opera House concert reputation by doing a jazz-concert trip that winter. Mr. Statler gave the idea his blessing, as long as we mentioned the Pennsylvania Hotel in our concert billing, so off we started for a whirlwind tour of the north-east, booked by William Morris and Sol Hurok. The serious music reviewers turned out at every city. The inevitable comparisons with Whiteman weren't bad. In fact, the Boston *Transcript* gave us the victor's nod.

"Last night the gods of symphonic jazz were feted anew when Vincent Lopez and his Metropolitan Concert Orchestra played at Symphony Hall. The crowd was as large and as enthusiastic as that which perviously turned out to greet his jazz contemporary, Paul Whiteman.

"The Lopez orchestra is intrinsically a better orchestra than Mr. Whiteman's, and Mr. Lopez is a firmer, more disciplined conductor than Mr. Whiteman. . . ."

I don't know what made the reviewer say I was a firmer, more disciplined conductor than Paul. Maybe it was the 102 degree fever I took onstage with me that night. I had come down with a rough case of New England flu and I still had the fever when the morning papers came out, but the marvelous reviews made it a happy delirium.

Our concert trip was an artistic success and a box-office record breaker, yet it brought me close to financial disaster. When the tour ended, vaudeville seemed my only hope to meet a payroll well above what I drew from the Pennsylvania Hotel, since radio income, those early days, was peanuts. So we hooked up with the Keith Vaudeville Circuit again. But the costs of my elaborate scenic effects, kept our accounts in red ink and I hired a financial manager, Henry Spitzer. After a week on the ledgers, he called a council of war.

"Vincent, how do you do it?" he demanded. "I can see how a new vaudeville presentation can cost you money on scenery, lighting effects, new orchestrations and the like, but it should start paying off somewhere along the line or why do you play vaudeville? To go broke?"

"To stay on top," I explained. "You can't afford to stand still in this business or in a couple of years you're out of business."

"What's all this column on 'incidentals'?" he questioned. "How can 'incidentals' mount up to a thousand a week?"

"They don't every week," I challenged, "but it's the same general idea—to stay on top. You think of some special effect you want to have that nobody else has, and you go for it."

"Then let's see if we can keep it under control," said Henry. "And what's the idea of paying the traveling expenses of the wives if they want to come along. Do the *wives* play in your band?"

"Having them along keeps the men out of trouble," I explained.

"And gets you in financial trouble," said Henry. "Tell 'em that starting today, the wives stay home or the men pay their expenses, not you."

The new rule was unpopular with the wives, but the boys loved Henry Spitzer for it!

At the end of a long auditing stretch, Henry came up with four specific recommendations: cut down the $75,000 a year payroll I carried in addition to band salaries!; convert the money I had borrowed from the ten percent (a month) loan sharks into a bank loan; wind up my corporation affairs to cut down legal expense; and find a way of using scenery and props that were gathering dust and storage bills.

The last was solved by the enterprising William Morris. "Vincent," he telephoned one day, "if you can work it out with Statler, I've got a two-month booking for you over in London."

"But I thought they keep American musicians out so there'll be more jobs for their own people."

"We can get around that," he explained. "They've heard of your concert at the Metropolitan and they want to know more about American jazz. Don't worry about the business arrangements. I'll take care of that end. Do you want to go? That's the important question."

"How much?" I asked, "that's an important question, too."

"Twelve hundred pounds a week," he answered. "For two dates, that is. You'd have to play the Capitol Cinema Theatre over there and open a new class nitery called the Kit Kat Club. People will have to be a member of the nobility to belong—or at least be recommended by one of the nobility. What do you say?"

Twelve hundred pounds British money then equalled $6,000 of ours, and a quick bit of mental arithmetic told me I couldn't lose anything on the deal. Anyway, it would be a two-month vacation from my local creditors, so I told Mr. Morris to go ahead.

Again Mr. Statler agreed to our temporary absence (with a substitute Lopez band) as long as we gave the Hotel Pennsylvania plenty of mention while we were abroad. He also permitted us to fill an overnight date that month in Washington, D.C., President Coolidge's second Inaugural Ball. Evidently President Coolidge had meant it when he told me he liked our music. My prized memento of the ball is a monogrammed baton he presented to me.

After shaking hands with me that night he added, "I still listen to you on the radio, Mr. Lopez, but I notice you're talking too much in between the songs."

I had adopted the practice of mentioning the names of the composers after announcing the numbers we would play! President Coolidge's nickname of Silent Cal was certainly well-deserved.

When the first of May rolled around, it brought alarming news about our London trip.

"Some of the creditors plan to attach our band instruments," Henry Spitzer told me in deep concern. "They're afraid you'll stay in Europe a year or so, and they insist on getting their money now."

Quick checks by telephone showed this might actually be done to force a settlement of what I owed. With no chance to borrow the money we solved our dilemma, by packing the instruments and scenery in new crates labelled "Gear Machinery," "China—Handle With Care," "Typewriters—This Side Up," and loaded them at night on the *Leviathan* on which we were to sail the next afternoon. We split the orchestrations among the band members (and the wives who were going along) so they could put it with their personal luggage. That left only me as a risk if a process server delivered an injunction. At five in the morning I slipped aboard the steamship and holed up in Bill Hamilton's cabin.

I was in a state of mild shock because at two o'clock our great trumpeter, B. A. Rolfe, told me he had decided not to make the trip with us!

"Sorry, Vince," he explained, " but I've got a chance to form my own group and play the Palais D'Or, the Chinese restaurant."

"Chinese laundry, you mean!" I said angrily. "They're open morning, noon and night. You won't like it there, B.A. Stay with us. You're practically a partner."

"In more ways than one," Rolfe agreed. "I'm like you in that I want my own outfit. Any other way, I'm not satisfied."

"Why didn't you tell me then?" I questioned. "This last minute stuff is murder."

Rolfe went on to splendid success at the Palais D'Or and then with the Lucky Strike radio program. He made good on the second chance fate had given him when two of my musicians found him hungry and broke, in a Child's restaurant.

As another good friend of mine would shortly say on radio, "Round and round it goes, and where it stops nobody knows."

Beryl Halley didn't like sneaking on shipboard to say good-bye to me. She'd been opposed to the trip all along.

"If we could make it together, Vincent, as man and wife, it would be wonderful," she murmured disconsolately as we shared lunch in Hamilton's cabin. "But all right. We'll skip it till you get back. Anyway, we have to think seriously about where we're going, dear. . . . You and I as two people in love—not Vincent Lopez and his orchestra."

"It's a promise, darling," I compromised. "I'll write to you every day and before you know it I'll be back in New York again."

She wasn't out of my arms until the Leviathan whistle sounded its "All Ashore!"

"I've heard that British girls are quite cold and reserved," she whispered on our parting kiss. "Don't you do anything to warm them up."

I made that promise, too.

Our creditor worries were needless. Nobody showed up with any legal papers. Nevertheless, I didn't go to my own cabin until the Leviathan was past the three-mile limit. Some of the creditors I'd worried about even sent me bon-voyage telegrams.

An overseas cablegram was delivered just after supper from William Morris, who had preceded us to England. With it, any "vacation" plans I'd had vanished. It read: MISUNDERSTANDING EXISTED STOP THEY WILL PAY TWELVE HUNDRED POUNDS ONLY IF YOU ALSO APPEAR IN "BY THE WAY" HIT SHOW STARRING JACK HULBERT AND

CECIL COURTRIDGE STOP CABLE ME IF THIS ALTERS YOUR ACCEPTANCE OF DATE.

Morris had timed his cablegram very well. What were we going to do—jump overboard with our instruments and swim back to New York harbor?

With all that work ahead of us, I decided to relax on shipboard at least and enjoy the trip. Jack Robbins, the music publisher, was aboard, plus movie actress Mae Marsh and the famous Ziegfeld Star, Evelyn Law and her mother. I enjoyed the relaxation of the voyage—but I also wanted to stay in action and most of the band shared my feeling. We felt the need for work and the sense of accomplishment it creates. A talk with Captain Hartley got an okay on our giving a series of jazz musicals on board, with everybody invited. And since the Leviathan was a little bit of the United States in a vast mid-ocean, we closed our concerts with the Star Spangled Banner. Somehow our national anthem had special meaning and a deeper thrill with a thousand miles of sea separating us from the homeland.

When Bob Effros commented on this, he added, "I guess the people of every nation feel that way about their national anthem."

That's when the lightning of recollection hit me. I had brought along the orchestration of a number we had to memorize.

"Special rehearsal ten tomorrow morning, fellows," I ordered. "We've got three days to memorize it. No reading when we play this one—'God Save The King!' "

Evelyn Law was making the trip with her mother. Considering some of my musicians, that was a good idea. One of my trumpet players, Will Blackson, was one from whom any unguarded girl needed protection. But Xavier Cugat needed it even more, and for another reason.

The third night out I was passing the cabin Cugie shared with Blackson when I heard muffled shouts for help. Fortunately, the door was unlocked and when I lunged in I found Blackson and another equally plastered musician trying to shove poor Cugat through the porthole, head first! I really blew my top. Blackson and his pal hauled Cugat back in immediately.

"We weren't going to shove him all the way through," Blackson explained. "We had a bet on whether Cugat could get out the porthole in case of a fire. He didn't want to co-operate."

"And you've got another drunken friend outside in a rowboat, I suppose, just in case you'd lost your grip," I exploded. "Do you want me to fire this guy right now?" I asked Cugat as he shook on the bed in exhaustion and fright.

"No. Don't fire him," he decided. "He didn't realize what he was doing. Just put me in another cabin!"

William Morris was waiting for us at Waterloo Station. He had brought along Jack Hylton, then England's number-one bandleader. Jack's band was lined up along the platform, to greet us. Luckily we were set up to play "God Save The King," so we skipped all the other luggage and hurried off the train with our instruments. The moment we began playing the British anthem, everybody in the station came to attention. There was no other sound. Even a switch engine ceased its busy chugging.

Jack Hylton must have suspected we'd have such a patriotic touch ready. When we finished the British anthem his band promptly answered with "The Star Spangled Banner." The melody was taken from an old British drinking song, "To Anacreon in Heaven," but Hylton's boys weren't too familiar with the ancient tune. They bogged down in the middle and we had to come to their rescue. We joined in on the last few lines, thereby finishing it nice and strong.

"Sorry about botching your national anthem," Hylton apologized to me after the handshakes and the reception ceremonies. "Hope you fellows don't feel angry about it."

"Forget it, Jack," I insisted. "After all, if it hadn't been for you British, we'd never have written the Star Spangled Banner!"

Three days later we got a star-spangled reception from our first British audience when we made our debut at the Capitol Cinema Theatre. I'd been worried because the stage was too small for the scenic effects we had brought all the way from America, and the motor working the electrically-operated curtain was slow, preventing a good start.

However, we opened fast and strong with "Follow the Swallow,"

—and I swallowed hard in disbelief to hear shouts of "Core!" "Core!" as we finished. Was that the Piccadilly version of the Bronx cheer? My face must have shown my reaction, for as we went into "Hello, Bluebird" a stagehand appeared in the wings, holding up a big cardboard sign on which was printed, "They're not booing. They mean *en*core."

After the show we encountered another unusual British custom. We were familiar with the Stage Door Johnnies lined up outside the theatre doors in New York; but in London it was women who lined up—Stage Door Jennies, let's call them. A flock of them were waiting for us with offers to show us dear old London town.

The next afternoon two solicitors, named Bull and Bevan, called on me to protest our jazz adaptation of the Gilbert and Sullivan *HMS Pinafore* music. "We represent Herbert Sullivan, who holds the copyright on his grandfather's music. It is his wish that you perform the music correctly or not at all."

"But I cleared all our music with your officials," I explained.

"Oh, playing *Pinafore* music is permitted, but not as you performed it! In jazz! Mr. Sullivan considers that a desecration, and we are prepared to have you fined accordingly."

"Well, how much would the fine be?"

"It could be as much as a thousand pounds," was the staggering answer.

By pleading ignorance of any offense, and invoking good will they owed to visiting Yankee cousins, I got off the hook.

"We'll advise Mr. Sullivan to drop the matter," they decided, "but on condition that you never play a jazz version of *Pinafore* again, even in the United States."

I kept that promise until we got back to New York. After all those orchestrations cost a lot of dough!

As the last-minute cablegram from William Morris had stated, we were also booked into a British musical called *By the Way* playing at the Apollo Theatre. It was a good show but its stage was also too small for our scenic effects. However, we hit our stride at the Kit Kat Club.

Chapter 38. MERRIE ENGLAND

A group of English noblemen had started the Kit Kat Club back in 1700. It had lapsed into obscurity, but in 1925, somebody sold the twentieth century descendents of its founders the idea of re-opening the Kit Kat as an exclusive club featuring the best in entertainment. It was a beautiful place with plenty of room for dancing, a writing room, a graceful balcony and an American style bar. It rapidly became the top club in London.

At eleven o'clock on the night of May 11th, the Kit Kat Club had its grand opening. There was a ribbon across the bandstand and no one—not even the band—could go on the stand until the ribbon had been cut. There were the usual speeches delivered by Generals, Admirals, Lords, Dukes and Earls. Everybody in royalty and society came to the Kit Kat Club. Although it was new, the Kit Kat Club quickly became the number one place for the elite.

When all the speeches were over the Duke of Marlborough, who we found out was really the sponsor of the whole affair, was given a pair of scissors and he cut the ribbon, officially opening the club.

To conclude the ceremonies, the Duke of Marlborough presented me with a beautiful ivory baton and I started the band off with "God Save the King" and "The Star Spangled Banner." Then we got the dancing and the fun under way with a song the British loved, "Sweet Georgia Brown." British reserve melted swiftly in the hot wave of jazz.

Later that night the Duke of Marlborough confided to me he'd been worried about using an American band to inaugurate the club, so the good reception we got meant as much to him as to us. A wonderfully easy man to talk with, the Duke became our good friend—and a pretty good substitute band leader. We learned something about human nature: everybody likes to lead a band. When news of his hobby made the London papers, quite a few titled Englishmen went in for baton waving when they visited the Kit Kat.

Friendly as the British were toward us, they knew where to draw the line with sharp decisiveness. On reaching London, I first put up at the fine old Piccadilly Hotel. I wasn't there two weeks before a famous American comedian of that day and a taxicab-tycoon friend of his arrived there and gave my name as a reference. When the hotel management checked with me, I gave the comedian my endorsement.

That same night they threw one of the loudest parties ever held in staid old London. At 2 A.M., when whisky bottles and phonograph records started raining out the windows the hotel went into action and tossed the entire crowd out into the Square. I saw the damage to the rooms the next day—and had my personal evidence of how a few misbehaving American tourists can give the rest of us a bad name!

With three dates to fill the only way I could get in any sightseeing was to walk through the town after we closed at the Kit Kat Club. Unlike New York, London was perfectly safe in the milkman hours. One beautiful May night I was out walking when I heard some wonderful harmonica sounds up ahead! There were certain special trills and effects that only one person in the world could produce, so I hurried my pace and sure enough, there was Borah Minnevich! With him were the dancers, Tony and Nina De Marco. They had just arrived in London. Delighted to see one another, we hailed a cab in order to keep the evening going at a spot I knew about. As it whizzed past, we saw that it was occupied. However, it came to a stop, then backed its way to our group.

"I say, Vincent," a pleasant voice called out, "can I share this cab with you and your friends? Cabs are hard to get this time of night."

It was the Earl of Essex and Sussex, whom I knew from the Kit Kat Club. He joined us.

Finding such vaudeville talent as Minnevich and the De Marcos got the production wheels going in my mind. Here was a chance to put that scenery we had carted across the ocean, to some use. When I asked William Morris whether he could get us something to replace our engagement at the Capitol Theatre he called up a Mr. Gillespie, who ran the London Hippodrome and made a deal for me to appear there with a full show—my orchestra and my scenic effects and Borah Minnevich, the De Marcos, Aileen Stanley and the Stanton Brothers.

The show was an improvisation—no plot to speak of, just an authentic representation of American entertainment and American jazz. Titled "The Jazzmaster," it played to enthusiastic theatre applause though it got mixed reviews. However, the Manchester *Guardian* critic understood what we were trying to put across:

"Nothing more solidly American has ever happened in London," he said. "Everything in the show is American, and it's as brassy and noisy as that young nation can get. American jazz seems to be concerned with the output of sheer noise and eccentric sounds. There are some among us who cherish the hope that when the children of jazz grow out of the nursery stage they will scream a little less lustily. However, the audience loved every minute of it, even when the whole devastating artillery of jazz sends some of us into shell shock.

"The musicians are widely skilled in the use of many instruments, even to their use for comic effects. Nor do they limit themselves to the musical form of art. At one time last night, a violinist laid aside his violin and revealed himself as a cartoonist! While the orchestra played a hectic jazz tune, he sketched a caricature of Mr. Lopez!" (Poor Xavier didn't get name credit for his art.)

"The maestro made a good subject for the 'sitting.' Despite the fierce beat of the music and the furious syncopation of the entire band, Mr. Lopez never relaxes a stoic calm onstage. He might be likened to a block of stone standing impeturbably in a wave of rushing sound. It is a marvelous use of the unexpected—a fine touch of showmanship."

What the *Guardian's* reviewer didn't know was that my "stoic calm" was my attempt to adopt British reserve and dignity. It was another phase I went through in the process of growing up; trying to be a type I admired instead of being myself. This led me into splurging on British clothes, discarding my American belts for British "braces," and acquiring some spiffy weskits. I so wanted to identify with them, that I even rented a "flat" at 49 Pall Mall, hired a butler, and to complete my British metamorphosis, started drinking tea for breakfast. This could have been excused as a defense measure. The "coffee" that butler of mine made would have killed me!

My adoption of British reserve went too far one evening at the Hippodrome. Just as I came offstage, to stand in the wings and watch the next act, a lovely young lady walked up to me and pleasantly said, "Hello, Mr. Lopez. I'm Lady Peel."

"How cha do," I responded ever so casually. When I looked back over my shoulder Lady Peel had vanished—and also vanished was my chance to meet England's superb entertainer, Bea Lillie!

One Sunday evening at the Savoy Plaza, I saw a Maharajah with a bevy of attractive Indian girls. Then I let go of my assumed British reserve and gave one of them a fascinated look. The Maharajah called me over and said, "Do you like this girl? She's yours!" And I think he meant it; but I didn't try to find out.

A place I got fond of was the Cabaret Club, the gathering place for London's Bohemian crowd. It was downstairs, a full flight, and the approaching customer was seen feet first. This produced an interesting betting game at a shilling a chance. The idea was to tell, when a woman's shoes started coming down the stairs, if she was British, or American. The British girls I got to know were experts at it. They beat me repeatedly, for the contours of the legs as they appeared one step at a time, proved too distracting to me.

We knew we were a genuine hit with the British when our band was invited to play for the Commemoration Ball marking the 400th anniversary of Christ College at Oxford University. Though our biggest disappointment on the trip over had been the absence of the Prince of Wales on a trip to Africa, the Commemoration Ball brought us the chance to meet Queen Mary, who graciously told us she enjoyed our music.

I found out later that the ball was just one of several functions she had presided over in that twenty-four hour period. Despite that heavy schedule and her advanced years, she looked as fresh as a British landscape.

Still we were glad to be going home though we all wanted to return to England again. I had become quite homesick for New York; so instead of applying for extended visas, we decided to close on schedule and sail back aboard the S. S. *Paris*.

Closing night at the Kit Kat didn't start off very well for me. I made a faux pas of the first order when a group of American stars dropped in for a visit. Sessue Hayakawa was one of them, and after complimenting him on his latest picture I turned to Mae Murray. Opening my mouth to say something equally nice, I put my foot in it.

"Don't you remember me, Miss Murray?" I asked. "I once worked as a part-time pianist at the Vitagraph Studios at Fort Lee to play mood music for stars like you and Olga Petrova and Pauline Fredericks."

"How interesting," Miss Murray acknowledge with a big smile. "It's strange I don't remember you, though."

"Well," I blundered, *"I was just a kid then!"*

Hours later I was still trying to forget my inane remark when two rather seedy-looking young men asked me over to their table. They seemed out of place there, and I wondered if they were out of money as well. It wouldn't have been the first time a stranded pair had asked me to sign the tab for them.

"My name's Campbell," one of them announced, "and my pal here is Connelly. That's how we hope to become known—as the songwriting team of Campbell and Connelly."

"Is it a song of yours you want me to introduce here—" I interrupted.

"Not here," Connelly explained. "We want you to introduce one of ours back in America. Frankly, we haven't had much luck with it over here."

"What makes you think it would go any better in the States?"

"You're familiar with the biblical remark that a prophet hath no honor in his own village?" said Campbell. "We're not known in our country, but if you introduce our song in America as the work of a famous pair of British composers, who'll know the difference? Besides that, we'll give you a third royalty interest in the song."

"You've got gumption making a proposition like this," I said.

"Beg pardon. We've got what?"

"Gumption," I explained, "is an American word meaning nerve."

"I see," he replied. "Over here, we call it 'cheek.'"

"Whatever it is, you've got it," I laughed. "I'll give your song a fair look, but don't count on anything."

"We want you to count on something, though," they replied. "Third ownership of the song. Here's a contract we brought along that we'll sign right now if you say so."

Visions of creditor swarms waiting for me at the Battery made the last remark interesting.

"It's a deal," I said. "What's the name of the tune? Sometimes a good title helps put it across."

"Maybe we could change it," said Connelly. "We call it 'Show Me the Way to Go Home.'"

"Don't change a word of it," I told them "'Show Me the Way to Go Home!' It suits me just fine, for we're going home tomorrow."

Needless to say, "Show Me the Way to Go Home" became one of the all time hits. There's hardly a language it hasn't been sung in. It made me a nice piece of change and zoomed Campbell and Connelly to the top in the British music-publishing field.

Aside from its great success, though, it was the perfect number to come across as we closed our trip to England.

Chapter 39. "WELCOME HOME"

Three days out on the Atlantic, taking a close look at the financial results of our London trip, I discovered that I had a long swim ahead of me to get out of my Sea of Red Ink. I was in a low mood when I got this cable from Henry Spitzer: TO WELCOME YOUR RETURN HAVE PREPARED PARADE UP BROADWAY AND BIG RECEPTION AT PENNSYLVANIA HOTEL HAVE BAND IN GOOD SHAPE TO MEET THE PRESS.

I kept expenses down with my three-word reply: ARE YOU CRAZY? —knowing Henry would understand that money matters were bothering me. Back came his three-worder: ALL IS WELL.

Then I *knew* he was crazy!

But Henry was in full possession of his faculties, for Mr. Statler underwrote the gala party at the hotel on our arrival night, and the only expense I had to cover was for two double-deck Fifth Avenue busses that met us as we docked at the pier.

I can still get emotional over the welcome-home we got. So for a touch of objective reporting, suppose we let a flashback to the *New York World* of August 2, 1925 tell what happened:

"When Vincent Lopez and his orchestra returned from their London engagement yesterday, a group of people from show business, regular business, and the political business met them at the pier. Once past the customs, the Lopez band members set up shop on the roof garden of a Fifth Avenue bus, second in line to a bus housing Joe Basile's brass band. After an exchange of musical greetings that followed the customary handshakes and welcoming speeches, the busses wheeled toward Broadway, the Basile and Lopez bands being followed by a caravan of cars carrying the attending celebrities.

"A convoy of taxis scurried alongside the busses and cars, with photographers snapping their cameras at any likely-looking news shot as we rolled up Broadway to 33rd Street, then west to the Hotel Pennsylvania where a big reception preceded the party to be given the returning wanderers in the evening.

"The Lopez music is still its same recognizable self, but young Mr. Lopez isn't. He has gone British on us, with his Bond Street suits, colored handkerchief, turn-down fedora hat, white spats and cane. This magnificent sartorial change had only one disadvantage. Some of his old pals down at the pier to greet him didn't even recognize him!

"This reporter managed to hurtle through the admiring throng at the Pennsylvania Roof last night and get a few words from Mr. Lopez about his London trip, in between sips he took at a cup of tea —a habit he picked up on his travels.

" 'What did I enjoy most about London?' he repeated our opening question. 'Well, I learned how to live! They do things right over there. No rush. No hurry. Take your time and you get just as much accomplished. We hurry too much over here and probably get less done. When I went overseas I was near a nervous breakdown. The British taught me how to lead a quiet life and get just as much accomplished. Relax. Take it easy. That's their secret. Now if you'll excuse me, I got a million things to do. . . .' "

One of the million things on my schedule that night was meeting the members of the music-publishing world who were out in full force, from song pluggers to the publishers themselves. It was an old familiar story they told, in a language I well understood: their reasons why the numbers they were promoting couldn't miss. Hence, when Henry Spitzer beckoned me to a corner table and introduced me to Morse Preeman, a music publisher from Los Angeles, I expected more of the same theme, whatever the variations. What I heard was new, strange music to my ears.

"Mr. Lopez," Preeman remarked after Henry left, "this isn't the first time we've met, but it's the first time you've met me. I've met you through your music and through some writeups on you that I've read."

"You sound like a Lopez fan," I smiled. "Please go on."

"I intend to," Preeman stated. "For your own good, I want you to listen to me carefully. I know from the newspaper writeups that you had spiritual training as a youth but I surmise that it has become rather secondary in your life."

"I guess that's true," I admitted. "I'm still interested in spiritual things but I don't find time for that side of life. I stay very busy."

"That's where you're making your mistake," he replied. "I'm not saying this to be dramatic, but unless you go back to the spiritual side of life—find a better way of living and thinking—you'll be through in a short time!"

"What do you mean, through?" I challenged. "We're just about tops in the music field. We're on radio, in vaudeville; we've got the best spot in New York here at the Pennsylvania Hotel. Are you kidding or just looking for an argument? I haven't got time for that."

"I'm saying this in your best interest," Preeman insisted. "Look how many careers vanish overnight in show business, or slide down to oblivion in a few years. Sometimes it's a lack of true talent, but often it isn't. It's something else. It's a lack of sincerity, it's a shallowness, an emptiness that the public detects. I needn't argue with you about it. You know it happens."

He had me stumped there, for it does happen. Here today, gone tomorrow is the fatalistic slogan of show business.

"All right, then, so we won't argue about it," I agreed, suddenly getting a new perception of what Preeman meant. "But what do you suggest? I admit I find a good part of my life empty and superficial. What am I supposed to do? Go back to the monastery?"

"That's out of the question," Preeman agreed. "And while it's a life of dedication, it can be a narrow path for some people. No, Lopez. I don't propose that you change your present way of living except to deepen and expand it. Otherwise you run the danger of becoming a very shallow, self-centered person. Haven't you suspected that, yourself?"

"It can certainly happen in this game," I admitted. "But I have no specific religious convictions to live by, if you're trying to say I should go to church regularly."

"It wouldn't be a bad idea at all," he countered. "I won't tell you to do it, though. That's a decision a man must make for himself."

"Then how am I to develop this interest in spiritual things?" I questioned. "What else do you have in mind?"

"Books," he answered. "The great books of all time and of all people. The books that express man's deepest thoughts about life, the meaning of things. The busier a man is with his personal career, as you are, the greater his need for books so he doesn't grow self-centered and thereby become shallow and superficial."

"I know something is missing in my life," I admitted, "but I'm not sure books can supply it. Why do you say I'm through unless I change my way of thinking?"

"Because you're like a kite flying through the air without a steady force to hold the line," he replied. "Sooner or later, an unguided kite smashes into the earth or gets tangled in a tree."

"I know what you mean," I admitted. "I've come pretty close to personal disaster a few times. Not a physical accident, but circumstances where I could have drifted off into a lot of trouble."

This was no exaggeration. There were hopheads, prostitutes, grifters and petty criminals in my coming-up years in Brooklyn and Buffalo. Some stronger force in my life had prevailed against their influence, but I couldn't be sure of that protection indefinitely if I rambled along without inner guidance.

"It's a soap bubble world I live in," I admitted. "Maybe you've made a point for me to think about. What books would you recommend I start with? Make it simple because I've been away from the deep stuff a long time, since I got out of St. Mary's."

"Well, how about something spiritual, mystical, and yet exciting?" Preeman suggested. "I'll send you a copy of a book I started with. It was written in 1886 by a man named Phylos and was about the lost continent of Atlantis."

"You mean that old legend about a continent west of Africa that sank thousands of years ago?" I smiled.

"It was more than a legend," Preeman replied. "Some of the greatest Greek historians and philosophers believed in Atlantis, Plato among them. In fact, after you read this book, I want you to go on from there and read what Plato wrote about Atlantis."

"Sounds interesting," I admitted. "But why should I read a book about a lost continent, anyway?"

"To acquire the first value of all learning," he explained. "Humility! To find out that we're not the ultimate in civilized man, talented man, educated and sensitive man: that a far greater civilization preceded ours and was lost in a wink of time, so to speak. The book I have in mind tells the story of that civilization, the story of Atlantis."

"Sounds as if it might be interesting," I agreed. "I'd like to read it."

"Good," he replied. "I'll send it to you as soon as I return to California. But don't stop with just this book. Let it act as a spur to your reading interests, and go on from there to even greater books."

"It's a promise," I agreed. "And thank you for your interest in me. Maybe this is what I've been looking for—this greater understanding of myself through good literature. By the way, what's the name of the book you'll send me? I'll be watching for it."

"You'll have it in a week," Preeman promised. "You'll find the title somewhat mystical. It's called 'Dweller on Two Planets.' "

Morse Preeman kept his promise and his prediction. He sent me "Dweller on Two Planets" and I found it fascinating. The story of Atlantis that it unfolded brought books back into my life. And with the great books of the world, the great people of the world came into my life. The mystery and spiritual halo that surrounds our existence if we but take the time to look up and behold it—that, too, became part of me as a new horizon slowly took shape and the narrow path of my own existence crossed the paths of my fellow men as we travel the steep hill toward Destiny.

This change in my outlook and my interests didn't take place overnight. Few lasting changes do. But Preeman had given me a start in that new direction, a flicker of interest in mankind that slowly grew into a flame—and then a torch that lit the road for me toward a better and a fuller life.

Religion has done it for many people. Dedication in other forms has been the light for many more. For me, great books of mystical design and spiritual quest formed the bridge that I hope has taken me from the ignorance of selfishness and the narrowness of prejudice over to the side of compassion and understanding that accepts man as he is.

The greatest Teacher of all history gave us that lone command: that we shall love one another.

Toward the end of the party, Henry Spitzer gave me some wonderful news, all the better because it was unexpected. While we were London-bound for ten weeks he had applied every cent of my side-income (royalties, bands, etc.) against my outstanding debts. I was now not only in the clear; I even had a modest bank account!

"You're a genius, Henry!" I enthused. "How did you do it?"

"You did it, Vincent," he said.

"I? How?"

"By getting out of New York for ten weeks!" he replied. "That's the secret of saving money in your case, Vince. Just leave this side-income alone. Make believe you're still in London!"

I wish I had followed his advice, or kept him on as my financial manager. However, he was wanted back in his job at Witmark's where regular hours and security beckoned. We remained the best of friends, and throughout all his life he asked me to do him only one favor. He had fallen in love with a German waltz that no one would touch in the jazz-frantic twenties. I began featuring it on the air and we found that Henry had been right. "*Zwei Herzen in Dreiviertel-takt*" became America's favorite waltz, "Two Hearts Beat in Three-Quarter Time."

Lovely Beryl Halley had met me at the pier, when we returned to New York but she missed most of the party at the Pennsylvania Roof that evening because of her own show. I made a date to meet her later at Gray's Drugstore. The news Henry Spitzer gave me that I was solvent again created a temporary resolve to stay that way, and part of the resolve meant fewer dates all around, less expensive dates when I did have them. Beryl understood.

"Let's just be friends, Vincent," she agreed. "No demands by either of us, except when we really need each other. As for taking me out, we can skip the expensive places. It's all right with me if you—well, if you meet me at the Automat!"

We didn't try to settle for mere "platonic friendship." It would have been silly to try it with such a beautiful girl as Beryl Halley. However, we saw each other less frequently, and with a bit less intensity. Our love affair was burning with a smaller though a steadier flame.

Beryl was one of Ziegfeld's most beautiful showgirls, and it seemed strange to me that despite our many dates I had never met her boss. Beryl fixed that a few weeks later by having me call for her at the theatre while he was still there. We walked into his sumptuous private office.

Flo Ziegfeld was never the one to make the other person feel comfortable.

"Oh, you're the orchestra leader who's been dating Beryl," he sized me up. "I have a rule against our girls going out with men from show business. They're better off meeting millionaires who want to marry them."

"Well, I'm no millionaire, I admit, but on the other hand I don't want to get married."

Ziegfeld never did figure out that remark. To tell the truth, neither did I. It was a spur-of-the-moment sentence.

Ten minutes later, with the conversation on thicker ice, I skated out toward the thin edge again by intimating that I'd like to have my orchestra in a Ziegfeld show. His counter-suggestion was that I might like to invest in the next Follies production. There matters ended.

I did play for the great Ziegfeld, however, at the time of the laying of the cornerstone of the Ziegfeld Theatre on Sixth Avenue. We taxied the entire band over from the Pennsylvania Hotel to play some famous song hits from past Follies shows. The customary courtesy check to cover expenses never arrived but I did form a lifelong friendship with Bernie Sobel (press agent for Flo at the time) which money couldn't buy.

All this time we had been extending our radio coverage, for I was convinced it was the shortcut to national recognition. Right after our London return, I ran into a two-horned dilemma that was bound to hurt no matter how I resolved it. The head of Keith Vaudeville, E. F. Albee, fashioned it.

"Make up your mind, Lopez," he insisted, when I met him at his office. "You can play vaudeville or you can play radio, but not both! You've got six weeks more under your contract with us. No renewal unless you get off the air."

"But people can't *see* us on the air," I protested. "That's why I put so much money into scenic effects. They get to like our music on the radio; then I tell them about what a good visual show we have and they came to the theatre. How can you lose on that deal?"

"That may be true in your case," said Albee, "but what about other acts? If they're heard over radio, that's it. No, Lopez, radio and vaudeville can't both survive. It's one or the other. Now, which one do you want to stay with?"

"There's a lot more to it than that," I challenged. "Mr. Statler has been very good to us at the Pennsylvania Hotel and he's depending on us to stay on the air. I can't overlook that."

"Nor can you overlook the money you make in vaudeville," Albee countered. "Does Statler pay you three or four thousand a week? And what about the ten thousand you've got tied up in orders for new scenic effects? What'll you do with them if you're barred from vaudeville?"

"You'd go that far?" I questioned.

"Further, if necessary," he warned. "This is a life or death struggle between vaudeville and radio—and we don't intend to lose!"

"You've lost as far as I'm concerned. If we go off radio we'll be practically forgotten in a year. That's just the pragmatic side of it, besides my obligation to Mr. Statler."

"*Pragmatic* side of it?" Albee echoed. "Say, that trip to England really did change you, didn't it?"

"That's not the point," I replied. "There's room in show business for doing the right thing. And this might be right in more ways than one. Radio can make my band even bigger than it has been to date."

"I thought you'd be smarter than that," Albee concluded angrily. "Go ahead and stick with Statler and radio. You're committing professional suicide."

"Maybe I am. If you're right then I'm killing myself and my band. But you may be killing all vaudeville, for everybody in it!"

We finished out our six weeks on the Keith Circuit, then said good-bye to vaudeville. But there was no way to cancel the new scenery order. The best I could do was hold up delivery so I wouldn't have a storage problem. The red-ink tide was rising again!

Chapter 40. CASA LOPEZ

The next day the chance came along to sign a clarinetist I had long admired. The name on his union card read James Dorsey but we all knew him as Jimmy. He must have liked our group, for a day after joining us he got me aside and said, "My brother Tommy is looking around. How about adding him to the brass section?"

"I thought you two fellows were always fighting," I replied. "There's enough trouble at rehearsals without a couple of scrappy Irishmen."

"We have our differences of opinion," Jimmy admitted, "but you've got our promise, Vince. You hire Tommy and we'll always be on our good behavior. First sign of trouble between us, fire us both."

So Tommy Dorsey joined our band, too, and there wasn't a single scrap between them while they were with us.

To meet my next instalment on the vaudeville scenery I had ordered and now couldn't use, I needed a $4000 loan—in the usual hurry. Two New York banks heard my proposition with horror: money to pay for equipment for vaudeville appearances I'd never make! It looked as if I'd land back in the clutches of the loan sharks again until Joe Gold, my pianist, found that Gene Geiger (a one-time theatrical producer) would lend me the money at a reasonable six percent.

It was a satisfying deal all around. I got the dough I needed; Gene got it back in ninety days with interest; and I gave Joe a raise in pay.

The first loan led to another . . . another . . . then another. Gene Geiger and I became pretty good friends.

"Look, Vince," he said, one evening when Beryl and I were visiting him at his ornate apartment on 47th Street, "you have a terrific radio following. You proved that in vaudeville where they always came out to see you; and you know it from the Pennsylvania Hotel. Why not capitalize on that popularity and open a night club?"

"In this town?" I questioned. "With the competition the way it is! Tex Guinan at her club! Jimmy Durante at the Club Dover! Harry Richman at his place! Jack White with the Club 18! We'd get murdered."

"Not with your radio following," Gene insisted. "Besides, it's your chance to use all those scenic effects you're paying storage on."

I told him to go ahead provided he could get the only spot in town I was interested in—the Rue de la Paix on 54th Street west of Broadway, which had a stage big enough for my scenic effects.

Geiger got the location for half its original cost. I'll never forget the night I got the news—October 5th, 1925. I was in Philadelphia conducting the pit orchestra, augmented with some of my key men, at the Fox Theatre. That night I was giving a party in my suite in the Adelphia Hotel, for the cast of *Rose Marie* and those of my musicians who had come down with me. In the midst of it the phone rang. It was Geiger telling me we had a night club, and urging me to take the next train to New York. I left the party going full blast, hopped the train for New York and signed as a night-club proprietor.

I was back in Philadelphia the next morning about 10 o'clock, and was met by a very sober-faced A.W. Baylitz, manager of the Adelphia. He had been one of my strongest sponsors at the Pennsylvania when he was manager there. I couldn't figure out what was bothering Baylitz. I'd never seen him so angry. When he said, "I want you to come up to your suite and look it over," I was more puzzled than ever.

What I saw was unbelievable. There was coffee on the walls, the chandeliers were swinging loose from their sockets and twisted into fantastic shapes. The furniture was broken. My clothes were strewn over the floor. I was told that one of the boys had tried to force my trunk out through the window. Luckily for me it wouldn't fit.

The damage bill came to four hundred dollars. I read the riot act to the boys who had staged the ruckus. I told them exactly how much I'd deduct from their pay each week until I got back the four hundred, and exactly how fast they'd be bounced out of my band if it ever happened again. To my surprise, they welcomed the discipline! Some musicians never grow out of the teen-age phase, and actually want a strong hand that allows plenty of leeway but pulls them up short of real trouble.

I felt a real thrill when the Casa Lopez was ready for our opening night. It was mine—in partnership, it's true—but something I owned and could work at building and improving. It was the realization of a dream that had sent my father and millions of emigrants like him, to a new world of hope and opportunity.

The Casa Lopez needed no "building and improving" in a physical sense. On opening night Mrs. Rudolph Valentino called it "The most enchanting room in the entire world."

The large foyer struck an immediate note of simple elegance. Its main furnishing was a $10,000 Ampico electric player piano that constantly provided piano music I had recorded for the Ampico Company. The piano was flanked by wall cabinets containing collector's items from all over the world. It was the only night club where people lingered as much as half an hour in the foyer, enjoying the music and the things to see.

On walking up a broad stairway to the Casa Lopez itself, the visitor's next point of interest was a radiant nude painted by Willy Pogany. There were other Pogany nudes to linger on when the visitor made the turn in the stairway and went up another half flight to the main floor. Pogany had fashioned the Casa after the Gardens of Versailles which Louis IV built for Madame Du Barry. The live greenery and the statuary brought a touch of Old World charm right to Broadway; it was quite a job and an expense, too, keeping the shrubbery alive indoors.

But outstanding in the decorative scheme were Pogany's murals and paintings. His nudes were in perfect taste. Pogany's work so impressed William Randolph Hearst that he commissioned him to decorate his estate at Wyntoon, California. For Hearst he did a Bavarian Garden surrounding a great oval lawn; and the murals portrayed the nursery tale of Goldilocks!

Although we had indirect lighting softly reflecting from the ceiling frescos, we also installed chandeliers in delicate French design that wealthy patrons later duplicated in their homes. Don't blame me if my enthusiasm carries me away. To a young man who less than ten years before had played piano in sawdust-floor saloons, the Casa Lopez was beautiful beyond description; but all that's left to tell of it today is words.

Our band played at one end of the room, backed up by a large stage. The big dance floor in the center was slightly elevated with a perimeter of tables around it, straight back to the Pogany-decorated walls.

On the floor above the Casa was another fabulous room for private banquets, laid out as a Spanish garden. Mayor Jimmy Walker brought important visitors from Spain to this room and their enthusiasm proved we hadn't let our friend Jimmy down.

But for me, the top floor topped everything, personally, for it was a luxurious double-apartment penthouse—one for Gene Geiger, one for me. Geiger was used to such quarters but for me the transition was an unbelievable switch to Shangrila! I resolved to do a lot more "living" and entertaining at home.

I was thrilled by our opening, but one member of our band didn't share my feelings. Xavier Cugat suffered a letdown when he learned that the "relief" band he would lead (an innovation we started in order to provide continuous music when our main orchestra took intermissions) would be hidden behind a scrim.

Our purpose was to make his tangos and soft Spanish music all the more alluring, but some jokers sold Cugat the idea we thought he was not good-looking enough to front a band! He retreated into a shell of grievance until the story came out and I convinced him there was nothing to it by putting him right in the floor show doing a violin specialty. He hasn't stopped grinning since. We also used his gift for sketching caricatures, and many a celebrity whom everything else failed to stir up went away happy with a profile by Cugie. The great George Arliss was so pleased with Cugat's first effort that he returned for more from other facial angles. Jimmy Walker was another fan of Cugat's artistry.

Besides other instrumental features that included Lopez at the piano, our show provided vocal entertainment by Gene Austin and the Radio Franks, the dance magic of Fowler and Tamara, and Frank Libuse for comedy. More about him later.

The show had to be good that night of October 15, 1925, to click with our opening night audience of connoisseurs. Show business was represented by Harry Richman, Jimmy Durante, Tex Guinan, Eddie Cantor, Phil Baker, Jack Haley, Bill Gaxton, Earl Carroll, George White, Sophie Tucker, Al Jolson, Irene Bordoni . . . but why go on? The Fourth Estate also turned out in force and we got good reviews from Walter Winchell, Ed Sullivan, Mark Hellinger, Heywood Broun, Karl Kitchen, et al.

An obscure comedian I had discovered at Edelweiser's in Chicago stole most of the honors that evening, the laugh honors, at least. The zany antics of Frank Libuse were unknown here, and we kept him under wraps, without a single line of publicity, until the première.

Part of his act was to pretend to be a waiter. He would greet a distinguished-looking couple at the entrance, walk them all over the place looking for just the right table—then suddenly lead them into the kitchen. There one of our regular waiters would rescue them before they got too peeved by the comedy bit.

Perhaps Frank's next couple would be seated promptly enough but there would be trouble with the menu. First Frank would hand it to the woman, then grab it from her with the remark that she wasn't paying the check anyway, and give it to the man, but take it back and tear it in two, presenting a half to each.

The more distinguished-looking the male guest, the more likely it was that Frank would frisk him for a flask—and usually find one! (The Casa served no liquor but we provided the rest of the setups.) A genius for sizing up the people who would stand for his nonsense, Libuse would pick the right woman for his crowning comedy touch in which he went into a passionate embrace and proclaimed his sudden but undying love.

Not even the celebrities escaped Frank. The night of our première, Mayor Jimmy Walker came in with a party of nine. Frank Libuse promptly went to work on them. Allowing enough time for the first drinks to be poured, Frank announced that their table was needed elsewhere! He whisked it up over his head and out toward the kitchen. That left poor Jimmy and his guests holding ten drinks with no table to rest them on. It also revealed a number of bottles tucked away under their chairs.

Jimmy was the first to realize it was a gag. He broke out laughing and that was the signal for the entire crowd to roar. Libuse walked back in to replace the table—with the smallest one he could find. While he was trying to help the group place their drinks (and bottles) on the impossibly small space, our regular waiters came back with the big table and chased poor Libuse right out of the club.

There was another celebrity, however, whom Frank Libuse left alone. She was a very shy person, and Frank's great human understanding exempted her from his "act." I didn't, though. I went over to her table and asked if she had a favorite song she'd like our band to play. She immediately named "Let Me Call You Sweetheart."

After we played it, she thanked us and I asked her why it was her favorite song. Was there a secret romance the public didn't know about? "No romance, Mr. Lopez," explained Gertrude Ederle (the first woman to swim the English Channel). "But my father had a record player in the boat that followed me—and that's the song that cheered me all the way across."

Our second triumph came when Gene Austin scored a hit with "My Blue Heaven," the wonderful new song we introduced for our show opener. Fowler and Tamara's dancing scored as big a hit. Finally came the test of our vaudeville routines. As the lights dimmed and the band picked up an exciting tempo, the curtain in back opened revealing Old North Church in Boston with a lantern blinking in the tower. This was the moment of decision! Would blasé New York nightclubbers go for that? Their delighted murmurs of surprise grew in volume as Paul Revere came on the scene, riding hard to warn the countryside of the approaching British. Paul was on a live horse, and the horse on a hidden treadmill that kept him from galloping offstage. House after house sped by on the moving scenery, with Paul Revere calling his alarm—and the music rising to a crescendo. At the very peak of excitement, the curtains closed slowly and the music finished on a note of victory.

The Casa Lopez was the biggest hit of Broadway!

Chapter 41. GOOD-BYE TO HOTEL PENNSYLVANIA

"Saturday Night Is the Loneliest Night in the Week" wasn't written about the night-club business. Sunday is the lonesome night, and we tried to brighten it by making it Celebrity Night at the Casa Lopez. Many a headliner helped us out, and was helped, in turn, by the chance to break in new material and see how it would go.

Running short on outside celebrities one night, we used our own Arthur Schutt to present "his interpretation" of Gershwin's *Rhapsody in Blue*. Arthur was the other pianist of the Lopez orchestra and he loved the chance to do some solo work of his own. His number went over big.

But when Arthur stepped forward on the dance floor to take his bows, Oscar Levant, a Casa guest that night, walked behind Arthur, sat down at the piano, and played the same piece. Being a close friend of George Gershwin's, Levant knew exactly how George intended his Rhapsody to be interpreted. His competing version outshone poor Arthur's.

Arthur sat down at a ringside table, undecided what to do. Levant had intended it as a joke, but Arthur took it as a professional insult. He glowered there as Levant played on, and when his rival stood up and bowed to the terrific applause, poor Art couldn't restrain his anger. He raced up with his fists swinging. Luckily, a couple of waiters and Frank Libuse broke it up. Schutt went steaming off while Levant just laughed it off. The press played up the episode and the Casa Lopez profited from the publicity. Some reporters even accused us of staging it.

We did, however, manufacture quite a few stunts to keep us in the papers. Remembering the Maharajah I had met at the Savoy in London, we dressed up a handsome Italian lad as an Arabian sheik and had him visit the Club every Sunday night. Two beautiful blondes always accompanied him. They saw to it that he got a ringside table; they translated the menu for him; they argued with the waiters—and the head waiter—on just how the sheik's special dishes were to be prepared; and then they "tasted" each dish as it was placed on the table to be sure their sheik wasn't being poisoned. The blondes didn't order anything for themselves—and that in itself is news in a night club. Instead, while their lord and master dined it was their duty to entertain him with fascinating conversation and flatter him with adoring looks. The sheik took all this in his stride, as if indifferent to such special treatment.

Actually, he loved the job—and why not? It paid twenty-five dollars plus a good meal. In those early days of his career such things were appreciated by that handsome young boy—whose name happened to be George Raft.

Whether the gentlemen from the press were credulous or skeptical, whether they ribbed us or played it straight, gags like this got the Casa Lopez in the papers.

By an item in his New York *Graphic* sports column, Ed Sullivan (who met his lovely wife Sylvia at the Casa Lopez) started an argument which wasn't settled until months later on the Atlantic City boardwalk. I had told Ed how, during World War I, I escaped the hoodlums who tried to mug me on Broadway by outracing them two blocks to the safety of the Pekin Restaurant. When I guessed-out-loud that I could still do the "hundred" in eleven seconds, Joe Moore —International Indoor Skating champion for six years—who doubled at odd jobs around the Casa Lopez, expressed doubt that *he* could do it in better than twelve seconds, even though he had been a sprinter and had stayed in top physical shape.

Sullivan picked it up from there with an item about the orchestra leader (me!) who could run faster than a professional athlete (Joe). This drew a lot of "doubting Thomas" mail so Ed arranged a race between Joe and me on a Sunday afternoon at Atlantic City. The local papers gave it quite a buildup. Mayor Bader himself fired the starting gun, and we ran the measured distance between a crowd that lined the boardwalk. I must have imagined those would-be muggers were still chasing me down Broadway, for I actually beat Joe to the tape by a couple of feet! Ed Sullivan got all the copy he needed for his sports column that day, and the Casa Lopez got a lot of publicity out of it.

In his poem "Resignation," Matthew Arnold wrote:

Yet they, believe me, who await
No gifts from Chance,
Have conquered Fate!

Put me down as someone who hasn't conquered Fate, under this definition, for Chance has brought me many gifts and the greatest gift of all—friendship.

In Christmas week of 1925 our band played for the Cholly Knickerbocker Milk Fund Party, Mrs. William Randolph Hearst's special philanthropy. The place was the Plaza Hotel and everybody who was anybody attended. Maury Paul (Cholly Knickerbocker) told me that society would be out in full force, so we surprised them with an opening number they certainly wouldn't associate with a dance band—the *1812 Overture* . . . in dance tempo! It drew a round of applause before we finished the first sixteen bars.

My band was set up right in the middle of the floor, with the crowds dancing around us. If I surprised society with our opening selection, society surprised me when the fashionable, very lovely, and very blonde Clara Bell Walsh (called Clarabell by her friends) walked straight across the floor, dragging a chair, which she placed next to me at the piano. She sat there all through our performance and carried on a conversation as if I'd known her all my life. It was anything but the stiff reception I'd been worried about from this crowd.

When I finished my piano solo, Clara Bell insisted on introducing me to all her friends. I had grown up with a rather different view of what the cream of society would be like. I discovered that people who possess true culture invariably possess another quality—friendliness.

Maybe I presumed too much on friendliness. Before I left I asked Clara Bell Walsh if she'd be my guest at the Casa.

"That sounds nice," she smiled. "I'd love to come over some evening."

"Well, let's not make it just any evening," I blundered. "New

Year's Eve is only a few days off and I haven't a date. Will you be my guest that night?"

The smile disappeared for a second—or rather froze into a look of unbelief. Then it returned and Clara Bell said she'd try to make it. She realized I wasn't being fresh—just appallingly naive!

My remark about a dateless New Year's evening was true. Beryl Halley had her show to do and a special party Ziegfeld was throwing for the cast would keep her from seeing me until the following afternoon for our own New Year celebration.

So I anxiously watched for Clara Bell Walsh to arrive at the Club, half believing she really would. Finally toward five in the morning I gave up and wished I hadn't been such a fool.

I wrote off Clara Bell as a person who had offered polite cordiality but nothing more. I was wrong.

The New Year wasn't quite a week old when one afternoon, as we were rehearsing some songs that would become the hits of 1926 (Ray Henderson's "Birth Of The Blues," Gershwin's "Sunny Disposish," and Berlin's "I'd Climb The Highest Mountain") Joe Moore broke in to say I was wanted on the telephone. I frowned my annoyance at the interruption.

"I tried to tell her to call back later," Joe explained, "but she says it's very important. Claims you know her—that she met you at the Milk Fund Benefit."

"What's her name?" I asked, half hoping it would be Clara Bell Walsh.

"A Mrs. R. T. Wilson," Joe remembered, rather slowly.

"Oh, *the* Mrs. R. T. Wilson," I said. "Just Mrs. 400 herself."

I had an idea that Mrs. Wilson might want our band for some social event but the news was even better. She and Clara Bell Walsh were over at the Embassy Club—and would I care to join them! They had their answer ten minutes later when I hurried out of a taxi and into one of the dearest friendships of my life. When Clara Bell greeted me with her warmest of smiles, I realized that a Happy New Year had simply come a bit late for me in 1926 . . .

Clara Bell was my guest at the Casa Lopez a few nights later, but she arrived much earlier than I had anticipated, and with Mrs. R. T.

Wilson. Frank Libuse sized them up at once as perfect foils for his horseplay and he gave poor Clara Bell the full treatment. He got Mrs. Wilson seated very ceremoniously and then rushed around to Clara's side of the table, took her in his arms and bestowed a Rudolph Valentino kiss on her. Clara Bell's quick mind realized this was a gag and she went along with it. But Mrs. Wilson thought they had run into a West Side madman! She sat petrified in her chair and was ready to scream for help when I reached the scene, got Libuse to desist from his amorous pursuits and apologized for the gag.

Clara Bell loved it! A few nights later she brought Mrs. Vincent Astor over with a small group, on the condition that Frank would give her the same reception. Mrs. Astor enjoyed the joke, too, and arranged for us to play it on other friends of hers on subsequent nights.

And so a chance meeting with Clara Bell Walsh took me across the threshhold of a new world—a world of wealth and graciousness, a world of culture and charm.

Just about that time I needed a new friend, for I lost an old acquaintance in the comfortable and satisfying deal we had going for us at the Hotel Pennsylvania. All the while I was building up the Casa Lopez, our band played the earlier part of the evening (until ten) at the Hotel Pennsylvania Grill. We had NBC wires in both places and we thought one engagement would strengthen the other: that some of our listeners would come to see us at the Pennsylvania for dinner, while the late starters would call on us at the Casa Lopez. It worked out pretty much that way but E. M. Statler wasn't exactly delighted.

"Vincent," he explained to me on Christmas eve, "I've put this off as long as possible because we're good friends, but I'll have to ask you to make a difficult decision between continuing with us at the Hotel Pennsylvania or going on with your Casa Lopez. It's got to be one way or the other, starting January first."

"But why, Mr. Statler?" I protested. "You don't think our music has suffered here because we play at the club, too?"

"No, no, Vincent," he assured me. "Your music hasn't suffered a bit. But our patronage has. We're still doing very well at dinner but the after-supper business has fallen off to almost nothing. The plain fact is that people who used to come here after the theatre now go to the Casa Lopez. Your substitute band just doesn't attract them. That's no good when the original Lopez orchestra is playing in direct competition."

"I appreciate the fact you're being so frank about it," I answered. "It makes it easier for me to be frank, too."

"Meaning that you choose the Casa Lopez?" he questioned.

"Well, why not?" I replied. "It bears my name. That's been a dream of mine ever since I began playing the piano. Giving it up would mean waking up from a dream I might never have again. Do I seem ungrateful—for all you've done for me?"

"Not a bit, Vincent," he put his arm around my shoulder. "Now that you've made the decision let me say I think it's the right one. A man can do bigger and better things when he works for himself. That's the principle America was built on."

I asked him if he had anyone in mind to replace me and he said he had thought of putting in George Olsen, who was then an up-and-coming bandleader. I told him he'd made a fine choice. There were no hard feelings between Mr. Statler and me. I remember him as one of the best friends I've ever had, and he treated me like his own son. To him I'll be eternally grateful.

And so on the same New Year's Eve that I had hoped would bring Clara Bell Walsh into my life, we played our way out of the Hotel Pennsylvania Grill. Our finale was "Auld Lang Syne," and we did it with rather mixed emotions. Mr. Statler shook hands with each of us and wished us lots of luck. Then we packed our instruments in the customary rush and made a beeline for the familiar taxis that awaited us on 7th Avenue. "The Casa Lopez," I absentmindedly told my driver.

"Sure, Mr. Lopez," he answered, "sure, I know where you're going."

At the moment I wished *I* knew where we were going. The Pennsylvania Hotel had become home to us—and the Casa Lopez was still a big gamble.

Chapter 42. VINCENT LOPEZ PARTNERS

I saw many famous people get their start, but one of the starts I wasn't aware of was that of a sixteen-year-old page boy, Sam Pearlman, who became one of the outstanding theatre managers. I had a talk recently with him about his page-boy start at the Casa Lopez. I remembered it because of his skill in keeping my current dates separated, if two or more of them showed up at the same time. Once he successfully kept four at bay while I got off with a lovely dancer named Ruby Stevens whom Hollywood renamed Barbara Stanwyck.

But Pearlman remembered his Casa Lopez start because it set him up financially.

"Are you kidding?" I asked. "On twelve dollars a week!"

"Oh, it wasn't the salary," Sam explained. "It was the liquor."

"We didn't sell it," I protested. "We observed Prohibition all the way."

"Sure you did," Sam agreed, "but the customers didn't. They brought their own and they brought plenty. Often they'd leave some under the table when they left—sometimes even a full bottle. I'd keep watching for a likely crowd, then move in when they left and beat the waiter to whatever liquor remained. Two or three such hauls and I had a fifth to sell other customers who hadn't brought enough. At $20 a bottle, that can add up—but not as fast as the big tips I often collected."

Expenses were catching up and getting past me again, so when the Casa closed for the summer I took stock of my personal, professional, and financial affairs and decided to do something about the last.

When I took my problem to Attorney Julius Kendler who was a good friend and a top-flight lawyer for show-business people, he had a real understanding of what would be practical and what would be impossible in my case. He gave me no admonitions about my personal life or about my professional expenditures. The only substantial cutback I could make, he said, was to dissolve the unwieldy corporation I had formed several years before.

"No wonder you're broke, Lopez," Kendler said. "You have more people living off you than King Solomon! What are you trying to prove? That you're a big business man as well as an orchestra leader? Okay, if you've got the time for it, but otherwise I recommend that you file bankruptcy—not as an individual, but as a corporation." We worked out a plan that would ultimately pay off 100 cents on the dollar. We knew the papers would pick up the item, and to make sure of fair play Kendler worded a news release explaining that the bankruptcy of the Lopez corporation didn't mean that Lopez was personally broke. It pointed out that income from my activities which had previously gone into the corporation would thereafter accrue to me, once all claims had been satisfied. Nevertheless, the story grew that I was up to my ears in red ink.

Following a brief vacation, our band swung back into activity with a short vaudeville tour, then a prize date at the Arrowhead Inn at Saratoga, New York, during the height of the racing season. Playing the races wasn't the only sport indulged there in those days. Saratoga was a pocket-size edition of today's Las Vegas, with the swank society crowd at the track all afternoon, then going indoors at night in further quest of Lady Luck at the gambling tables.

I caught the fever, too. I went over to Tommy Dykes' place. I must have lost two or three hundred dollars and was about to finance a new stack of chips when Joe Moore told Dyke, who was a good friend of his, "There's Lopez over there at the crap table and he's losing."

Dyke came over to me, nudged my elbow and said, "You're Lopez, the orchestra leader, aren't you?"

"That's right," I admitted. "Nice place you've got here."

"Didn't I just read that you're in bankruptcy?" he went on.

"That's right, too," I admitted.

"Well, look, Vincent, I think your luck is suddenly gonna change. We don't want to take anybody who can't afford it, so play this same table a while longer and when you get back your money, quit. Understand?"

I got the message and to my surprise I won my money back in a few minutes. A real coincidence (!), and I thanked Mr. Dyke for it as I left.

There were a lot of society people in Saratoga. Quite a few of them had become Casa Lopez patrons, including my good friend Clara Bell Walsh. I added a number of new social-register friends, notably Mr. and Mrs. Joseph Widener. Their horsey talk got boring but I loved the attention they gave me. A society reporter from the New York *Graphic* spotted the news angle. Here's an extract from her column of August 25, 1926:

"Guess who is being lionized by the 400 at Saratoga this season. Vincent Lopez, the orchestra leader! The Wideners took him up after meeting him at Clara Bell Walsh's parties and he's been trotted out for all their friends to see quite regularly. Ella Widener simply adores him as a dancing partner, for Vincent's average height is just perfect for her tiny figure. At the Arrowhead Inn the other evening, Ella parked her chair right at the bandstand and wouldn't budge until Vincent desisted from his chores at the piano and danced an entire set with her. The crowd adored it. . . . Incidentally, if the maestro is bankrupt as the papers say, how come he has rented a beautiful cottage where he entertains not lavishly but quite intimately and well."

The very last day of the track season I was seated at a large table at the Club House with Clara Bell and several of her friends when a very polite man walked up to me and asked if I was Vincent Lopez. I told him I was and naively inquired if he wanted an autograph.

"Some other time, maybe," he replied, "but right now I've got something for *you*. This summons, answerable in New York City on September 30th."

The legal mumbo jumbo of the document puzzled me, but with the help of some of my friends at the table I deduced that several major stockholders (and creditors) of Lopez, Inc., planned to enjoin dissolution of the corporation unless I settled their claims within a month. I promptly forgot about such relatively slow things as race horses and put through a fast long distance call to Gene Geiger in the city. After all, the Casa Lopez was to reopen shortly, and he was concerned about legal red tape that might tie me up outside the state. Gene had plenty of money (he was then helping Warner Brothers finance the Vitaphone talking-picture process) and I asked him to lend me enough money to settle the mess outright.

"I thought you'd come to me sooner or later, Vincent," he remarked, "so I've been considering it and I've got a proposition for you. I'll put up the money and I'll get the right people to iron out the whole thing for you—but on one condition."

"Name it, Gene," I agreed. "Anything within reason."

"Oh, it's reasonable enough," he assured me. "Up to now we've been partners in just the club, but from here on I own half of *you*. Everything you earn from your activities, I get fifty per cent!"

"My corporation's been getting a lot more than that," I laughed with relief. "It's a deal."

But it was out of the financial frying pan into the fire of partnership frictions!

Since Gene had a big stake in Vitaphone (and an even bigger stake in me) it was no surprise that a few months later the Lopez band made a Vitaphone short that got world-wide distribution. I've forgotten what it was like, but Bob Effros, one of my men on trumpet, will always remember it.

In those early talkies, techniques had not yet been perfected. With each day's shooting we had to pick up, positionwise, exactly where we had left off. One night poor Effros dislocated his shoulder when there were still important takes to be made that featured the trumpet section! With the help of chiropractor Ed Crozier, who stayed on the set and kept pushing Bob's shoulder back in place when it threatened to pop, we managed to finish the picture before we moved Bob into the hospital.

On October 8, 1926, the Casa Lopez reopened with a brand-new show. But the overtones of new trouble began to sound in my ears. Evidently figuring his ownership of me at 50 percent, Gene Geiger started taking control in several ways—some subtle, some obvious. In the pretense of "consulting" me, if I didn't go along with his "suggestions," he became insistent—even demanding. The result was unending friction.

All my life I have resented the "authority figure" which the books on psychology describe so accurately. I'd had enough of such authority from a tyrannical father. I could do little about the situation in that phase of my life, but Gene Geiger ran into trouble playing papa to me.

It was a woman who understood me best at that time, better than I understood myself. Without chiding or sermonizing, Clara Bell Walsh sized up my hectic and too numerous romances.

"Vincent," she explained, "you've found out something from your marriage and from the few other serious loves in your life. You've learned that a woman in love wants to dominate you. She can't help it. Your love is what she wants most of all in life, and she tries to protect it and make it secure."

"You're talking about jealousy, aren't you?" I suggested.

"That's a name for it—an oversimplification," Clara Bell went on. "But most women in love are possessive, and they can't help trying to secure what they want. They turn the bonds of love into ropes."

"I know the feeling," I concurred. "Especially around my neck!"

She laughed, but then seriously added, "I don't know why you're the way you are, Vincent, but I've seen it in a few other men who don't have it in their power to make a woman truly happy. As soon as romance becomes serious with them and the poor girl does what her nature compels her to do becomes protective, assertive, and a bit demanding—your type Romeo wants out. That's true, isn't it?"

"Yes," I admitted. "I really love the girl, until she tries to stake me out as her claim."

"Exactly," Clara Bell agreed. "Then come the tears, anger, bitterness—"

"The story of my life," I admitted. "What should I do about it?"

"For the present, until you change, if you ever do," she recommended, "stay pretty much the way you are now. Have your romantic flings but no deep romances. And if a girl mistakes it for the real thing straighten her out before—well, before she gets hurt."

"What about you and me, Clarabell?" I asked. "We're such very good friends, you know. Have you ever thought it might turn to romance?"

"With a man like you, Vincent," she smiled, "a girl is better off settling for friendship. Just let's not make it too platonic."

Chapter 43. I FIND NUMEROLOGY

I've always had a lot of friends in the newspaper world, and a secret wish to join the fraternity as a writer (a wish that ultimately came true). Wise men have observed that there's only one way to become a writer: putting the seat of your pants on a chair and working. I tried an easier method the first time. Harry Hershfield was then the president of an informal writers' organization called the Cheese Club. Thinking I might be elected an honorary member at least, and with the publicity possibilities also in mind, I threw a wingding of a party for the Cheese Club at the Casa Lopez.

For entertainment we put on our regular show but it was topped by the impromptus by the guests, notably a song and dance bit by Jimmy Durante and Walter Winchell entitled "She Doesn't" that definitely implied she did! Then Harry Hershfield closed the affair with a monologue that had even my musicians exhausted with laughter, absolute proof of success.

But the invitation to join the Cheese Club never arrived. I think I learned something else about life through the episode. If there's something you want very much, don't try to get it from a fairy godmother.

Although I wasn't doing any writing that time, I was continuing the reading I had begun soon after my return from England. During my reading I became fascinated with the life story of Pythagoras, a Greek mathematician and philosopher of the sixth century B.C. Pythagoras built his philosophy on the idea that there is an order, rhythm, or pattern in life—based on mathematics, since the universe is a marvel of mathematics—that has great influence on the individual and on entire nations, civilizations, and the world itself. The gist of Pythagoras is contained in Shakespeare's lines:

There is a tide in the affairs of men,
Which, taken at the turn, leads on to fortune;
Omitted, all the voyage of their life
Is bound in shallows and in miseries!

Those lines from *Julius Caesar* convinced me I should know more about Pythagoras and his philosophy that "number" is the first principle of the universe (from which the term Numerology is derived). I mentioned my interest to Clara Bell Walsh one evening and found she too was a numerology enthusiast.

"Why don't you study it seriously, Vincent?" she suggested. "Maybe it's what you need to give your life more purpose and meaning."

I nodded. "If there's anything to this idea that timing is important in what a person does, maybe I can find out when to take steps to get out of my deal with Gene Geiger."

"That's really troubling you, isn't it," Clarabell said. "You probably resent the authority he tries to wield over you. But it might be the wise and mature thing to overlook it."

"But it's come to involve a lot of money, Clarabell. The Metropolitan Theatre in Boston offered us $10,000 to play there for a week but Geiger vetoed it. Then Coral Gables in Florida bid $12,000 a week if we'd play a full month there. He ruined that deal too!"

"I can understand his not wanting you away from the Casa a whole month," Clarabell remarked, "but a week wouldn't have been bad for business. He was unreasonable there."

"Then the Cadillac people wanted us just overnight and were willing to pay $10,000. Geiger said the price was $12,000; but when they agreed to pay it, he ruined everything by insisting they cover the transportation expenses, too! They signed somebody else then."

"That doesn't make sense," Clarabell agreed. "Maybe he *is* trying to dominate you, even though it costs him money. You do need advice, Vincent, on how to handle this."

"I've seen Julius Kendler and he says the contract is unbreakable," I went on. "My only chance is to buy Gene out, but I don't have the kind of money he'd want. Maybe he'll be more reasonable next year, if I time it right."

Clara Bell said she knew of a woman numerologist who was consulted by quite a few people in society—and by some show people too, she added.

"Who?" I asked.

"Well, I know of one man who followed her advice closely for many years, until one time when she said the year was unfavorable for him to make a trip abroad. He went anyway."

"Who was he?" I wanted to know. "And what happened to him?"

"He went to Europe and died there," Clara Bell answered. "His name was . . . Enrico Caruso!"

That settled it.

I met the numerologist, whose name was Asa Cochran, and told her the difficulties that were troubling me mentally.

"Mr. Lopez," Asa Cochran said. "This isn't the year for you to buy Mr. Geiger out or try to force any change in your contract with him. That solution will be easier for you three years hence, but at present let things stand as they are. Relax about them and learn to accept what you can't readily alter. You'll be a happier person for it."

"Well, I'll try, but it won't be easy. And I doubt that I'll be happy about it."

"Perhaps you're right there," she answered, "for at this very moment something is occurring that will change your entire life."

"Change my entire life?" I questioned. "At four o'clock in the afternoon? Well, you've intrigued me, at least. I'll let you know if you were right. I'll be back later."

"Yes, Mr. Lopez," she answered. "Indeed you'll be back."

Chapter 44. THE CASA LOPEZ FIRE

I hurried to the Audubon Theatre where we were playing a vaudeville date. The manager met me at the door and asked me if I'd heard the news.

"What news?" I brushed him off. "Tell me later, Jack. I've got only five minutes till we're on."

"Okay, Vince," he agreed. "Maybe it's better that way."

The show didn't go over very well. My musicians seemed strangely tense and made mistakes.

"What's the matter with you fellows today?" I demanded as we walked off after tepid applause.

"Haven't they told you?" Bob Effros asked. "Don't you know?"

"Told me what?" I snapped. "What's going on here, anyway?"

Norman Spencer, the theatre manager, then put his hand on my shoulder and said, "Vincent, prepare for a shock. The Casa Lopez is on fire. It's a three-alarm job and the radio news says nothing can be saved."

I ran out of the Audubon stage-door entrance and waved down a passing taxi.

"The Casa Lopez is on fire. The Casa Lopez is on fire," I kept repeating.

"Yeah, I know," the cabbie replied. "Heard it on the radio when I was getting a cuppa coffee . . . Hey! You're Lopez!"—and he stepped hard on the accelerator.

The Casa Lopez on fire! How bad was it? Could anything be saved? Had Gene Geiger covered it with enough insurance? What would the band do now? Would I be so much in debt that I'd never recover? Who were the friends I could turn to for help? These were the thoughts that raced through my mind as the cab dashed through the city's heavy traffic.

Then I suddenly thought of what Mrs. Asa Cochran had said about an event that would change my life. Change it in what respect?

—to what degree?—better or worse? At that moment my mind was full of questions without answers.

We ran up against police lines two blocks from the Casa so I left the cab and talked my way past the police captain who didn't want to let me get any closer to the fire.

"Sure, I know you're Vincent Lopez," he explained, "but what good can you do in there? The place went up like kindling wood. Maybe you'd better not even look at it."

However, he finally let me by and I ran to the club and who was there but B. A. Rolfe.

"Vincent, I got here a minute after I saw the flames as I was walking along 54th Street," he said. "I ran inside to try and save Bill Kessler's drums, but there wasn't a chance. The whole place was a wall of flame by then. It must have gone up in a minute so they couldn't salvage a thing. You're just an unlucky guy."

"I don't know about that," I disagreed. "If the Casa was such a firetrap with all those drapes and oil paintings and shrubbery, suppose it had caught fire when we had a big crowd inside. Maybe I'm luckier than we think."

No one realized just how lucky we had really been until the disastrous Coconut Grove holocaust killed hundreds of people in Boston because it occurred at two in the morning instead of two in the afternoon!

Here is the *Morning Telegraph's* account of the fire:

Throngs Watch Firemen Fight $200,000 Blaze.

Fire late yesterday completely destroyed the palatial Casa Lopez at 247 West 54th Street. The seven-story building, which formerly was used as an automobile club, was badly damaged. The fire started through defective electrical wiring in the bandstand which was used in the elaborate stage shows.

While making his rounds the porter of the club saw smoke coming from the rear of the dining room. He went to the kitchen and as he opened the door, he was met with a blinding flame. He summoned a policeman, who sent in the alarm. Subway construction nearby was temporarily halted by the fire and reserves were called to handle the Broadway crowds which jammed the street. No one was in the club at the time. The greatest damage was done to the Casa Lopez. Its great ballroom and spacious dining rooms were completely destroyed. The gorgeous musicians' stands, the Spanish Room and the Glow Room were burned completely.

The only part of the Club not damaged by the fire was my own bedroom on the top floor. Miraculously it had escaped damage and that was the only thing left of what had been America's most beautiful night club.

Ironically, an elaborate dinner had been held at the Casa Lopez the preceding night by two hundred members of the Fire Underwriters' Association. This made a good twist ending for the news story, but for me there was far more irony in an advertisement that appeared on the same page. It announced that Paul Whiteman was opening a new night club where Rector's used to be.

Not because of tradition that the show must go on, but out of a sense of loss that I must somehow overcome by increasing my activities, I went back to the Audubon Theatre the night of the fire and played the final performance.

Then I headed for a hotel room once more, since my beautiful penthouse was a thing of the past. I had a tough time dropping off to sleep that night, and the last thing of which I had conscious thought was the prediction Asa Cochran had made that afternoon.

"At this very moment, Vincent, something is occurring that will change your entire life. . . ."

Chapter 45. DOWNWARD

Offers of help poured in after the fire. One call I will never forget came from George Olsen, suggesting I come back to the Hotel Pennsylvania. "This is your right place, Vincent. A lot of your friends still come here expecting to find the Lopez orchestra. We're doing very well, but we haven't really replaced you. I'm pretty sure Statler would like to have you back."

"Thanks, George," I answered with my emotion plainly showing. "Your friendship in making this offer is something I'll never forget. But I think the best thing for the band and me is to go on the road until we get this bad break out of our minds."

"Might be a good idea at that," he agreed. "New places, new faces—it could be just what the doctor ordered."

George Olsen was right about the new faces and new places. In Atlanta, Georgia, where we played an engagement at the Capitol Theatre, I ran into my good friend, Jan Garber, the orchestra leader, who was and remains the idol of the south. Through him I went to many parties. At one I met Laura Candler, daughter of Asa Candler, founder of the Coca-Cola industry. She was like a beautiful flower; we dated many times the two weeks I was there and became very good friends. To my surprise, I started to get serious about Laura and I thought she felt the same way.

At our farewell party the night before returning to New York, Laura told me she was going to the National Park Seminary, a very exclusive school for girls in Washington and asked me to come down to see her. I said I would do more than that, bring my band and play for the fall Seminary dance at my own expense. I took it from there and arranged with the school authorities for the Lopez band to play the date—free.

When I returned to New York, I told this to my partner. Profit-minded Gene told me I was crazy.

"Not crazy," I said, "just a guy in love."

"Six of one, half a dozen of the other," he replied.

Later in the season, when we arrived at the Seminary for the dance, I learned that our orchestra would have to play from the balcony above the dance floor and the students weren't permitted to mingle with the musicians. When Laura added her protest to mine we were granted permission to meet on the balcony during the orchestra's twenty-minute intermission. Still and all, the thought of being with her again was wonderful until she walked in wearing a beautiful gown and a look of disappointment. There was an elderly woman with her.

"Vincent," she explained, "this is Mrs. Patterson. She's my sorority mother and she—she wants to meet you."

It was a polite way of saying that Mrs. Patterson would act as our chaperon for the precious third of an hour that was ours. A duenna, I realized! My father would have thought himself back in his beloved Portugal.

During the Christmas holidays later that year Laura arrived in New York with her parents. I immediately sent a corsage of orchids to her hotel with a card saying, "I will wait until I hear from you, which I hope will be soon, as I am very anxious to see you."

Laura called me and said, "Vincent, many thanks for the beautiful orchids, but I cannot accept them as my parents have other plans." This was another blow.

Several years later I met Laura in New York. Her smile of welcome was so warm I impulsively kissed her, and then realized this was our first kiss.

While our band was on tour that summer, Gene Geiger was hard at work on plans for a second Casa Lopez. He found a spot over the old Winter Garden on 50th Street and Broadway that could be reconditioned for a lot less than the fortune we had put into Casa I. The inadequate insurance we had carried meant we had to wield the economy axe all around, including salary slashes for the band.

I held out against the reductions, but Geiger forced his decision through. It turned out as I feared. Only two of our men stayed, hoping for a return of better times. The others, simply stepped over to competitive orchestras. Gone was Cugat, gone the Dorseys, etc., etc. From the top of the heap we slid down to mediocrity and almost into obscurity.

"You don't need a top band in a night club, Vincent," Geiger argued. "When we get the place going and pay off some of the bills, hire back your old musicians and you'll be on top again professionally."

It was the familiar case of the business man, the financier

oversimplifying artistic problems. Rebuilding an orchestra is a task that might have stopped even Hercules.

On October 13, 1927, the second Casa opened. Jimmy Walker was on hand, as he had been at the opening of the first Casa two years earlier, and so were Nora Bayes, Harry Hershfield, Mrs. Joseph Widener, Clara Bell Walsh, the Chauncey Olcotts, Mrs. Napoleon Bonaparte, Louise Groody, Jimmy Johnston, Richard Watts, Texas Guinan, Lee Shubert, Ward Morehouse, O. O. McIntyre, Bugs Baer, Abel Green, Walter Winchell, Ed Sullivan, Karl Kitchen, Mark Hellinger, etc. A lot of people sent telegrams. The one from Paul Whiteman was most prophetic: IF FIRED OR FIRE, DONT WORRY. I CAN USE A SECOND PIANO.

The second Casa Lopez being but a cheap imitation of the first, we lost our society patronage (except for a few old friends). The wreck of the Lopez band got rid of the rest of the customers. Geiger's notion that any sort of music would do for a club proved fatal. Our outside engagements tided us over for a while; but the word along Broadway that my band had cooled froze all interest in further bookings.

Oversimplifying as usual, but this time with more dangerous results, Gene Geiger decided that what we needed was some real publicity—a story that would put the club on page one. I must have been pretty desperate or I never would have let them talk me into it. It started in the busy brain of Irving Strouse, who also handled a dance team named Roseray and Cappella. Simone Roseray was a good-looking woman and Cappella a handsome young man who resembled her somewhat—not strange, since she was his mother. No one knew it at the time, for it would have ruined them professionally. Geiger had hired them for the new Casa Lopez. Strouse's publicity idea was to plant stories in the gossip columns that Roseray was madly in love with me and miserable because I was spending my time with two Ziegfeld girls. The stories caught on so well that he and Geiger came up with an idea that Roseray should fake a suicide. With that harvest of publicity, people would flock to the Casa Lopez to see the two principals, and we'd get out of the red ink.

Geiger and Strouse hired a couple of private eyes to be on hand near the lake in Central Park early in the morning. They next got a doctor who was willing to sit by in a cab. Then, as dawn broke, Roseray came up in another cab, took off her fur coat, and ran toward the lake. She was supposed to jump in, but instead she waded out. The water was so cold that she only got her ankles wet before she decided it wasn't worth the chill and started to scream and head back to shore.

When the private eyes saw she was only one-twentieth wet, they picked her up and dunked her, then rescued her. Meanwhile a prearranged someone had leaked the news to the papers that Roseray was going to commit suicide and before the doctor had finished treating her, reporters were on hand to hear Roseray moan that it was Vincent Lopez who had driven her to that act of desperation.

Well, we got the headlines all right and the phone at our office rang all day long. Geiger pretended to be trying to hush the affair up, but added enough fuel to keep the fire going. However, Geiger and Irving hadn't figured on two newshounds named Mark Hellinger and Walter Winchell. It didn't smell right to them and they questioned me. Later Johnny O'Connor of the *Morning Telegraph* tipped me off that there was rough water ahead. He was right, for the newspapermen really gave me the works. Editorials were written condemning this "suicide" as a publicity hoax. About the only journalist who didn't join the "thumb Lopez" campaign was Johnny O'Connor. That was the beginning of a long friendship.

"What can I do about this mess, Johnny?" I asked him.

"Nothing," he said. "You should never have let it happen. The word is around that you're poison and you won't be mentioned in the papers for a least a year." It was a sentence of execution for the Casa Lopez. Oddly enough, Roseray and I must have been drawn together by our mutual misery, because we started going together.

The talk went around that Lopez was finished. Without my top-flight band I couldn't draw a decent crowd into my own night club and the newspapers were giving me the silent treatment. Even my partner Geiger told me I was through.

That night I began to think what had I accomplished since I left the monastery. Was this outside world for me, or was I broken in spirit? I began to analyze all the different places I had worked, how I had started building my life into the music world. I was never more down than after I left the monastery and found myself in the milk business—yet that was when I got my first break at Clayton's. After several years of comparative success, I was jobless and broke when I got my chance at the Pekin. Perry's was closing as Labor Day approached and I had no idea where to go next when Pat Rooney walked by and grabbed me for *Rings of Smoke*. When his *Lovebirds* didn't do so well and it looked like the end of the line again, I tied up with E. M. Statler and the Pennsylvania Hotel and great new things happened that I never even dreamed could come about. Here I was at another crossroads in my life. Where was I headed?

What helped to keep my head above water and our spirits from being broken, were the lucrative outside engagements.

Leo Lewin, a contact man for Irving Berlin, knew that I booked outside college dances and special parties. He buttonholed me one afternoon and said, "There's a young college kid in town and he needs some local jobs to get his union card in New York. Will you help him?"

I said, "Where is he? Bring him in."

"He's sitting right outside," said Leo.

I booked Leo's young musician to play that night with one of my orchestras at the Judge Gustave Hartman Israel Orphan Asylum benefit at the Commodore. There were over 2500 people dancing at the party that night and this young fellow was playing fourth sax. Twice in the middle of the party he asked me, "Mr. Lopez, would you mind if I sang a song while the orchestra is playing?"

I said to him, "Just go back to your seat and play the sax. I can't imagine anyone singing in this big ballroom with people laughing and talking and all the noise going on." (There were no speaker systems in hotel ballrooms in those days.)

He did this once more and I sent him back to his seat again.

Around 11:30 I went over to talk to Judge Hartman and was gone about fifteen minutes. When I got back to the band I was just in time to catch the last strains of a song that my newly-hired sax player was crooning through a megaphone. He didn't see me because he had his eyes closed all through the number.

"What are you trying to do with that thing?" I asked when the song ended. "Who asked you to sing?"

Ignoring my question he turned to me and said, "How was it?"

I said, "How was what?"

"My song."

"Do you imagine that anyone heard you in this big ballroom? Do me a favor and go back and play the saxophone."

When the party was over, I found him waiting for me.

"Look young fellow," I began, "if it's about singing for my band, forget it."

"It's not that, Mr. Lopez," he assured me, "I just want your autograph."

I smiled. "What'll I write on it?"

"Just say, to my friend Rudy Vallee."

Chapter 46. THE ST. REGIS YEARS BEGIN

The sentence of execution for the Casa Lopez was finally carried out on March 18, 1928. In the tradition of show business we gave our finale the best we had and bowed out smiling. Clara Bell Walsh came over with her friends for a farewell party. In her party was J. J. Atkinson, manager of the swanky St. Regis on Fifth Avenue. When he said good-bye he said he hoped to see me again quite soon. I passed it off as merely a polite remark.

The following afternoon my conversation with Gene Geiger was anything but polite and casual! He blamed the Casa debacle on me personally. "You're through, Lopez," he said. "That's been our trouble and I didn't realize it. The parade has passed you by!"

"It's that second-rate orchestra your crazy sense of economy saddled me with. But I'll overcome that. I'll get some of my old boys back and form a real band again."

"What'll you use for money? And how about the dough you owe me personally, aside from our partnership?"

"I'll pay it back somehow," I promised. "And I'll get the money to rebuild my band. I've got friends who'll help."

"Walk out on me and I'll slap a suit against you the very next day," Gene coldly announced. "The band you've got is pretty good and it's getting better. Good enough for dates out of town where you haven't slipped yet. You're finished on Broadway, Lopez, but they still love you in Topeka—I hope."

That night in my hotel room I brooded over the things Gene had said. True enough, there were orchestras getting by with no better music than ours. I couldn't risk a suit by Geiger now. Another bad publicity item could kill me in show business. It looked as if I'd be taking that long road trip Gene proposed—but then the telephone rang.

"This is J. J. Atkinson of the St. Regis Hotel. I met you last night at the Casa Lopez, Vincent, and I enjoyed your music. I hope you're not tied up with other commitments."

"No," I replied. "We have some nice road offers, but we could play some local dates before we leave, if that's what you have in mind."

"Oh, no. It's something regular we have in mind," said Atkinson. "We're going to open a beautiful roof garden at the St. Regis. I won't beat around the bush, Mr. Lopez. Your orchestra isn't exactly the sort of instrumentation we have in mind—but you're the man we want. Are you interested?"

"Very much," I replied.

"Well, there are a few details we have to iron out, but if everything goes all right we'll soon have a contract ready for signing."

I tried to get Gene Geiger on the phone immediately so I could crow about the good news, but he didn't answer. The next morning at ten he rang me, and his voice was pleasant for a change.

"Vince," he said, "let's forget about yesterday afternoon. I closed a deal last night for the Woodmansten Inn up near Pelham. The Westchester society crowd hangs out around there and I figure you'll be a hit with them."

"When did you find that out, Gene?" I quizzed.

"I said let's forget yesterday."

"And the road trip to Topeka?" I needled him.

"Of course, of course. We've got a great setup at the Woodmansten. Wait'll you see it. You need my dough to finance the place and I need you and your band to put it over. We can make some real money on it."

"They like me at another society place," I went on a bit childishly, but I needed that moment of retaliation. "They made me an offer last night."

"No kidding," Gene snapped. "Where? Who?"

"Oh, a little place over on Fifth Avenue called the St. Regis."

"Great, Vince," Gene enthused. "I've got some ideas on how we can capitalize on a place like that!"

"Look, Gene," I interrupted. "You call the turns at the Woodmansten Inn. It's your place and your money. I'll go along with whatever you decide there. But the St. Regis is my deal, understand? You'll get your half, but you'll have nothing to say about what I do there. Let's get that straight right now!"

Just as my father had retreated when I challenged him years before so did Gene Geiger now.

As the weeks rolled on toward summertime after our Woodmansten debut, I realized our band was getting very good but I didn't appreciate just how good until Al Jolson chose the Woodmansten Inn as the place to bring Ruby Keeler the evening she became his bride! And he found a lot of his best friends there as part of the crowd that night!

It was all of a month before I heard from J. J. Atkinson again. He'd been running an investigation on me! It couldn't have been too puritanical an inspection, for I made the grade personally. Now all I had to do was make it professionally—at the St. Regis.

Atkinson left the band instrumentation up to me, and this was a problem, for our Woodmansten band didn't quite suit one of New York's finest hotels. A chance meeting with Joe Ribaud, an old friend, rescued me. Joe had once played the guitar for me but had switched over to the management side of the business. I poured my troubles into his receptive ear.

"I can handle it for you, Vince," he said. "I know just what those Fifth Avenue places go for—music on the soft side with plenty of strings. I can organize the brand new band you need in two weeks."

"OK, go ahead," I said.

Call it luck, call it a hunch, but that quick decision gave me a fresh start and gained me a lifelong friend. However, I'll admit I had some doubts when I met my new band for our first rehearsal. It was made up of three violins, a viola, a cello, an accordion, three saxes, just one trumpet (muted, at that) plus a rhythm section of bass, drums, guitar and two pianos with Lopez at the solo piano.

"Joe," I protested when I saw the setup, "this is a band? With a big crowd dancing, people won't even hear the music."

"They will at the St. Regis Roof, Vince. I checked on the acoustics, and this band is perfect for it. I know what the society crowd likes, and this band—plus your piano—will be sensational."

"You may be right but I'm glad I've got my regular band at the Woodmansten just in case . . ."

"Listen, Vince," Joe insisted. "At the Woodmansten, you're just another pop orchestra—a good one, but nothing really great. I'm telling you that heading this group you'll be back on top again in no time. You can write your own ticket at the St. Regis for as long as you want to be there, unless you do something foolish."

"What makes you think I'd do something foolish?" I asked.

"I don't know. I don't even know why I said it," Joe admitted. "Forget it, Vince."

I did forget it at the moment, but it was something I should have remembered all my life! Instead, I had to learn the value of humility the hard way. By humility, I don't mean excessive meekness or a retreat from a full and satisfying life. But failure to appreciate success, and taking chances with it for the sake of personal gratification, is a dangerous and foolish form of pride.

I left so much to Joe Ribaud that I didn't even see the St. Regis Roof until the afternoon of the night we were to open there. Joseph Urban had done a magnificent decorating job, fully living up to the reputation he had established by creating the backgrounds to set off the feminine loveliness assembled by Flo Ziegfeld.

The St. Regis foyer, with walls of orange silk embroidered with figures of gold, set the scene for the elegance of the reception room that was completely panelled with mirrors. Then came the main room itself with a high vaulted ceiling that gave the effect of golden branches against a blue sky. Its walls were done in a deep blue, and Urban had attempted (and succeeded in) a daring decorative touch —an emerald green carpet that seemed a perfect blend of the sky and the sea. However, I instinctively felt there was something missing as J. J. Atkinson proudly showed me around.

"Absolutely fabulous, Mr. Atkinson," I agreed. "But may I ask a silly question? . . . *Where's the bandstand?*"

By some amazing oversight (for which we fire a poor clerk but tolerate in a genius), Urban had forgotten to provide a bandstand or even stage lighting for the orchestra and the brief floor show! It was about two in the afternoon when I spotted the trouble, but Urban got together a double crew of carpenters and electricians and ten minutes before the first guests arrived in their evening gowns and dinner jackets, the last worker had left the place.

When the dinner crowd plainly showed they loved the music of our unusual instrumentation, I beamed a big smile of relief and thanks to Joe Ribaud who was again playing the guitar. My smile was even bigger the next day when I saw the press reviews, especially from the society columnists.

What could be a better story to read than Cholly Knickerbocker's in the New York *American* of June 6, 1928:

Society's newest aerial dining and dancing rendezvous opened last evening in a gala blaze of colorful surroundings, people, and the strains of Lopez's music. So great was the demand for reservations that more than a thousand guests were turned away after accommodations for 500 were exhausted, with the result that another opening will be held tonight! . . .

Nothing quite so magnificent as the St. Regis Roof has ever been attempted, and to the famous Joseph Urban goes the credit for providing Mayfair with the most beautiful place in New York. In perfect décor, he has thought of everything. [Everything except a bandstand, I could have corrected Cholly.]

The political field was well represented by Mr. and Mrs. James Walker, Mr. and Mrs. Franklin D. Roosevelt, and others. Society was out in full force, among them the Tony Biddles, the Dan Toppings, the Donahues, Mr. and Mrs. Stanley Menken, the Huttons, the Joseph Wideners, Samuel Riddle, Charles Minot, Mrs. Jacob Hays, the John Scott Brownings, Joseph Tate and his lovely wife, Mrs. Napoleon Bonaparte, the Cornelius Vanderbilts, J. H. Louderback, and the always-welcome, Clara Bell Walsh.

Strangely, though, the only representative of show business I spied was Marie Dressler. Maybe the rest of them delayed making their reservations and will be there tonight. Let me warn them that the strict rule is dinner dress. Even the most conservative blue suit isn't enough at the St. Regis this season.

. . . The music is provided by a splendid new orchestra led by Vincent Lopez. Although this is Mr. Lopez's first venture to the East Side of the city he was completely at home the entire evening and made an immediate hit with the society crowd. Each time he played the piano, most of the dancing stopped and large groups gathered around him to applaud for more. It seems to me there's an affinity between the "400" and the "88", at least when the "88" is played as entrancingly as Mr. Lopez does it. I predict he will be a favorite at the Roof for the entire summer.

Cholly Knickerbocker was a conservative prophet. Our band remained a fixture at the St. Regis for the next seven years. At the moment, though, his forecast of a three-month engagement delighted me.

When opening night was over and congratulations were out of the way, J. J. Atkinson mentioned another oversight to me—one of his own.

"Vincent," he explained, "you saw the cream of society here tonight, and you'll be playing for them every night. The best known people from the finest American families will be your fans, and I liked the way you were at ease with them. But, the St. Regis gets its patrons from all over the world, and sometimes we entertain royalty.

That means a bit more work in store for your band, learning their national anthems."

And no visit of royalty ever found us short of the appropriate anthem—even when the King of Siam visited the St. Regis a few years later.

"Incidentally," Atkinson went on, "I didn't want to tell you this earlier in the evening for fear it might cause you some nervousness, but the distinguished-looking man who sat just to the right of the bandstand this evening is a confrere of yours in the music world. He remarked to me that you have great technique with your right hand."

"And what's the matter with my left?" I bristled.

"You'll have to ask him the next time he visits us," Atkinson laughed. "Keep his name in mind. It's Sergei Rachmaninoff!"

Chapter 47. MY FOUR LIVES

For the next year or so, my life was a tale of two opposite worlds: the St. Regis where I mingled with the cream of society, and Woodmansten's less formal crowd. There was a contrast in everything: in the different music I provided and the different conversations I engaged in when the band was off the floor and I was visiting friends at the nearby tables. Then there was the contrast between the vivacious showgirls at the Woodmansten and the society matrons and their debutante daughters at the St. Regis.

However, there must be a universal and perhaps primitive appeal to piano music, for I was accepted with equal enthusiasm by both. Before long I had my first date with a debutante and I found that romance is a common denominator for all women.

My life had become complicated and busy enough after we opened at the St. Regis, when an offer to appear in Earl Carroll's *Vanities* came along. My success at the Woodmansten and the St. Regis gave Earl Carroll the idea that I would be just the right touch that would help the *Vanities*. After some tough bargaining we made a deal that I conduct the overture. It shortened my appearance at the St. Regis Roof but Gene Geiger had arranged the date and we convinced Mr. Atkinson it would be good publicity for the Roof.

Shortly before we were to go into rehearsal for the *Vanities* Marie O'Connell, a newspaperwoman, came to see me and said, "Mr. Lopez, I'll come right to the point and save time for both of us. I've been commissioned by a wealthy woman to get a few songs into a Broadway show."

"Out of the question," I snapped. "A million other amateur song writers want the same thing."

"These aren't amateur numbers," Miss O'Connell said. "Her two nephews are the composers and they've had several songs published. What they need is to get their material into a Broadway show, so that important publishers will pay some attention to them."

"That would certainly help," I admitted, "but why pick out the *Vanities?*"

"Well, I heard the score isn't the best in the world and even if these numbers are just average you stand to gain $12,000, Mr. Lopez. The woman I represent has more money than she can ever spend. She wants to do something for her nephews while she's still alive and is willing to pay you $12,000 to include their new songs in your part of the show."

"I can't do a thing like that," I protested. "It's just throwing money away."

"Not if the songs are any good," Miss O'Connell disagreed. "Even if they don't hit, at least the kids will have an important show in their credits—and that can mean a lot to their future chances. You know I'm right on that, Mr. Lopez. And why don't you let my client decide for herself how to spend her money? She considers it an investment in their future. Who are you to say she's wrong?"

"I'll think it over. The songs have got to have a reasonable chance, and Earl Carroll has to agree."

"Fair enough," she concluded. "I've got the manuscripts right here. Look them over and let me know."

The tunes weren't bad at all, so I put the proposition to Earl Carroll that same afternoon, offering to split the $12,000 with him.

"Well, its okay with me," said Carroll, "on one condition. I've got to meet the benefactor. I'm looking ahead to my next show. She might be a favorite aunt to her nephews, but maybe she'll be an angel to me!"

And so it was arranged. I wrote Earl my personal check for $6,000 on the spot—I already had a cashier's check for $12,000 to cover it.

"Vincent," he grinned, "I don't think I'm far wrong when I say the pleasure is all mine as I pocket this check. By the way, how much did I pay you for being my demonstration pianist? Or have you forgotten that detail?"

"I've forgotten the details on a lot of the money I've made," I added, "but not that one. You paid me fifteen a week."

Unfortunately for the wealthy Mrs. Penfield of Connecticut and her two nephews who wanted to crash Tin Pan Alley in a hurry, "Once in a Lifetime," which they did not write, was the only hit song of the 1928 *Vanities*. However, having their numbers in a Broadway show did get them "in" with the big publishers for later songs they wrote and they made pretty good money from the royalties. Poor Mrs. Penfield wasn't that lucky, though. Earl Carroll met her, charmed her, and talked her into putting money into his next show, *Fioretta*, which was an expensive flop.

I kept my $6,000 safe, and not only from Earl Carroll. After I had banked it at the Harriman National, some inner sense told me to deposit it elsewhere. I withdrew the money just three days before it closed its doors.

Then I picked another loser!—the Bank of the United States, which later failed. However, that same inner warning came to my rescue and I went to the bank while it was still solvent and asked for my full account!

"Why not leave a nominal amount here, Mr. Lopez?" the vice-president suggested. "That way you won't have the red tape of opening a new account with us later. Shall we give you our cashier's check for, say, all but five hundred dollars?"

I went along with the idea—and never collected a dime of that "nominal amount."

Several years later Ed Sullivan asked me to make a trip to Sing Sing with Glen Gray and his Casa Loma Orchestra and several other great acts. They were going up just for the day on an entertainment mission. While there I met the former president of the defunct Bank of the United States. He was serving a long term that I'm afraid was instigated more by a desire for vengeance than a legal search for justice. His bank had gone to the wall at the start of the Big Depression.

Foolishly, I mentioned to him the $500 I had lost in his bank's failure. He burst out crying—and I learned a badly needed lesson in tact.

To come back to the *Vanities,* it marked a triumphant return to Broadway for Carroll. W. C. Fields was the star but another performer pressed him hard for the laughs by means of a piano he used as a prop. It was Joe Frisco and his audience-fracturing take-off of Helen Morgan perched atop a piano—"one of the finest features of satire ever seen in the American theatre," to quote from one of the press reviews. Martha Morton, Gordon Dooley, Ray Dooley, Barto and Mann, Adler & Bradford, Joey Ray, Dorothy Lull, and Beryl Halley all came in for mention, not forgetting Lillian Roth and the showgirl Dorothy Knapp, whom Earl Carroll billed as the most beautiful girl in the world.

I personally preferred a showgirl Ziegfeld had brought from England where she won a beauty and talent contest he had conducted. Her name was Blanche Satchell and she had the same British beauty that Jean Simmons has today. Through Bernie Sobel, Ziegfeld's publicity man, I managed to meet her and life, which had been anything but dull since the St. Regis, suddenly acquired an extra glow. I was in love again—not seriously, but nevertheless with a lot of enthusiasm and joy. However, I continued to see Beryl Halley quite seriously—and an occasional newcomer to the date list which included a recent debutante or two from the St. Regis. These were wondrous days for me of youth and love.

Professionally my day began at 6:30 P.M. at the St. Regis. At 8:30 I was due at the *Vanities.* By 9:30 or thereabouts my chauffeur whizzed me into the long driveway at the Woodmansten Inn. The

Cadillac had hardly cooled off when we had it going again to get me back to the St. Regis by midnight. Unless a special dance or party date had been booked, my professional life wound up by 2 A.M., when my personal life took over.

Before it ended, 1928, which had started off so badly for me, saw me more firmly entrenched than ever.

Chapter 48. BOOM BOOM

As the fall season arrived, Atkinson wanted me to identify my name and presence more definitely with the St Regis Hotel "You're a success here, Vincent. For goodness sake take advantage of it and give us more time here. I'm not complaining, understand. It's just that I've taken quite an interest in you as a young man we like—both Mrs. Atkinson and I—and we don't want you to kill your career, if not yourself, with overwork."

I thought it over and quit the *Vanities,* where I hadn't been happy anyway, though Earl Carroll and I remained good friends. My last recollection of him was in 1948 when, passing me in an open car with lovely Beryl Wallace beside him he slowed down to wave me a happy "hello." The next morning's papers carried the news of the plane crash that took their lives.

I got another time break that pleased Atkinson when Geiger closed the main room at the Woodmansten Inn for the fall and winter, keeping just a wing of the place open with a small band for dance music. Devoting most of my time to the St. Regis, pleased Atkinson but annoyed Geiger. Arguments became the order of the day between Gene and me.

When Atkinson closed the St. Regis Roof at the end of the summer we immediately moved downstairs into the equally sumptuous

Seaglades Room, also decorated by Joseph Urban. Mr. Urban rated top honors of 1928 as the absent-minded professor of the year. When the Seaglades was ready, we found it as impressively beautiful as the Roof had been, but again *without a bandstand!* It required more frantic last-minute carpentry for us to open on time. Otherwise the première went over perfectly. Ramon and Rosita had left, but we found another marvelous dance team in Veloz and Yolanda to maintain the happy combination of dancing that delighted the eye and music that pleased the ear.

I became busier than ever. Atkinson reopened the Roof after fashioning it into an ultra-swank club to make it even more exclusive. Through it I landed weddings, coming-out affairs, and other lucrative party dates.

I hesitated to ask the big money Atkinson suggested I charge for these occasions until I learned that flowers alone often cost $5,000! I didn't use my Seaglades Room orchestra for these events, there now being plenty of top musicians available who were familiar with my library and my style. Every Friday and Saturday night we had "Lopez Orchestras" going in five or six different places at which I put in a brief appearance. My last stop was the Mayfair, at the Ritz-Carlton, where one of my bands played from midnight to 6 A.M. Now and then we'd add a benefit to our timetable and the St. Regis crowd went out of their way to support these charities.

The bucks came fast but went as fast. Some went as loans to pay the rent for an apartment or two when a show folded and a lovely dancer lost her income. I was badly fooled on that story once, for the girl used her borrowed rent money to finance a trip to Cuba. Strangely enough, it proved a good investment for me. She returned with ecstatic news about a Havana hit tune called "El Manisero," with a wonderful dance rhythm called the Rumba. I paid no attention until my NBC announcer, John Young, mentioned having heard it in Havana, too, and was just as enthusiastic. I had it orchestrated and introduced "The Peanut Vendor" at one of my St. Regis Roof broadcasts. It started the still active trend toward Latin American music.

While I was at the St. Regis we broadcasted every night except

Sundays over NBC from 11 to 11:30. Different announcers were assigned to open and close the program. One of my favorites was the aforementioned John Young, who later joined the diplomatic service. Announcers weren't exactly overpaid, but most hotels provided them with free meals when they handled a sustaining program. The unwritten rule was to order something in the middle-price range, but John ignored it. One evening after studying the menu he specified the most expensive item: guinea hen under glass with all the fixings. The waiter hesitated a moment, then gave in. John got his guinea hen, took two fastidious bites, complained it wasn't cooked right and demanded another! He got it, too, but also a polite notice that free meals at the hotel were a thing of the past for him. Annoyed, John returned the following night with a grocery bag containing coffee and hamburgers which he proceeded to unwrap and munch while the crepes suzette flamed all around him!

That cost him exile from the St. Regis, but "it was worth it," Johnny told me later. "They wouldn't serve me free guinea hen, so I gave them an expensive bird!"

Great-hearted Clara Bell Walsh was always going out of her way to help people. Noticing that I looked run-down she made an appointment with her doctor for me. Before I know it I was in the hospital having my tonsils yanked. When I returned home to recuperate, Clara Bell brought me a beautiful Siamese cat to keep me company. I named the cat Clara Bell and what a great friend she was to me for the five years she lived. Coming home at 3 or 4 o'clock, in the morning, she would tell me in no uncertain terms, that I ought to get home earlier, that she had been waiting up for me. If I didn't go to bed, but sat down at my desk to write something, Clara Bell would jump on the desk and knock the pen out of my hand. Before I could do anything she would run away making the weird sounds Siamese cats make. So I usually had to give in and go to bed! Then she would stay at the foot of the bed with one eye open. When she thought I was asleep, she would retire into a hole in the box-spring of the bed. I didn't find that out for a long time; she did that just to be near me.

New York was a city to fall in love with that year. Nobody paid attention to the overtones of financial trouble ahead. Money was plentiful everywhere. Herbert Hoover was in the White House and even busboys were buying RCA stock on margin.

Charity balls and coming-out parties, the rooms of the St. Regis filled with people in evening dress, show-business prosperity all reflected the seemingly permanent America boom. You heard one phrase everywhere: "How's the market doing?"

Since everyone seemed to be in the market, J. J. Atkinson asked me one day was I in, too. He was glad to hear that I wasn't and said something prophetic. "Keep away. That market is going to crash and when it does it will be the worst thing that happened to this country."

"Are we in for a change?" I asked.

"I'm sure of it. You can see the signs in the very music you play, Vincent! The hot jazz tunes are on the way out. What are some of the hits right now?"

I did a quick mental recap. "There's 'Am I Blue,' 'Deep Night,' 'Moanin' Low,' 'Stardust,' 'Why Was I Born.' Say, they are on the subdued side, aren't they?"

"I'm afraid they're a sign of what's ahead." Atkinson repeated. "Vincent, keep your money out of Wall Street. Mrs. Atkinson and I would hate to have anything happen to you."

Chapter 49. I THRIVE IN THE DEPRESSION

At first, business didn't suffer much at the St. Regis in spite of the crash—which came, as predicted. If the socialites did any economizing, it wasn't apparent. For me, the tide continued to rise in income and achievement. As the overall number of parties decreased, I got more of them. I played for a smart party in Newport, Rhode Island, given by the now-famous "hostess with the mostest," Pearl

Mesta. The popular Tony De Marco went along and broke in a new dancing partner that night. He confided to me that they needed more rehearsals, but no one noticed the difference. The next night we played at the twenty-fifth anniversary of the F. W. Roeblings. The motif was to set back the clock to 1905, with the guests in appropriate costumes and our orchestra offering turn-of-the-century tunes.

Radio now came on with a rush. I got into the swim on January 7, 1930 with my first major program for the Pure Oil Company arranged by Bertha Brainard, NBC's programming genius. Eddie Cantor and Frank Parker, as guests, helped us launch the first show. My thirteen week contract (which ultimately ran twenty six) seemed to fill the cup of success. The very next day it ran over when the swank Everglades Club in Palm Beach, Florida, hired one of my orchestras at a price that brought me $400 a week, merely for the use of my name.

I was also getting somewhere in a creative sense, for I started the innovation, on the St. Regis radio shows, of quick interviews by the leading radio critics. Jack Foster of the *World-Telegram* led the parade, then came Louis Reid of the *American*, John Skinner of the Brooklyn *Eagle*, Ben Gross of the *Daily News*, Nick Kenny of the *Daily Mirror*, and a host of others. Many had never been on radio personally and they learned how tough it can be on the transmitting end!

I'll never forget the night that Nick Kenny was on the program. While we were having a voice leveling before the show, our engineer called me over to tell me something. He said the "boys across the street" said you can't use him—he has a voice like a foghorn. I said he might be a welcome relief, because he has something to say, and people will enjoy him no matter what he sounds like. And furthermore, he's the radio editor of the *Daily Mirror*.

When the Pure Oil program terminated for us, I was put out by NBC's apparent indifference. When I mentioned it to J. J. Atkinson, he thought up a solution in a jiffy.

"You know the NBC brass lunches in our Oak Room," he reminded me. "Join me there tomorrow. Never mind the questions. Just be there."

I was there, of course—and so was Bill Paley, of CBS, whom Atkinson had invited! We talked shop, including a casual mention of putting the Lopez orchestra on his network. When luncheon was over Mr. Paley said to Atkinson: "You're very clever [looking around the room]. With all these rival NBC executives surrounding us, whatever you have in mind you'll be able to get from them!"

He was so right. A few days later John Royal, one of the top executives of NBC, called me and said he had an hour's afternoon show, straight across the board, Monday through Friday, 3 to 4 o'clock, with a half-dozen or more sponsors. It was called "The Women's Radio Review." One of the sponsors was Elizabeth Arden, who did her own commercials. She was nervous but added a lovely touch to the show.

I got a kick listening to a young fellow seated at a small table explaining the virtues of Lydia Pinkham's pills into his microphone. He was so convincing we all got a boot just listening to him—and watching him. One afternoon I went over and said, "One of these days you'll be one of the top announcers of America! You're great!"

His name—Ben Grauer!

My progress in radio had its setbacks, too. I inaugurated another program idea at the Salle-Cathay Room of the St. Regis on Saturday afternoons with Eddie Cantor as my first guest of honor. But the publicity it drew brought an overflow crowd of Cantor's show business pals from Broadway into the St. Regis' sacred portals. Afraid it would miff the regular attendance, J. J. Atkinson pronounced his ban that same evening: "Discontinue those Saturday broadcasts, Vincent. We don't want the hoi polloi from the other side of town."

That wasn't J. J.'s only mistake, either. Thanks to Joe Ribaud, my contractor, who discovered him, I added a marvelous singer-instrumentalist to my orchestra. He signed his paychecks Pinky Perlstein. Atkinson took a dislike to him and told me to get rid of him. But Pinky went on to success as the featured soloist at the Roxy and Paramount theatres and ultimately made the Metropolitan Opera Company. By that time, however, he had changed his name to Jan Peerce.

Since I couldn't explain why I let him go, Pinky naturally resented it. Some years later I booked a package show into the Jamaica Theatre on Long Island on the stipulation that Jan Peerce be part of it. When Joe Ribaud offered the job to him, he said, "My regular price is $350 a week. If I were doing this job for you personally I'd go on for nothing. But since it's for Lopez, the price is $750!"

Maybe I should have taken a sabbatical from women for a while. I was quite impressed one day to meet a real (or supposed) Russian countess by the name of Olga Valder. After a few weeks she sent me a couple of etchings as a gift, presumably so she could come up and look at them. I didn't particularly want the etchings, but I put them in the closet and stuffed her letter in my files, after a routine thank-you note. Not long afterwards I got her demand for $500 for the etchings. I promptly wrapped them up and returned them, but her lawyer sent me a threatening letter anyway. I took her original letter to my lawyer, who started investigating. It turned out that the Countess had lifted the etchings from the Monterey Hotel. I can understand her needing a little ready cash—but I was such a soft touch she probably could have gotten it just by asking. I don't like to be made a sap of any more than the next guy.

Shortly after this incident Atkinson okayed a short leave so I could pick up an extra ten thousand playing at the Thomas Edison Exposition in Cincinnati. There I was invited to a luncheon given for President Herbert Hoover, at the Gibson Hotel. The President had said that he didn't want any entertainment, but he changed his mind when Mr. Blackwell, chairman of the luncheon, told him it would be Vincent Lopez playing the piano. The President then said I was one of his radio favorities. While the porters were pushing in the piano one of its legs broke. However, I managed to play it with the help of Mr. Blackwell who lay flat on the floor and propped up the legless side with his two hands, and I started in to play, "Nola," "Flapperette," and "Doll Dance." President Hoover got quite a laugh out of it and later, when we were shaking hands, said he wished he could put a prop under the nation's economy as readily as we had under the piano. . . .

With all this success I suppose I should have been happy. Instead,

I was discontented and had a confused inner feeling of frustration. My good friend Clara Bell Walsh sensed that, and knew that I was seeking spiritual knowledge. A friend of hers, Nella Webb, knew Clifford Cheasley, an outstanding numerologist. So Clara Bell arranged a seemingly casual meeting one Saturday afternoon at the St. Regis. I found him very interesting. Cheasley said that he had been listening to me on the radio and felt that some time he would meet me. He thought I had spiritual qualities and would some day need help to find myself.

"Can you teach me your spiritual approach to things?" I asked him.

"I can teach you nothing," he replied. "However, I can awaken you so that you can teach yourself! That is, if you genuinely want to learn."

"I think I do," was my answer. "I've been getting more and more interested in books about the spiritual side of life. I feel that I'm seeking for something my subconscious mind tells me is there despite the denials of my conscious mind."

My search for the spiritual didn't end with Cheasley. In fact it was the very materialistic pursuit of keeping in physical shape that led to my meeting someone else who had a profound spiritual influence on me. I used to keep myself physically fit at Riley's Health Club. Knowing I was interested in the occult and spiritual world, Riley mentioned a man by the name of Edgar Cayce to whom, he said, some doctors sent almost incurable patients for a reading.

However, it was through Clara Bell Walsh that I met Cayce. She introduced me to David E. Kahn, through whom I met Morton H. Blumenthal and his brother Ed. Our conversation touched on my spiritual interests and they asked me if I would like to meet Mr. Cayce. What I had been told about him was confirmed by my own impressions. He could describe your past incarnations, sending his mind back thousands of years. He helped hundreds of sick and unhappy people.

I visited Virginia Beach on the 15th of December to meet Mr. Cayce in person. I wasn't sick but I wanted to talk to the man who had done so much for afflicted people. Since then a dozen books have been written about him (notably *There Is a River* by Thomas Sugrue of the New York *Herald Tribune* and the *American* Magazine).

Mr. Cayce impressed me as being a very humble man, yet I could sense a powerful force within him. Along with his unexplainable power to heal went his unshakeable belief in reincarnation, a subject the mystics have studied since the first great temples of religions were erected. Practically all the oriental religions are based on it.

My reading took place one afternoon in the presence of Mrs. Cayce, who was the conductor, Gladys Davies, the stenographer, Dr. M. Brown, Morton H. Blumenthal, Thomas House and myself. Reclining on the sofa, Cayce entered a trance. He traced my reincarnations from Atlantis, through Mesopotomia, Greece, and Egypt to my last one in Italy.

Then and later, I was deeply impressed by Cayce. The world lost a great man when he passed away.

I had always been interested in reincarnation and I knew there was a great possibility of its being a fact. There are many things that happen in this world which can be explained convincingly and believably only on the basis of reincarnation, but this is almost a forbidden subject for the reason that most people do not understand it. I made up my mind at that time that I would make a study of it.

Further search for spiritual answers led me to quite a deep study of reincarnation. When I think of all the different things that were happening, it seems that the material and the spiritual were trying to show their pattern to me. First it would be physical, or material, and then it would be the spiritual and I knew that I had to find a balance between the two.

Meanwhile my troubles with Geiger were increasing. J. J. Atkinson wanted me to break the partnership up. I, like Barkis, was "willin'," but it wasn't easy.

Then on April 2, 1930 the Woodmansten Inn burned down. The band was promptly switched over to the Pelham Heath Inn and Geiger started pressuring me to appear there more often to pull in the crowds. Then I got a letter from Atkinson saying that he didn't want Geiger to advertise that I was appearing there with my orchestra.

When it looked as if I were going to be turned out of the St. Regis, I went to Mrs. Asa Cochran for her numerological advice. She recommended no immediate action. But when I learned that Atkinson was thinking of bringing Jack Denny's orchestra in from Cincinnati to replace me, I hurried back to Mrs. Cochran for another consultation.

"Now! the time is favorable to resolve things," she stated. "You needn't wait another day. In fact, Mr. Geiger will take the initiative with you this evening."

As we were driving in his car to the Inn about 10 P.M., that night, Gene brought up the subject that I was trying to put into words.

"You and I aren't getting along very well, Vince," was his understatement of the year. "How about buying me out?"

"How much?" I exclaimed, hardly believing my ears.

"One hundred and fifty thousand dollars," he replied. "And in cash. No notes. No checks."

That was a fantastic figure, but at least a basis for bargaining. I finally got him to agree to take $80,000.

I immediately went to Atkinson and told him, "I can get rid of Geiger for $80,000."

"Make the deal as fast as you can," Atkinson said, "but not at that price. Tell him I'll give him fifty brand new thousand-dollar bills but not a cent more. Don't worry any more about it," Atkinson concluded, "I'll have the money for you and some pretty good news as well."

Atkinson was wrong about Geiger accepting $50,000. I had to enter a side agreement with him to pay off another $30,000—a deal I didn't tell quick-tempered Atkinson about. We all met at the St. Regis on July 9th. That afternoon Geiger signed my release, took the fifty grand, and our stormy partnership was ended.

Shortly afterwards I signed a ten-year, million-dollar contract with the St. Regis, the first in history for a band leader. I was guaranteed $100,000 a year, out of which I had to pay the band. Since Atkinson had put up the money to buy Geiger out, he came in for a 25% cut on everything I made (net) other than at the St. Regis, so I was assured of always being able to get away and play other engagements.

J. J. Atkinson was a wonderful partner. He always listened to new ideas and would let me try them out even when he felt doubtful. He had somewhat the same protective, father-like attitude that Dick Harding had had for me. He didn't push me around like Geiger and any advice he proffered was for our mutual good, not just for himself. He thought I paid too much for arrangements, musicians, publicity, and the like, but he knew how to criticize without making a person feel like a low-life. He helped make my stay at the St. Regis one of the better periods of my professional life, even though, as a person, I was having a hard time finding myself.

Chapter 50. NATURAL AND SUPERNATURAL

I kept on working very hard and making plenty of "jack," but I still hadn't learned how to keep it. This was one of my chief troubles at this period. But the worst was that I was turning hot and cold musically—good one night, mediocre the next. In show business there is no surer road to oblivion. As these depressing thoughts swirled around me one sleepless night, I asked myself, "What is it I need to straighten myself out and stop making the mistakes that can ruin me?" I asked the question aloud, and an answer came out of the silence. I put it into words as I sat there in the darkness.

"No one ever grows beyond the need for prayer. And the books you've read—haven't they said the same thing?" So came my resolution to put aside some period of each day for prayer and meditation. But there were still years ahead of living and learning before I realized that such resolutions must be backed up by courage and discipline.

In a more practical way, I also resolved to make the most of my new contract with the St. Regis and devote myself completely to the place. It was another unkept resolution although, at the beginning, I had no alternative. Gene Geiger had committed me to bookings which I covered somehow.

One of them was the Piping Rock again, at Saratoga. On arriving there, I was amazed to find no radio wire at the club. Arguments about it were futile, so I shelled out the cost of the wire—two hundred a week. To stay in the public eye in those days, one had to stay in the public ear.

Station WGY took advantage of our microphone-mindedness by including us in the first radio program beamed to our good neighbors in South America. I headed my Latin American offering with Ernesto Lecuona's wonderful piano solo, "Malaguena," and scored a hit . . . but nobody offered to foot the wire charges.

My good resolutions went overboard at the sight of Saratoga's gambling tables. I dropped several hundred dollars at roulette each night, and more by day, at the races. I had only one lucky day, when Ben Bernie's brother Jeff took twenty from me on a 30-to-1 shot named Foxhall that came in by a slender nose.

I began to look for other long shots, with somewhat bigger noses, but just then my ex-partner Gene Geiger did me a good turn by showing up at Saratoga for some "action." He got it, dropping $50,000 on cards, dice, roulette, and the ponies in less than two weeks. He gambled away almost every dollar he got from our deal. I learned wisdom from that example.

What went out foolishly in gambling came back in party dates. Squeezing them in made airplane travel a must. Despite the uncertain schedules of those days we never missed a date.

Robert Goelet hired Meyer Davis' band and ours, for his big party at Newport. Davis' band was all set up by thc time we arrived, with an illuminated electric sign proclaiming its identity. Goelet's patrician sense of decorum was outraged.

"Take that damn sign off your piano!" he thundered at poor Meyer. "Do you think this is an advertising convention?"

Luckily we didn't have an illuminated sign. It was something I had overlooked!

We worked in almost a dozen other parties during the summer, none in better taste (or for bigger money) than the one Mrs. James B. Duke gave at her Rough Paint estate in Newport for her debutante daughter, Doris.

It was news of Doris Duke's aunt, Mary Duke Biddle, who was married to Tony Biddle, one of society's most personable and well-liked men, that awaited me when we returned to the St. Regis for the fall season. Mrs. Biddle, I should add, owned the St. Regis.

"You'll read about it in the papers soon, Vincent," J. J. Atkinson told me. "Tony and Mary are divorcing."

"What?" I asked in total disbelief. "Why, I considered them the two happiest "marrieds" I know." And I went on. "I wonder if she'll still ask me to play 'At Dawning.' That's her favorite number. I had the idea it was connected with her marriage."

"I'd say she'll still want *you* to play it, Vincent," came Atkinson's surprising reply. "And play it right *to* her. I happen to know she likes you—a great deal."

A $10,000 date we played was in Cincinnati to celebrate the extension of airmail service to that city. A giant cabinet had been built, its four sides painted as airmail stamps. Early in the morning we packed ourselves and our instruments inside this simulated stamp. When the crowd arrived we started our music, causing a stir of wonderment as to where it came from. Finally the cabinet opened and the Lopez orchestra came into view for a big hand and corresponding write-ups in the press.

Publicity breaks came with considerable ease that year. However, some of the things that happened to me that I couldn't get into print would have made still better copy.

For instance, although Prohibition didn't end until December of 1932, 3.2 per cent beer became legal on May 14, and New York celebrated with an all-night binge. A "beer parade," led by Mayor Jimmy Walker, started the celebration in the afternoon. There was a strange hope afloat that the revived beer industry could revive business in general, so everybody got into the welcome act—making news that crowded other stories out of the papers. Our party at the St. Regis that evening, which dapper Jimmy attended, wasn't covered, though the Mayor's attentions to Blanche Satchell, my romance at the time, would have had all the columnists talking.

There was another publicity story that the New York press ignored: my appointment as a Kentucky Colonel (which came through while I was in Cincinnati). However, at just about that time, O. O.

McIntyre gave us a one-line item praising our Dixieland music, in his syndicated "Day to Day" column. It got us a plush date at the Suburban Gardens in New Orleans. It was a big success, and a wealthy, and influential citizen of Louisiana insisted on my having a parting drink with him. The band went home ahead of me; I followed on a later train.

Half an hour after the porter made up my compartment bed, he stuck his head back inside to trace the terrible groaning he heard. It was me!—deathly ill and almost unconscious. I was half-paralyzed with the pain and fright, for I don't think there's any situation more terrifying than to be taken sick when travelling alone on a speeding train. Rounded up by the head conductor, a doctor in the sleeper ahead diagnosed my condition and administered a strong emetic. Fifteen minutes later I was able to answer his questions.

"Yes, doctor," I gasped. "I had a couple of drinks with a friend just before I got aboard."

"Mr. Lopez," he informed me. "That was no friend. The drink he gave you was heavily doped."

"Could it have killed me?" I asked.

"I doubt it," was his professional opinion. "You've got the constitution of a horse. But why would a friend want to poison you?"

"I can't imagine, doctor," I honestly stated. "But there's nothing I can do about it. The man I had that drink with is one of the most influential people in the South."

I might have added (but didn't) that he was the best friend of a certain New Orleans newspaper editor whose beautiful wife had tried to date me.

Anyway, it was another great story which I couldn't feed to the papers.

In my spiritual search I took up séances, but they never convinced me. Newspaperman H. Allen Smith was mildly amused by my interest in the occult, but the famous Dunninger (whom I knew from vaudeville) was downright annoyed.

Referring to a famous medium of that period, he said, "I don't care what this great Nino has done. "I'll prove he's a fake! Arrange a séance with this Nino at which I'll be present."

That wasn't difficult to do, and I asked H. Allen Smith to attend, as well. Several other friends of mine were present, including the ever-trusting Clara Bell Walsh, Eddie Wolf, my publicity man, looking for an "angle," and Mrs. Wolf.

Nino was in form as we turned down the lights to induce his trance. His was a marvelous performance of going slightly out of this world. Soon he had his "control" in touch with us, a long dead Italian named Palladino. After some unintelligble conversation Palladino groaned a demand for some water. When Eddie Wolf got up to fetch the water the sepulchral voice said, "Don't move! Don't move! The water is coming."

And it came—torrents of it in the darkness! I thought a spiritualistic miracle had occurred. But Dunninger's voice rasped. "The sprinkler system! The overhead sprinkler system in this old hotel room!" he shouted. "Some stooge has turned it on for him!"

Somebody moved toward the lights, and the water stopped as suddenly as it had started. When we looked up, the fire-alarm sprinkler jets high on the ceiling were still dripping. Despite his soaking suit Dunninger was all for further scientific pursuit of the mumbo-jumbo. This time we tied Nino in a chair so he couldn't get near any of the controls—water, lights, or even the drawn shades. He was getting angrier by the minute, at Dunninger who now heckled him openly. Suddenly Nino and his chair rose from the floor and catapulted across the room—toward Dunninger!—but missed him and landed in the lap of Mrs. Eddie Wolf, who screamed and went into her own trance—a good old-fashioned faint!

That broke up the séance and when Nino had left we turned to Dunninger for an explanation of how the man had sailed six feet or more through the air, with a chair strapped to him.

"Very simple, very simple," Dunninger intoned. "Rage can build up almost superhuman strength in a man!"

But none of us bought the explanation.

I guess our best publicity break of those years came when we were selected to play at the dedication of the Empire State Building on March 2, 1932 in a breezy broadcast over Station WOR which took place on the Observation Roof. We took care of the music, Lou Holtz and Harry Hirschfeld attended to the laughs. Then Governor Al Smith came to the microphone and topped everybody with the warmth of his personality and humor.

Fascinated by the view from the roof, I stayed around after the ceremonies and looked out over the Big Town that lay sprawling before me, crisp and cold in the March air. Looking south, my eyes took me to Brooklyn and my imagination carried me right on out to Clayton's, Minden's, McLaughlin's and all the other places of my post-monastery days. I tried to locate where Pacific Street lay and visualized the brick house that had been my childhood home . . .

Somewhere off in the northwest distance lay St. Mary's where Father Sebastian might still be laboring in the scholastic vineyard. A sudden desire filled me to visit Dunkirk again and see how many of my old friends were still stationed there—and if Father Aloysius had ever managed to play the "Cannonball Rag!"

But it was Manhattan that interested me mainly—the Manhattan of my present sphere. I could pick out the landmarks that had been my own career milestones: the Pekin, the Pennsylvania Hotel, the regal-looking St. Regis up Fifth Avenue, the Palace Theatre and somewhere off in the same direction was the Hollywood Theatre—and I was due there in a few hours for my show! My sight-seeing came to an abrupt end and I hurried to the elevators that would drop me back to street level and the mundane matters of making a living.

Talent-agent Abe Lastfogel had booked me into the Hollywood Theatre for that same month, and Lou Holtz was our co-star. Lou's genius for spur-of-the-moment comedy flashed through in our very first stage show. Lou knew we were reviving a favorite scenic effect of mine—the ride of Paul Revere. As the curtains opened there was the church, the lamp in the belfry, the off-stage shouts of recognition (all heard above our music)—then onstage came Paul himself, on a big white horse whose hoofs flashed over the treadmill that kept beast and rider stationary.

It was always good for applause—but on opening night at the Hollywood the applause was followed by an even bigger laugh when Lou Holtz came dashing onstage as we took our bows. He was dressed as Paul Revere, his Colonial coat half off, his shirt all the way out, and he was gasping for breath as he shouted, "I almost didn't make it!"

Chapter 51. CHICAGO IN ITS WORLD'S FAIR DAYS

It's the tradition of the theatre that many a romance begins at the stage door, but what might have been the most important romance in my life wound up there!

Mary Duke Biddle and I had just driven over from her home to the stage entrance of the Hollywood Theatre, where I was winding up my engagement with Lou Holtz. After this we were booked for a month out of town. Mary didn't know about the trip and I had put off telling her. Repressing the news had made me uneasy, which Mary had noticed—as a woman always does. The storm I had felt brewing all through our luncheon broke when I said I was taking the band to Buffalo. Ten minutes later, when we kissed—quickly, almost casually . . . each of us knew it was good-bye. When I got back to New York a month later, Mary had left for Europe.

My enchantment with Mary had begun long before her divorce, but even after she and Tony Biddle parted I held back any sign of showing it. One night, at the St. Regis roof, Mary asked me to play "At Dawning," and added to her usual thanks a comment that was warm and personal. A few nights later she called me over to ask me to dance.

"But Mrs. Biddle," I protested, still uncertain how to act toward my own employer and one of the richest women in the world. "I don't dance very well. Why not let me get you an expert . . . that young fellow Veloz who's in the floor show here . . ."

"Listen, Vincent, I'm Mary, not Mrs. Biddle, to you from now on."

In the months that followed, Mary and I often danced till dawn at the El Morocco, Stork Club, Leon and Eddie's, etc. When we dined out, her favorite restaurant was Voisin. I was invited frequently to Mary's Sunday dinner parties when she entertained socially at the beautiful Biddle estate at Irvington-on-the-Hudson. During Thanksgiving week that year, the society editor of the New York *Journal*, May Christie, and Australian explorer Sir Hubert Wilkins were also Mary's guests. Sir Hubert fascinated us with tales of his submarine trip near the North Pole in 1931.

He knew the Arctic, all right, and he also had a vision of the space age to come.

"There's no doubt about it," he told us one night, "Man will build an airship that can reach the moon. The only problem is the expense. Mr. Lopez, how would you like to take your band along?"

I joined in the general laughter but declined the trip as too risky. I suggested he take me along on his next Arctic submarine trip instead.

"There would be even more risk there," he warned.

"Polar bears?" I hazarded.

He smiled. "No, I have a theory that the Gulf Stream is pulled down into a huge cavern at the North Pole and carried straight through a channel in the hot earth to emerge in the Caribbean and start its long journey again. . . ."

Meeting such people had its subtle effect on me. However, men of more practical bent continued to play the most important part in my life. One of them was Jules Stein, head of the Music Corporation of America. From the reputation I had built at the St. Regis and the gossip column items that linked me with Mary Duke Biddle, Jules decided that the Lopez orchestra would be ideal to play the new Urban Room at the Congress Hotel in Chicago, to which the management hoped to lure the society crowd.

Stein had no trouble persuading me, and he convinced Atkinson as well. He sold him the idea that one band grows a bit stale in the same room . . . should be replaced occasionally, then return with fresh audience appeal. In short, Jules worked out a three-way contract whereby I went to the Urban Room in Chicago; Anson Weeks and his orchestra came East to replace us; and the St. Regis Corporation sanctioned the arrangement. However, this meant terminating my connection with Abe Lastfogel of the William Morris Agency. Abe had built up our band for its theatre dates, and I hated to end our business relationship. At lunch the next day at Leone's I told him emphatically that I hoped it wouldn't end our friendship.

"Of course not, Vincent," he assured me. "These things happen in show business. As a business man I hate to lose your band, but as your friend I don't like to see you do this because it's not good for you."

"I've explained all that, Abe," I protested. "This way I open up a deal I might need in the future."

"Keep building yourself *right* at the St. Regis and you won't need it," Abe replied. "You've got a ten-year contract and you can retire a wealthy man if you want to. Why risk all that with something that might go wrong?"

"You mean this isn't really such a good deal for me?" I questioned.

"I know it's a better deal for MCA," said Abe. "Jules has always wanted to cut in on a big society hotel. Well, he's made it. You're going to Chicago, and one of his bands will be at the St. Regis. As Ted Lewis would say, 'Is everybody happy?' "

At the St. Regis that night Clara Bell Walsh asked me if I remembered that lovely husband and wife team that had appeared on our celebrity program last week.

"You mean Burns and Allen?" I replied. "What about them?"

"They're getting tired of vaudeville, and vaudeville seems to be slipping anyway. I'd love to help them. What do you suggest?"

"Tell them to get into radio," I advised. "Albee was right years ago when he said that radio and vaudeville couldn't both survive."

"But they're not sure they have the right material for radio. Would they be funny if you couldn't see them in person?"

"To me Gracie Allen would be funny to listen to even if they shut her up in a mausoleum," I insisted. "And there isn't a better straight man than George Burns. I'm positive they'll go big on radio."

It was my understatement of the year. . . . and the next two decades.

Just before we left for our date at the Schroeder Hotel in Milwaukee that preceded our engagement at Chicago's Urban Room, I met another performer headed for fame. On Joe Ribaud's recommendation (he was my contractor) I hired him to play first saxophone and clarinet. He was a brilliant musician, but the talent that bordered on genius had a temperament to match.

We had been holding extra-long rehearsals to get the right edge on our performance at the Urban Room, and I guess at the preview engagement the Schroeder Hotel offered us, I worked the boys unusually long. My new man got madder by the minute. As we finally closed with the familiar "Shave and a Haircut . . . Bay Rum" signature he placed his clarinet in its case very carefully, then walked up to me and said, "Mr. Lopez, haven't you ever heard of Abraham Lincoln?"

"Of course I've heard of Abraham Lincoln," I popped in astonishment. "Why?"

"You should know, then, that Lincoln *freed* the slaves," he retorted. "You're not an orchestra leader; you're a slave driver. I never worked this hard, and I don't intend to. Not even for the extra money you pay." With that, he gave his notice.

Yes, indeed; I don't need a magazine article (or Ava Gardner) to tell me how temperamental and explosive is Artie Shaw.

Our Saturday night opening at the Urban Room on October 1, 1932, was a smash! The crowd was with us all the way. A number of our friends had come out from New York for the occasion, headed by Mr. and Mrs. J. J. Atkinson and Clara Bell Walsh. We made some new friends that night, too, notably a team of entertainers whose real-life names of Correll and Gosden were then little known, but who had hit the radio jackpot as Amos 'n' Andy.

So began a successful run that made us feel we'd done the right thing in signing with MCA in order to establish another "base of operations." We worked hard to make good in Chicago, against the dozen or so fine bands already established there. A special rivalry sprang up between Ben Bernie and me. Ben, playing capacity at the

College Inn, used a celebrity night idea on which he evidently thought he held a patent, although we had featured it at the St. Regis for years. When we started celebrity nights of our own at the Urban Room, Ben did a fast burn and promptly declared a personal vendetta on me—all in fun, of course. His main theme as he used his dry voice and sly wit on me, was that I'd make a swell one-arm paperhanger since I was strictly a one-hand pianist!

"When you hear him on the radio, folks," Ben would observe, "remember it's only the treble notes Lopez is playing. Yowsuh, yowsuh. Lopez can play the piano only with his right hand. He keeps his left hand in his pocket—counting his money . . . Yowsuh, yowsuh. . . ."

One night, I went over to see Ben at the College Inn, for a rebuttal involving a piece of rope. Don't jump to the conclusion that I intended to hang poor Ben. However, when he introduced me with the anticipated remark about my one-hand virtuosity, I said, "Ben, you really believe I can play only with my right hand, don't you?"

"Yowsuh, yowsuh," he admitted. "We *hear* your left hand playing, but that's really a midget pianist you keep hidden in the piano."

Ben got a big laugh with that, but I topped him without saying a word. Instead, I had his trombonist tie my right hand behind my back with the rope I'd brought along—then took over at their piano and played "Some of These Days" with my left hand only.

Of course, a couple of Chicago columnists were there as my guests to cover the event and when Ben saw the syndicated column stories, he wouldn't talk to me for a month!

I didn't really appreciate and enjoy Chicago until we went back there a second time—to go into a tailspin at the Urban Room! It happened the following May, after we went back on a two-month visit to our home base at the St. Regis. We had done so well on our first visit that MCA quickly rescheduled us for the Urban Room. But the Congress Hotel, in the meanwhile, had opened two more rooms for dining and dancing!—with Leo Reisman in one and Carlos Molina in the other. This was to accommodate the World's Fair mob who walked themselves to exhaustion by day and didn't feel much like dancing at night.

However, opening night on our return to the Urban Room brought us a crowd starred with such celebrities as Texas Guinan, Rudolph Friml, Sophie Tucker, Paul Whiteman, Burns and Allen, George Gershwin, Oscar Shaw, Ernest Truex, Billy Gaxton and others. My friend Victor Watson, editor of the *Herald-Examiner,* was there with Walter Winchell, who got a specially big hand when he stood up to take his bow.

When we introduced these big names and they stood up to take a bow, Winchell got a terrific hand but Arthur Brisbane was practically ignored. Winchell turned to me surprised and said—nodding toward Brisbane, "That's the man that really deserves the great applause!"

A big surprise awaited me during our first week. Two representatives of an advertising agency came in for dinner one night, then asked me to join them at their table.

"Lopez," they stated, "two weeks from tonight you start playing for the Real Silk program. You and your orchestra will get $1,500. Is it a deal?"

It was that quick and simple. We had to get ready in a hurry, but that didn't concern me. Alice Joy and Jane Froman were the vocal stars of the program, and with such performers we didn't need much time.

But after several weeks at the Urban Room what we needed was customers. Our chances of lasting out the engagement kept going down—and my emotional outlook down with it. I wanted desperately to stay in Chicago, not only because our radio show originated there, but in order not to admit that we could have a failure. I did something about it—cast around for other local opportunities where we might finish out our midwest visit until we were due back at the St. Regis. I even consulted local astrologers, fortune tellers and palmists.

It was while I was holding a lovely woman's hand that a possible answer to our problems arrived. She suggested that I talk to a Chicago impresario named Eddie Liebensberger about putting my band in the 225 Club, which he owned along with Gus Winkler. Eddie's counterproposition was that I reopen a swank place called the Opera Club, as a full-third partner. "With your New York society background we could draw the Chicago society swells there."

We were almost at the contract-signing stage when sensible Dorothy Gullman, my publicity girl, cooled me off. She changed my mind for keeps by bringing Harry Richman over to our closing week at the Urban Room in order to sell him the idea that we were the right band for his Chez Paree show. Just a couple of dance sets convinced Harry and then the two of them convinced me.

I got out of my previous tentative commitment with a simple telephone call in which I told Liebensberger that the St. Regis didn't want me to enter the proferred deal. He was gracious about it and said he'd get someone else. He never did, though. The night I opened at the Chez Paree, a desperate Eddie Liebensberger committed suicide in his palatial home—and his partner Gus Winkler was rubbed out by gangland bullets!

My first near contact with the Chicago underworld had occurred during our first date at the Urban Room. The Congress Hotel management had given me a luxurious suite on the top floor. A few days after I moved in, a couple of odd-looking characters knocked on the apartment door and asked if they could look in one of the bedroom closets to see if the previous occupant (a Mr. Brown) had left an important missing document there. I told them to go right ahead.

When they were through one of them remarked, "You've been real nice about this, not makin' a fuss. We'll tell Mr. Brown you're an okay guy."

"Thanks very much," I responded, not particularly caring.

But an hour later, out of curiosity, I asked the manager about my predecessor, Mr. Brown.

"Brown isn't his real name, Mr. Lopez," he said. "He's better known as Al Capone."

For the record, we opened at the Chez Paree on October 6, 1933. Harry Richman emceed the show which included Frances Langford, Ina Ray Hutton, Rose Marie Deering, and the Chez Paree "Adorables." Closing night at the Urban Room we had played for forty-five people. Here we had a crowd of over twelve hundred with I don't know how many turned away when the ropes went up at ten. It made all the difference in the world to the band and me. The special spark that snaps and crackles when things are going right gave us an extra charge that we put into our music. And so the ropes stayed up, with the twelve hundred capacity reached almost every night. In a couple of weeks we were back at the top literally and emotionally.

Among the many people I met while at the Chez Paree was Charles "Buddy" Rogers, one of our regular patrons. Promptly at one each night he would put in a long distance call to Hollywood. At the other end of the line, of course, was Mary Pickford. I never saw a man so obviously in love as he was as he talked to "America's Sweetheart" two thousand miles away.

One night he didn't have to make the phone call. Miss Pickford had come to Chicago, and Buddy brought her to the Chez Paree. We dedicated one of the year's hit songs to them: "The Touch of Your Hand"—made especially appropriate by their soon-to-come marriage.

Another romance flourished right under my eyes when Martha Raye fell in love with my vocalist Arthur Beddows. She met him at the Chez Paree almost every night, but one evening Arthur suggested a more expensive date at the swank Edgewater Beach Hotel. Martha put on the delighted act, then came over to my table in tears.

"How can I go to the Edgewater Beach in this crummy old coat?" she explained to Dorothy Gullman. "They wouldn't even let me in the back entrance with this on."

"Don't let that worry you, Martha," Dorothy generously suggested. "Wear my mink. Come on, now. I insist."

Martha gave in to the idea with obvious delight. Her date that night was a big success and her memory of it just as excellent. Several years later while Martha was doing a movie in Hollywood she saw Dorothy come on the set as a studio visitor. Typical of her, Martha Raye stopped the cameras and rushed over.

"Dorothy Gullman!" she shouted. "Remember the coat you loaned me! . . . The Chez Paree! . . . Arthur Beddows! . . . Vincent Lopez!"

Dorothy tried to help another young singer during our Chez Paree days.

"This girl can't miss, Vincent," she said. "Good voice, beautiful face, marvelous figure—sign her for the band and she'll be a sensation."

It took some persuading (after all, I didn't use a girl vocalist with the band), but finally I agreed to audition her. "But if she's so good," I grumbled, "how come she's running an elevator at Marshall Field's?"

I never got around to the audition, though. Too bad—the elevator operator at Marshall Field's was Dorothy Lamour.

However, I made a delightful discovery at the Century of Progress Exposition, when I visited it. The hit of the show was Sally Rand and her fan dance. Sally Rand was an old friend whom I had known in New York as Helen Beck! We'd had several dates together . . . and spent them (she) talking and (I) listening to her plans for going places.

Helen certainly made good on those plans when she became Sally. Later that year, Sally Rand, Amos 'n' Andy, and the Lopez orchestra broke all the records at the Chicago Theatre.

A lot of talent and would-be talent showed up at the Chez Paree to audition for the floor show. Probably because he came back so often I took note of a friendly-eyed young man sitting patiently in the lobby almost every evening, with his arms around a strange-looking suitcase, which later proved to contain millions of dollars for that young man. He finally got his chance when a performer was stricken with an illness; and that was how Edgar Bergen and Charlie McCarthy hit the big time.

But tragedy too, came to Chicago that year. Texas Guinan was in town for the Exposition, along with Bee Jackson, the first dancer to smash with the Charleston. Back in New York I had frequently dated Bee, and it was natural for our acquaintance to renew itself in Chicago.

One afternoon I had lunch with the vibrant, happy girl. She suggested that I order salad.

"I don't go for them, Bee," I explained. "I've got a good appetite, and salads don't satisfy me."

"Well, we girls have to watch our weight. See that other table? Texas Guinan's having salad, too."

But the salads in Chicago, the year of the World's Fair, were contaminated with amoebic dysentery from which hundreds died, including beautiful Bee Jackson and vivacious Texas Guinan.

While at the Chez Paree I also fronted the show at the Chicago Theatre where I got to know Mary Garden, Al Jolson, Bing Crosby and others. Jolson was truly incomparable. He was the Mr. Show Business of his era, the secret of his success was his love for people whom he wanted to give the emotional release of laughter and tears. When Paramount made *The Big Broadcast of 1932,* Bing was the biggest star in that hodgepodge of famous names. Although Bing's part was shot in Hollywood, Paramount wanted me to lead the band for his songs and since my commitments at the St. Regis held me in New York we did it the hard way: Bing sang his numbers for the soundtrack on the Coast, and with a special record of them to guide me, we then dubbed in the music out on Long Island! Paramount then spliced them together. When the picture was finished it seemed that Bing was singing and we were right there accompanying him. But it wasn't till he came to Chicago for the première that I met Bing—although we had worked in the picture together!

Chicago was less formal than New York, and more competitive in the music field. New bands were coming up there, with the new jazz concepts that soon blossomed out as swing. Equally good were the Chicago exponents of the sweet style, with Wayne King as the established head, the newcomer Hal Kemp, and Kay Kayser. Rising in popularity for their Dixieland were Bob Crosby and his Bobcats.

One of my most memorable Chicago recollections dates back to December 5, 1933, when Prohibition was thrown out the back door. A week before that Harry Richman said to the customers, "Lopez and I have a bet. On the night of repeal you will see Lopez under the table—no, you'll see Toots Lopez under the piano!" Well, I had made a lot of inquiries on how to tame a drink, and was told to buffer it with olive oil. Taking drink for drink, Harry went into a crying jag and at two A.M. had to be taken home, while I was still up on my feet.

Chapter 52. NEW YEAR TO NEW YEAR

1933 had been no bargain economically for America, with the "bank holiday" in March and abandonment of the gold standard in October, but the New Year's Eve crowd in Chicago that night gave no thought to that. The party ran until six in the morning. From there we went over to the Vincent Bendix home (of washing-machine fame). Quite a crowd turned up, and when breakfast was slow in reaching the table, Louise Groody, Harry Richman, and Phil Baker nominated me to fill in as their short-order cook for ham and eggs.

It seemed like a lot of fun, but as I was standing at the enormous kitchen range dropping eggs into frying pans my memory swept back to boyhood days when I had cooked the meals at home during my mother's illnesses. The recollection got me quite misty-eyed and as soon as I could get away to the telephone, I put in a call to my mother and sister back in Brooklyn, wishing them a happy New Year. It was too late for such greetings to my father. He had died several years before.

The reflective mood was still on me when I got back to my own room, so instead of going to sleep, I wrote in my diary. I recorded the last day of '33 as the closeout of a year which had set me some pretty hard tasks—a dangerous tailspin at the Urban Room, but a marvelous comeback at the Chez Paree. That got me wondering about the New Year—what it would be like. From curiosity as much as anything else, I consulted my numerology books and tried to piece together the pattern that would apply to me.

The substance of it was that I could expect a great deal of activity, sudden and unexpected changes over which I could exert little or no control. My immediate reaction was doubt, for we were a solid click at the Chez Paree and could seemingly write our own ticket on how far we'd go, how long we'd stay. Finally, I hit the pillow, wondering if I had somehow misread my pattern.

The telephone woke me in the early afternoon. It was long distance from New York—J. J. Atkinson calling from the St. Regis.

"How nice of you to phone, Mr. Atkinson," I began. "I want to wish you a happy New Year, too."

"Oh—yes, happy New Year to you, Vincent," he answered. "But this is more a business call than personal. We've got to have you back here at the St. Regis no later than March 1st."

"That's awfully soon," I said. "We're going great here."

"I'd advise you to arrange it somehow, Vincent," said J. J. "In fact, the hotel insists on it, and if you can't return, I'm afraid they'll cancel the contract. You've been gone longer than the terms allow, anyway."

I hung up the receiver with a new respect for numerology. . . .

Later that afternoon, Jules Stein of MCA, then in Chicago, also put through a call to back up Atkinson's demand and to report some great news for me in radio. Our Realsilk show had wound up just two weeks before, but Stein had another program for me, sponsored by Plough's Penetro and St. Joseph's Aspirin. Our first show was to go on that very week—January 3rd!

"How did you arrange it so quickly, Jules?" I asked him. "You didn't have it when you phoned me a few days ago."

"It broke very fast, that's all," he explained. "I met Abe Plough on the train to Washington. He told me about expanding advertising plans for their products, and I told him about you. Before we even got to Philadelphia we had the deal set up. Thirteen weeks with an option for another thirteen that I'm sure they'll exercise. It looks like a big year for you, Vince. Plenty of action."

Newspaperman Victor Watson gave me a farewell party the night we closed at the Chez Paree, and I was still so excited about my numerology score on predicting events about myself that I offered to do some forecasts on the guests at our table. I don't know how accurately the others turned out, but I hit it on the nose for District Attorney Dwight Green, an up-and-coming young man in Illinois politics.

"Mr. Green," I predicted, "some day you will be the Governor of this state."

And a few years later he was in the Governor's mansion.

I left Chicago in a blaze of glory, and went back to the St. Regis and the Seaglades, where we opened with a bang. Clara Bell Walsh and many others were there to greet us. It was a real ball of fire. The sadness I had felt at leaving Chicago dissolved in the old friendships in New York.

Our band was still getting a lot of important party dates, and benefits arranged by organizations as money-getters. I was playing such parties as the June Ball sponsored by Mrs. Randolph Hearst and Mrs. Vincent Astor for Mrs. Franklin D. Roosevelt's unemployed girls, the Cobina Wright Circus Ball and one that I have played for years—the Israel Orphan Asylum Benefit. In fact, this goes back to 1921, when I first met Judge Gustave Hartman and the lady who later became Mrs. Gustave Hartman. I have played this engagement every year from then up to the present, and it is a "must" on my calendar.

All this activity, plus a degree of nonchalance and the satisfaction that success builds up over the years, blinded me to the big changes that were beginning in popular music. The Dorseys, Artie Shaw and others who had been in my band pioneered in new jazz forms. Swing was on the way, but I ignored it. I no longer tried to bring anything new to our vaudeville dates. I had even put our old scenic effects into storage. We were tops in radio, which needed no scenic effects! So ran my short-sighted reasoning.

Format changes in our Plough radio show put major emphasis on big-name guest-stars (Milton Berle, Jack Dempsey, Lenore Ulric, Peggy Joyce, Edward G. Robinson) with a relative newcomer, Ed Sullivan, as master of ceremonies. I think this was one of Ed Sullivan's first radio shows. He did a very good job, was friendly and affable, but he seemed like a scared little boy when he started. He was that way, too, when he started television, but look at him today!

About that time we added a feature performer to our band who soon became famous on radio, coast to coast. He was Clara Bell Walsh's discovery, rather than mine.

We were rehearsing at the St. Regis Roof one afternoon when a phone call interrupted. "Don't be angry, Vincent," said Clara Bell, detecting the annoyance in my voice. "You'll thank me for this. Just listen."

The next sound I heard seemed to be two people whistling "At Dawning."

"Isn't he wonderful!" Clara Bell enthused. "Isn't he wonderful?"

"He? You mean to say that was just one guy?"

"That's right," she stated. "His name is Fred Lowery. I'm sending him over. But there's one thing I want to explain in advance. Fred is—almost totally blind."

Having denied him the gift of sight, nature compensated Fred with wonderful artistry at whistling (which, by the way, is one of the oldest forms of entertainment). We put him on that very night at the St. Regis Roof, and he stopped the show. He was one of the few entertainers—if not the only one—who auditioned successfully by telephone!

In the meanwhile I was made uneasy by rumors of financial troubles at the St. Regis. Business was good in the dining rooms, but all hotels were doing poorly in room rentals. The management group Atkinson headed asked for a drop in the interest charges on mortgages held by the Astor family which also owned the land. Knowing that Mary Duke Biddle was very rich, the Astors refused.

Internal squabbles arose. In their own way the cream of the social world can heat up a feud as hot and furious as the mountaineers. When the bankruptcy action finally broke, the Astors offered a mere $250,000 for hotel furnishings that had recently cost over $2,000,000. When Mrs. Biddle and the St. Regis corporation objected, the quarter-million offer was withdrawn and the suggestion made that they throw the furntiure out in the street! Mary Duke Biddle wound up with $9,500,000 less in the family fortune when the bankruptcy was over and the hotel ownership transferred.

On June 30th my good friend J. J. resigned from the St. Regis. He called me into his office and said that this was the finish of our contract. He had told the receivers to keep me on as long as they could. But things moved rapidly. On July 4th, our twenty-six weeks for the Plough radio show terminated and Guy Lombardo took my place. On the day I closed at the St. Regis, Freddie Martin took my place with a smaller band.

We were suddenly out of two jobs, but not out of work. Alerted by my forecast of the uncertain year and the column mentions of foreclosure at the St. Regis, I had asked Jules Stein to have immediate theatre bookings ready. As a result, we opened in Baltimore on July 6th!

"Whatever happened at the St. Regis?" Jules asked me, disappointed at the way things had turned out. "Did you say the wrong things to the wrong people? Take sides in the bankruptcy?"

"I stayed out of it, Jules," I assured him. "If I made any mistakes it was leaving the St. Regis so many times and staying away so long. But never mind the past, where do I go from here?"

"Try vaudeville a while, Vince," was the best Jules could offer. "We'll keep you booked pretty steady, but if you get any chances elsewhere, take them. And how about making some changes in your band? Have you thought of that?"

"My band's all right," I insisted. "We've got some great sidemen in it. I know about the new music styles, but they're just passing fancies. We'll stick to what we've got."

What we had was plenty good enough for out-of-town dates, but New York was another story. Our first date back at the Capitol Theatre, after a succesful swing of the Eastern Seaboard, produced an audience that resembled a September 30th turnout at the baseball park of an eighth place team! New Yorkers remembered our interesting scenic effects, and when we came up with nothing more spectacular than a straight music presentation they felt cheated.

Nevertheless J. J. Atkinson hadn't lost faith in us. He phoned me about a new connection he had made, and asked me to meet him that afternoon over at Radio City.

"Wonderful news, Vincent," he announced. "See this skyscraper? Right on the top floor they're going to build a beautiful restaurant that will have everything and a tremendous view of the whole island. How would you like to have your band play there?"

"In an office building?" I questioned. "It would never go, J. J. People want to get *away* from business surroundings when they go out at night. Where would the glamour be?"

"In the beautiful room—we're calling it the Rainbow Room," he answered, "plus a fine band. I've had several offers, but this is the one I'm taking. Will you join me in it?"

"No, thanks," I foolishly declined. "Maybe you can take a chance with your future and the Rockefellers with their money, but I can't afford the gamble."

While Atkinson got someone else for his Rainbow Room, Sonny Werblin and Bill Goodheart of MCA came up with a coast-to-coast trip that would wind up at the glamorous Beverly Wilshire Hotel in Beverly Hills. With hopeful thoughts of getting the band into some movie musicals, I signed the contract.

On our way west we played the Sky Club at Pittsburgh, near the airport. I auditioned a young singer there whom several of the fellows in my band urged me to hear.

"Will you drop everything else and join our band?" I enthused. "Work in as our vocalist as we go along, and I guarantee that when we hit Hollywood you'll have a dozen movie offers in a week. You're the greatest thing I've heard since Bing Crosby!"

"Well, I don't know," he wavered. "We were married just last summer and my wife doesn't like me to be away on long trips. Could I look you up when you come back to New York? Meanwhile I think I'll continue with Freddie Carlone's band around here."

"Get in touch with me any time," I disappointedly answered him. "Better still, where can I get in touch with you when we're back east?"

"Oh, that's easy," he answered. "Just drop me a line: Perry Como, Canonsburg, Pa."

While in Pittsburgh I visited St. Paul's Monastery of the Order of the Passionist Fathers. It was there that I would have fulfilled my novitiate if I had finished at Dunkirk. My good friend Father Sebastian was there and he was delighted when I dropped in. He took me around, showed me holy relics and the catacombs where they buried the deceased fathers. The sacred atmosphere thrilled me, but I knew it was not my destiny. I knew, too that behind the physical and material things I was doing my spiritual background would come to the fore some day.

My visit to California in September 1934 was my first. We were to open the Gold Room of the Beverly Wilshire Hotel, a tough place to play since the room was full of massive pillars and half the customers needed periscopes to see us. All the Hollywood luminaries turned up for opening night. I fell victim to the movie-hero fever and sent out for an autograph book for the signatures of Nancy Carroll, George Raft (what a renewal of auld lang syne it was to see him), Loretta Young (she's the page one signature in my autograph book) Mary Brian, Rudy Vallee (the kid I hadn't let sing with my band), Sylvia Sidney, Virginia Bruce, Ralph Bellamy, Jean Hersholt, Ralph Rainger, Louella Parsons, and dozens more.

Another signature was Thelma Todd's. In fact her boy friend, who later was accused of killing her, signed his name right above hers.

Two celebrities at the opening who were particularly nice to me were Gloria Swanson and Herbert Marshall. "This isn't the room for you, Vincent," Gloria said. "It hurts your band, I've heard you often enough on radio to know how you really play."

"What can I do about it? I'm signed up and we'll have to make the best of it."

"Not necessarily," said Gloria. "There's a beautiful room upstairs —the Florentine Room—that would be marvelous for you. It needs redecorating, but I'll do it personally if you can work out the switch."

"Thank you for taking such an interest in us, Gloria," I said, "but we'll be here only a few months and I guess we'd better put up with things as they are. If it were a long-term date, I'd certainly take you up on it!"

Maybe I should have followed through on it. Shortly after we left, the hotel opened the Florentine Room with Orville Knapp's band and it was a success.

From what happened at the Beverly Wilshire I realized that my band was losing its spark. Cary Grant called my attention to it. "Sure we love you, Vincent, but we can't keep on loving the same thing all the time. In marriage that's called monogamy, but in music it's monotony!"

The only evening that really went over with the movie crowd was Celebrity Night. One of the guests I introduced on our last Celebrity Night was Ralph Rainger, writer of "Love in Bloom." We sat down at the piano together and played it as a duet. We received a terrific hand. A week later he was killed in an airplane accident.

We closed at the Gold Room on November 4th, almost two months ahead of time. I was relieved because we were not making the success we should have. A great opportunity, but I was not ready for it. So I relaxed and gave myself some time to see and enjoy California. It's a marvelous state. As for Californians, I found them in between the indifferent New Yorkers and the impetuously friendly Chicagoans.

Abe Lastfogel's prediction that we would be back at his William Morris office proved correct. Since MCA had no spot for us we let Abe book us into Miami—my first time in Florida. There were several stopover dates for us in Texas that restored our self-confidence. From also-ran status in Beverly Hills we hit star-attraction importance at the Baker Hotel in Dallas, then topped even that success with a sellout to 6100 dancing students at a University of Texas prom in Austin!

Florida turned out to be a big surprise in many respects. However, *the* surprise awaited me at Miami's Deauville Club.

"Hello, Vincent," the owner greeted me. "Remember me from Pabst's Restaurant in Brooklyn? Remember the raid the cops made on us that New Year's eve?"

It was Frank Zagarino who had wanted to replace me with Jimmy Durante years before and who still owed me that last week's pay. I never did collect the thirty dollars, but it didn't matter now. He more than made it up with the salary he was paying for the band at Deauville.

We opened on New Year's Eve. The night was hot and muggy. Even our bounciest tunes put few people on the dance floor. I never in my life played to a deader crowd.

"It's only eleven," I said to my men. "They'll get going by midnight."

They were as good as gone at twelve . . . as good as gone home! The bodies were still there, but the spirit. . . . We went into the customary "Taps," "Auld Lang Syne," "For He's a Jolly Good

Fellow," "Happy Days," etc., as 1935 made its appearance; but that crowd just sat there staring, as if wondering why we were whooping it up!

"Well, fellows," I remarked as we ended the last number to absolute silence, "let's wish each other a happy New Year. Nobody else seems to be doing it, and I can't understand why."

Since that New Year's night wound up so early, I didn't seem to have much to write in my diary about it until I remembered an encounter in front of the Deauville. It was a very misty afternoon and an old lady suddenly appeared alongside of me.

"You're Mr. Lopez, aren't you?"

"Yes."

"I'm surprised that you're going to work here."

"Why?"

"If you had studied your astrological and numerological aspects, you would have known this place is not for you. It's full of wrong vibrations. You won't be here long and this place will never go over."

Truer words never were spoken.

I closed my diary for that year with "So long, 1934 . . . please don't come back. . . ."

Chapter 53. I SEE AMERICA

Deauville was an oval-shaped building flanked by two tall yellow towers. It stood on Collins Avenue between sand dunes, facing the ocean. It was to have been operated by Tex Rickard and Nat Evans, who owned the Brook in Saratoga. Great plans had been laid for gambling and the protection was all paid, when Tex Rickard died. Evans and his crowd gave the place up after two years.

Lucy Cotton Thomas had taken over and rented the gambling

concession to Frank Zagarino. Frank got nowhere in his attempts to swing protection for his games of chance, without which there wasn't much use operating. I asked him how Nat Evans had managed in prior years.

"They had a system," he explained, "but they couldn't afford to keep it going. They kept a few big trucks on the alert in case a raid was set in motion. All they could get was about an hour's warning, but the trucks got here inside of ten minutes and moved out the gambling equipment. There was an extra payoff along the line right away, and by eight o'clock the same night the tables were back in place."

Unable to afford the protection money and the 24-hour trucking service Frank Zagarino turned to name talent to keep the Deauville open. My orchestra, the dance team of Baron and Blair, and Hollywood's Lillian Roth were expected to lure the customers. I had known Lillian from our days together in the Earl Carroll *Vanities*. I liked her but she didn't like me. I guess our vibrations didn't click.

Vibrations were not the problem when Helen Morgan replaced Lillian Roth as headliner. For reasons known only to her she arrived a whole week early—and promptly went to bed with a case of "nerves." I had just returned from an afternoon cocktail party at Manna Zucca's beautiful home when Zagarino met me in the Deauville lobby.

"You got to do something, Vince," he insisted. "This Morgan woman is in such a state that I don't think she'll be able to open the new show for us."

"That's a whole week off," I argued. "Unless she's a hospital case, she'll be all right by then. What's wrong with her?"

"I don't really know," Frank went on. "I just left her and she says she has a terrible attack of nerves. From what I could see, it was getting worse by the minute. Somebody's got to straighten her out. Will you talk to her and get her to see a doctor?"

When I reached Helen's apartment, the front door was wide open, and when I got no response, I walked right on into the bedroom. Helen, looking tired and drawn, had relaxed into deep slumber, but I decided to wake her up and discuss the illness she complained of.

"I'll be all right, Vincent," she claimed. "Just a bad attack of the jitters, that's all. Sometimes life catches up with a person and . . . I'll get over it."

"Let's not take any chances," I insisted. "You might need medicine, or just some vitamins. I'll get you the best doctor in Miami, and we'll see what he thinks."

"Never mind getting a doctor," she replied. "I feel like this sometimes—all keyed up and nervous about the future. But I snap out of it in time. Just seeing someone I know helps. I'm glad you thought enough to drop by, Vincent."

Over a cup of coffee, Helen and I had a long discussion about show business, the good parts and the bad, the likeable people and the unlikeable. By telling her some of my troubles, I got her mind off her own.

Helen gave a marvelous performance on the 21st, and I was deeply thrilled by her special artistry as I played for her at the piano. She had talent that could captivate an audience and envelop them in the sheer magic of make-believe . . . and that's the secret of showmanship.

Business was excellent at the club for a change, but our happy smiles became a desperate grin once more when our luck and Helen's health ran out again. The ups and downs of show-business people involve more than the booking dates they land. . . .

My little old lady suggested that I visit Professor Seward, Miami's leading astrologist for a reading. He was off somewhere on a trip, but his daughter Juliet was taking his place. I found her most interesting and accurate. Everything she told me came about. She mentioned that everything was confused—until the 25th—and from that time on the situation would be relieved.

Since she confirmed that the vibrations at the Deauville were no good for me, I decided to make whatever arrangements I could to get away. That very afternoon I ran into Mike Yoder and Frankie Curtis who liked my band at the Deauville and wanted to make a buck. They suggested that I play at the Biscayne Dog Track, which was not doing any business. They were sure that if I played there between the races and brought in a visiting celebrity each evening, it would perk up business. The money part of our informal agreement was very good but there was no assurance of our being paid.

Nevertheless I gave it my OK, even though I had no idea how to get out of my contract with Zagarino by February 4th, the date they wanted me to start at the track.

But destiny was busy as usual. January 25th came along and I remembered what Juliet Seward had told me about watching out for that day. She was so right! Frank Zagarino told me he wanted to release the band because his latest attempts to get the green light on gambling had failed. To his immense relief I told him I had felt this coming on and booked myself into the Biscayne Dog Track.

He laughed and said, "So you're going to the dogs."

Little did he know that we would do such terrific business that the Hollywood (Florida) Dog Track grabbed us immediately after the Biscayne track closed. And on the day I started at Biscayne the Deauville went into receivership.

Getting by the first week at the dog track took a bit of luck, for we later found out they were just about down to their last dime—didn't even have the money to pay for dog food! A lot of people who liked our band but couldn't afford night-club prices came to the track and business was sensational. Some were so unfamiliar with dog-track procedures that when they'd come up to get an autograph, they asked us how to put a bet on the races.

What a change from Deauville! We played two numbers between each race, had a different celebrity performing with us each night (such as Helen Morgan, Rudy Vallee, Jimmie Fox, Ed Sullivan, etc.). We were finished by eleven and then visited the swank places that were going broke because other forms of gambling were taboo while the race tracks had been legalized. Our bandstand was outdoors and we got more fresh air in a week than most musicians inhale over an entire year. Florida, which had looked like a disaster, became an outstanding success for me and, furthermore, we were pioneering another form of entertainment that opened up new employment for bands.

This was a big travelling year for me. In April I headed north. We went to Niagara Falls and played at another gambling place, the Hollywood Restaurant in North Tonawanda near Buffalo. Gambling was OK there and business was great.

From there we worked our way into the Middle West, down south into Texas and made a lot of friends. We played all the big cities of Texas. Fred Lowery, our whistler, was a show-stopper there for more reasons than his talent. He's a Texan himself and the Panhandle State loves a local boy who makes good.

While I was on the road my old boss, J. J. Atkinson telephoned me that he was handling the Ambassador Hotel on Park Avenue. He and his partner Mr. Thorne would like to have me back in New York immediately to open their new Trianon Room. I accepted. We were doing fine on the road, but I have always felt that a band is better off at a place it can call home. Maybe it's simply that the security I had lacked from my twelfth birthday on, when I left my home for the monastery, has always impelled me to "seek anchorage."

I arrived with my orchestra three days ahead of our slated opening. I had my boss, J. J. take me over the room; I wanted to see what vibrations I would receive. With exquisite taste, Maurice Fatio and Christop Castou had produced a modern adaption of the elegant Louis XVI court style. The lighting effects were to be operated from the bandstand. There were fourteen switches with a dimmer control which I had innovated at the Pennsylvania Hotel, used again at the St. Regis, and now here. The décor was delicate, but cold—a great deal of white with gold trim and a ceiling in black also with gold trim. As impressed as I was, I felt its coldness. I knew I would have a tough assignment.

The opening night was a sellout, a Henry Street Settlement benefit of which Mrs. John Fell was chairman. New York society really supports such occasions.

Besides my orchestra of fourteen men were Maxine Tappen, girl vocalist; Fred Lowery, whistler; and Dorothy Stone and Charles Collins, a dance team. Although the Trianon Room seemed to have everything I felt that it was *too* smart. As the weeks went by we merely managed to get by. One bright spot was the night José Iturbi and his daughter came in. We played duets together on the piano and to my surprise Iturbi went to town with the "Twelfth Street Rag."

The worst night was Christmas Eve. The Trianon Room was

empty. J. J. tried to cheer me up. "Maybe it's just a freak night, Vincent. Let's see how things go on New Year's Eve. Anyway, I'd like you to play a special affair at the Rainbow Room on the 29th. It will give the boys a lift to entertain a crowd again."

The Rainbow Room—the restaurant in an office building for which I had predicted swift failure! "We'll be glad to play it," I assured him, "and I won't need the elevator to get me there. I'm going to kick myself up every flight!"

New Year's Eve at the Trianon Room proved absolute disaster. I had toasted off 1934 without any regret that it was finished. How much better if 1935 had never arrived! Time was changing all around me and I seemed to be out of rhythm.

Chapter 54. WHAT THE NUMBERS TOLD ME

Although I had relinquished formal religion, I retained a firm belief in God and an interest in the spiritual side of life. But I claim no exemption from "weakness of the flesh," and material things kept attracting me. It was in quiet moments of reflection, in long hours of troubled doubt and in urgent crises that I turned back toward the Creator, just as the needle of a spinning compass seeks the north.

I was convinced of an order and purpose not only for the universe but for each individual life. No wonder, then, that numerology, whose main concept is that our lives have a specific pattern, attracted me. It's philosophy holds that personal salvation comes not from acceptance of a particular creed, but by our own effort. That idea avoids the fatalism of the eastern religions and the western beliefs that man is lost unless he finds and accepts a redeemer.

Using New Year's Day as a time to reflect on the lessons of the past and the possibilities of the year ahead had become a ritual with me. I sized up 1936 as a year with plenty of mistakes to learn from. My sixth sense told me I'd been wrong in two vital respects: taking on the Trianon Room, and not tackling the new swing style that the Johnny-come-lately bands had brought with them.

However, instead of facing up to these realities, I settled for such standard good resolutions as not to procrastinate, not to spend so much time on new romances, etc.

My Trianon Room band had both the old and the new style musicians. The new style was headed by Tony Pastor, whose distinctive way of singing and playing was becoming very popular. Had I recognized his talent it would have helped me bridge the gap. But I kidded myself that Park Avenue would never go for swing. Then business got even worse after New Year's, and I prayed for guidance.

In a conversation with Esta Silsbee, my secretary, we came to the conclusion that it would be a good idea to offer the profits from my outside engagements to J. J. Atkinson to help cut down the losses. In other words, go on the road for four weeks, put a smaller band in the Trianon Room while we were away, and see how it would make out.

Atkinson was genuinely touched when I outlined the arrangement. He promptly took it up with the bondholders and came back with a glowing smile.

"They wouldn't dream of it, Vincent. First of all, it would mean having you away from the Room for a month, which they don't like. Secondly, to a man they want me to tell you they have confidence that you can put the Trianon across!"

It was Clara Bell Walsh who came to my rescue. She got busy in her social set and I put Tuesday nights aside for a Night of Fun with Clara Bell Walsh. The first one started off with Baron Wrangle as master of ceremonies and celebrities from all walks of life, but chiefly radio personalities. Business promptly picked up. But I also took this as a warning to change with the times. Just as radio had replaced vaudeville, the new jazz music was sweeping the old aside. I had told Albee off bravely enough on the vaudeville issue, but this time I couldn't tell myself that we were falling behind in the game and here was the seventh inning—time to stand up and do something.

It was at one of these celebrity nights that I first met Fred Allen. He would come to the Trianon Room with his lovely wife, Portland Hoffa, and sit off in a corner. Now and then I'd see him making notes on a scrap of paper, probably for his next radio script!

Princess Laura Rospigliosi, with whom I became fast friends, was living at the Ambassador. She had come from a family of great wealth and had married a title.

Highly influential with the Park Avenue set, the princess had a working arrangement with J.J. whereby she got her living quarters there and a commission besides on all society functions she swung our way. She helped keep the Trianon Room running by applying the Elsa Maxwell technique, with infinite grace and charm.

An idea of mine that attracted the smart crowd involved using socialites as singers. Some were really good, notably Miriam Fairbanks of the Fairbanks Scale fortune of Chicago, and Florence Weicker of the Squibb family. They got us reams of publicity in the society columns. All this helped to perk up business, but not enough.

One night, after I had finished, I stopped at the Famous Door where Mike Reilly and Ed Farley, two former musicians of mine, were packing them in singing "The Music Goes Round and Round." I offered to feature them at the Trianon Room at $400 a week, which was more than they were getting, but their answer was "No." Then, as I looked around I saw many of our society customers in that little hole in the wall!

Several months later I had a novelty hit of my own that helped start a silly craze, and at the same time brought us back into the spotlight. It was a tune called "Knock, Knock, Who's There?" which Johnny Morris, my drummer, and I had polished up after Jimmy Tyson and Bill Davis brought us their rough manuscript. That tune inflicted a fiendish game upon an America already suffering through the depression. Just a couple of verses will revive the pain of it for readers who remember the silly craze:

Knock! Knock!
Who's there?
Delia.
Delia who?
Delia cards off the top.

Knock! Knock!
Who's there?
Tarzan.
Tarzan who?
Tarzan stripes forever!

Heywood Broun wrote in his "It Seems to Me" column: "The best Knock! Knock! has been made up by me. It goes 'Knock! Knock! Who's there? A gang of vigilantes armed with machine guns, leather straps, and brass knuckles to knock the breath out of anybody who persists in playing this blame-fool Knock-Knock game!' "

But all our frantic efforts failed to keep the Trianon alive, and in the spring my suggestion of a small substitute band while I took the Lopez outfit on the road was accepted by Atkinson and the bondholders, with the stipulation that the profits be applied against the Trianon deficit.

On returning from my road trip I was greeted with the news that the Trianon would close May 2nd for the summer and it meant that this would be our last week there. Although I turned over the profits from our tour, I felt no regrets.

Losing a home base of operation put us on the road again. Railroad and plane expenses were high, and one night talking to my ex-trombonist and friend, Tommy Dorsey, whose band opened at the Lincoln Hotel, I said, "You travel a lot, Tommy. Got any ideas on how to keep transporation costs down. Do you find it cheaper to charter a plane or take the scheduled flights?"

"Charter a plane?" Tommy looked appalled. "Are you kidding? Get yourself a bus, Vince, and pile 'em in it."

"What about your girl singer?" I went on. "You have special accommodations for her, I suppose."

"Oh, sure," Tommy answered. "She gets the entire back seat so she can lie down."

Tommy was certainly irrepressible, and sometimes irresponsible, when he was a sideman with my band. Starting a group of his own put a business head on his shoulders. That's what usually happens to sidemen when they become leaders.

Another important opening was that of George Hall's fine band at the Hotel Taft Grill Room, which I attended with Princess Rospigliosi. My sixth sense told me that some day I would be playing here. I suddenly thought of my little old lady from Miami, and how she might say the "vibrations" were right.

Long Island became our home base for the summer when we were booked into the Pavilion Royal on Merrick Road on June 25th. Sick of living in a swank but confining hotel suite, I swung to the other extreme by renting a twenty-room house. It was a good place to relax in and I felt the urge toward study and prayer.

Sometimes prayers seem to get no answer; other times the answer is slow and uncertain; but on this occasion the answer came swift, clear and loud. First the J. Walter Thompson Agency signed me to do a radio show for Nash cars with Floyd Gibbons as master of ceremonies; then Nat Kalcheim, of the William Morris office, booked us into the Broadway Paramount Theatre; and Bob Christenberry asked us to open the Hotel Astor Grill Room that fall!

Christenberry thought we could attract some of my society patrons to the Astor, but I was doubtful. I wasn't sure they would go for trailing their ermine wraps and bouffant evening gowns downstairs and past the men's room and barber shop in order to reach the Grill.

But my dependable friends of the carriage trade didn't let me down during my stay at the Astor.

It was at this time that I started dating the very young, attractive, and exotic Diosa Costello. She knew everything there was to know about Latin rhythms, and the increased success of my band with Latin-American music can be credited in part to what she taught me. One night I took her to the Club Yumuri (now Birdland), a favorite haunt of mine that featured Latin music. It was a Sunday, their celebrity and amateur night, and I insisted that she go out on the floor and do her stuff. Her version of "Shoeing the Mare" brought down the house.

Later, she wanted to join my band, but I wouldn't agree to it. She went on to a big success as Bloody Mary in *South Pacific* and now is a star. Another big mistake on my part, for she would have been sensational with the band.

Bob Christenberry was a boss who could keep business and friendship far apart. He didn't hesitate to tell me the truth about my band.

"You've been standing still," he said. "Better take a close look at the competition, the way you used to when you were feuding with Paul Whiteman. When the Grill at the Hotel Pennsylvania opens tomorrow night, go down and look over the new king, Benny Goodman."

Benny's opening was a sellout. The best I could do on getting there after we had finished for the night at the Astor, was to stand in the doorway and look in over the crowd. Goodman's clarinet solos shook the place with applause, but the terrific beat and wide open brass section shook it even more. The younger crowd loved it though some of the older patrons filed out practically holding their ears.

I spotted Mrs. Statler coming out with her party, although she didn't see me, and overheard her comments as she left, "I don't care how popular they are," she was saying, "they will simply have to tone down their music and play softer or we'll have to make a change."

I knew Benny Goodman from the many conversations we had had together when my band was at the St. Regis. I hope Mrs. Statler didn't get around to suggesting changes in the style he had so patiently developed. His answer would have been a pretty forceful, "We'll play my way or else!" Benny is one of the quiet gentlemen of the music world, but he has a will of iron.

As I stood on the outer circle of the crowd that night taking in the fact that a new cycle of rhythm had rushed onto the scene and over me, I felt so downhearted I didn't even wait to get inside to congratulate Benny. Instead, swallowing the lump in my throat and blinking back the tears in my eyes, I went home. The next day I telephoned my friend Nick Pisani who had been my assistant leader at the St. Regis and now was playing with Ray Noble at the Rainbow Room. I asked him to drop by at the Astor Grill to give me a frank evaluation of my band.

He gave me the harsh truth. "Not only is the band lousy, but you're not the pianist you used to be."

"Will you help me straighten it out, Nick?" I almost pleaded. "I just mean the band. I'll have to straighten myself out, I realize, and that means going back to some fundamentals, not only in music but in my personal life."

"I can help you on one condition," Nick agreed. "Give me the full say on changes—who goes, who we get, the type of music we play."

"Anything you say," I replied. "I'll work with you and give you all the help I can."

"All right," Nick answered. "There are three men I want right away. Buddy Morrow on trombone, Charlie Spivak on the trumpet, and a young guy named Glenn Miller to do our arrangements. You'll notice the difference in a week."

Nick was a little optimistic about the time, but in a month we had a terrific new band going and started to click again. The Nash radio show was going over very well and I had more time to take inventory of myself, with Nick Pisani helping me. The next few months were successful as far as money was concerned. Radio, vaudeville, our hotel date, and the special parties we landed had me more solvent than I had ever been.

The 1936 election night at the Astor, was a great sight. The Grand Ballroom had been taken over by the Republicans and I played there that night instead of in the Grill Room. The place was decorated with big sunflowers for Kansas-born Alf Landon, who was running against Roosevelt.

At that time I was beginning to have the power to make accurate forecasts, and as I stood on the bandstand, looking at the sunflowers all over the ballroom, and hearing the Republican crowd having a good time while waiting for Landon to be elected, Bob Christenberry came over to me with a question. "I forgot to ask you before,

Vince, but have you worked out this election with your numerology? Which way is it going?"

"I'm sorry you asked me that, Bob," I said. "I don't like to disappoint you, but Roosevelt is going to beat Landon."

"Are you out of your mind?" Bob exploded. "It'll be close, maybe, but the Republicans will win. Wait and see."

The waiting and seeing were just about over by ten that evening—and so was Bob's party.

Chapter 55. CALIFORNIA INTERLUDE

Clara Bell Walsh's Tuesday cocktail parties at the Plaza Hotel were a must for me. At one of them I was introduced to Melba Melsing Meredith Smith, who played the guitar and sang folk songs. She looked exotic, she had a deep throaty voice, and her social connections were excellent. With Christenberry's approval I put her on for the supper show and it brought us a society crowd. Through Melba I met Gloria Vanderbilt who had wit and an intriguing speaking voice which did things to you.

Everything was riding along nicely when I got a call from Bill Goodheart of MCA telling me the Nash program was going to California with Grace Moore co-starring with me. But they wanted me to take only two key men and an arranger. This was another time I had to turn to prayer to make the right decision, and again my sixth sense guided me.

It was tough to scrap that band, because we had fine musicians in it. I tried to talk my arranger, Glenn Miller, into accompanying me at a steep increase in salary, but he regarded the break in jobs as a chance to form his own orchestra.

"Mr. Lopez, how do you think I'll make out?" he asked. "Not just your professional opinion, but by your numerology forecast."

"Professionally there's no doubt that you've got what it takes, Glenn," I assured him, "and as for your pattern under numerology, it spells success."

And his career bore out this prediction. It was a sad day for millions when his plane crashed. But he left a lasting monument in his music.

On April 28th I arrived in Los Angeles and was met by Max Sturgis from the MCA office who was putting the rest of my band together for me. All the time I was required to give the Nash program was three hours of rehearsal Friday, and the half-hour broadcast on Saturday afternoon. That left me plenty of time to renew old friendships in the movie capital.

But friendships are transient in Hollywood, so I turned to the eternal things California offers in its majestic scenery. After my first broadcast on Saturday I drove to Yosemite Valley, the most beautiful place I have seen. There man really knows how infinitesimal he is in the sight of God, who gave to nature such overpowering grandeur. I stayed at the Awanhnee Hotel, which is truly a traveler's dream. From the full-length windows of the dining room you could see Glacier Point and Mt. Baldy. I woke up the first morning I was there with a keener feeling for the greatness of the universe, the smallness of me, and the mercy of a Creator who might remember me among such of his handiworks. David must have had similar feelings when he wrote some of his psalms.

Then followed week-long visits to the Redwoods, Riverside, Catalina Island, Palm Springs, and other scenic places.

That glorious vacation ended when the twenty-six weeks of the Nash radio show were over. The final program was followed by a party for the cast, which I remember best for a photo and a kiss from lovely Grace Moore.

I headed back east on a quickly arranged tour of one-nighters with a group of Coast musicians, including the talented LeRoy Holmes. The farther east we went, the colder those Californians got, and the more homesick for their sunny state. Soon after we reached New York they headed west again, and I was left without a band, except for LeRoy Holmes and my two key men, Nick Pisani and Johnny Morris.

But not without a friend! Some time before, a sudden need for quick cash forced me to take on a partner again, to the tune of $10,000. The tune got pretty sour when he tried to make decisions for me. Word got around that I was in urgent need of ten grand to buy him out.

I had just managed to get to sleep about four one morning when an insistent knock on the door awakened me. It was a Western Union boy, accompanied by a house officer, with a thick envelope to deliver. I signed for the envelope, threw it into a corner, and fell back into bed. In the morning I discovered that the envelope contained $10,000 in cash and a note saying, "Buy your partner out—A Friend."

The impact of this was so great that I burst into tears. Some unseen power was always there to help me! Although there was no name signed to the message I could guess who had sent it. I bought my partner out and eventually paid back the money to the mysterious donor.

With the help of Nick Pisani and Manny Heicklen I assembled a combination mostly of my original musicians. We got good road dates including Billy Rose's Cleveland Aquacade. Following Cleveland, we played the Drake Hotel in Chicago and, as 1937 ended, we were at the Gibson Hotel in Cincinnati. We had a solid beat, a number of sidemen not topped anywhere at swinging it; but we couldn't catch up to the newer bands to which we had abdicated our leadership. Still 1937 had been a good year for me in many ways; and according to numerology, I knew that 1938 should be a year of fulfillment.

Chapter 56. HOW TO HIT THE HEADLINES

I wonder if the old, lush days of publicity will ever come back for bandleaders. Paul Whiteman and I got front-page mentions galore when we were feuding for the King-of-Jazz sceptre—which we eventually divided like a wishbone, with Paul getting the bigger half. While such publicity was still easy to get I let loose an idea that brought me plenty of headaches as well as clippings. It was a 1938 brainstorm of my public relations man Joe Glaston about re-writing "The Star-Spangled Banner" so it would be more singable. I had long noticed that even professional singers with years of vocal training dreaded the high notes of the 17th, 18th, 29th, and 30th bars, whose range defies anyone but an Yma Sumac with her three-octave span.

I came up with a more singable version that dropped all the F naturals to D natural, bringing it within the reach of baritones and altos. My premise was that many Americans don't sing their own national anthem because they *can't* sing it—and therefore never learn the words. I claimed it should be sung (as well as loved) by everyone, instead of being left to the occasional voice that can span its range.

I got support for my proposal from some American Legion Post commanders and from Mrs. William A. Becker, President-General of the Daughters of the American Revolution. The press services gave the story a big play and newspapers all over the nation accorded it feature coverage. Soon the mail poured in, at first favorable but soon swinging sharply to disagreement, criticism, then outright threats against me! The Ambassador Hotel had to discontinue accepting telephone calls for "that so-and-so Lopez. . . . who does he think he is? etc., etc."

When I played the Hippodrome in Baltimore, a Mrs. Reuben Ross Holloway let loose a front-page blast against me from which I quote: "Lopez doesn't know how to play music anyway. I always turn him off on the radio. 'The Star-Spangled Banner' was written in the midst of battle and is an inspiration from the heart and mind that should never be changed. Each note in it is a jewel to me. I'm going to tell the Daughters of the American Revolution that even considering Mr. Lopez's idea is a desecration of their ancestors.

"And as for Mr. Lopez, I won't write to him, but he'd better not come to Baltimore again. There are too many loyal Americans here, and we won't tolerate that kind of an insult. We are going to hang Mr. Lopez in effigy."

Nevertheless, I did play Baltimore again. Mrs. Holloway didn't have a lynching party out to greet me, but she and some twenty patriotic cohorts picketed the Hippodrome Theatre. The papers played it up, the curiosity seekers came out in droves, and dear Mrs. Holloway helped us set a new attendance record.

Mrs. Holloway apparently thought that Francis Scott Key had composed the music as well as the words of our anthem. But the music had been written half a century before, as the official drinking song of the Anacreontic Society of London, a social organization whose "patron saint" was a Greek poet who wrote ecstatically of wine, women, and song! When some of its members migrated to the colonies they started branches here and our Francis Scott Key was a member of the Baltimore group.

Key, a lawyer, was an amateur poet as well, who assured himself of a correct meter by making his verses fit the rhythm of well known songs. He liked the beat of his society's official song, "To Anacreon in Heaven," and wrote a number of other lyrics to it besides the famous one he wrote when he was held aboard the British ship from which he witnessed the bombardment of Fort McHenry. Consequently, Key's inspiration involved only the *words* he wrote. These he originally titled "The Defense of Fort McHenry" and he promptly sold the verses to the Baltimore *Patriot,* which published them with the suggestion that they be sung "To the tune of 'Anacreon in Heaven.'" An actor then appearing at the Holiday Street Theatre in Baltimore took up the suggestion and, finding himself with a hit, promptly published the song! With good theatrical sense, he changed the title from "The Defense of Fort McHenry" to "The Star-Spangled Banner."

I explained all this in a letter to Mrs. Holloway. It was like trying to cool off a blast furnace. To this day I sincerely believe our anthem should be made singable for average voices instead of being limited to sopranos with operatic range.

Although my version of "The Star-Spangled Banner" was granted a copyright, and mention of the new version was published in the *Congressional Record,* my dream of revising it so everyone could sing it went glimmering when the D.A.R. shelved its president's proposal. Next year the onrush of World War II ended all chance of changing it in our time.

Another 1938 activity of mine that got coast-to-coast newspaper mention were the jazz appreciation lectures I gave at New York University. They were well-attended and I made the most of it by inviting prominent columnists to sit in with the college students. Swing was the national rage in jazz rhythms and everybody had his own version of how it originated and what it meant in the American culture. My viewpoint was original if nothing else. Let's look over some of my old lecture notes:

"Why does the younger generation like swing?"

"Well, nature gives us music as an emotional outlet, and young people are highly emotional, not having learned to suppress their feelings as members of the middle-age set do. The adult person abides by the dictates of the social code that emotions be controlled in general, at least to some extent. Many younger people, taking example from this suppression, carry it too far and suppress themselves in an extreme degree. They thereby build up an irresistible need for letting themselves go, and swing or jazz music provides the opportunity for responding to this urge! This is not a bad thing at all for human beings. Music has always been an outlet for emotions that can even cure physical ills."

As for how the term originated, everybody and his favorite uncle has an opinion on that question. My NYU students found the idea that it is an African derivative of a native word which meant "hurry up" most logical. They also readily bought my claim that jazz was the perfect expression of the tempo and atmosphere of the machine age in which we live.

My students seemed to agree with everything I said, especially when I stopped talking and let the piano speak for me. The College of Arts and Pure Science was satisfied, too, and invited me back for the next semester. And like the absent-minded professor, I didn't even notice that the school never sent me a check for my services!

Throughout the centuries, medicine has tried to use music therapy in cases of mental derangement. I think I was the first to try swing music. I suggested it to the superintendents of certain mental institutions in the late thirties. A number of attempts had been made to improve despondent victims with the soft strains of chamber music, but it was my opinion that such music only made the patients more melancholy. I felt that the insistent, lively rhythm of jazz and swing might have the opposite effect. Several institutions asked me to try out my "Swing Therapy" on their patients.

The results were reported to be good. At the Philadelphia State Hospital, Dr. Albert Wooley told the press that "many of the patients who had previously been impervious to all attempts to rouse them from their stupor applauded the swing music with real enthusiasm and stamped their feet in time with the music displaying the first interest they had shown in years." Dr. C. H. Bellinger, head of the Brooklyn State Hospital, put the experiment on a scientific basis by submitting one group of patients to the swing therapy while keeping an equal number out of the experiment. All cases involved were chosen (as he put it) "for their unresponsiveness to socialization."

The participating group certainly socialized that night. The New York *World-Telegram* gave the event a lot of coverage:

As the music progressed, many of the inmates displayed a growing interest that began with an effort to keep time but soon became active participants. A man who had refused to move for more than a year, except when forced to walk by an attendant, jumped out of his seat and improvised his own dance steps. A woman who rarely even budged stood up and sang "Strutter's Ball," while we played it.

Hospital physicians expressed themselves as satisfied with the experiment today and felt convinced that it should be continued and studied carefully. As a group, the patients exposed to the swing therapy were far more expressive and social for the next twenty-four hours than were those who were omitted from the experiment. All agreed that the lively, pulsing swing music had far greater effect on the mentally depressed than the more classical forms of melody. In this regard Mr. Lopez's belief seems pretty well verified.

"You could see the patients enjoyed it," said Dr. Wooley. "It made them happy. We know it has value. There is so much that we don't know about treating mental disorders that we are willing to try anything. Who knows? Perhaps swing music will set off a latent spark in some patients that will lead to complete recovery. Mr. Lopez is to be complimented for his idea."

We continued our swing-therapy efforts for several months, but the interest of the medical profession diminished. I'm not yet convinced that we weren't on the right track.

Chapter 57. I DISCOVER BETTY HUTTON

Among the lesser press clippings of those days was this item: "The new Lopez orchestra is a suave-swing outfit which appeals to the feet, the ears, and the heart of listeners. In the group of 17 are Fred Lowery, an extraordinary whistler, and a fifteen-year-old girl singer whom Lopez recently found in Detroit. She's Betty Jane, a personality girl for whom the maestro predicts a brilliant future."

"Betty Jane" became Betty Hutton, and the "brilliant future" I predicted soon became a reality.

I first saw Betty Jane at the Continental Café, an obscure night spot across the street from the Book Cadillac Hotel in Detroit. At first I wasn't much impressed by her jumping around with a microphone and interrupting her songs to do some jitterbug steps. Nevertheless, when my friends Mr. and Mrs. Haskell Bliss dropped in from Chicago, I took them to see her.

"I'll say she's different," Haskell agreed. "I think it's her thyroid gland. Overactive, you know."

"No, it isn't a physical condition," his wife disagreed. "She's simply out of her mind!"

I had to admit we'd never seen anything like Betty Jane at the old Urban Room where I had met the Blisses.

Spotting me at the Continental, the manager of the place came over to rave about her. "She can't miss, and I ain't the only one who says so. Ted Lewis was in here a couple nights ago and he said she's wonderful. I'll admit she don't seem like much the first song or two you hear, but this kid has really got something."

"Well, whatever she has," Mrs. Bliss commented, "I hope she doesn't give it to anyone else. I don't know how she stands that pace of hers. It wears me out just listening to her."

Nevertheless, I stayed around and listened . . . and the longer I listened the more I agreed with Ted Lewis.

Later that night I telephoned Charles Gentry of the Detroit *Times* about her. With his help on promotion, I was running a contest for a personality-girl singer, and I wanted him to put Betty Jane in it. But when the two of us caught her act at the Continental the following night, Gentry had his doubts about her.

"Look," I insisted. "You'll agree at least she's unusual and different. She's a regular dynamo."

"So she's a dynamo," he agreed. "That doesn't make her a singer. We're looking for a good band singer in this contest. Aren't you?"

"No, that's not what I'm looking for," I replied. "Good band singers are a dime a dozen, even in Detroit. I want somebody who has the potential to make it big—become a star."

"She'll never be a star," Gentry disagreed. "It isn't only that she can't sing. Her feet are too damned big. Take a look!"

"So what?" I grew stubborn. "I'll buy her the right shoes."

After Betty Jane had won the contest I found out she had only two suitable numbers, "Dipsy Doodle" and "I Want To Make

Rhythm." Building a career on a couple of rhythm tunes called for patience on my part but infinitely more on hers. I told her so as we were en route to the Palace Theatre in Fort Wayne and her première with the band.

That night she came into my drawing room to talk over salary and her routine. Her face glowed with excitement and gratitude. She gave me an impression of angelic innocence and I began to doubt the wisdom of signing her on. The vaudeville hops ahead of us could make a little angel awfully homesick—and reviews or listless audiences would discourage an angelic temperament. I was soon to learn that cherubic-looking Betty Jane had the determination and the reactions of a hellcat!

Her appetite, though, was that of a healthy, growing teenager. After a quick rehearsal, I took her to breakfast at Berghoff Gardens, the spot for entertainers in Fort Wayne. The boss was quite a character and reminded me of Primo Carnera.

"Let's start with orange juice," I suggested. "Then how about eggs? Would you like some ham and eggs?"

"No," said Betty Jane, "I'd like a steak!"

It was the same when we went back for a late lunch. At dinner, after we finished our second show, Betty Jane finished her third steak. After the last performance, she felt hungry, so back we went for another steak.

"What is this, Betty Jane?" I asked, "this steak kick of yours. Are you on a high-protein diet?"

"I'm so sick of scrimping along on hot dogs and hamburgers," she confided, "that I promised myself I'd just have steak every meal if I ever made enough money."

Betty Jane fascinated me. I enjoyed taking her to breakfast, lunch, dinner, supper.

The afternoon theatre audience is always a tough one. Betty Jane put her all-out energy into her act, then ran off to almost no applause. I could see her sobbing bitterly in the wings.

"Don't let it hurt you that way, Betty Jane," I consoled her. "This is a dead audience, anyway. Wait till tonight. You'll wow them."

"You're damned right I'll wow them!" she blazed, the tears stopping and her anger taking over. "I'll tear this lousy theatre down with applause!"

It would be nice to say that she was a smash that evening, but it wouldn't be the truth. Her start was slow. Often she'd make a little curtsy as polite applause greeted her number—a curtsy which resembled something a doting mother might have taught a high-school girl to make at an amateur play—then run into the wings and burst out crying. But she was learning with each performance. Every day she added some new attention-getter. I kept telling her stardom was a matter of time, but she was terribly impatient.

We went back to Detroit for a one nighter at the Greystone Ballroom run by Frank Staltenkemp, who, with his wife, had made a sort of pet of Betty previously and had been very kind to her. They had hired Betty to appear there with some of the local bands. They didn't think she should go in there with me, however, since they felt it would detract from the pull of the Lopez orchestra to have a local singer.

"I don't see that at all," I told them. "I want her in." And after some hasseling I got my way.

That night before we left Betty told me about her sister Marion, who was also a singer working at the original Nut House behind the bar in Detroit. I went to hear Marion sing and was very much impressed with her beauty. I arranged for her to open at the Henry Grady Hotel in Atlanta, Georgia, for my good friend, Carling Dinkler.

We tried to push things along for Betty with a fast publicity build-up. She loved every line printed about her. When somebody ran a photo as well, she was practically rapturous. A write-up in *Radio Guide* meant more to her morale than the offer of a radio show. Attention was the motivation that made her tick.

When we played the Earle Theatre in Philadelphia, lovely Benay Venuta was the main attraction, leaving only a minor share of the audience applause for Betty Jane. Again bitter tears in the wings . . . tears that kept right on flowing despite my assurance that soon she'd get the most attention.

"That's it," she decided. "What I've got to do is to get their attention."

Between shows she bought a blouse, skirt and saddle shoes, already becoming the symbol of the jitterbug era. I didn't see her until she was ready to go on.

I couldn't get her out of that outfit; I had to let her try it once. When it got her even less applause, Betty Jane went back to regular attire.

Tough competition from celebrities kept plaguing poor Betty Jane as our tour continued. In mid-February when we hit my all-time favorite town, New Orleans, I met Cary Grant on the street and invited him to our opening at the Tulane Room of the Jung Hotel. He brought along Seymour Weiss, Managing Director of the Roosevelt Hotel. As soon as the crowd spotted him, it was no longer my opening but more like the première of a Cary Grant picture. The usual autograph rush mounted to the souvenir-grabbing climax and Cary lost his tie, tie clasp, coat and shirt buttons and one sleeve off his sports jacket—before a flying squad of waiters rescued him!

One thing Grant didn't lose, however, was his good disposition and his famous smile. I complimented him about it the next day and asked how he could lose a good coat and be such a sport about it.

"Well, Vince," he grinned, "I've got another coat. When I had only one coat nobody wanted to tear it off me."

Betty Jane's performance was lost on that crowd. However, for the rest of our date there she did very well. The rough edges were wearing off and the diamond in Betty Jane was beginning to show through.

New Orleans is such a friendly town that we hardly got to sleep the entire week we were there. I would have stayed longer, but we were due at the Royal Palms in Miami, Florida on the 25th, where Harry Richman had voluntarily taken a $500 cut in his salary as M.C. so the club could squeeze us into their budget for a month.

Ella Logan was also in the show and it took only a hint from me to get Betty Jane to watch every trick and nuance of that top vocalist's style.

"I'm not going to copy anything she or anybody else does," Betty

Jane insisted. "But maybe from the way they do it, I can find a way to improve my own style."

By that time, however, Betty Jane's "Dipsy Doodle" and a couple of other numbers were so terrific that other singers were watching to learn from her!

Harry Richman left the Palms and Joe E. Lewis came in. For some reason Joe thought I didn't like him, which wasn't true at all. I don't know where he got the idea, unless it was that he was so used to having everyone around him busting up with laughter that my deadpan made him think I didn't enjoy him—and if you don't laugh at a comedian, he'll be sure you don't like him. Joe always worked it into the act that there was someone in the club who didn't like him, then added, "But I'll grow on him." He did, too.

Betty Jane and I loved the races and nearly every afternoon we went to Hialeah, while it was open, and then to Tropical Park. I was out about $3,000 by the end of the month, but I gave it one more try. In the last race my sixth sense topped my better judgment with a hunch on an 81.40 to 2 shot—Ranicilla, ridden by Carroll Bierman. I put a hundred on it, kissed it good-bye when my horse broke poorly, then watched in astonishment as he came thundering on, took the lead in the stretch, and lasted just long enough to keep his nose in front at the finish. I had my $3,000 back and was almost $1,100 ahead! That night Betty Jane had two steaks at a little restaurant we both loved. It had a California-sounding name, The Rose Bowl, but we remembered it for some wonderful Florida nights we spent on the open porch, surrounded by the glow of soft candlelight.

The same night I tried the dice game at the Royal Palms and my luck stayed with me. Bill Dwyer, who then owned Tropical Park, was at the next table, losing. He came over to bet on my rolls and began to recoup fast. I had to quit at show time but Bill seemed well set for the evening, about $1,000 ahead. An hour later, when I got back, Bill was in the red again.

"Hey, Lopez," he entreated, "will you give up being an orchestra leader and just roll dice for me! C'mon and get back in the game."

But this time my sixth sense told me my lucky streak had run out and I declined Bill's offer.

I really began to get sweet on Betty Jane. It was against my better judgment and against traditional show business wisdom. Betty had a way of doing things that would make you want to kill her. Then she'd smile at you and you'd forget all about it! But the bitter words and bitter feelings in between!

Chapter 58. THE WAY OF THE HURRICANE

We worked our way back to New York through a series of one-nighters. On April 13th I was at the MCA office talking to Bill Goodheart, who was handling most of my bookings, and I told him that I would like to open at the Taft Hotel because I thought it would be a great bet. Every time I passed that hotel something attracted me to it. I felt the vibrations would be good.

Little did I realize that I would actually open there in 1941 for a long run. But Sonny Werblin said, "Billy Rose wants your band to open at the Casa Mañana on May first. He's lined up a terrific show, and a couple of months there can do you a lot of good with the public."

"I've heard that line before, Sonny," I broke in. "Doesn't that bit about doing us a lot of good with the public mean we sign up at bargain rates?"

"It does," Sonny admitted. "But you know Bill Rose. He gets people at bargain prices, but click for him and you can even up by naming your own price. It's worth the gamble."

"A 41.20 to 1 shot came in for me at Miami," I laughed, "so why shouldn't I bet on this one, too. If Rose knew how tired I am of road trips he'd charge me money for the Casa date—and I'd pay him!"

We filled in the remaining weeks with one-nighters to keep our suave-swing in top form, and I put in some time working out a better professional name for Betty Jane. Putting the principles of numerology to work I came up with a name that had the right rhythm and number balance to attract attention—Betty Hutton.

Our Casa Mañana opening on May first was one of the greatest things that ever happened in this town. The stars included Lou Holtz, Helen Morgan, Harriet Hoctor, Georgie Tapps, and Paul Sydell and his trained terrier, Spotty. To top it all I introduced, for the first time in New York, my new suave-swing orchestra.

The immediate future didn't dawn any too well for Betty. A long-smoldering feud with Joe Glaston, my press agent, burst into flame when Betty asked him to put a big blow-up picture of herself out in front of the Casa Mañana. But that spot was reserved for Rose's bigger stars.

"Whatever gave you the idea your picture should be featured?" he began.

"Vincent said it was all right," Betty explained. She didn't add that I had simply told her to take care of it herself when she broached the idea of having her photo featured. I had thought she would clear it through Joe and Billy Rose, but impetuous Betty went right ahead and got a full-length, life-sized, colored monstrosity of herself. When it came to putting it out front, Joe said, "No. Billy Rose doesn't want it."

The argument was referred to me when it reached the all-out stage. Maybe I should have upheld Joe Glaston, but I got off the hook with the explanation, "Look, Joe, she's just a kid, but she has a real chance of being a star some day. A setback now to her confidence could ruin her chances."

"What do you want me to do?" Joe replied. "Ignore Billy Rose?"

"Let's compromise," I suggested. "Put her picture in the inside lobby." And Joe did. We had some press interviews lined up for the following afternoon, and more or less on the spur of the moment I introduced Betty as America's Number 1 Jitterbug. The columnists liked the title; Betty loved it—and everybody was happy for a few days.

Even a better break arrived the next week when Paramount signed us for a movie short that would feature Nan Wynn, Sammy Cahn,

Jean Ellington, and Betty Hutton! I was surprised when Betty didn't share my enthusiasm over appearing with such stars.

"What's wrong?" she echoed my question. "Oh, I like the idea of doing the short, but I hope it doesn't hurt my future. I wouldn't want the public to think of me as only a band singer!"

When I explained the importance of being in any sort of presentation with the big names of show business, (even a benefit), I found that Betty really didn't have much background or knowledge of the entertainment world. Names like Pat Rooney and Eddie Leonard meant nothing to her. Even Al Jolson was just a guy who got somewhere singing mammy songs in blackface! Her only real interest in show business lay in becoming an important part of it herself.

Not long after, I got her a screen test with 20th Century. They looked at her and said before she tested, "She ought to be a brunette." I was against it, but Betty agreed. I was tired of fighting. The dark hair spoiled her looks and after the tests they said, "Has possibilities but isn't ready yet."

Betty Hutton first really clicked when we played the Annual Swing Carnival at Randall's Island with Martin Block, and the jitterbugs there really whooped it up for her. She came off crying again.

"Now what's the trouble, dear?" I asked, in puzzlement. "Why are you crying?"

"Because they liked me so much," she explained between a fresh batch of boo-hoos.

Then she clicked at the Casa Mañana, too, when Billy Rose brought in a new stage show with Jimmy Durante, Ross Wyse, the Presser Sisters, and Nick Long, Jr., assisted by a young stooge whom Nick had named the Mad Russian (not to be confused with the Mad Russian of the Eddie Cantor radio show).

"Watch this guy, Vince," Nick said to me, "he's going to be a great comedian some day." Nick was predicting the rise of Danny Kaye!

One night the Mad Russian and Betty came to me and outlined a dance that Nick Long had choreographed for the three of them to work into the show. Billy Rose had okayed it and I liked it, too.

"There's only one difficulty," the Mad Russian explained, "we need five bucks to get Betty a special shirtwaist."

I kicked in with the fiver and that night they just killed the audience with their act, about as funny a dance as I've ever seen. After that the audience really took notice of Betty when she came out to sing with the band.

"Summertime and the livin' is easy," according to the Gershwin song. That summer wasn't easy at all for me. First, I had to talk Billy Rose into releasing us for a month so I could keep my verbal agreement (of the preceding year) to play the Piping Rock Club at Saratoga again. Then Betty complicated our trip by getting me to let her sister Marion join the band. I had secured several jobs for her since Betty had come into my life, and now I welcomed the opportunity to have beautiful Marion along with us as company for Betty. My sixth sense must have been asleep.

Pete Sullivan, the Piping Rock boss, wasn't inclined to listen when we arrived at Saratoga and announced that both Betty and Marion were with the band and would be in the floor show (along with Russell Swann, Adelaide Moffett, and dancers Dario and Diane).

I had to argue vehemently to keep them in. But after all, they were on my payroll and didn't cost Sullivan a dime. A week later he was convinced I had a million-dollar hit—in *Marion*, not Betty!

"I don't go for this jitterbug stuff," Pete stated, "but I'll take your word for it that Betty's the best. Nevertheless, I still prefer Marion, and so do most of our patrons."

"Marion is a good band singer," I insisted, "but Betty is the real entertainer. You can see that with your own eyes, can't you?"

"What I can see with my own eyes," Sullivan answered, "is one of the loveliest girls ever created. And that means Marion. *Your* eyes can see that, can't they, Lopez? . . . Or can they?"

I guess my eyes *had* been noticing Marion's unique beauty after she joined our band, or perhaps I was going out of my way to make things pleasant for a newcomer.

Betty worked up a peeve and took off from Saratoga, saying she was going home and didn't know when she'd be back. She was back four days later to say that Detroit bored her after all and she felt her place was with the band.

"It's good to have you back, dear," I welcomed her. "Let me tell you what a wonderful job Marion did while you were away. . . ."

Things were velvet smooth for a while. We closed at Saratoga ahead of schedule because gambling had been shut down, but they paid us for the entire season. The day after closing Betty got all dolled up and headed for New York to audition for a musical.

My protest that she wasn't ready meant nothing. You could no more stop Betty with words that you could hold back a tidal wave with a snow shovel. She came back without the part, with the reluctantly imparted news that the producer had given her the same advice at the audition.

Since we had some free time, I took Betty to lunch at the Mt. Royal Hotel in Montreal, where the head waiter happened to be one I had met in London. Everything went well until the time came for coffee when he asked me if we wanted a large cup or a demi-tasse.

"I want good old American coffee," Betty said in a voice which carried for several tables. "None of that damned foreign stuff."

"Great sense of humor," I said to the waiter whose eyebrows had traveled half way up to his hairline . . . and he was a little bald, too.

Back to Boston, where we went into the Ritz-Carlton Roof featuring both the Huttons who weren't received with any hosannas. After a few days the green-eyed monster started giving Betty trouble again. I know she liked Marion, but Betty's competitive spirit was always working overtime.

Glenn Miller, who was then playing in Boston, was looking around for a girl vocalist. Nick Pisani, my violinist and friend, had formerly been with Glenn Miller and he thought he was doing me a favor by putting in a good word for Marion with Glenn, since she and Betty were always squabbling. One night when I came on the bandstand there was only one Hutton, Betty. I later found out that Marion had left of her own accord. She understood Betty's fiercely competitive spirit and decided to get out of the way.

The day we finished at the Ritz-Carlton in Boston it was raining pitchforks. The next day I left in my car with Betty and told the chauffeur to try and make New York as soon as possible because of the threatening skies. We left in the nick of time. The roof of the

Ritz Carlton was blown apart and they had to shut down for the rest of the season. Luckily, no one was hurt, but the hurricane of 1938 took an awful toll of life elsewhere in New England.

With Marion out of our professional lives, I thought Betty and I would have clear skies ahead. But we were riding into a hurricane of our own.

Chapter 59. LETTERS, I GET LETTERS

Betty had been gone but a day or two on her quick trip back home from Saratoga when I received a most affectionate letter from her that showed how volatile her moods could be—and also how deep and meaningful.

"Dearest Vincent," the letter read. "Hello! Well, this is my first day home, and believe it or not, I wish I was back. I miss you like I never thought I would miss anyone in my whole life. It didn't hit me how much I love you and need you. Without your guidance I'm dead, I realize now.

"I know I'm just rotten mean to you, and at times I don't know how you can stand me, but believe me when I tell you that there will never, ever, be anyone in my life that I respect as much as I do you. When I come back, I'll show you how much I've changed.

"I'm awfully impulsive and headstrong and I make a lot of silly mistakes, but if you're just as patient with me as you have been, maybe I'll turn out to be what you want me to be. Down deep I mean well, and maybe some day you'll look a little deeper than the surface."

Betty's letter made me realize that I was on the verge of falling in love again, and I had the sense to realize too that a love affair between a man in his thirties and a teen-age girl would probably wind up in quicksand.

All my life, I mused, I had been repeating the same mistakes, not only in matters of the heart but in those of the mind as well. I looked back on the partnerships that had foundered, the Lopez corporation which had made money for others but only trouble for me, my failure to establish a solid position for myself at the St. Regis. . . . I remembered too that in none of my love affairs had I ever been able to feel deep emotional attachment toward the woman. Again the rush of firm resolutions to change my life somehow! First and foremost, I resolved not to "fall in love" again until I knew the true meaning of love.

I also put a vital business decision into effect by returning to the William Morris fold for my bookings. Our run at the Casa Mañana was ending, although Billy Rose wanted us back soon and insisted that I give him priority on the band for an engagement at the coming New York World's Fair.

With Abe Lastfogel's familiar and welcome help, we put together a marvelous vaudeville show that we opened at the Shubert Theatre in Newark. In my package were Abbott and Costello, Estelle Taylor, Dr. Hoffman and Betty Hutton, with the midnight ride of Paul Revere brought out of storage for its scenic effect. The surprise hit of the show at Newark was Betty Hutton whose reputation as America's Number 1 Jitterbug was really catching on.

Betty later capitalized on her Newark success by demanding the star spot in the show at the New York Paramount (following instead of preceding John Boles), plus big-letter mention of her name in lights on all three sides of the marquee! Things had become wonderful between us again, and I went to bat for Betty and got her demands accepted.

It took only one show for Betty to realize that John Boles was the greater performer and that the audience thought so too. After our opening show Betty came back to my dressing room.

"Vince," she began very seriously, "they liked John Boles more than me, didn't they?"

"Well, I guess he did make a terrific hit," I said. "But you were great, too, honey."

"But not that great," she said. "I know you wanted the best spot in the show for me, but I don't rate it yet, so will you please change it. Let Boles have my spot."

"Well, it makes sense, Betty," I agreed.

At Betty's request John Boles got top billing—an unheard of voluntary act in show business, but that was Betty Hutton!

At the Stanley Theatre in Pittsburgh, a run of rainy weather kept us indoors between shows, and I was drawn into endless poker sessions with Bud Abbott and Lou Costello. I had a run of luck, with Lou the big loser—his fault because he insisted on doubling the stakes. Finally, Abe Lastfogel wired me to stop playing Stud with the boys because they were asking for salary advances. When I told the boys, Costello yelled, "This is a free country. If I wanna lose my money playing poker, it's my constitutional right to do so and nobody's gonna stop me. Besides, I'm gonna clip you tonight, Lopez. No limit to the size of the pot."

Our poker games ran long into the night—and Betty's anger about having to eat alone ran far into the following day! If I didn't play poker, Lou would sulk about not getting a chance to come up even; if I played, Betty had to be pacified over the broken date. Soon she resolved matters by dating others . . . and then our arguments started all over again.

On Sundays it was the custom of road shows to move over from Pittsburgh to nearby Steubenville, Ohio, to avoid the Pennsylvania Blue Law. One night, after the show, some friends of mine took me over to the Half Moon Club, which featured the double attraction of a good floor show and wide-open gambling. There I met a very beautiful and talented youngster.

"Sign her up, Vince," Nick Pisani suggested. "It's only a question of time before Betty walks out on you, and this doll could step right into her show."

"It's true, she's left us, but she always comes back. I think I'll take a chance with Betty. But this girl is very good. What's her name?"

"She's Irish," Nick replied. "Her name's Helen O'Connell."

We got back to New York in April where I started to make some changes in my band and recorded for Bluebird records with my suave-swing orchestra. Drummer Bob Spangler had left Jan Savitt's band to join us, and the terrific job he did on "Dark Eyes" made that disc an obvious winner even as we cut it. I got Betty to record a novelty tune called "Igloo." It wasn't very good, probably because there was no big audience out front and the rather indifferent recording crew insisted that she stand still at the microphone so they could get a good tone balance.

Troubles began to mount. We went back into the Chez Paree in Chicago with comic Romo Vincent, dancer Harriet Hoctor and filmdom's Lupe Velez as co-star. Lupe Velez displayed a large streak of temperament and would only do two shows a night instead of the customary three. I think the reason was that she didn't have enough material. Her uncooperativeness hurt business and the bosses asked me to talk her into doing a third show. All I got for two hours of trying was an offer of one of her Chihuahua dogs.

I wanted Betty to have a good spot on the bill, but the owners refused, saying she might be America's No. 1 Jitterbug, but she was a big zero in the Loop. I had to knuckle under since they were paying the bills, but Betty felt I was letting her down.

Maybe because Eddy Duchin was a fellow pianist or perhaps because, as a bandleader, he understood such problems, he asked Betty and me to join him at Rickett's for supper. He was waiting for us when we arrived. Betty seemed quite nervous and in a minute I knew why.

"Vince," Duchin said, "I want to tell you what's going on and that's why I wanted your singer here, too, so she couldn't complain that I did this behind her back."

"If this has anything to do with our personal lives, Eddy," I interrupted, "I'd rather you forget it."

"I wouldn't even touch that," he replied. "But it's your professional relationship that's involved. This singer of yours has been around looking for a job with my band. The salary she wants is preposterous, but I thought you should know that she wants to pull out and leave you high and dry."

"She wouldn't do that," I answered. "She has a contract with me and I still own the name Betty Hutton."

If Hutton was going to take off I wouldn't be left high and dry. Sonny Schuyler was singing with the band at the time and when I heard a girl named Penny Parker, who sang like Bonnie Baker, I added her. Now I had a boy singer and two girl vocalists.

Things between Betty and me got worse both professionally and personally. One night she missed an important broadcast and we had an argument about it. An hour afterward, a bellboy delivered the following note:

"Dearest Vincent—This is the hardest thing to tell you, but somehow I will. I won't talk to you, because you don't understand me. I'm sorry as hell about the broadcast. I'm the meanest bitch that ever walked and always will be. So if you don't see me at all, you won't be half as unhappy. I stink in every language, and I know it—but that's me.

"As soon as this engagement is over, I'm leaving for parts unknown. I've said this before, but this time I mean it! I'm really through with this business because I make everyone unhappy and it's not for me . . . Goodbye . . . I'm sorry. . . . Betty."

Every time Betty "retires" from show business, I look back at this letter and smile. Betty Hutton can no more quit the entertainment world for keeps than she can command her warm, impulsive, unpredictable heart.

These song lines must have been written for us:

When an irresistible force such as you,
Meets an old immovable object like me,
You can bet as sure as you live,
Something's gotta give!

It gave—but good—in Memphis, at the Claridge Hotel. The climax of a two-week argument came on the dance floor that night with a violent shove I foolishly gave Betty that sent her spinning across the polished dance floor. That night, she took off once more for Detroit—and home.

My manager Manny Heicklen said, "We've plastered Birmingham with ads about Betty Hutton, America's No. 1 Jitterbug, Vince. I didn't even stop to check with you on this. I sent Betty a telegram warning her she has to fulfill her contract."

"Betty and I are always arguing," I replied, "and it's wearing us both down, Manny. Let it stand this way. If we can't give Birmingham America's No. 1 Jitterbug, we'll give them a runner-up. The last time we played New Orleans, Mr. Langstreet of the Jung Hotel said he knows a girl singer who's enough like Betty to be her twin—or we can make her a twin in a hurry."

"I don't believe it," Manny replied, "but it's worth a try."

A couple of phone calls established the fact that the girl, Ann Barrett, was singing with Leighton Bailey's orchestra at a place called The Grove in Baton Rouge, Louisiana. I left Memphis in my car at nine the following morning and got to Baton Rouge around six. By eight o'clock I knew we had the girl who could replace Betty! Ann Barrett had the bounce, the youth, the enthusiasm—and probably a better voice.

I explained the situation to Leighton Bailey and he released Ann from her commitments with him although she meant a great deal to his band and it took a completely unselfish person to let her go.

She left with us for the return trip to Memphis that same night and slept in the back seat of the car. We reached Birmingham at 5 P.M. and Manny Heicklen was at the hotel to meet us. "Vince," he said, "I got some news for you . . . Good news, I hope."

"Great," I stated. "I could use some. What is it?"

Manny took a deep breath. "Hold on to your hat, now," he stated. "Betty is back!"

I now had three girl vocalists to make my life a song!

The William Morris agency kept us snowed under with engagements, but it was work without much satisfaction in it. We were living out of half-opened suitcases, with little or no rest, and it was no wonder Betty and I were soon edgy toward each other again.

When we played the Eastwood Gardens that August, back in Betty Hutton's home town, Detroit, she decided to throw a party for all the relatives and school friends. Betty had a ball doing it. No girl was ever happier playing hostess, or more naive and childlike. It was a marvelous week for everyone and Betty was the sweet, compelling kid I had fallen in love with before ambition had begun to gnaw at her.

We were building up Ann Barrett, for I could hardly send her back after persuading her to leave Leighton Bailey's orchestra. Caps on her teeth, a new hair-do, smart clothes,—and Ann had turned into a very attractive girl. I deliberately had her copy some of Betty's style and mannerisms in putting a song across, for it was simply a question of time before my band would need her as America's No. 1 Jitterbug. Ann learned her lesson so well that she could out-jit Betty.

The break came in October while we were in Indianapolis. This is the letter of resignation which Betty sent:

"Dear Vincent—Due to the fact that I feel I've gone as far as I can in this field, I would like to leave after Minneapolis and go into a different field. I don't want you to feel that I have any malice toward you. You've done everything in your power to make me a success and I deeply appreciate it. But now I feel it is time for me to leave, for the good of both of us. I'm going back to New York."

I knew this parting was for keeps, but I wanted it to be amicable. So instead of rushing for a lawyer, I hurried to the telephone and asked Betty to have dinner with me. We fiddled through some empty conversation and then I agreed to manage her and have the William Morris Agency book her.

"Lots of luck, Betty," I toasted her. "Now what would you like to order?"

"A steak—a BIG one!"

I burst out laughing. At least one thing hadn't changed in the year and a half between our first and last meals together—Betty's appetite!

Chapter 60. NEWS PROPHET

On September 1, 1939, while playing a one-nighter in Dubuque, Iowa, I picked up a short-wave broadcast of a political speech by Adolf Hitler. I understood no German, but I was amazed at the effect of Hitler's voice. It had hypnotic power, and I can understand how it lured so many millions to their deaths. It was after this speech that Germany invaded Poland—and the second World War was on.

Few at that time realized what vast changes were in the making. When I asked the boys in the band the next morning if they had stayed up to listen to Hitler, one of them answered, "Are you kidding? Who listens to that nut?"

For show people, as for everybody else, the show must go on. For us, the show went on to San Francisco, a city I really grew to love. Our opening at the Rose Room of the Palace Hotel was tremendous. Among the people there were Pierre Monteux, Igor Stravinsky, Leo Carillo, Freddie Martin, and Jack Dempsey—some new friends, some old ones. As an added surprise New York's social set was represented by Mrs. Cobina Wright, Sr. She was there to root for Cobina, Jr., who was appearing with us as a society singer and certainly helped bring in the "right people."

Cobina was a hit and was succeeded by Pierre Monteux's niece Nancy, who was followed in turn by Nina Tobin. Nina, whose dad was a mogul in the Hearst empire, opened on Ash Wednesday, and everyone said the place would be empty. Thanks to her, it was jammed.

Although I loved San Francisco, I had a let-down feeling toward my work while I was there. Maybe I missed my effervescent Betty. One way or another, my interest in the band lessened—and with it grew a feeling of dissatisfaction with things in general and myself in particular. However, two events came to my rescue.

One night, on the bandstand, I received a large package that had come by first-class mail. I opened it in between dance sets and found it was a half-filled stamp album with a note from Miss Merrill Parrish Hudson, a friend of mine in Memphis, Tennessee.

"Dear Vincent," she wrote. "This stamp album was left with me, but I realize it will take somebody with a more inquisitive mind and a deeper interest in history to make the most of it. So I feel you should have this album . . ."

My trombonist, Morty Bowman had married my new vocalist, Ann Barrett. Maybe the fact that he had acquired a romance soon after I lost one had prompted him, just the day before, to suggest that I keep a stamp collection. This seeming coincidence got me interested and I got a big lift out of it! The new hobby refreshed my outlook on life. I have become quite a stamp collector, perhaps to the point where I have earned the imposing title of philatelist.

My new hobby led to some interesting encounters. One day while on a tour in Canada I stopped at a post office to see if I could pick up any unusual stamps. The clerk began whistling a very familiar tune—it was the closing theme from my Pennsylvania Hotel broadcasts, written for me by Owen Murphy. I looked at him in astonishment, and he explained that he had recognized me by my voice, since he had been listening to me over the radio for years. To prove it, he recited the words to the song:

On the radio we said hello, but now farewell we'll say.
And so you'll understand, this is Lopez speaking,
Hotel Pennsylvania, 33rd Street and Seventh Avenue.
And if you come to New York Town, we'll greet you with delight.
So from the radio we've got to go.
We're signing off.
Goodnight, everybody!

I had no idea that anybody but me had ever memorized it. We ended up very chummy, and I picked up some very well-centered stamps. (If you're a philatelist, you'll understand what I mean.)

The other incident was a bid from the San Francisco Chronicle to do a daily column on numerology. I decided to apply the principles of numerology to world figures and I led off with a numerological study of Hitler. But the feature editor politely pointed out that they had plenty of political pundits; what they wanted from me were forecasts on San Francisco debutantes!

I wrote my copy in the way they wanted and pulled many letters requesting forecasts. Soon I had another hobby! Since that 1939 start in San Francisco I've written forecasts for hundreds of people, in the hope that the guidance numerology provided would be helpful in their lives. That hope was borne out. In my files are hundreds of letters of thanks for observations that spurred people to successful actions or even changed entire lives.

Our stay in San Francisco was up on February 16, 1940, with Ray Noble slated to take our place as we headed rather aimlessly back east on a series of one-nighters. Discouraged at the prospect, I resorted again to prayer to improve our lot. Three months and many prayers later I still seemed to be without an answer.

Our band was deteriorating in morale, if not in music. We all sensed the need for a "home base" again. If nothing along that line turned up, my key men were bound to leave me . . . and then the slide downhill would become faster than a San Francisco cable car gone haywire.

Matters seemed at their worst when we rode into Fond du Lac, Wisconsin, on a warm May evening for a three-day home exhibition at which we were to play four shows a day. As we took our bows for the last performance of the second day, the stage manager handed me a telegram. I ripped it open.

"Hold on, fellows," I shouted as I read the message from the William Morris Agency. "This is what we've been waiting for: ALL OTHER ENGAGEMENTS CANCELLED STOP BILLY ROSE WANTS BAND FOR THE AQUACADE."

It seems as if God was always there to pull me back from the brink of disaster.

Billy Rose wanted me to open his Aquacade at the New York World's Fair on May 11th. There was not a moment to lose and I wouldn't have lost it anyway. They made a fuss at Fond du Lac about my sudden departure, but I was to rehearse the Aquacade show and open in four days. Billy Rose is a great one for requiring immediate action in others once he makes up his mind. I left by plane.

Our wheels bumping as we made our landing at La Guardia woke me up from my sleep. Before the motors cut off I recognized Ed Fishman of the William Morris office and the late Jack Rosenberg, then president of the Musician's Union, Local 802, waving toward me from the end of the ramp.

"Great news, Vince," Ed reported. "Not only have you got the Aquacade but you also have a sponsored radio show!"

After the four months I had just gone through I could hardly believe my ears.

We started our Aquacade rehearsals that same afternoon. The empty World's Fair buildings fascinated me, and despite my resolution on the plane to work like crazy I turned most of the rehearsal job over to Dave Mordecai, my assistant conductor, while I took in the sights. In fact, throughout the engagement I simply led the overture, then turned things over to Dave for the rest of the show. My part in it involved four minutes of conducting, plus a piano solo—"*Nola.*" My determination to work harder dissolved into the easiest job of my life. The wheel of fortune had spun my number again.

The day before we opened I arrived in a taxi with a heavy trunk suitcase. No taxis were allowed in the Fair grounds and I was struggling along with my heavy load when a young man came up to me and said, "Do you need any help?"

"I certainly do," I admitted, "Guess I shouldn't have taken a chance on going it alone."

"Never say that," he admonished. "Always take a chance on anything and go it alone."

When we reached my cabana back of the Aquacade, a long way from the entrance gates, I said, "You sure were a life saver. You wouldn't happen to be my guardian angel in disguise? What's your name?"

"I'm afraid I haven't got the disposition of a guardian angel," he laughed. "My name is Mike Todd."

And that was my introduction to that famous showman.

Mike's penchant later in life for showering his lovely bride, Elizabeth Taylor, with expensive jewels and exotic gifts brings to mind an episode at the Aquacade involving Billy Rose and his bride of a year, Eleanor Holm. Eleanor was the female star of the show, with Buster Crabbe as her co-starred swimming partner. The Rose's wedding anniversary was nearing and Billy was trying to get a rare type of diamond Eleanor wanted. Billy had several jewelers on the trail but they hadn't run one down. However, with his usual confidence, impresario Rose kept telling her she'd soon have the bauble to go with the others he'd lavished on her.

The Rose anniversary arrived with the jewelers still delivering only promises. Eleanor, denied the treasure, became hard to live with. Finally, about a half-hour before the show went on, one day, Eleanor asked him if he had the diamond.

Billy, crestfallen, shook his head.

"All right," she exploded, "I'm not going on."

"But, dear," Billy frantically argued, "you can't do this! This is part of the theatre, and the show must go on."

"Well, put it on then," Eleanor flatly stated, "with my understudy! She hasn't worked all summer. I'm taking a night off."

With only fifteen minutes to go Billy told the stage manager, "Miss Holm isn't going on. Get her understudy ready."

When the stage manager told the girl "You'll have to go in tonight for this number. Mrs. Rose is not going in," the girl stood up and said, "Going where?"

"In the Aquacade, of course" was the hysterical answer. "You'll have to take her spot."

"Take her spot?" the understudy said in a daze, "but I can't swim."

Somehow her audition the preceding April had been limited to what she put into a bathing suit, not what she did in it! One of the regular girls of the swimming line of 125 did the number that night and next day Eleanor was over her huff.

I couldn't have met such an emergency, either. Eleanor Holm and Buster Crabbe tried to get me up to the dog-paddle stage at least, but I have a horrible fear of the water and simply can't relax in it. Poor Buster finally gave up on me as a pupil. "Lopez," he said, "I've taught many a pupil the proper stroke, but you're the only guy who almost gave *me* one!"

There was plenty of kidding around at the Aquacade show and

it's a wonder I didn't wind up in the deep end of the pool because of the horseplay. Comedian Frank Libuse would stop at nothing for a laugh. He worked with a girl named Margo, who wore a flowing velvet gown of deep maroon. One night when the laughs were few and far between, Frank tripped her right into the pool! He got his laugh, all right, but it was an expensive one. Margo bought a new gown twice as expensive—and charged it to Frankie.

Frank's stunt must have given Fred Waring's Glee Club group an idea. On closing night in October they gave soloist Everett Marshall a dunking, but it wasn't in fun. Marshall's temperament had irked the boys and they waited for the chance to deflate him. They handled it with military precision, closing in on him slowly as he started the last sixteen bars of his encore number, then edged him into the pool just as he finished the last note.

The gala-mood audience got the idea at the last second and howled with delight. Although Marshall was burning up, he couldn't do anything but laugh it off.

On September 29th I started the radio program, "Show of the Week" over the Mutual Broadcasting System. It went on from 6:30 to 7 Sunday nights and did not interfere with my appearance at the Aquacade. Buddy Clark was master of ceremonies and our guest star comics included Milton Berle. The producer, Norman Livingston, gave me free rein in the music end of the show, and our association developed into a lasting friendship.

The free time between shows at the fair gave me an opportunity to study numerology and metaphysics. A lot of people asked my help in changing their names (as I had done for Betty Hutton) and wanted me to make predictions about their probable future by numerology.

A publicity man named Russell was discussing the war with me, late in May 1940, and the talk turned to Italy's possible intervention. "What do you say about that, Vince? Will Mussolini play it safe or get into it? Can you give me a yes or no answer under numerology?"

"I'll do better than that," I replied. "I'll give you the date. Italy will enter the war—on June 10th."

"Well, that's sticking your neck away out," Russell commented.

"I'll do a story on that for the big papers. You'll look like an awful chump if it doesn't happen, though."

"Send out the story," I replied.

Only one columnist ran it—Danton Walker in the New York *Daily News.* But a week later it made all the front pages: MUSSOLINI ENTERS WAR. PRESIDENT ROOSEVELT CALLS IT A STAB IN THE BACK!

And the dateline?—June 10, 1940!

On June 13th the New York *World-Telegram* acknowledged getting the prediction I had made and apologized for not using it.

It might be interesting to cite just a few other such forecasts that I collected from the newspaper articles and reprinted in my book *What's Ahead.*

On August 27, 1940, in Danton Walker's column, I said that President Roosevelt would be re-elected, and that "Hitler will not die in the year 1940." My prophecy of "the break-up of Roumania and the end of Carol's rule, with complete loss of power and territory in the fall of 1940," came true in September. I said, "Italy stands to lose Ethiopia in 1941," and she did. I wrote that "Stalin will continue to play along with Germany until 1941." In answer to the question "Will Hitler win the war?" I went on record to the effect that "England will survive and grow stronger as Hitler's power wanes." The spring of 1943, as I then saw it, promised "internal revolutions, intense suffering and a change in the political setup with new leaders assuming power," conditions for Germany similar enough to 1916 and 1917 to have been remarked by nearly all the commentators in the summer and fall of that year.

On March 21, 1941, I said, "Before 1944, this war will have merged into another war." This came to pass, of course, through the Japanese attack on Pearl Harbor, creating a second war in the Western Hemisphere.

I wrote, again in Danton Walker's column, on March 21, 1941, that "Yugoslavia will be lined up with the Axis. Prince Paul will be deposed and a puppet government set up under another's rule, probably the eighteen-year-old King Peter. This should occur between March 21st and April 1st." It took place March 27th. I added, "Greece will undergo decisive changes in her government regime and could lose an ally (not England, however) in April." This also happened, since she lost Yugoslavia.

I said that the Nazis would march into Greece, but would avoid invading Turkey, and also that May 10th would mark the beginning of Hitler's decline, the latter prophecy fulfilled when Rudolf Hess broke away from the party on that date.

Overnight I received bids to comment on world affairs. My forecasts have become a ritual in Hy Gardner's space in the *Herald Tribune* shortly after each New Year and also, from time to time, in Nick Kenny's column in the *Mirror*. I also preview my forecast columns for Hy on his television programs. My batting average so far—85%. The prediction I made in 1954 that "When Russia wised up China she signed her own death warrant," seems to be heading for the grandstands as a home run!

Soon my predictions of world events came into prominence and a whole new field opened for me which has had a decided effect on my life and career since.

But while I was gaining prominence in numerology throughout 1941 I was losing it in the music world. No important hotel date turned up after we closed the Aquacade, so we kept on the move with one-nighters, vaudeville appearances, and our radio show. Then came a chance to open on Broadway again at a place on 50th Street and Broadway called the Hurricane. It had never blown anybody any good, but we needed the New York job.

The opening night was big with Billy Rose and Eleanor Holm lending it an extra splash, but a week later the club suddenly lost its liquor license—and its management closed the place, leaving me with the unpaid tab for the music and entertainment.

I called everyone together on Saturday morning. "Let's keep the place open without liquor. We have a lot of big parties for tonight and can't let them down."

Most of the kitchen crew had lammed out of there but the entertainers Peggy Fears, Marty May, a dance team, and my secretary, Esta Silsbee, called up friends and relatives and got them to come down and fill in. People were surprised to come in on Saturday and be told we weren't serving liquor, but the big parties stayed. We provided them with setups, and bottles appeared from somewhere.

"Oh, this is fun!" one of our women guests exclaimed. "Just like Prohibition days! Doesn't it make you feel young again?"

We got by that Saturday, but the following week showed we were in a losing battle. Peggy Fears was the first to call it quits. Marty May stayed on, and everybody agreed to a cut, but after a ten-day struggle we threw in the towel.

Everybody got paid. I came out of the Hurricane with a net of $22.00.

To top this off, my friend Jimmy Petrillo had come up with a storm of his own: the decision that each radio station carrying a "co-operative" network program must figure in the amount of salary paid the musicians performing on the show. Maybe James C. had no alternative, but in our case it was killing the goose that laid the golden egg. Our program costs went up prohibitively, and our "Show of the Week" was canceled.

That put us on the road again—and set my thoughts back to New Year's day of 1941, when I had examined my outlook under numerology and found that the first several months of the year would be very difficult and would be influenced by decisions beyond my control!

But the forecast I'd labored over so intensely on New Year's had indicated improvement in our lot as the year went on. I wondered when the tide would turn.

I got my answer via telegram while we were playing a fill-in date at the Totem Pole in Boston. It was an offer from *American Astrology* Magazine to write a monthly forecast column—at a dollar a word!

Chapter 61. THE TAFT BECOMES MY HOME

I was at the Ambassador Hotel on April 25, 1941, when I received a call from Willard Alexander of the William Morris office that changed the pattern of my life.

"Vince," the voice at the other end of the line said, "Remember saying that the Hotel Taft would be a good spot to reorganize? Well, it's yours if you want to try it. We can book you into it this summer. You won't be happy about the money though. Strictly union scale for the entire band and fifty a week for each of your two singers."

"How about me?" I asked.

"Their best offer," he said apologetically, "is double the scale for you. But don't hang up. You play only from 12:30 to 2:30 every afternoon and from 6:30 to 9:30 every evening. I'm sure you can make a lot of money there with outside dates."

Willard had played his ace card with that last remark. I needed extra money. I had picked several losing "war babies" in the stock market, and additional thousands had gone into the ponies. Still more had followed the well-trodden path of wine, women, and song. I was $30,000 in debt.

"All right, Willard," I said, "I have had this feeling about going into the Taft, and regardless of money I'm going to take it."

My meeting with Alfred Lewis, manager of the Taft, was on a very friendly basis. We signed a contract for three months at the Hotel Taft Grill Room, to start on June 29th, a Sunday night; and when I inscribed my signature I had a strange feeling that this would make a big change in my whole career. The contract date just left me time to squeeze in a two-week date at the New York Paramount, where I co-starred with Milton Berle. Maybe opening night worries were on my mind, but Uncle Miltie and I didn't get along very well on that occasion.

I had run into a phase when I had trouble getting along with people. If there's a lesson involved, it's this: Don't get heavily in debt. It's not only bad for the debtor; it's bad for his friends as well!

(I think this has been said before, and said better, but it can't be said too often.)

On the day of our Taft Grill opening, I was sitting in my car outside the hotel with Manny Heicklen, my personal manager.

"Why did you ever take this place, anyway?" he wondered out loud. "It's never done much for the bands that played here. This place is strictly for the masses."

"You mean the common people, Manny?" I smiled. "You know what Abraham Lincoln said about them—God must love them a lot. He made so many of them."

"On the money they're paying you," Manny grimly commented, "you'll soon be *one of them!* If you went $30,000 in debt on good dough, how do you expect to make out at this place?"

"I don't know," I admitted, "but some sixth sense told me to take this date, and I'm going to give it a real try."

The Taft Grill Room is below the main floor and can be reached by a staircase in the main lobby or by an entrance from Seventh Avenue. It's a large room with plenty of space for dancing. The bandstand is at the far end of the room. On the main floor, in the Village Room, Charlie Drew was the attraction.

Despite the heavy rain, our opening that Sunday night, June 29, 1941, was a success. I started at seven o'clock with fourteen musicians, myself, and Ann Barrett and Sonny Schuyler as vocalists, at a salary of $1,225.40 for all of us. When I gave the downbeat for the first number I felt inspired as I had on October 24, 1921, when I opened at the Pennsylvania (now the Hotel Statler).

At the conclusion of "Dolores," the final number of the first set, I gave the downbeat for the "Nola" sign-off and left the bandstand to mingle with some friends. The first table I stopped at was that of Mr. Alfred Lewis, the manager, who introduced me to Mrs. Lewis.

"I think you're very good for the Hotel Taft Grill Room," she remarked graciously, "and the Grill Room is going to be very good for you. Mark my words, Mr. Lopez, your band will be here a long, long time."

I smiled and said, "If you consider three months a long time, then you're right."

"No," she shook her head, "I mean much longer than that."

Mrs. Lewis was playing Nostradamus that evening without realizing it. Our three-month engagement has been extended repeatedly so that we hold the all-time record in that regard. Indeed, we soon dispensed with the formality of contracts.

"Let's put it on this simple basis," Mr. Lewis finally suggested. "The Lopez orchestra is here as long as you want to stay. And we'll go along with you as far as we can on the outside dates you get for your band. Just arrange for a substitute outfit and you can have short leaves of absence."

It was the sort of informal agreement under which I work my best.

Despite the tough competition of Johnny Long at the New Yorker, Harry James at the Lincoln, and Tommy Dorsey at the Astor, just down the street, we did a terrific business that summer and fall.

It makes me laugh every time I think of one incident. No matter how crowded we were Mr. Lewis would say, "We're losing money." We had lines straight back to the kitchen, the Grill Room jammed with more than six hundred people and Mr. Lewis would still tell me we were losing money. At last I said, "The place is jammed, so why do you say you're losing money? How do you figure that?"

He said, "See all those people out there. They can't get in here, so I'm losing money."

I got wise to him then.

New Year's Eve at the Taft is something to write about. During the afternoon Max Goldenberg, of Mr. Lewis's staff measures every foot of the place so they can squeeze in more tables. If a guest moves a half-inch he'll be in another person's lap.

Lou Mindell, the staff manager and Russell Levy, the engineer, would also help with the hectic preparations.

At a quarter of ten Mr. Lewis starts rushing around saying to the waiters, "Wake up you Schnell." Then he gets up on the bandstand in front of the mike and starts yelling "Get the pepper and salt shakers ready. Get the dishes out. Get the forks and knives in place. See that all the caps and favors are out. People are waiting by the hundreds upstairs and you're holding me up. Last year you were five minutes late." He also tells them, "Don't push any beer. You can't make any money doing that. We have to pay your salaries. Even me I want to get paid." He goes on and on giving out with his comedy and at the finish he says, "Thank you very much and a happy New Year!" At midnight he always greets me the same way, "Here's hoping we'll be here together next year."

During this period Betty Hutton was back in New York starring as Hattie in the musical, *Panama Hattie*. I found the chance to say hello, but while our dates were friendly, they were less than cordial and often cool.

However, Betty was red-hot in Hollywood and they wanted her for a movie right away. The producers were willing to release her from *Panama Hattie* only if a good replacement could be found. That led them to ask me to release Ann Barett whom I had groomed to take Betty's place and who, at some moments, could out-Betty the Hutton-tot herself.

I owed Betty Hutton less than nothing, but I didn't want to stand in Ann Barrett's way, and although I had Ann under contract I let her go with my blessings. I replaced her with Nancy Gay, whose name I changed to Karole Singer, after a numerological analysis. We started her at fifty a week but soon she was making an additional $200 a week on outside engagements. She wouldn't renew her contract, but bought her name, Karole Singer, from me.

It's funny but most girl singers seem to give a band leader trouble. Many of my colleagues won't have a girl singer for that reason. There's always trouble—quarrels with some musician in the band, or with you. I finally realized the secret of getting along with them—not to try to understand them but try to *accept* them as they are.

I also had trouble with Sonny Schuyler, my male vocalist who was under contract not only for his singing, but as a song writer. I spent about $2,000 on arrangements for the songs he wrote, but nothing happened until one day we were talking about numerology and he said, "How about changing my name like you did for Hutton." Sonny Schuyler had been his change from his original name, Selig Shaftel. After a numerological study I changed his name to Sunny Skylar which has a stronger vibration in his pattern toward success.

Right after that we went to Camp Upton on the Coca-Cola Spotlight Band Show. I heard Sunny, who was riding in my car mumbling to himself. Suddenly he exclaimed "I think I have it! How about this for a song?—

"Said the private to the sergeant, 'Don't you think the bugle blew too soon?'

"Said the sergeant to the private, 'You can sleep till noon.'

"Move it over, move it over, move it way over there;

"There's another dirt load coming up the road, so MOVE IT OVER there."

"Move It Over" was a sensation at every Army show at which we performed, and it became a popular hit as well.

Changing his name to Skylar had helped him as changing her name had helped Betty Hutton.

Sunny clicked with other songs, among them "Intermission," "Workers' Train," "Don't Cry," etc. He also wrote English verses for Spanish songs, one of which was "Besame Mucho." A year later Sunny was on his own.

I never could understand Tin Pan Alley's dearth of inspiration during the war years of 1941-1945. However, when the writer of "Bell Bottom Trousers" brought his song to me, I felt sure it was a potential hit. We played it 144 times on the air without getting it off the ground—or so I thought.

One day the writer offered me $500 for my part of the contract. I asked him why and he said, "Well, nothing's happening with it."

My sixth sense told me to say nothing doing. I immediately called the publisher and found there was over $5,000 in royalties accruing for my share of the song. "Bell Bottom Trousers" became a real smash and I made over $16,000 in royalties! It came closest to World War I hits like "Over There" and "Tipperary."

The war gave band business a terrific boost, but it brought problems as well. We lost most of our young musicians to the Army, and we had to change from our accent on strings to brass á la Benny Goodman, Artie Shaw, and Glen Miller. That's the mood of wartime—noise, swing, lots of life. I had a tough time selling the change to the hotel and even a tougher time facing the costs of a whole new library. Nevertheless, it was a matter of change or fade out. We changed.

On the air I had started a "Luncheon With Lopez" daily radio program. I owed the title to NBC announcer Ray Nelson. On our first broadcast he suddenly suggested, "Vincent, let's call this 'Luncheon With Lopez.'" We did.

After we came into the war I started dedicating our "Luncheon With Lopez" programs to Army camps. By telephone or telegram we let the Commandant know his camp was up for special mention that day. The outcome was a tremendous popularity with the Armed Forces. Indeed, the first thing many a soldier did when he came to New York on leave was to drop in at the Grill to catch our band in person and take away an autograph. Many brought sweethearts, wives, or parents along.

The WAVEs, who were in training at Hunter College, came down in droves on weekends. One Saturday afternoon I impulsively put some of them on the air for a quick interview. The idea caught on, and soon we were packed with WACs, nurses, WRENs, Women Marines, etc. Some nights it seemed that we had enough of the Armed Forces on hand to take Berlin all by ourselves.

But the war that laid the golden egg for the band business also forged the sword that now threatens to kill it. I refer to the entertainment tax, originally levied as a wartime measure. At one time it went as high as thirty per cent. People went along with it in the hectic days of victory, but now it is an intolerable burden on live entertainment. It seems to me that in these days of high-tension living people need the relaxations which show business offers. The unfair entertainment tax is sapping the nation's morale.

Easy war money meant lots of outside dates for us, which we handled in addition to our regular shows at the Taft and three radio shows at one time. We also made some movie shorts, and theatre dates were available whenever we could find the time for them. For all these activities we got top money, so I was able to begin to pay off my debts. This I did systematically each week, holding back just enough salary to live on and enough money to keep the band on the road back toward the top.

When I was in the clear again, I celebrated by putting my next two thousand dollars of earnings into Wall Street. This time, however, I was lucky. Additional investments caught the wartime rise in stock prices and I was soon way ahead financially, with a firm resolution to stay there, and with a good auditor, Charles Steinglass, to keep me there.

The war also put me ahead in the field of numerology. I am proud of the 85% accuracy of my predictions. The November, 1941, issue of *American Astrology* Magazine carried my column forecasting important occurrences in Hawaii that would put the military brass in trouble. Linked with the prediction was the remark that Japan would become our ally! Then came Pearl Harbor—and an explosive laugh of derision for my prediction on Japan. People forgot the first part of the prediction. They are now beginning to remember the second part, for each passing year makes all the clearer Japan's role as our ally in the Pacific.

All during the late 30's I had been struggling for self-command, but I made little progress until I settled down at the Taft. Then I decided that it was now or never, for unless I changed at that point, there was every chance of my career ending the way I started it, playing honky-tonk piano.

About the only ironbound stipulation (which I obeyed to the letter) in my contract with Mr. Lewis was that I be on the bandstand when my band was playing.

The reason for this clause was that before I came into the Taft the late Ben Bernie had been appearing there with his band and he had always come in twenty minutes late, or just in time to do his broadcast. After the sign-off he would say to the boys, "I'll be seeing you," and be off to the race track. The night Paris fell to the Germans he said, "I can't work any more tonight. Paris is gone!"

"What has Paris to do with my crowd?" Mr. Lewis wanted to know. "You stay here and work."

"I can't work. Paris is gone, Paris is gone!" Ben wailed.

Ben Bernie could get away with anything, but every band leader that worked in the Taft Grill after him had to be on the bandstand—and no excuses.

When I first came into the Grill, they were serving $1.25 dinners—everything from soup to nuts. They were lucky to sell two cocktails the whole evening. In time I brought the drinking crowd to the Taft—the crowd you make money on in this business. The management had wanted to get the masses. Now they got the classes, too.

My friend Dorothy Gullman was in town and I asked her to help me get some publicity, which she did. The nights I was not working extra jobs, we made the rounds of the different cafés, El Morroco, the Stork Club, etc. One evening, at the Stork Club, Tallulah Bankhead called me over to her table and started talking about astrology and numerology. Like most people of great talent she seemed to be searching for a greater understanding of life.

Evelyn Nesbitt Thaw would sometimes come to see me at the Taft. She was a deep believer.

My analysis of people who were high-strung, and creative showed that they found it difficult to strike a balance. I think they are constantly fighting an inner battle between the material needs of life and the spiritual demands of their personalities. They are the first to admit that there is more in life than meets the eye.

Chapter 62. THE LIGHT THAT SHINES

As World War II progressed, things got tougher. The food shortage made it hard to get a decent meal in a restaurant. As a long-term bachelor (my wife, from whom I had separated, had died), I depended on eating out, when not at the Taft.

What bothered New Yorkers even more was the shortage of taxicabs! Gasoline was rationed, performers in cafés had to be fingerprinted, there were curfews, etc. It reminded me of World War I, but it didn't have the same intensity, or the excitement. But everybody was making money—and spending it. Our band became more and more popular and we were dated for one party after another. We made appearances at Army camps, officers' clubs, and pop-music concerts aboard the Navy's big ships.

The nation grew more dependent than ever on their radios for news and entertainment, especially in the suburbs where gas rationing kept Mr. and Mrs. America at home. We were on the air almost constantly, for music has always been the backbone of radio entertainment. The personality announcers also made a comeback. Two of the best of them, still on the scene today, were connected with my programs. On our commercial for Borden's the studio audience warm-up was done by the irrepressible Bert Parks, and Louis Sobol was the M.C. of our show.

Equally talented was Barry Gray, one of the announcers on our "Luncheon with Lopez" programs. It was then on a "sustaining" non-sponsored basis, and he was always bemoaning this fate. In a directly opposite reaction, was Lonny Starr who liked a sustaining spot since it gave him greater leeway for his wit. Barry has a good sense of humor, too, but he saved it for later when he got his own sponsored midnight show on WOR. Then he filled the air with good-natured jibes about all the money I was making.

"I give you today's subject for a new Horatio Alger book," he'd say. "Vincent Lopez, the only man ever to wear out the steps of the Manufacturers Trust Company bringing in his bankroll!"

Then the whole nation was jolted when the weary, war-worn Franklin D. Roosevelt succumbed to a stroke late in the afternoon of April 12, 1945. The news reached us at 5:55 P.M., and when I went to the Grill Room Mr. Lewis, who was waiting for me, said we would not have any music and that I should make the announcement of the President's death. When I did, my voice broke. I wasn't crazy about President Roosevelt, but for the first time I understood what he had meant to our nation in two crises: the depression and then the war for survival.

New York was literally stunned for days. At the Taft, we didn't resume our music for four days. Even after that, people seemed subdued and saddened by a deep sense of personal loss. The part Franklin D. Roosevelt will have in history hasn't been finally determined, but the place he held in the hearts of Americans that day was undeniable.

We broke out of our gloom on May 8th—VE Day. There were the same wild scenes of excitement as in November, 1918, with this difference: a younger America, a more naive America perhaps, had celebrated Armistice Day with a spontaneous abandon. Its 1945 counterpart was just as frenzied, but not so spontaneous. People celebrated because it was expected of them. What moderated the jubilation, perhaps was the spectre of protracted warfare with Japan that might take a million young American lives. Happily, on August 14th, I was able to make another victory announcement over the Taft Grill loudspeakers—VJ Day.

Again there was not the old spark in the celebration. Perhaps it was the thought of the terrifying new force of atomic destruction that had come into being.

My musicians celebrated the end of the war with enthusiasm. Believing the freeze Uncle San had clamped on salaries would soon be over, they served me with notice the same night that they wanted more money, better outside jobs, more comfortable transportation and so on. They picked the wrong time. Uncle Sam had slapped his 1944 amusement tax on show business, the most enduring "temporary" tax ever invented.

We got an unexpected publicity break when Margaret Truman slipped away from her Secret Service guards and came to the Taft Grill with a handsome escort, whose name we never did learn. I stopped at her table, had a pleasant chat, and added her autograph to my own collection. Margaret complimented my piano solos, remarking that her dad was a pianist, too. I asked her to visit us again and got her very lovely smile and nod of agreement.

In the meanwhile, however, the hotel publicity man had been busy with phone calls to the newspapers. One result was a feature story by Anne Viviani in the *Daily News;* another result was not so pleasing. The Secret Service man Miss Truman eluded lost his job because of the episode—and Margaret never paid us that promised return visit.

Sometime later I recorded an album of piano music. I had a special set up made up in vinylite with a gold cover, to present to President Truman. I had an appointment to meet the President, or at least I thought I had. On my arrival I was met by General Vaughan, who regaled me with some wonderful anecdotes for a full hour—then broke the news that the President couldn't make it but would certainly appreciate having the album. That was the last of that.

It might have been overwork brought on by our expanded wartime activities and the hectic period that followed. Anyway, I began to deteriorate physically. When my piano technique was affected, I became alarmed as ever when threatened with a reverse in life. I returned to the religious training of my early years and intensified my prayers and meditation, especially in the early morning hours. And I jotted down the thoughts and insights which occurred during meditation. One such thought I noted at the time was a feeling of an important impending change.

One night on the bandstand I looked up from the piano just after realizing my fingers were stiffening up—a terrifying feeling to a pianist. At that moment I found myself looking into a pair of large brown eyes that possessed warmth, sympathy, understanding, and a touch of humor.

Involuntarily, I smiled. The eyes I looked into showed a split second of indecision, then returned my smile. The glance I had cast in their direction changed to a long look of interest, and the eyes I had found broadened into a lovely face . . . crowned by dark brunette hair . . . and supplemented by a petite figure.

My eyes imparted a quick question: May I drop over and introduce myself? Again the sudden look of indecision, followed at once by another smile that spelled out her permission. I went over to introduce myself and said, "I am Vincent Lopez." She looked up and smiled and said, "Hello, I'm Betty Long."

Ten minutes later, it seemed I had known her—or at least had been waiting for her—all my life.

"Miss Long," I explained when I returned to her table the second time, "I'm so glad you dropped by, and I hope you believe me when I say that I came over to meet you because something very deep inside me says it's most important that we know each other."

"Well, good," she answered. "Let's hope that inner voice is right. And I have something to confess, too. I was startled when your eyes beckoned to me, because of something that happened just before I left for New York . . . No; it sounds a bit silly. I'd rather not talk about it."

But at my urging she did.

"A group of my teacher friends suggested I go with them to a spiritualist meeting and I went along out of curiosity. The woman who conducted the meeting said that on my trip to New York I would meet a short, dark, well-built man who would be deeply interested in music. . . . Doesn't that describe our meeting?"

"I'm glad you went to the spiritualist," I laughed. "Otherwise you might not have returned my smile."

"I won't take it too seriously," she added. "She said other things about the man I would meet that obviously aren't true of you."

"Like what?" I pressed.

"Oh, that he was in great need of guidance," came her reluctant answer, "that his way of life is undermining his health and happiness; that he is in a crisis of some sort. As she put it, he has to be born again. That can't be you."

"Don't be too sure," I protested. "We all need help, don't we? Maybe you're the one to help me."

"I don't see how that's possible. I'm on my way to California tonight. I don't know when I'll be coming back east . . . and then I will be in Massachusetts."

"At least give me your address," I urged. "We can write to each other."

And so it was that I met Betty Long, Bible student, nurse, real estate broker, designer of women's clothing, and song writer. She continues to use the name Betty Long professionally—but, she is Mrs. Vincent Lopez.

Betty had been gone several weeks when one afternoon I felt very sick, as if my vitality were going away from me. My doctor said I needed a long rest, but the band business permits a maestro no such luxury. I had to keep going, and he agreed on condition that I secure a nurse, especially for the circulatory treatments needed to bring back the full use of my hands and overcome the arthritic stiffness that was settling in my arms and legs.

I immediately thought of Betty Long. I called Massachusetts to find out if she had come back from the Coast and, luckily, she answered the phone. I asked her if she would come to see me as I was concerned about my health. She agreed and came to New York, to find me sick in bed.

Betty took over just in time, for my physical decline had almost reached the breakdown stage. It wasn't easy for me, or for Betty either. She set me a severe daily routine. After my luncheon and dinner session in the Taft Grill Room I would go back to my suite on the sixteenth floor for a rest period, treatment for the circulation of my blood, and prayer and meditation.

As soon as I felt improved, several weeks later, I was all for getting back on the old merry-go-round of good times, careless diet, and an overload of work.

"Look here, Vincent," Betty declared, "I like you far too much to see you lose all you've gained. Maybe that spiritualist was right in saying the man I'd meet needed to be reborn. You need a different outlook on life. You can't pray and meditate only when you need help, then forget God when He answers your prayers. We've made a good team as patient and nurse in getting you back to health, why don't we try the same teamwork on the spiritual side?"

"Pray together?" I questioned. "And share our meditations?"

"Why not?" Betty replied. "When two or more meet together in His name, God is also there."

To the slogan that families which pray together stay together, let me add the statement that prayer and meditation brought Betty and me together as no other force possibly could.

When the mind is elevated to a truly spiritual plane, the superficial side of life is seen in its true aspect. For example, I no longer worry about the material part of my existence. I know I must make a living, and that the problems of my business and my social life must be met and solved. But they no longer seem all-important to me. I value success and I dislike failure, but these are not "eternal verities" for me anymore. I know for sure that man does not live by bread alone. He needs spiritual understanding, for which prayer and meditation are the surest paths.

Man must give up narrowness of interest, selfishness and the pursuit of personal satisfactions.

The true path of life is not discovered only through religion. It is to some extent philosophic and esthetic. Plato described it when he said, "Before virtue the gods have set much toil. Can we ascend by any other means the lofty tower which will be a fortress to us all our days?"

Betty and I have shared the thrilling experience during meditation of simultaneous insight. We first experienced it on a quiet afternoon. I visualized an island or planet hanging in space, with the most beautiful body of blue water and sky surrounding it. A deep feeling of peace seemed to radiate from it.

"Isn't it beautiful?" I heard Betty say—and I realized the same picture had appeared to her! In response to my questioning, Betty described the vision I saw in exact detail!

"This can't be a dream or an illusion," I suggested. "Somewhere in space this scene is a reality, and we have been able to look upon it together!"

Since then, I have found that the encyclopedias of religious thought and experience record many such happenings. Often the vision or manifestation (no word exactly describes it) lacks specific detail but is full of color and light. The Bible is full of instances involving supernatural light.

This strange manifestation of beautiful light and color can accompany deep meditation, as Betty and I have often experienced. It is not simply light in the ordinary sense. With it comes a wave or force which it quite indescribable—a force so compelling that there have been times when I feared it. It is this force, I believe, which gave the Christian martyrs serenity in the face of torture, which guided the Pilgrims and the Quakers to a land of religious freedom, which causes an Albert Schweitzer to dedicate his life to the suffering people of Africa.

I cannot imagine what force produces the illumination but I am *not* imagining the illumination itself. After all, if the experience of seeing electric light had been described to a person a hundred years ago, he would have dismissed it as an illusion. I'm convinced that when the world reaches a more spiritual plane the supernatural illuminations reported in the Bible (and other religious works) will be better understood. I can only say that, today, profound meditation can produce experiences which for the present are inexplicable.

Though unexplainable, the results were undeniable in my case. My health came back in a sudden sweep that amazed my worried friends. Skin tone reappeared, the "touches of arthritis" left me, and I could play the most difficult compositions better than before! People asked me what marvelous vitamins I was taking that worked this health miracle. When I prescribed prayer and meditation, they were puzzled. They had lost their faith.

Any prescription which does not include faith isn't worth the paper it is written on!

Chapter 63. ALPHA TO OMEGA

There is an old Portuguese proverb that he who has not learned has not lived. I believe I have learned to live, not by the emotional acceptance of a religious code or a set of philosophical utterances, but the hard way, from life itself, through suffering, and causing others to suffer. I'm afraid there's no other sure way of learning for most of us.

In navigation, man finds out where he is, how far he has travelled, by comparing his present position with his previous position at the last measurement. I'd like to do exactly that in measuring my own course. Two great New York hotels will be my points of reference: the St. Regis and the Taft. I compare the Lopez of the St. Regis against the Lopez at the Taft. And since comparisons should be specific, I'm going to set up ten areas of human thought, outlook, and conduct that largely guide our existence.

Over the intervening years, from the St. Regis to the Taft, I have moved from disorganization to discipline. This is reflected not only in matters of major importance but even in the matter of punctuality. Being punctual has helped me immensely, and for anyone who seeks to change his own habits in the direction of tidiness and discipline I recommend making the start by developing stop-watch punctuality.

For a second rule, I changed from financial chaos to bankbook stability, with my earnings safely invested in blue-chip stocks and in my stamp collection. I entered the Taft engagement $30,000 in debt, but within a few years wiped out the red ink and kept it out. Steady and rising income at the Taft, our comeback in commercial radio, and plenty of top-paying outside dates were important, of course, but the Lopez of the St. Regis had the same favorable conditions and couldn't stay solvent.

Rule three required me to switch from excessive touchiness to a sense of humor about myself. Life can make us thin-skinned through upsets and uncertainties, but there's no need to carry a chip on one's shoulder, waiting for a careless or frivolous remark to knock it off. There's an oversupply of grim humor in life itself and many people get a laugh at the expense of others. We must simply learn to live with it. Man's sense of humor was apparently given him to harden him against the grimness of life. At the St. Regis I let myself feel hurt by things that now I would laugh off.

There's nothing funny in my fourth point: That a man must move from materialism to consideration for others. So much of our quest for materialistic things brings out the worst in us! Against this the major religions and philosophies have thundered . . . in vain. But materialism is a self-defeating force. Man is a spiritual being essentially, and achievement at the expense of one's fellowman becomes empty.

Certain decisions made by the Lopez of St. Regis days unnecessarily hurt other people. He "won out" in several romances that proved meaningless. The more mature Lopez of the Taft realizes the emptiness of such victories.

My fifth rule is extremely important: the need to move from self-centeredness to interest in others. Here again, the major religions and the great philosophers have always taught that man must "lose himself" in something greater than his own single existence. Some mystics try to lose themselves in a contemplation of life on a higher plane. So be it—for them. For me, an interest in people serves a greater purpose.

When one is young one does not realize the value of friendship. At the St. Regis I had many friends whom I failed to appreciate. Today, at the Taft, I have learned to value friendship. It is a two-way street not to be traveled by one who is too wrapped up in his own concerns to notice the friends who would travel the road of life with him.

Following this path, I found myself in a new world of joyous experience and emotion.

My sixth rule is that the "staccato" type of personality doesn't really pay off. In an artist it is sometimes excused as temperament; in others it is merely explosive temper. It must be controlled if we are to get the most out of life. I don't say there is no place for justified anger. The most serene Man the world ever knew drove the money changers from the temple with angry words and blows. But an excitable temper is something else again, and learning to govern it has helped bring serenity into my life.

Like the seventh commandment, my seventh rule of learning involves the change I made from frivolity to fidelity. The Lopez of the St. Regis was incapable of constancy toward a woman. That all changed when I met and married Betty Long. In marriage any departure from this rule is playing Russian roulette with one's happiness.

Again, this was a truth beyond my discernment in the earlier days.

It took years of living, plenty of discipline, and endless hours of prayer to reach and understand it. Oh, there was another important ingredient from which the change was made: the right woman, who was Betty. Rodgers and Hammerstein certainly put some sound advice in their lyrics of "Some Enchanted Evening."

It was a truly enchanted evening when I saw Betty in the crowded room of the Hotel Taft Grill. At that moment, she was a stranger . . . but I soon made her my own. Then fidelity became a matter of delighted choice.

Which brings me to point eight—the change I managed to make from constant rebellion against life whenever anything went contrary to my wishes, to concentration on the things I can actually change, and acceptance of those I can't. I guess there is a bit of the rebel in each of us. The example was set in the Garden of Eden, no doubt. However, flying off the handle because of every reverse in our lives lacks wisdom. I don't recommend blind submission to everything that occurs. Somewhere in the middle of the road lies the path to travel, and I gradually found it. Maybe the following passage from Philippians 4:11 helped me: "I have learned in whatever state I am therewith to be content unless I can change the circumstances."

Rule nine replaced a general aimlessness in my personal life with a sense of purpose and accomplishment. While that had largely governed my professional life, it had been missing in my personal life. The Lopez of the St. Regis had always settled for the frivolous rather than the constructive. I found that I lost nothing materially, yet gained so much, by deepening the spiritual content of my life.

Finally, I may sum up my tenth point, as a change I gradually made from anxiety to confidence. There I had two problems to overcome: fear of myself and fear of others. Long after I had conquered the first, the latter remained to plague me. Facing an audience had always been an ordeal for me, not that I doubted our band or my own ability at the piano; but I feared that people were hostile and critical by nature.

Professionally, this gave me an "inferiority complex." Prayer helped somewhat. It brought inner security that partly overcame my doubts about the essential goodness and friendliness of most people. In my early days at the Brooklyn saloons, I often had to overcome sheer terror when it was my turn to go on. A good bit of that feeling had dissolved by the time we reached the St. Regis but too much remained. What rid me of it for keeps was a miracle of our century—television!

As had been the case with radio, I got into television more or less by chance. A young TV producer named Gerry Gross dropped in at the Taft Grill early in 1949 and suggested I give television a try. I'd told him I'd try anything, then promptly forgot the conversation. Gerry didn't. He was back in a few days with the news that I would be on the Ed Sullivan show that week with Russ Morgan. TV in its early days was that fast and informal.

I was scared going to that rehearsal for my first television show. I kept hoping something would happen to cancel it. I felt more and more jittery waiting for Sullivan to show up. He was late. I had just leaned over to Gerry Gross to say, "Let's get out of here," when Sullivan appeared. He came over to me and said, "Vincent, I'm so glad you were able to make it. It's a pleasure having you." With that my confidence returned. Ed asked Russ Morgan and me to cook something up for the show.

When Sunday night came we were both at our best. I teamed up with Russ to do "Twelfth Street Rag." Ray Block, the musical director of the show conducted while doing a shag and tearing up sheets of music and throwing them into the air. The audience loved it. When we were finished, I knew TV was for me.

So a few weeks later, when Gerry asked me would I like to do a daily TV series, I told him to go ahead on it. About two hours later he gave me a ring from one of the house phones at the Taft and said, "Let's go to Lindy's for lunch. I have great news for you." On the way he said, "I have sold you on Dumont for fifteen minutes, five times a week. I am not sure of the exact time, but I think it will be about 3:15 in the afternoon. You just have to play the piano, that's all."

"That's all," he said, but I knew that just playing a piano on television would never hold any audience. Something has to happen. TV must be visual as well as audio. So I made up my mind to do more than play.

The next day I went with Gerry to see Dumont's program director, James L. Caddigan, whom I liked from the start. He said, "Well, Vincent, we've made arrangements for you to start this Monday."

However, the interval was long enough for the old doubts to return. A guest appearance was easy enough, the doubts whispered, but could I swing a daily television show? Would it be too much work—the Hotel Taft engagement, outside dates, recordings, radio shows, guest appearances, etc.?

But my doubts and worries were needless. Our Dumont show was a hit from the start and it lasted two and a half years. As M.C., I introduced over two hundred guests including such headliners as Forrest Tucker, Fanny Hurst, Cab Calloway, Fanny Ward, Juanita Hall, Eddie Albert, Pat Rooney, Kurt Weill, Osa Johnson, Ella Fitzgerald, Quentin Reynolds, Maxine Sullivan, Billy Gaxton, Horace Mann, Fritzi Scheff, Doretta Morrow, Tommy and Jimmy Dorsey, Lionel Hampton, Martha Wright, Mark Dawson, Janice Page, Joyce Matthews, Rudy Vallee, Bert Wheeler, Mrs. Gustave Hartman, Ruth Donnelly, Lawrence Welk, Conrad Nagel, Joey Adams, W. C. Handy, Diana Barrymore, Linda Farrell, Earl Wilson, Nick Kenny, Ray Heatherton, etc., etc.—in fact personalities from all walks of life. It was like writing my own Who's Who in show business.

On one of my programs I had the pleasure of interviewing Xavier Cugat. At that time a beautiful young singer named Abbe Marshall was one of my feature vocalists and I noticed that Cugie couldn't take his eyes off her. After the program was over Cugat said to me, "Who is that girl?"

I asked why.

"I must have her telephone number," he replied, and he kept bothering me until he got it.

A few weeks later Abbe Marshall didn't appear on our show. Cugie had captured her. She eventually became Abbe Lane—and later Mrs. Cugat.

I took to television like a duck to water. I had prayed hard to make good, and the answer to my prayers arrived when I suddenly thought of television simply as an invitation from a family of friends to come into their living room and entertain them. This simple thought overcame my innate fear of people as a critical, aloof audience. Prayer pointed my way to this answer, and it was an answer that significantly changed my life.

Hal Hough of WCBS-TV recognized this new ability of mine when he signed my band to do "The Vincent Lopez Show." Hy Gardner also recognized my newly-acquired ability to talk about my numerological forecasts with the ease and informality that television required.

But to go back, I would like to describe that studio at Dumont where I did my first shows. It wasn't much bigger than the coat room at the Taft Grill. Nevertheless, programs were put on back to back there—meaning that the room was divided into two sets. As one show finished, the cameras dollied a few feet to the other end of the studio to pick up the next program which had been rehearsing in the meanwhile.

For my first show on Dumont, I decided to have as guest Russ Morgan, who had bravely gone through the Ed Sullivan show with me. What a show that first one was! There was no rehearsal, but I had sent some records over to Les Tomlin, my director, the idea being that I would play along with them. Well, two little things prevented that. One was that, because of technical difficulties, it was hard to get the sound of the record back to me so that I could synchronize with it. Secondly, somewhere along the line, the records had been put in a warm place and had warped. The music which came out wasn't the best this side of heaven. In fact, it sounded as if it came from the other place. Then, to add to the confusion, the floor manager came up to me and yelled, "Who's first?" I didn't know what he meant, but I said, "What do you mean who's first? I'm supposed to play, this is my show, and I'm first." Later on I found out all he meant was what was the first camera shot on the show.

Finally we were ready and the first number I played was "Kitten on the Keys" without the recording. Then I interviewed Russ and told his horoscope. Russ is usually a very funny guy, but during the interview he wasn't saying much, so I asked, "What happened, Russ? You're supposed to be funny."

That woke him up, and he answered, "Oh, I forgot to put out my wash this morning!" From then on it was all right.

From my experience on radio I knew that one piano sounds thin, so I decided to make it a two-piano show. At the other piano right from the start was Ray Barr.

Television came to play a very important part in my life. On January 25, 1950, Jim Caddigan, whom I was working for at Dumont, came in to see me with Gerry Gross at the Hotel Taft Grill. "How about doing a show from the Taft Grill Room, in addition to your daily shows?" he asked.

That was some order. I had to get clearance from Mr. Lewis, manager of the Taft, and the musicians' union, Local 802. I had two days time to do it—but I managed it!

We had been the first band on radio, and we became the first band with a regularly-scheduled "remote" TV show. It was called "Dinner Date With Lopez," and every Saturday the program read like a Who's Who of show business.

Here's what Roy Walters said about it in his syndicated TV column:

Vincent Lopez, conductor of the "Dinner Date" telecast at 8 over the Du Mont Television Network, is a man who really believes that variety is the spice of life. Leading guestars of show business appear on this sparkling variety program. But great as these performers are, Lopez realizes that too much of anything can be overdone, even when it's good. So he insists on variety. The result is excellent television, a technique of rapid-fire timing that enables him to move from one act to another so smoothly that the speed of the operation goes unnoticed, and that seems to be the lesson which TV must learn in order to avoid the killing fault of monotony.

It was good advice that Roy Walters offered, but did television take it? Let program scheduling answer the question. One year it's a surplus of quiz programs, the next a surfeit of westerns, then something else catches on and is repeated endlessly!

I think I've learned important things from the process of living. It took me quite a time, though. Suppose we give television more of that ingredient. Maybe it will learn, also.

To add a few summarizing sentences that supplement my ten points of learning, I have found nothing new yet something precious and rare. Socrates said in his parting message to his sons that they should value virtue and peace of mind above riches and pleasure.

Substitute riches and pleasure for virtue and peace of mind and you will fill the champagne glass that life offers you with mere ginger ale. You will take its beautiful gold setting and place therein a dull pebble!

This wisdom of understanding was offered to me early in life in my studies at St. Mary's Monastery. I rejected it then, for I wasn't ready for it. But I kept groping for it, moving toward it, and finally it was mine in my slow but sure return to the spiritual and to God.

The man of the world had completed the cycle—back to the boy in the monastery!